THE PHILOS

THE
PHILOSOPHY
OF
BEING

M E T A P H Y S I C S   I

GERARD SMITH, s.j.
*Professor and Director of the
Department of Philosophy,
Marquette University*

LOTTIE H. KENDZIERSKI
*Associate Professor
Department of Philosophy,
Marquette University*

Printed in U.S.A. by
Marquette University Press
Milwaukee, WI 53233

IMPRIMI POTEST:

Leo J. Burns, S.J.

PROVINCIAL, WISCONSIN PROVINCE,
MARCH 25, 1960.

NIHIL OBSTAT:

Francis J. Breidenbach, Ph.D.,

CENSOR DEPUTATUS.

IMPRIMATUR:

✠ Francis Cardinal Spellman,

ARCHBISHOP OF NEW YORK.

DATED JANUARY 17, 1961.

The nihil obstat and imprimatur are official declarations that a book or pamphlet is free of doctrinal or moral error. No implication is contained therein that those who have granted the nihil obstat and imprimatur agree with the contents, opinions or statements expressed.

6th Printing, 1990

LIBRARY OF CONGRESS CATALOG CARD NUMBER: 61-5281

PRINTED IN THE UNITED STATES OF AMERICA

TO CHARLES J. O'NEIL
Professor of Philosophy
Marquette University

FOREWORD

It so happens that this book was written after *Natural Theology* (New York, The Macmillan Company, 1951). We hope, nevertheless, that if not in time, at least in the now acknowledged space-time complex the horse is still before the cart. Dr. Kendzierski and I are co-authors. She is mainly but not alone responsible for the notes. I am mainly but not alone reponsible for the text.

We have received much help from Father William J. Stackhouse, S.J., Assistant Professor of Philosophy at Marquette University, who gave the nod to every line; from Father Edmund W. Morton, S.J., President of Gonzaga University, and from Father Clifford Kossell, S.J., Dean, Mount St. Michael's Scholasticate, Spokane, Washington, who toiled through the reading of the difficult section on Relations, and contributed to it most wise suggestions; from Drs. Kenneth L. Schmitz and James H. Robb, Assistant Professors of the Department of Philosophy of Marquette University, who allowed every bit of the book to be read at them. Father Francis C. Wade, S.J., Assistant Director of the Department of Philosophy of Marquette, gave us the administrative comfort we could not have done without. Miss Esther Diehl, Secretary of the Philosophy Department, typed the manuscript with a faithfulness, speed, and accuracy which leave its errors chargeable only to us.

Gerard Smith, s.j.
Lottie H. Kendzierski

TABLE OF CONTENTS

THE PHILOSOPHY OF BEING

I · WHAT METAPHYSICS IS ABOUT

read to Chapter Two

Metaphysics is a science or knowledge about being as being.[1] Everyone, of course, always knows "being" in some sense. A mathematician, for example, knows being as quantified, a biologist knows being as living, and a gas station attendant knows being as oil, air, water, autos, patient and impatient customers, and so forth. Now, a metaphysician professes to know being as common to, or involved in, whatever anyone else knows or can know.[2] That is what a metaphysician means by being as being.

AUTHOR'S NOTE. Throughout the text, notes will be quoted alternately in Latin or English. Whenever a good English translation of St. Thomas' work was found, it was used and indicated in the General Bibliography. The Latin was used, in preference to an English translation, whenever it was found to be more beneficial to the reader.

[1] On metaphysics as the science of being as being, see Aristotle, *Metaphysics*, IV (Γ), 1, 1003a 21-23; IV, 2, 1003b 15-1005a 17; XI (K), 3, 1060b 31-1061a 17. St. Thomas Aquinas, *In Metaph.*, Prooemium; *In IV Metaph.*, lect. 1; Cathala, n. 533; lect. 4, nn. 571, 587; lect. 5, n. 593; *In XI Metaph.*, lect. 3, n. 2194; *In Boet. de Trin.*, V, 1 and 4. See also J. Maritain, *Distinguer pour unir, ou les degrés du savoir*, Paris, Desclée de Brouwer, 1932, pp. 3-37; *Sept leçons sur l'être, et les premiers principes de la raison spéculative*, Paris, Téqui, 1934, pp. 5-21, 51-70; *Court traité de l'existence et de l'existant*, Paris, Hartmann, 1947, pp. 23-78; J. Owens, C.Ss.R., *The Doctrine of Being in the Aristotelian Metaphysics*, Toronto, Pontifical Institute of Mediaeval Studies, 1951, pp. 147-180; *St. Thomas and the Future of Metaphysics*, Milwaukee, Marquette University Press, 1957, pp. 1-61.

[2] The distinction between metaphysics and the other sciences may be found in Aristotle, *Metaphysics*, IV (Γ), 1, 1003a 23-26: "None of these other [the special sciences] treats universally of being as being. They cut off a part of being and investigate the attribute of this part; this is what the mathematical sciences, for instance, do." See *Metaphysics*, VI (E), 1, 1025b 1-1026a 32; XI (K), 3, 1060b 31-1061b 17. See also St. Thomas, *In II Sent.*, d. 3, q. 3, a. 2; *In Metaph.*, Prooemium; *In I Metaph.*, lect. 2, n. 47; *In V Metaph.*, lect. 1, nn. 530, 547; *In VI Metaph.*, lect. 1, nn. 1145-1165; *In XI Metaph.*, lect. 4, nn. 2206-2210; *In Boet. de Trin.*, II, 1, ad 6; V, 1; *Contra Gentiles*, I, 1.

However, a metaphysician has a hard time explaining what he means by *that*. The reason is this: when one quite understands what a metaphysician means by "being as common to, or involved in, whatever anyone else knows or can know," one knows a considerable amount of metaphysics and until one knows a good deal of metaphysics, it is very difficult to know what a metaphysician is talking about. The situation is like that which often confronts surgeons: they cannot operate until the infection clears up, and the infection won't clear up until they operate. Nonethelesss, in the matter of explaining what metaphysics is about, the circle, more vital than vicious, can be broken by a student who has average intelligence, a desire to learn, and, above all, humility.

Humility, in the order of learning, is largely a matter of docility. A docile learner looks in the directions to which the teacher points. Once a learner has looked in the proper directions, either he will see for himself, and then he can forget the teacher; or else he won't see anything, in which case there was perhaps nothing to see in those directions. This would mean that the teacher was a quack to start with. If, however, the teacher is not a quack, and if the student still sees nothing in the direction to which the teacher is pointing, the learner must somehow be at fault. The fault is usually indocility. Indocile students don't try to see, or else they try to see what they wish to or what they say they see.

The Multiplicity and Unity of Being

What metaphysics is about may be seen in the following or some similar way. Many things have much in common. Identical twins, e.g., have so much in common that they are often indiscriminable except by the fact that one twin is here and the other is there. Yet no thing has so much in common with another thing as to *be* that other thing. For, if one thing were another thing, there would not be two things, and this is against the fact that there are two things. Indeed not only is one thing not another thing; one thing is not even able to be another thing—not, that is, if it is to stay itself. For, if a thing could stay itself and be another thing, it could be, because it is itself, and it could also not be, because it could be another thing. This is an impossibility, a zero which is not a zero, a being which can be itself and also not be itself, because it can be another being's self. In sum, it is against the fact that two beings are one being, the fact, namely, that there are at least two beings; and it is impossible that one being, staying itself, could be another being, else there couldn't be two beings. Identical twins are not so all-fired identical as to be one of them, else there would not be the other, and there *is* the other. Nor *can* identical twins be just one of them, else they *couldn't* be twins at all.

Metaphysics tries to understand the situation just described, that is, it tries to understand plurality, multiplicity, the fact that there is more than one being. In order even so much as to understand the data, plurality, that is, we may find it helpful to keep on paraphrasing the situation, viz., to be an existent is to be one existent, yet there are many existents.

The following paraphrase might help. All things have this in common: they are existents, actual (you) or possible (your future children).[3] On the other hand, the commonness of the status of being an existent is not such a commonness as to cause many existents to be one single existent, else there could not be many existents.

The status of being an existent (actual or possible), then, is such that *each* existent fully enjoys it. This feature of that status is called the *unity* of being. Yet no one existent so fully enjoys that status as to exclude another being from enjoying it as well: *every* being enjoys that status. This feature of that status is called the *multiplicity* of being. Thus being as being is the status of an existent which is both *one* such status and *many* such statuses. Being is one and many.[4]

[3] Were things neither actual nor possible, they would neither have anything at all in common, nor would they have any differences. They would be nothing, and "nothing" can neither distinguish nor unite. Try to distinguish or unite the two holes in two doughnuts without the two doughnuts.
[4] Plato, in the words of Socrates, is not certain as to the name he will give to the science which deals with being as one and many: "And if I find any man who is able to see 'a One and Many' in nature, him I follow, and 'walk in his footsteps as if he were a god.' And those who have this art,

The Question Which Multiplicity and Unity Raise

This multiplicity and unity of beings as existents, actual or possible, raises the question: why are there any existents at all, actual or possible? And one has not quite grasped the situation if one asks, why does the multiplicity and unity of beings as existents raise *that* question?

Let us, then, review the situation. The status of being an existent, actual or possible, is not confined to any one actual or possible existent. For, if that status were so confined, there would be no other existent, actual or possible, except the one to which that status is by hypothesis confined. Yet we know that there are many existents, actual or possible. In sum, the prerogative of being an existent, actual or possible, is not the exclusive prerogative of any one existent; it is the prerogative of many existents, actual or possible: being, i.e., the status just described, is many. On the other hand, the status of being an existent, actual or possible, does not *have* to be the prerogative of many existents; certainly, not of all these we see. Peter could, for example, be an existent without Paul. All that is strictly required for Peter to be an existent, actual or possible, is that it be *he* who is an existent, that *his* status of being an existent be confined to him *alone*, and not to him *and* to someone else. The reason is: this someone else, if his were Peter's status, would *be* Peter, and so there would not be Paul. Nevertheless, Peter is an

---

I have hitherto been in the habit of calling dialecticians; but God knows whether the name is right or not," *Phaedrus*, 266b. Plato's analysis of the unity and multiplicity of being may be found in *Parmenides*, 128a–129d; *Sophist*, 244a–245e; *Philebus*, 14a–17e. Aristotle's historical exposition of the problem of the one and many in being is found in *Metaphysics*, I (A), cc. 1–10; IV (Γ), cc. 1–8. St. Thomas' commentary on Aristotle, and his analysis of the problem is found in *In I Metaph.*, lect. 1–17; *In IV Metaph.*, lect. 1–17.

On the problem of the one and many in being, see also E. Gilson, *L'être et l'essence*, Paris, Vrin, 1948, pp. 21–45; *Being and Some Philosophers*, Toronto, Pontifical Institute of Mediaeval Studies, 1949, pp. 1–40; A.C. Pegis, "The Dilemma of Being and Unity," *Essays in Thomism*, N.Y., Sheed & Ward, 1942, pp. 151–183; 379–382; L.-B. Geiger, O. P., "De l'unité de l'être", *Rev. des sciences phil. et théol.*, Vol. XXXIII (1949), pp. 3–14; G. Smith, S.J., *Natural Theology*, N.Y., Macmillan, 1951, pp. 12–17.

existent without Paul, who may or may not exist, for we see Peter
with or without Paul. In sum, the status of being an existent, actual
or possible, is the prerogative of one existent at a time, so to say; it is
not the *single* prerogative of *many* existents together, else there
could not be many existents: being, or the status of being just
described, is one. Thus we have it that the status of being an existent,
actual or possible, is both one status, i.e., it is confined to that very
thing's status which is an existent, and it is also many, i.e., it is also
all other existents' status. Being, which is the status of being an
existent, is one and many. Such is the situation.

As the inevitable spark from flint and steel, so from the multiplicity and unity of being comes the inevitable question: why are
there any existents at all?[5] Observe, the question arises not from the
unity alone of the status of being an existent. Surely, a being must
enjoy its *own* status of being an existent, else *it* would not be an
existent. Surely, if x is an existent, it must be x which is an existent,
not something else. To think otherwise is to think that the existent x
is not the existent x. Nor does the question arise from the multiplicity
alone of the status of being an existent. Surely, many beings, each an
existent, enjoys severally the same status. Surely, if x and y are
existents, then they *both* exist, actually or possibly. To think otherwise is to think that two existents are not two existents.[6]

The question arises rather because there is nothing in being an

[5] See Aristotle, *Metaphysics*, I (A), 2, 982b 4–10: "And the science which
knows to what end each thing must be done is the most authoritative of the
sciences, and more authoritative than any ancillary science; and this end is
the good of that thing, and in general the supreme good in the whole of
nature. . . . this must be a science which investigates the first principles and
causes; for the good, i.e., the end, is one of the causes."
See also St. Thomas, *In IV Metaph.*, lect. 1, n. 546; *Contra Gentiles*, I, 1.
Fr. Owens, basing his analysis on *Sum. Theol.*, I, 44, 1, ad 1, *Contra Gentiles*,
I, 22, and *De Ente et Essentia*, ch. 4, has developed, in a historical and sys-
tematic way, the meaning of the cause of multiple being, "The Causal Proposi-
tion—Principle or Conclusion?" *The Modern Schoolman*, Vol. XXXII, n. 2
(January 1955), pp. 159–171; Vol. XXXII, n. 3 (March 1955), pp. 257–270;
Vol. XXXII, n. 4 (May 1955), pp. 323–330.
[6] Aristotle, *Physics*, I, 3, 186b 38–39: "For the subject cannot be a *being*
unless 'being' means several things, in such a way that each *is* something."
See St. Thomas, *Comp. Theol.*, I, cap. 102; *In I Metaph.*, lect. 10, n. 154;
Sum. Theol., I, 11, 3, Resp.; I, 39, 3, Resp.; *De Ente et Essentia*, ch. III; ed.
Marietti, n. 18.

existent which demands that there be two existents. Why, then, two? Nothing in unity can explain multiplicity, nor is there anything in multiplicity which can explain unity. One existent (unity) has all that it takes to be an existent; two (multiplicity) are not needed in order that there be one. Why, then, two? On the other hand, that there be two existents (multiplicity) cannot of itself explain why either of them (unity) is an existent. Of course one might try to say that there is no need of an explanation for there being two existents, but the only reason why one could say that would be because to-be-an-existent is to be two of them, and that is contrary to fact. One existent is not and cannot be another. Besides, to say that there is no need to explain why there are two existents because to be an existent is to be two of them, is merely to try to say that two existents are not two but only one. Yet they are two. Why?

The situation must be reexpressed until the question jumps at us. There is nothing wonderful about Peter being an existent, actual or possible, provided only that it be *he* who is an existent. This is the unity of being, i.e., that situation of being an existent which demands that *that* situation be *one* thing's situation. There's nothing wonderful about 'that; after all, if *x* is, it must be *x* which is. Nor is there anything wonderful about Peter and Paul both being existents, actual or possible. This is the multiplicity of being, i.e., the situation of there being two existents which demands that *that* situation be *two* things' situation. There is nothing wonderful about that: after all, if there are two existents, there are two existents. What is wonderful is this: many existents, each enjoying the status of being an existent, need not, indeed cannot, enjoy that status solely upon the score that there are many of them. Yet they do enjoy that status. Why? The question (I am still repeating) would not even arise if there were only one existent. For, either you would be that one existent, or you wouldn't. If you were not that one existent, you would not be around to raise the question; and if you were that one existent, you would be quite content intellectually with that, because you would see that to-be-an-existent is to be yourself, and to see that is as satisfactory as to see that a toot is a toot. What else indeed could a toot be if not a toot? Just so, what else could an existent be except yourself if you were the only one? But such is not the complete case. The complete case is this: there are many existents, and we cannot see why there should be many existents upon the score that they are all existents, any more than we can see why there are many toots upon the score that all toots are toots. Of course all toots are toots. That is not remarkable. The remarkable thing is that there *are* many toots. Now, *that* is unintelligible upon the score that all toots are toots. To see this, recall the story about the irate policeman who asked the motorist why he tooted his horn. "I always toot it," the motorist replied. That was no answer, precisely because the motorist was saying that a toot is a toot. So it is, but that fact doesn't explain why there *is* any toot, and this is what the policeman wished to know. It is the same wonder we have when we are faced with many existents: although an existent is an existent, quite as a toot is a toot, there's nothing in the status of being an existent which demands that there be many existents. Why, then, are they many?

One who sees the situation will agree that it is wonderful enough. The difficulty here lies in seeing the situation. We must strive to see it, as the man, who has always seen black on white, tries and suddenly sees white on black.

Summary of the Question

At any rate this is the situation: in order that there be an existent there need not be many of them; yet there are many existents. And this is the question: why, then, are there many existents?

because they have been caused.

The Answer to the Question

The answer to that question is as follows: many existents are caused to be existents, actual or possible, and are therefore caused to be many by a cause which has what it takes to do the job, or has what it takes to be able to do the job.

We have now stated three propositions. (1) The status of being an existent is both one and many. (2) This status of being many existents is caused. (3) This status is caused by a cause which has what it takes to do or to be able to do the job.

The knowledge of these three propositions is what is known as metaphysics, and it will be the purpose of this book and Natural Theology to generate the knowledge of those three propositions. This book will try to generate the knowledge that multiple being is caused being, an insight which already contains in solution, so to say, the third insight: the cause of multiple being is uncaused.

* * * * * *

While many reasons lead me to introduce a student to metaphysics in the way I have, the principal one is this: whereas a student can, with patience and effort on the part of the teacher, grasp the metaphysical situation and the metaphysical question it raises, no one (I have found) learns any metaphysics before grasping that situation and that question. To expect a student to learn the metaphysical problem of the divisions of the sciences, e.g., before he knows any metaphysics, is like asking him to pull himself up by his bootstraps.

At any rate, it seems clear that one can think metaphysically without knowing fully the nature of such thinking. And the proof is that you have just done such thinking. It is not too hard to do. When you ask a child why he beats a drum and are told, "because I always beat it," you are not quite satisfied with the answer. Nor should you be satisfied with this answer to the question why there are many existents: "there are many of them." It won't do. To see that it will not do is to think metaphysically, and to see what will do in order to account for the situation is the science of metaphysics.

Suggested Reading

The Nature of Metaphysics:

Aristotle, *Metaphysics*, IV (Γ), 1–2; VI (E), 1; XI (K), 3.
St. Thomas Aquinas, *In Metaph.*, Prooemium; *In IV Metaph.*, lect. 1;

In VI Metaph., lect. 1; *In XI Metaph.*, lect. 4; *In Boet. de Trin.*, V, 1; *Contra Gentiles*, I, 1.

Eslick, L., "What is the Starting-Point of Metaphysics?" in *The Modern Schoolman*, Vol. XXXIV, n. 4 (May 1957), pp. 247-263.

Henle, R., S.J., *Method in Metaphysics*, pp. 1-73.

Klubertanz, G., S.J., "The Teaching of Thomistic Metaphysics," in *Gregorianum*, Vol. XXXV (1954), pp. 9-13, 192-201.

Maréchal, J., S.J., *Le point de départ de la métaphysique*, Vol. V, Bk. II, sec. 1, pp. 38-53.

Maritain, J., *Distinguer pour unir, ou les degrés de savoir*, ch. I; *Sept leçons sur l'être*, Leçon I and III; *Court traité de l'existence et de l'existant*, ch. I.

Owens, J., C.Ss.R., "A Note on the Approach to Thomistic Metaphysics," in *The New Scholasticism*, Vol. V, n. 28 (1954), pp. 454-476; "The Intelligibility of Being," in *Gregorianum*, Vol. V, n. 36 (1955), pp. 169-193; *The Doctrine of Being in the Aristotelian Metaphysics*, pp. 147-180; *St. Thomas and the Future of Metaphysics*, pp. 1-61.

Paulus, J., *Henri de Gand. Essai sur les tendances de sa métaphysique*, ch. I.

Robert, J.-D., O.P., "La métaphysique, science distincte de toute autre discipline philosophique, selon saint Thomas d'Aquin," *Divus Thomas Plac.*, Vol. L, nn. 3-4, pp. 206-222.

The Problem of Unity and Multiplicity in Being:

Plato, *Phaedrus*, 266b; *Parmenides*, 128a-129d; *Sophist*, 244a-245e; *Philebus*, 14a-17e.

Aristotle, *Metaphysics*, I (A), chs. 1-10; IV (Γ), chs. 1-8.

St. Thomas Aquinas, *In I Metaph.*, lect. 1-17; *In IV Metaph.*, lect. 1-17.

Forest, A., *La structure métaphysique du concret selon saint Thomas d'Aquin*, pp. 25-45.

Geiger, L.-B., O.P., *La participation dans la philosophie de s. Thomas d'Aquin*, pp. 77-84, 156-217, 238-258, 365-398.

Gilson, E., *L'être et l'essence*, pp. 21-45; *Being and Some Philosophers*, pp. 1-40.

Marc, A., S.J., *L'Idée de l'être chez Saint Thomas et dans la scolastique postérieure*.

Pegis, A. C., "The Dilemma of Being and Unity," *Essays in Thomism*, pp. 151-183, 379-382.

———, *St. Thomas and the Greeks*.

Smith, G., S.J., *Natural Theology*, pp. 12-17.

The Cause of Being:

Aristotle, *Metaphysics*, I (A), 2.

St. Thomas Aquinas, *In IV Metaph.*, lect. 1; *Contra Gentiles*, I, 1.

Anderson, J., *The Cause of Being.*

Forest, A., *La structure métaphysique du concret selon saint Thomas d'Aquin*, pp. 46–71.

Gilson, E., *Being and Some Philosophers*, pp. 156–157.

Owens, J., C.Ss.R., "The Causal Proposition—Principle or Conclusion?" *The Modern Schoolman*, Vol. XXXII, n. 2 (January 1955), pp. 159–171; Vol. XXXII, n. 3 (March 1955), pp. 257–270; Vol. XXXII, n. 4 (May 1955), pp. 323–330.

II · PASSIVE POTENCY IN A BECOMING BEING

Summary of the First Chapter

Since in metaphysics nothing is less repetitious than repetition, we shall now repeat what we have already seen. This much we have seen: there are many existents, actual and possible. And this: the reason for there being many existents cannot be because to be an existent is to be many of them, nor can it be because to be many existents is to be any one of them. Whichever way you try to explain the unity and multiplicity of the status of being an existent, your mind goes blank. Your mind goes blank because the status of being an existent has disappeared, like the doughnut with only the hole left. The status of being an existent has disappeared, by such pseudo-identifications, because on the one hand if to-be-an-existent is necessarily to be many of them, then there is no one existent unless absolutely every other actual existent is always actual, and unless every other possible existent is always possible. Yet Aristotle was an existent when Peter was not, and Peter could be without Paul, and Peter's unborn older brother cannot now exist at all, although he might have. Now, all those propositions must be denied if to be an existent is necessarily to be many existents, because any one of these actual existents just mentioned existed without the others having to be actual, and many of the once possible existents are no longer possible. On the other hand, if to be many existents explains why one of them is an existent, then the many, which cannot explain themselves, explain that one—the many are one. In sum, if there is only one existent, there aren't many, and this is against the fact; or, if there be many existents because to be one of them is to be all of

11

them, then the many are that one existent. This latter situation is impossible.[1]

Make a dry run to test the matter. Say: to be sick is to be many sick people. Nonsense. Upon that basis, everybody would be sick. Or say: to be many sick people is to be one sick person. Nonsense. On that basis, there are not and could not be many sick people. The only difference between the identification of many sick persons with one sick person (or *vice versa*), and the identification of many existents with one existent (or *vice versa*), is that the disaster in the second case is complete. Conceivably, everybody could be sick, although everybody is not. But nobody could even be, let alone be sick, if to be an existent is to be every one of them or *vice versa*.

In order to keep our mind from going blank when thinking that to be an existent is to be one and also to be many (this we do think, because this is the fact), we must think, not that the many are one, or *vice versa*, but that the many are caused to be.

Preliminary Consideration of a Cause

It is self-evident that the number of fish in Lake Michigan is odd or even. Not that a given number of fish is odd or even. That is impossible. One given number like 3 is odd; another given number

---

[1] Aristotle criticizes the identification of being with unity and multiplicity in the following texts. *Physics*, I, 2, 185a 1-10: "For just as the geometer has nothing more to say to one who denies the principles of his science— . . . so a man investigating principles cannot argue with one who denies their existence. For if Being is just one, . . . there is a principle no longer, since a principle must be a principle of some thing or things. To inquire therefore whether Being is one in this sense would be like arguing against any other position maintained for the sake of argument (such as the Heraclitean thesis, or such a thesis as that Being is one man) or like refuting a merely contentious argument—a description which applies to the arguments both of Melissus and of Parmenides: their premisses are false and their conclusions do not follow." *Physics*, I, 2, 185b 20-22: "But if (c) all things are one in the sense of having the same definition, like 'raiment' and 'dress,' then it turns out that they are maintaining the Heraclitean doctrine, for it will be the same thing 'to be good' and 'to be bad,' and 'to be good,' and 'to be not good,' and so the same thing will be 'good' and 'not good,' and man and horse; in fact, their view will be, not that all things are one, but that they are nothing; and that 'to be of such-and-such a quality' is the same as 'to be of such-and-such a size.'"

like 4 is even. A number, however, is odd or even until it is given, e.g., by counting the fish; but until it is given a number is odd or even.[2]

It is the same with the status of being an existent. It is self-evident that an existent is caused or uncaused. An existent could be either caused or uncaused, but not neither; nor can we know which it is, caused or uncaused, until we examine. See well what this means. It means that nothing in the status of being an existent demands that it be caused or uncaused, no more than does anything in the nature of number demand that it be odd or even. All that is required for an existent to be an existent is that it exist, actually or possibly. Causality is not necessarily the reason why there is an existent, not necessarily a principle of being. Causality is a principle, a source, a reason why there is an existent only when examination reveals that the existent examined must be caused.[3] Causality is a principle of caused being, not a principle of being, and that a being be caused must be demonstrated. In short, "to be caused" is a predicate of a being when it is proved that a being is caused, pretty much as "odd" or "even" is a predicate of a number only after examination has shown whether the number is odd or even.

[2] St. Thomas makes this point in *Sum. Theol.*, I, 19, 3, *Resp.*: "There are two ways in which a thing is said to be necessary, namely, absolutely, and by supposition. We judge a thing to be absolutely necessary from the relation of the terms, as when the predicate forms part of the definition of the subject: thus it is necessary that man is an animal; or as when the subject forms part of the notion of the predicate: thus it is necessary that a number must be odd or even. In this way it is not necessary that Socrates sits: hence it is not necessary absolutely, but it may be so by supposition; for, granted that he is sitting, he must necessarily sit, as long as he is sitting."

[3] That the existent demands a cause, see Aristotle, *Posterior Analytics*, II, 8, 93a 5: "Now to know its essential nature is, as we said, the same as to know the cause of a thing's existence, and the proof of this depends on the fact that a thing must have a cause." St. Thomas, *Sum. Theol.*, I, 44, 1, *ad* 1: "Though relation to its cause is not part of the definition of a thing caused, still it follows as a result of what belongs to its nature. For, from the fact that a thing is being by participation, it follows that it is caused. Hence such a being cannot be without being caused, just as man cannot be without having the faculty of laughing. But, since to be caused does not enter into the nature of being absolutely, that is why there exists a being that is uncaused." On this same point, see *Contra Gentiles*, I, 22; *De Ente et Essentia*, ch. 4; J. Owens, C.Ss.R., "The Causal Proposition—Principle or Conclusion?"

Why Plurality Needs a Cause

There is this about an existent which demands that it be caused: its status of being an existent is enjoyed by many existents, no one of which is the other. In short, plurality demands a cause because it is plurality.[4]

We may see why plurality must be caused by examining, first, the plurality within one given being; next, by examining the plurality between one given kind of being and another kind; last, by examining the plurality among different beings, whether they do or do not differ in states and kinds.

The last case is the honest-to-goodness, sure enough metaphysical situation, and the job of explaining that situation is a metaphysician's job. The first two situations are situations in qualified being. We do not necessarily find those qualified situations of being when we examine merely the status of being an existent. The status of being an existent need not be qualified or unqualified, one or many, although in fact it is all that. Those statuses of a qualified existent, however, are situations with which a metaphysician can profitably begin, first, because they are better known than the status itself of being an existent; second, because what he has to say about unity and multiplicity in their regard is pregnant with what he will have to say about the unity and multiplicity of the status itself of being an existent. A metaphysician in other words makes preliminary and side remarks about qualified statuses of an existent before he discourses upon that status itself of an existent, which may or may not have given qualifications. For, though metaphysics gets no help or hin-

---

[4] In *Contra Gentiles*, II, 15, St. Thomas shows that plurality demands a cause: "But being is predicated of everything that is. Hence, there cannot possibly be two things neither of which has a cause of its being, but either both of them must exist through a cause, or the one must be the cause of the other's being. Everything which is in any at at all must then derive its being from that whose being has no cause. . . . Again, everything that can be and not-be has a cause; for considered in itself it is indifferent to either, so that something else must exist which determines it to one. Since, then, it is impossible to go on to infinity, there must exist a necessary being which is the cause of all things that can be and not-be."

drance from the sciences, the philosophy of nature, or the philosophy of man, nevertheless the metaphysician and those who are learning metaphysics are helped by first examining plurality in qualified being. Further relations of metaphysics to the fields of knowledge will be discussed later.

We shall, then, examine three cases of unity in plurality: (1) the case of an existent which is plural in its states, e.g., John unmusical and later musical; (2) the case of one existent *kind* of being which turns into another existent *kind* of being, e.g., the inorganic turns into the organic, and *vice versa;* (3) the case of one existent which, whatever be its states or kind, is not another existent.

In case (1), John's becoming musical is *John's* becoming (unity), yet the musical is not the unmusical (plurality). In case (2), *something* must be common to the organic and the inorganic (unity), yet the organic is not the inorganic (plurality). In case (3), one existent is an existent (unity), yet one existent is not another existent (plurality).

The Need of a Cause of Change

In case (1), and in the two cases thereafter, it is essential to recognize the facts. Yes or no, does John become musical? If you say *yes* to that or any other similar question, you commit yourself to saying that there exists a changing or becoming being. Now, you don't have to commit yourself to saying there exists a changing being, precisely because you don't have to commit yourself to saying there exists a being. You could say, e.g., that we merely think there is a being, but there isn't. Or you could say that there exists a changing being because we *must* think there does, which is to say that a changing being is our *thinking* that there is a changing being.[5] You could say that or things like that, but if you do, you have against you the evidence of facts. The facts are, John does become

[5] On Aristotle's refutation of sophism, see *Metaphysics*, IV (Γ), chs. 3–8; IX (Θ), 10, 1051b 7; G. Smith, S.J., *The Truth That Frees*, Milwaukee, Marquette University Press, 1956, pp. 2–7.

musical, gets bigger, moves from here to there, and so on. There is
no proof of these facts; nor are they self-evident. They are simply
evident.[6]

A self-evident situation is such that it cannot be otherwise, e.g.,
2 plus 2 equals 4. None of John's situations as a changing being is
such that it couldn't be otherwise. Nor is there any proof that the
description of the above situations of a changing being, viz., becoming musical, bigger, etc., fits the case of John. Proof is based upon
self-evident and evident propositions, and neither the self-evident
nor the evident proposition can be proved.[7] The only reason why
we know that things change is the evidence that they do. These two
evidences, that things change and that they exist, are given together
in the sensory-intellectual knowledge of man.

As we said, you may, if you wish, deny this evidence, but if you
do, you are committed not merely to being cautious about given
evidence—that is a virtue—but also committed to being cautious
to the point of denying evidence itself—that is a vice. Caution
carried to the point of refusing to commit oneself to evidence is
like vanity: as a virtue it is inexcusable. Just so, it is no virtue to
deny evidence. Let it then be clearly understood that realism
acknowledges that things exist and that they change. Realists don't
prove these propositions or claim them to be self-evident. They
take them as evident, and if they be naive in doing so, theirs is the
naïveté of the human race.

Realism understands the fact of becoming in the following com-
mon-sense way: John-becoming-musical is no longer unmusical, and
is not yet musical; he is on the way to being musical.

---

[6] Aristotle asserts the evidence of change in *Physics*, I, 2, 185a 12-14: "We
physicists, on the other hand, must take for granted that the things that exist
by nature are, either all or some of them, in motion—which is indeed made
plain by induction." St. Thomas makes the same point in *In II Phys.*, lect. 1, n.
148: ". . . it is ridiculous to try to demonstrate that nature exists, since it is
evident to sense that many things exist by nature which have in themselves the
principle of their own motion."
[7] On the nature of demonstration, and evident and self-evident knowledge,
see Aristotle, *Posterior Analytics*, I, 2, 71b 18-72b 4; St. Thomas, *In IV Metaph.*,
lect. 6, nn. 597-608.

Passive Potency

Only two suppositions can make that fact so described intelligible: first, there is in John a passive potency; second, there is an active potency or cause of John's becoming.[8]

To explain the first supposition. We say that a monkey cannot write a symphony. We also say that the baby Beethoven cannot write a symphony either. Both statements are true. Yet the "cannot" does not have the same meaning in both cases. The monkey cannot write a symphony in the sense that there is no supposition possible upon which he could. The baby Beethoven cannot write a symphony in the sense that he cannot while he is a child, but there is a supposition upon which he could, viz., if he were to grow up and learn how. Clearly, it is not the monkey's or the baby Beethoven's lack of symphonies which differs. Both have written nothing. The monkey and baby Beethoven, nonetheless, differ because, whereas the monkey absolutely cannot write a symphony, the baby Beethoven can, even though he doesn't and cannot now. The baby Beethoven is able to write them; he possesses the ability to write, and the name of that ability is passive potency.[9]

---

[8] On passive potency, see Aristotle, *Physics*, III, 1-2; *Metaphysics*, IX (Θ), 1-9; St. Thomas, *In III Phys.*, lect. 2; *In V Metaph.*, lect. 14, n. 955; *Sum. Theol.*, I, 25, 1, *Resp.* On active potency, see Aristotle, *Physics*, III, 3; St. Thomas, *In III Phys.*, lect. 5. On action and passion in change, see Aristotle, *Physics*, III, 3, 202a 12-22: "The solution of the difficulty that is raised about the motion—whether it is in the *movable*—is plain. It is the fulfilment of this potentiality, and by the action of that which has the power of causing motion; and the actuality of that which has the power of causing motion is not other than the actuality of the movable, for it must be the fulfilment of *both*. A thing is capable of causing motion because it *can* do this, it is a mover because it actually *does* it. But it is on the movable that it is capable of acting. Hence there is a single actuality of both alike, just as one to two and two to one are the same interval, and the steep ascent and the steep descent are one— for these are one and the same, although they can be described in different ways. So it is with the mover and the moved." Aristotle repeats this text in *Metaphysics*, XI (K), 9, 1066a 26-34. St. Thomas makes the same point in *In XI Metaph.*, lect. 9, n. 2312; *Sum. Theol.*, II-II, 90, 3; *Contra Gentiles*, II, 16. John of St. Thomas speaks of change as the act of a being in potency—from the cause, in the effect, *Cursus Philosophicus, Ars Logica*, Pars II, q. 19, a. 2; ed. Reiser, t. I, p. 627b 19; *Phil. Nat.*, Pars I, q. 14, a. 4; Reiser, t. II, p. 312a 11.

[9] There is a feature about the ability to write a symphony which is also

Be very sure that you see, first, that passive potency (the ability to write symphonies) is in *no* sense the actuation of that potency, is in *no* sense the actual writing of them. Many have tried to understand passive potency as a diminutive act, as if the actual writing of symphonies were under wraps within the ability to write them, like peas in a pea shooter or the rabbit in the hat—there all the time, and needing only to have the wraps pulled aside, or the peas blown out, in order to reveal the passive potency for what it was all along, namely, an act in hiding, so to say. No. Its actuation is in no sense within passive potency. Next, be very sure you see that the actual writing so affects the writer that it is *he* who writes when he does write; it is *his* potency to write which his writing actuates. The reason is: it is *he* who can write even when he doesn't, and when he does write it is *he* who is writing.

Change Explained

Such being the nature of passive potency, we are now prepared to understand change or becoming. Consider this diagram: $x^{-1} \longrightarrow x^{+1}$. Let x be a man, let -1 be his qualification as unmusical; let $+1$ be his qualification as musical; let the arrow indicate the process of his becoming musical. At any spot along the arrow, namely, x's becoming musical, x is no longer -1 (unmusical), nor is x quite $+1$ (musical): x is *becoming* musical. X's becoming $+1$, therefore, is a composite of two factors: (a) the actuation of x, because x is no longer unmusical, (b) which actuated x is still in potency, because x is not yet musical. Act and potency, then, these compose a changing being. In other words, since any point in the process of becoming

"active," but this feature would occur only to one who knows something about active potency. We must not let one knowledge get in the way of another, even if we have that first knowledge. So here: we must not let the fact that Beethoven did write symphonies get in the way of seeing that he could write them even when he did not and could not the while he was a baby. At any rate, if the example fails, try another one: a tree cannot see, and neither can a blindfolded man; nevertheless, the "cannot" doesn't mean the same thing in both cases: the tree absolutely cannot see; the blindfolded man can —if the blindfold is removed.

something is the actuation (act) of the potency of a being to become that something, and since that very actuated being itself is still in potency with respect to further actuation, therefore becoming is the act of a being in potency as such. The "as such" means, "while the being is still potential."[10]

One or other paraphrase of the description of becoming may help us see the matter.

Becoming Is a Continuous Process[11]

Let the becoming in question be a change of temperature of x. Do not think that when x changes from 1° to 10° there is a spot along the arrow (during the becoming, that is) when x is 2°, another spot when it is 3°, etc. Should you take a reading of x's becoming 10°, and should the reading show 4°, this would mean that at that time x was not *becoming* 4°, it *was* 4°. X's becoming 4° would have been during the interval from 1° to 4°. So for any other reading.

Becoming Is not Replacement

Let us say the same thing in another way. X's becoming is not a series of states of x, one state replacing another, like a series of tiny inserts. Should you think it was, you would have missed the specificity of motion. The motion or change is precisely the inter-

[10] Aristotle, *Physics*, III, 1, 201b 5–7: ". . . clearly it is the fulfilment of what is potential *as* potential that is motion. So this, precisely, is motion. Further it is evident that motion is an attribute of a thing just *when* it is fully real in this way, and neither before nor after." See also St. Thomas, *In III Phys.*, lect. 3, n. 292.

[11] Aristotle, *Physics*, III, 1, 200b 16: "Now motion is supposed to belong to the class of things which are *continuous*; . . ." Aristotle argues for the continuity of motion in *Physics*, VI, 1, 231b 15–232a 18, especially 231b 27–30: "Now a thing that is in motion from one place to another cannot at the moment when it was in motion both be in motion and at the same time have completed its motion at the place to which it was in motion: e.g., if a man is walking to Thebes, he cannot be walking to Thebes and at the same time have completed his walk to Thebes. . . ."

val *between* the states or inserts, if any. *There* lies the becoming. To think you can compose motion out of a series of discontinuous states, no matter how small the interval between the different states may be, this is to think that there is no change. For, these states, being discontinuous, are not states of becoming; they are states of being *before* or *after* a being has become. Of course, you might try to think that the discontinuous states came so fast that they give us the illusion of continuity, like the discontinuous states of each picture in a motion picture film. But precisely, each *picture* in the film *is* discontinuous, whereas the state of becoming of the *thing pictured* is *not* discontinuous. Were the state of becoming of the thing pictured as discontinuous as are the pictures of that state, then you would have totally different things, just as you have totally different pictures of it. But the state of becoming is not made up of totally different things. It is made up of one thing, whose becoming-different is precisely an actuation which is still potential to further actuation.[12] Thus we are back at the definition of a thing in motion: the act of a being in potency as such.

Becoming Is the Actuation of the Potential as Such

Let us say the same thing again. Assume something actual, like bricks, mortar, steel, etc.: building material. Assume that this building material can become a building. Then the change of this building material into the building is the becoming of the building. Thus, the becoming of a house consists in bringing building materials from that state of being which *can* form a house into the state of

[12] Aristotle, *Physics*, I, 7, 190a 14: ". . . there must be an underlying something, namely that which becomes, and that this, though always one numerically, in form at least is not one." *Physics*, I, 7, 190a 33-37: "Now in all cases other than substance it is plain that there must be some subject, namely, that which becomes. For we know that when a thing comes to be of such a quantity or quality or in such relation, time or place, a subject is always presupposed, since substance alone is not predicated of another subject, but everything else of substance." See also St. Thomas, *In XII Metaph.*, lect. 2, nn. 2429-2430.

becoming a house. After the movement of constructing a house is over, the buildable is no longer in act; the built, the house, is in act. The buildable in act is the buildable in the process of being built, and the act of the buildable (the becoming of the house) lies precisely in the buildable's becoming builded.[18] Thus, movement implies a potential factor (the buildable) which has not as yet lost all its potentiality in the course of becoming actual, nor has it gained all its actuality, precisely because it is still in the process of becoming actual. When the buildable has lost all its potentiality, then it is no longer in movement; it is in act. Act nullifies the potentiality to itself, but in movement act does not completely nullify the potentiality thereto, because the act of the potential (*as* potential) or of the being in potency (inasmuch as the being is still in potency) is precisely not fully in actuation, not fully act. Thus, becoming differs from actuation as incomplete act differs from complete act: movement is incompleted act, and act is completed movement. Movement is neither the purely potential nor the purely actual: it is the actualization of the potential inasmuch as the potential is still potential, and the actual is not fully actual. In sum: (1) before movement there is only the building material, not the house; (2) after movement there is only the house, not the unactuated material, nor the material-becoming-actual; (3) in between, the interval when motion takes place, there is no longer the purely potential house, nor as yet the actual house; (4) in that "in-between" there is

---

[18] Aristotle, *Metaphysics*, XI (K), 9, 1065b 17–1066a 7: "When the 'buildable,' in so far as it is what we mean by 'buildable,' exists actually, it is being built, and this is the process of building. Similarly with learning, healing, walking, leaping. ageing, ripening. Movement takes place when the complete reality itself exists, and neither earlier nor later. The complete reality, then, of that which exists potentially when it is completely real and actual, not *qua* itself, but *qua* movable, is movement. . . . it is the complete reality of the potential, and *as potential*, that is movement. That it is this, and that movement takes place when the complete reality itself exists, and neither earlier nor later, is evident. For each thing is capable of being sometimes actual, sometimes not, e.g., the buildable *qua* buildable; and the actuality of the buildable *qua* buildable—or the house. But when the *house* exists, it is no longer buildable; the buildable is what *is being* built. The actuality, then, must be the *act of building*, and this is a movement." Aristotle says the same in *Physics*, III, 1, 201a 15–17. See also St. Thomas, *In III Phys.*, lect. 2, n. 287; *In XI Metaph.*, lect. 9, n. 2297.

that which is potentially a house *becoming* a house, not that which is potentially a house not becoming a house, as in (1). Movement is thus, once more, the act of a being in potency in so far as the being is still in potency.

Becoming in Terms of Its Termini and Privation

Another description of change. You may describe motion in three ways: (1) bricks become a house; (2) something not-a-house becomes a house; (3) bricks, which are not a house, become a house.[14] The first description takes account of the permanent element in change, viz., bricks, the *terminus a quo* of change. The second description takes account of the impermanent element of change, viz., the something not-a-house, a something affected with privation. The third description takes account of both the permanent (bricks) and the impermanent (something-not-a-house) elements of change. These two elements, the permanent and the impermanent, are not inseparate in thought, for to be bricks is not *necessarily* the same thing as to be something which is not a house because, though bricks are not a house, lumber is not a house either. Now, the numerical identity of bricks with something which is not-a-house might cause you to miss the point that it need not be bricks which is not a house, for though bricks can become a house, so also can lumber. If you miss that point, you miss the point in understanding change, viz., the permanence or persistence of the subject of change, viz., bricks or lumber, or whatever can become a house.

Becoming in Terms of Its Subject

Another description of change. As we saw, Coriscus-walking-to-the-marketplace is an actuation of Coriscus, because he is no longer

---

[14] In describing the three ways of motion, Aristotle uses the example of a man becoming musical, *Physics*, I, 7, 189b 35–190a 4: "We can say (1) the 'man becomes musical,' (2) what is 'not-musical becomes musical,' or (3) the 'not-musical man becomes a musical man.'"

at home where he is merely able to walk to the marketplace; yet that actuation is still potential, because Coriscus while walking to is not yet at the marketplace. Now, as material or stuff *out of which* the composite, Coriscus-walking, will be made, Coriscus at home is *not* the composite of Coriscus-walking. Nevertheless, as material or stuff *in which* his walking is taking place, Coriscus *is* identical with Coriscus-walking. Coriscus-walking is, therefore, a composite of two components, himself and his walking, neither of which components is the composite. The composite is Coriscus-walking, a changing "permanent," or, if you will, a "permanent" which is changing. You cannot find this composite at either end of the process (the x^{-1} or the x^{+1} stage), because before Coriscus walks there's no change, and after he has quit walking change is over and done.

However, at either end of the process you do indeed find a composite of Coriscus and qualifications *other* than his walking, and the composite of him and those other qualifications are exactly like the composite of him and his walking; that is, you find at either end of the process a composite of components, neither of which is the composite; rather, the composite is the components. In other words, a becoming being is always becoming in some respects, and so it is always a composite. Becoming, which is continuous, is a constant characteristic of becomers, though they are not always in the same *kind* of becoming.

"The act of a being in potency as such" is therefore a description not only of a section or cut of a changing being, but also a description of a changing being's total duration as a being: it is always being actuated in some sense, and its actuation is always potential to some further, or different, actuation, or to the loss of its present actuation. Do not think, therefore, that the "permanent" factor of a changing being is related to the impermanent factors as a man is related to his hat, or as a kernel is related to its shell. You could have a hatless man and a shelled nut, but there could not be a permanent factor in changing being unless that permanent factor were changing, always changing in some respect. Were the permanent factor *not* always changing, there would be no changing being, except at certain periods, and to think of the permanent factor as not changing except at certain periods is not to think of changing being but of a changing and unchanging being; worse, it is not to think of a changing being at all, because there is no "period" where a changing being is not changing in some sense.

Hume so thought of that permanent factor.[16] If we name that permanent factor "substance" (from *sub-stare*, to stand under), and if we conceive substance as related to its impermanent factors, which are named "accidents," as being able to be without any accidents, then we must think that substance hides unchanged beneath its accidents as a man hides beneath a veil. Moreover, since such substance *never* steps from behind *such* a veil, we might as well dispense with substance altogether. This is exactly what Hume did. By this procedure he failed to understand changing substance as a subject of accidents. Changing substance as a subject of accidents cannot be without any and all accidents whatsoever. Moreover, its relation to its accidents is the relation of a component to components, i.e., substance with accidents is the composite; without some accidents, changing substance, whether becoming or already become, but not in all respects, is inconceivable and inexistible.

[16] See D. Hume, *A Treatise of Human Nature*, Bk. I, Part IV, sec. V; ed. L. Selby-Bigge, Oxford, Clarendon Press, 1928, pp. 233-234:

"For thus I reason. Whatever is clearly conceived, after any manner, may exist after the same manner. This is one principle, which has been already acknowledged. Again, every thing, which is different, is distinguishable, and every thing which is distinguishable, is separable by the imagination. This is another principle. My conclusion from both is, that since all our perceptions are different from each other, and from every thing else in the universe, they are also distinct and separable, and may be considered as separately existent, and may exist separately, and have no need of any thing else to support their existence. They are, therefore, substances, as far as this definition explains a substance.

"Thus neither by considering the first origin of ideas, nor by means of a definition are we able to arrive at any satisfactory notion of substance; which seems to me a sufficient reason for abandoning utterly that dispute concerning the materiality and immateriality of the soul, and makes me absolutely condemn even the question itself. We have no perfect idea of anything but of a perception. A substance is entirely different from a perception. We have, therefore, no idea of a substance. Inhesion in something is supposed to be requisite to support the existence of a perception. We have, therefore, no idea of inhesion. What possibility then of answering that question, *Whether perceptions inhere in a material or immaterial substance*, when we do not so much as understand the meaning of the question? . . ."

Ibid., Appendix, p. 635: "If perceptions are distinct existences, they form a whole only by being connected together. But no connexions among distinct existences are ever discoverable by human understanding."

Becoming and Privation

Privation or the −1 factor is not a principle of being. It is a principle of the beginning of movement.[16] Things are not (privation) what they will become, but we cannot say they are not what they are, or that they are not, absolutely, what they are becoming. You do not have to be a bad man in order to *be* a good man. You have to have been a bad man if you are to *become* a good one. All that is required to be a good man is to be one, but to become a good man, one must have been a bad one. Were one a good man, one would not need to have become good; one could always have been good. When it is said, then, that contraries come from contraries, this means that in order to become the +1, the potential must have been affected by the coefficient of privations, namely, the −1. Things cannot become what they already are, nor need a thing have become what it is: in order to become something, a subject or patient must not have been what it is to become.[17]

[16] Aristotle discusses becoming and privation in *Physics*, I, 8, 191b 13–16: "We ourselves are in agreement with them in holding that nothing can be said without qualification to come from what is not. But nevertheless we maintain that a thing may 'come to be from what is not'—that is, in a qualified sense. For a thing comes to be from a privation, which in its own nature is not-being—this not surviving as a constituent of the result." See St. Thomas, *In I Phys.*, lect. 13, n. 113: "Therefore it must be said that matter is never without privation because when it has one form it is with the privation of another form. Therefore, while something which comes to be (as musical man) is in the state of becoming, there is in the subject, when it does not yet have the form, the privation of the musical. Thus, the *per accidens* principle of musical man in the state of becoming is nonmusical because this happens to man while he becomes musical. But when he already has this latter form he has along with it the privation of another form. Thus the privation of the opposite form is the *per accidens* principle of existing. Therefore it is plain according to the intention of Aristotle that privation, which is given as a *per accidens* principle of nature, is not some aptitude for form nor an inchoation of form nor some imperfect active principle, as some say, but it is the very lack of form or the contrary of the form which happens to the subject." See also *De Principiis Naturae*, c. 2 in *Opuscula Philosophica*; ed. Marietti, n. 343: "Sunt igitur tria principia naturae, scilicet materia et forma et privatio; quorum alterum, scilicet forma, est id propter quod fit generatio; alia duo sunt ex parte eius ex quo est generatio. Unde materia et privatio sunt idem subiecto, sed differunt ratione."

[17] On the three principles of change: the subject, term and opposite, see

Becoming in Terms of Identity, Distinction, and Difference

Let us now describe change in terms of identity, distinction, and difference. That is identical which is itself, e.g., this mark ($\sqrt{}$) is identical; but these two marks ($\sqrt{}$ $\sqrt{}$) are not, because one mark's "self" is not the other's. Observe, to be identical or to be oneself is a necessary condition in order that there may be, and in order that we may know there is, an existent. For, unless an existent were itself, *it* would not be; something else would by hypothesis be the "it," and so that something else would be something else again, and so on indefinitely. Now, such a series of supposed "selfs" is impossible, because, none being its *own* self, none of them is a "self." Our knowledge reflects this status of the identity of an existent with itself, for unless we saw the identical thing the next time we took a look at it, or indeed, even while we are looking at it, we should never know that *it* was an existent. Yet we do know that a given thing exists, and so we know that it stays identical with itself. "Identity" is an abstraction from the "identical," and it is a characteristic which each identical thing has, viz., it is itself.[18] "To be distinct" means nothing unless there be something to be distinct from. It is the same for "to be different." Hence, that is distinct or different which is not something else. "Distinction" and "difference" are abstractions from the "distinct" and the "different." Sometimes "distinctions" and "differences" are used concretely, and then they mean as above a different or distinct thing. Sometimes, and more usually, "difference" and "distinction" name the reason why distinct or different things differ. Should that reason be described, "differ-

---

Aristotle, *Physics*, I, 7, 190b 10-15: "Thus, clearly, from what has been said, whatever comes to be is always complex. There is, on the one hand (a) something which comes into existence, and again (b) something which becomes that—the latter (b) in two senses, either the subject or the opposite. By the 'opposite' I mean the 'unmusical,' or by the 'subject' 'man,' and similarly I call the absence of shape or form or order the 'opposite,' and the bronze or stone or gold the 'subject.'" See also *Physics*, I, 7, 190b 28-35; *Metaphysics*. XII (Λ), chs. 2-3; St. Thomas, *In I Phys.*, lect. 12.

[18] On identity and difference in becoming, see note 12 of this chapter.

ence" also names that which the description of difference describes. To illustrate, say "Peter is wise." Peter stays identical as a specific kind (the *man* kind) of individual, whether wise or stupid; yet Peter-wise is different from Peter, and from Peter-stupid, and the differences are stupidity and wisdom.[19]

The problem is this: how may Peter, when he is becoming wise, stay identical, as he must if he is to be an existent, whereas he is not identical because he changes?

We may as well face it. Peter-becoming is not ever fully himself, not ever fully identical. Nor does he quite lose hold upon being himself while he is becoming wise. His identity is not perfect, not absolute, and this is exactly what we should expect; for if he were quite identical he would not be *becoming*, and if he were not at all identical it would not be *he* who is becoming. This is what we might expect in a becoming being, but we have not yet stated the grounds of such expectation, we have not yet answered our question: why is a becoming being not fully itself, and yet is itself withal?

The answer is as follows. A becoming being must be a composite of two components, neither of which components is the composite; both of the components together are the one composite. If a becoming being had no components, e.g., Peter and his becoming-wise, it could not be both identical with itself (as it is, for Peter-becoming is the same specific kind of individual) and unidentical with itself (as it is, for Peter is not the same before his becoming as he is during it; and, what is even more important, even during his becoming Peter does not remain quite identical, because he changes). Without two components, a becoming being would be both identical and unidentical with itself in a *single* factor, and two contradictory predi-

[19] See Aristotle, *Categories*, ch. 5, 4a 10–20: "The most distinctive mark of substance appears to be that, while remaining numerically one and the same, it is capable of admitting contrary qualities. From among things other than substance, we should find ourselves unable to bring forward any which possessed this mark. Thus, one and the same color cannot be white and black. Nor can the same one action be good and bad: this law holds good with everything that is not substance. But one and the self-same substance, while retaining its identity, is yet capable of admitting contrary qualities. The same individual person is at one time good, at another bad. . . ."

[handwritten margin note, top: essentially you have to have two components which are different otherwise you are a contradiction.]

[handwritten margin note, left side: the components they have to be totally distinct]

cates of a single factor are a contradiction in terms—like saying *Peter is and is not identical*, or, *is and is not changing*. Our minds go blank at that situation, because a blank has moved into our thinking instead of a changing being, that is, we are not thinking of anything at all any more. With two components, however, a becoming being could be identical with itself according to one of them, and unidentical with itself according to the other. It could, but upon two conditions: (1) the components must be so distinct that of one we must be able to say *it is not the other;* (2) yet the components must be so united that we must say of the unit which they cause that it, the unit or composite, is becoming.

We must go into this a bit. It is easy to see and say that becoming involves a subject of becoming. How, indeed, could there be becoming when nothing becomes? It is also easy to see and say that a subject which is *not* becoming is distinct from that same subject when it *is* becoming. How, indeed, could Peter be identical with his becoming, unless he were becoming before his becoming, which latter situation would be against the fact? The difficult thing to see is this: Peter, who is one component of Peter-becoming, is not the other component, viz., the becoming-wise, *the while Peter is becoming;* yet the two components cause one composite, of which you must say that it, the composite, is becoming. Not only, therefore, is Peter *not* his becoming *before* he becomes, he is not even his becoming *while* he becomes; yet it is *he* who is becoming, because, while becoming, he is a composite, and it is this, the composite, which is becoming; the composite is not Peter apart from his becoming, nor is it his becoming apart from Peter. The separate factors of becoming do not become.

We must have this again. Assume the fact: Peter is becoming wise. Before becoming wise, Peter is *not* his becoming; else he would not become, he would have been, wise. Nor is Peter during his becoming identical with his becoming, because upon that hypothesis Peter would not be Peter unless he were becoming, and that is against the fact: Peter stays Peter, before, during, and after his becoming. Yet Peter becomes wise. Conclusion: Peter-becoming is a unit of two components, and it is this unit which is a becoming being; its separate components are not a becoming being. Not even the component which is Peter? Is not even *that* component becoming? No, not if you speak of that component as uncompounded with its becoming; that *uncompounded* component is not becoming. But if you mean that Peter, as compounded with his becoming, is becoming, yes, he is becoming. Notice, though, that he is a composite, and that it is as a composite that he is becoming. This is to say that the composite is becoming, and this is perhaps the central insight into change.

Let us insist upon that insight. The components of a changing being are so distinct that of one you must say *it is not the other.* The composite of those components is identical with itself according to the subject of becoming, and that same composite is unidentical with itself according to the other component, viz., its becoming. To understand how that situation is possible is to understand change. Now comes a statement of that understanding, the central insight: besides being identical according to the subject of change (Peter is identically the specific kind of individual, before, during, and after change), the composite *differs* also according to the *very same subject* by which it stays the same, because becoming so affects the subject of becoming that it is the *subject* which *differs;* furthermore, besides being different according to the accident of its becoming, the composite remains *identical* also according to the *very same accident* of becoming by which the composite differs, because "becoming" is the becoming of the *same* subject. This is the insight, and it is completely unintelligible if the subject and its becoming are each principles of sameness and difference in the same order. But they are not. The subject is the principle of sameness and difference in the order of potency; its becoming is the principle of sameness and difference in the order of actualization or act. To paraphrase, consider this: the subject of becoming is the principle of *sameness* in the order of potency, because it is the same Peter who *can* become different (potency), that *does* become different (act); the subject is also the principle of *difference* in the order of potency, because it is that Peter, who *is* becoming different (act), who *could* become different (potency). Consider next: "becoming" is the principle of *sameness* in the order of act, because Peter's *becoming* different (act) is his *own,* the same Peter's (potency), becoming;

Peter's becoming different causes him to be different.

"becoming" is also the principle of *difference* in the order of act, because Peter's becoming different (act) causes *him* (potency) to differ. In sum, "becoming" (act) actualizes a subject, causing the subject to be the "*same-different*" and, because the "difference" is the difference of the same, it also causes the subject to be the "*different-same*"—in the order of act. The subject (potency) is actualized, causing the composite to be the "*same*-different" and, because the "same" differs, the subject also causes the composite to be the "*different-same*" in the order of potency.

By this time you may feel you have had just about enough of this. However, we may console ourselves with the reflection that this is pretty much all there is to the insight into a becoming-existent. We may now coast.

It is thoroughly misleading to say that a subject of change stays the same, whereas its accidents vary, because it is precisely its accidents which cause the *subject* to vary. We have tried to say that the subject of change varies in its accidentals, and if we have succeeded, the basic reason is this: the subject is distinct from its becoming as "is" differs from "is not." The subject is *not* its becoming; yet it is the subject which becomes nonetheless.

#1 Peter individual is the same who becomes different
#2 Peter becomes different = one who could become different

Other Explanations of Becoming

Others explain change in other ways. All their explanations must suppose some sort of distinction between a subject and its becoming, and so it is the kind of distinction they propose which divides them among themselves and from those who distinguish subject and becoming as above.

Nominalists propose a nominal distinction: a subject is distinct from its becoming only in words, as *man* differs from *homo*.[20] Such an explanation is subphilosophic.

[20] The nominalist position is best expressed in the following. William of Ockham, *Sent.*, I, 2, 6, *Resp.*; in *Guilhelmi de Ockham anglici super quatuor libros sententiarum subtilissimae quaestiones earumdemque decisiones*, Lugduni, 1495. Ockham says that universality has no real existence outside of the

Conceptualists propose a conceptual or mental distinction between a subject and its becoming, but a mental distinction of a peculiar sort.[21] So far as I know, no conceptualist distinguishes a subject from its becoming as *animal* is distinguished from *rational*, or as a *definiendum* is distinct from its definition. Such distinctions are indeed mental. They are mental as a potential conceptual understanding of *man* by the concept of *animal* (which concept of *animal* is an *actual* understanding of man so far forth as man is an *animal*) is distinct from the further actualization of the understanding of *animal* by the concept of *rational*. The *definiendum* is distinct from its definition as the obscure from the clear. But these two concepts of *animal* and *rational* are transcriptions of what in man are identical: it is the identical man who is both *animal* and *rational*. So for the definition and the *definiendum*. Now, no conceptualist worth his salt distinguishes a subject from its becoming in that way.

Conceptualists distinguish a subject from its becoming as one mode of being from another. They mean this: to be a *subject* of becoming is one way of being a becomer; to be *becoming* is an-

mind: "Illud quod est universale et univocum non est aliquid realiter ex parte rei, distinctum formaliter ab individuo." Locke says much the same in *An Essay Concerning Human Understanding*, Bk. III, ch. 3; ed. A. Pringle-Pattison, Oxford, Clarendon Press, 1924, p. 230: "It is plain, by what has been said, that *general* and *universal* belong not to the real existence of things; but are the inventions and creatures of the understanding, made by it for its own use and concern only signs, whether words or ideas." See also D. Hume, *A Treatise of Human Nature*, Bk. I, Part I, sec. VI; ed. L. Selby-Bigge, p. 16: "We have therefore no idea of substance, distinct from that of a collection of particular qualities, nor have we any other meaning when we either talk or reason concerning it. The idea of substance as well as that of a mode, is nothing but a collection of simple ideas, that are united by the imagination, and have a particular name assigned them, by which we are able to recall, either to ourselves or others, that collection. But the difference betwixt these ideas consists in this that the particular qualities, which form a substance, are commonly referred to an unknown *something*, in which they are supposed to inhere; or granting this fiction should not take place, are at least supposed to be closely and inseparably connected by the relations of contiguity and causation."

[21] The conceptualist position may be seen in Descartes, *Principles of Philosophy*, Part I, Princ. LX; ed. E. Haldane and G. Ross, *The Philosophical Works of Descartes*, Cambridge, University Press, 1931, Vol. I, p. 243: ". . . we can conclude that two substances are really distinct one from the other from the sole fact that we can conceive the one clearly and distinctly without the other." See also Kant, *Critique of Pure Reason*, Bk. II, ch. 1; in T. M. Greene, *Kant Selections*, N.Y., Scribner's, 1929, pp. 100–106.

other way of being a becomer. They go on: you may if you wish call the subject of becoming the potential or potency, and you may name its becoming the actual or act, but the potency and act (the potential and the actual) are in the becomer only as two different ways of being the same thing, viz., a subject-becoming.

This sort of distinction is very seductive. It permits us to understand becoming as a full-blown subject, and it permits us to understand the subject of becoming as a balloon with the wind let out of it. Such an understanding of the matter is attractive, because we can thus reduce becoming, which we can't conceive, because it doesn't stay put long enough for us to conceive it, to a subject which we can conceive, because it does stay put. The distinction won't work, not if you can't let the wind out of a subject of becoming without having it cease to be even so much as a subject of becoming. Such is the case. Just as a dead lion is not even a lion, so a subject of becoming, deflated of its becoming, is not even a subject of becoming. A subject of becoming *is* becoming, or else it *isn't* a subject of becoming at all. Granted that, granted that is, that a subject *before* its becoming is not becoming, not, therefore, an honest-to-goodness existent which is becoming (what indeed *could* an existent subject of becoming be which is *not* becoming?), we must grant that, while becoming, a subject is not even *then* its becoming. Why not? Because if it were, it would be an existent which *is*, not an existent which "is *becoming*," different. Now, we started out to explain an existent which is *becoming* different. It would be strange indeed if we wound up that explanation by saying that a subject of becoming is, but is not becoming, different; and this is exactly what those who distinguish subject and becoming as one mode of being from another must mean, whether they like it or not. For, even if one mode of becoming, viz., the subject, is not another mode of becoming, viz., the becoming, the two modes in *their* supposition are nevertheless modes of the same thing, viz., modes of becoming, and that is unintelligible if "to be different" is not the same as "to be becoming different." Better say, then, that the two supposedly distinct "modes" are not modes of becoming at all. They are two distinct principles of one mode of being, the mode of becoming-being, and they differ as "is" differs from "is not" in this sentence: the subject is not its becoming. This is the sense of the real distinction between potency and act in the matter of becoming.

Becoming Explained by "Adequate" Concepts of Potency and Act

The real distinction of a subject from its becoming is often propounded as a distinction between adequate concepts of potency and act.[22] Such concepts are assumed, and rightly, to reflect the ontological status of potency and act; it is they and not only the concepts of them which are distinct. Perhaps this manner of expressing the real distinction, namely, as a distinction between adequate concepts, differs only verbally from saying that the real distinction is a difference between "is" and "is not." At any rate, the expression, "adequate concepts," does not seem felicitous.

Concepts express what things are. Neither potency nor act expresses what things are. There are no concepts, adequate or inadequate, of potency and act. "Potency" is an abstraction from the "potential," and act from the "actual." Nevertheless the concrete "potential" means this: that which is not, but can be, actual. The concrete "actual" means this: that which is, but is not potential. The difference between the potential and the actual is thus a difference between "is" and "is not." Of course, if the "is not," said of the potential, were an absolute negation of the "is," said of the actual—like the negation of the hole, said of the doughnut (*the*

---

[22] On adequate concepts of potency and act, see note 8 of this chapter. St. Thomas, *De Princ. Nat.*, c. 1, n. 338: "Quoniam quoddam potest esse licet non sit, quoddam vero iam est, illud quod potest esse et non est, dicitur esse potentia; illud autem quod iam est, dicitur esse actu." See *In IX Metaph.*, lect. 1, n. 1776; *Contra Gentiles*, II, 43; II, 53; *Sum. Theol.*, I, 9, 1, *Resp.* See also E. Gilson, *The Christian Philosophy of St. Thomas Aquinas*, N.Y., Random House, 1956, pp. 174–186; R. Arnou, S.J., *Metaphysica Generalis*, Romae, Typis Pontificiae Universitatis Gregorianae, 1941, pp. 28–32, 124–125; A. Farges, *Théorie fondamentale de l'acte et de la puissance*, 7th ed., Paris, 1909, especially p. 21; L.-B. Geiger, O.P., *La participation dans la philosophie de s. Thomas d'Aquin*, 2nd ed., *Bibliothèque Thomiste*, XXIII, Paris, Vrin, 1953, pp. 77–84, 156–217; A. Forest, *La structure métaphysique du concret selon saint Thomas d'Aquin*, pp. 167–257.

doughnut is not the hole in it)—then surely the potential would not even be able to be actual, just as the hole absolutely cannot be the doughnut. When, however, "is not" is said of the potential, it negates only the "is" of the actual; and the "is" which is said of the actual negates only the "is not" of the potential—as dough, not the hole in dough, negates the actuality of the doughnut, and the doughnut negates only the unactualized, but not the actualized, dough. The "abstractions" of "potency" and "act" are merely short-hand expressions of the "is not" of the potential, and of the "is" of the actual. But the "nonbeingness" of the potential, and the "being-ness" of the actual are not states, either separately or in combination, of a being which is becoming. Being which is becoming is not com-pounded of states of being at all. Being which is becoming *is* a state of being, a state of being which is compounded, not of two states, but of two factors of *one* state of being, viz., being which is becoming. Being which is becoming is, *mirabile dictu!* becoming, and that state is a composite of the potential (which has not yet fully become) and the actual (which is no longer potential, and not yet fully actual). It is vain to try to express these two factors of a becoming being by anything less than two judgments. You may, of course, tag those two judgments with the names of potency and act, just as you tag Sienkiewicz' characters with letters instead of their names, and this will effectively shorten the expression of your thinking. But the expressions of thinking need not necessarily express the thinking; expressions of thinking may express only what thinking has been done, not the thinking which is being done. The thinking which is being done when you think of "potency" is ex-pressed in some such way as this: potency is a principle by which that which is not actual can be actual; and when you think of "act": act is a principle by which that which can be actual is actual. I speak, of course, only of the actual and the potential in a becoming-being.

Suggested Reading

Change:

Aristotle, *Physics*, I, 2; I, 7; I, 8; III, 1; VI, 1; *Metaphysics*, XI (K), 9; XII (Λ), 2–3.

St. Thomas Aquinas *In I Phys.*, lects. 12 and 13; *In II Phys.*, lect. 1; *In III Phys.*, lect. 3; *In XI Metaph.*, lect. 9; *In XII Metaph.*, lect. 2; *De Princ. Nat.*, ch. 2.

Potency and Act:

Aristotle, *Physics*, III, 1–3; *Metaphysics*, IX (Θ), 1–9; XI (K), 9.

St. Thomas Aquinas, *In III Phys.*, lects. 2 and 3; *In V Metaph.*, lect. 14; *In IX Metaph.*, lect. 1; *In XI Metaph.*, lect. 9; *De Princ. Nat.*, ch. 1; *Sum. Theol.*, I, 9, 1, *Resp.*; II–II, 90, 3; *Contra Gentiles*, II, 16; II, 43; II, 53.

John of St. Thomas, *Ars Logica*, Pars II, q. 19, a. 2; *Phil. Nat.*, Pars I, q. 14, a. 4.

Arnou, R., S.J., *Metaphysica Generalis*, pp. 28–32, 124–125.

Farges, A., *Théorie fondamentale de l'acte et de la puissance.*

Forest, A., *La structure métaphysique du concret selon saint Thomas d'Aquin*, pp. 167–257.

Geiger, L.-B., O.P., *La participation dans la philosophie de s. Thomas d'Aquin*, pp. 77–84, 156–217.

Gilson, E., *The Christian Philosophy of St. Thomas Aquinas*, pp. 174–186.

Owens, J., C.Ss.R., *The Doctrine of Being in the Aristotelian Metaphysics*, pp. 251–256.

III · PASSIVE POTENCY IN MULTIPLE KINDS OF BEING

Summary of the Second Chapter

In order to explain how it is possible that an existent may be an existent which is becoming, we must, as we saw, say that in it there must be a subject of becoming (passive potency) which is not identical with its becoming (act). Peter while becoming wise is not identical with his becoming wise; yet it is Peter who becomes wise. We have insisted that the distinction between a subject and its becoming is not as between two existents, nor as between two different conceptual transcriptions of an identical existent (e.g., an *animal* and *rational* are two different conceptual transcriptions of an identical *man*), nor even as between two real states or modes of an identical existent. Rather, the distinction is as between two principles (potency and act) of one mode or state of an existent, namely, the state of an existent which is becoming. The distinction, in other words, is as real as the one between Peter and Paul; only it is not between two existents, each set up in existential housekeeping, like Peter and Paul; it is as between two partners in one existential house. The last figure of speech fails in that the two partners which are potency and act are not, separately nor even when together, existents at all. It is only the composite of the two components which is an existent that is becoming. Passive potency or the ability of an individual of a specific kind to differ in its accidentals *enables* a becoming being actually *to differ* in its accidentals and yet to remain the same specific kind of individual.[1]

[1] Observe carefully that passive potency *alone* does not explain why some existents are becoming. The explanation of that lies partly in another factor,

36

What It Means to Differ in Kind

We must now discern the grounds of the possibility of there being an existent of a specific kind. Those grounds will still be passive potency and its act, but with a difference.

To ask why there can be an existent of a specific kind is to suppose that there are specifically different kinds of individuals, and so we must now see why there are.

If there were no specifically different individuals, if, say, a man were only accidentally different from a horse as a man becoming wise is only accidentally different from himself, and so for all the rest of individuals, it would follow that to be an existent is to be one kind of existent, whatever that kind might be. Now, it is impossible that all existents be of the same kind if we accept the following data.

To begin with, some individuals don't look to be the same kind as others. A man doesn't look like a fish. This, of course, could be only a matter of appearances. When, however, we say a man doesn't look like a fish we mean more by our "look like" than meets the eye. We mean a man does not have the same intelligible contour as a fish. We mean that his intelligible contour, which is the specific kind of being he is, is not the intelligible contour of a fish, not the kind of being which a fish is.

To illustrate what an intelligible contour means, let us assume a circle: a plane figure bounded by a curved line everywhere equally distant from the center. Let us next assume that the circle is so slightly squashed that its line is eccentric from its former center by, say, one one-millionth of a millimeter. Ask, is the new figure a

---

namely, in active potency. With active potency or efficient cause we are not at present concerned. No doubt the question why components compound (why *does* Peter become wise? why *do* unidentical components get together?) is a crucial question, but before it can be answered, one must have seen that components *can* get together. Passive potency enables us to see why they can, because passive potency *enables* the two principles of a subject and its becoming to *get* together. Passive potency does not on its own get together with its act, but without passive potency there would be nothing for act to get together with. A man can't become wise unless he is able to, even though his ability to become wise will not of itself explain his actually becoming wise. A man's ability to become wise explains only why it is *he* who becomes wise if and when he does, and that explanation is simply this: he *can* become wise.

circle? You must say *no*, even if you can't *see* the difference between
the two figures. The eccentric figure is not the circle, and you see
this, not with your eyes, but with your mind. The intelligible vision
which the definition of a circle puts before your mind is not the
intelligible vision which the eccentric figure does, and the reason is
this: a circle is *not* the eccentric figure: a difference as between *yes*
(yes, a circle is a circle) and *no* (no, a squashed circle is not a
circle).[2]

The question now is this: do some natural bodies differ as some
mathematical bodies do? Is being one specific kind of body so different from being another specific kind of body that of one kind you
must say, it is not the other kind, just as you must say, this kind
of mathematical body is not that kind?

You must, and for the following reasons.

Before stating those reasons, we must recall, because it is preliminary to the answer, what has already been stated concerning a
changing being. The differences of a changing being are differences
in it, else *it* would not be becoming. To see that much is to see that
differences, accidental to be sure, belong to being. Parmenides
thought that differences did not belong to being, and that is why he
thought there were no differences.[3] This Parmenidean block to
thinking about changing being as changing has been eliminated, at
least so far forth as accidental differences are concerned: *they* at
least belong to a changing being. If they do, the way to seeing how
essential differences also belong to being is open. But the way to
seeing the latter situation is blocked if there are no accidental differences *in* a changing being. Let us then repeat the explanation of the
first situation lest we be hindered from seeing the second.

If you suppress the subject of accidental traits, you eliminate a
changing being. If there is no subject of accidental traits, which
subject differs accidentally and not merely its accidental traits, then
there's nothing left for accidental traits to distinguish. If a man does

[2] See G. Smith, S.J., *The Truth That Frees*, pp. 11–27.
[3] Of Parmenides, Aristotle says: ". . . Parmenides seems in places to speak
with more insight. For, claiming that, besides the existent, nothing nonexistent
exists, he thinks that of necessity one thing exists, viz., the existent and nothing
else . . . ," *Metaphysics*, I (A), 5, 986b 28–30. See *Physics*, I, 3, 186a 23–186b 1.

not become wise, there's nothing becoming wise. Hence, it is he, the man, who becomes wise.

Our question, then, is not this: is it a subject of traits which its traits distinguish? Of course it is the subject of traits which its traits distinguish. What else could it be if we accept the fact of change? Our question is rather this: how far does the distinction between some beings go? All the way to distinguishing one *kind* of being from another, all the way to distinguishing the necessary traits of one being from the necessary traits of another being? All the way.

Why There are Different Kinds of Beings

And now for the reasons why.

Between a subject and its accidental traits there is a loose connection. We cannot, precisely because that connection is loose, say that a man is by definition wise, or stupid, or fat, or lean, etc. A man may indeed have all those characteristics, successively, or sometimes in combination, but he would be a man without any given accidental traits, though some of these traits are given. Let us name those accidental traits, nonnecessary, and the nonnecessary traits will mean such traits which a subject need not have, although if it does, it will necessarily have them for as long as it has them. Socrates, although he need not run, will, if he runs, necessarily run.[4] Of course. Yet it is not necessary that Socrates run.

[4] On the necessary and the contingent, see St. Thomas, *Sum. Theol.*, I, 19, 3, *Resp.*: "There are two ways in which a thing is said to be necessary, namely, absolutely, and by supposition. We judge a thing to be absolutely necessary from the relation of the terms, as when the predicate forms part of the definition of the subject: thus it is necessary that man is an animal; or as when the subject forms part of the notion of the predicate: thus it is necessary that a number must be odd or even. In this way it is not necessary that Socrates sits: hence it is not necessary absolutely, but it may be so by supposition; for, granted that he is sitting, he must necessarily sit, as long as he is sitting." *Sum. Theol.*, I, 86, 3, *Resp.*: "Contingent things can be considered in two ways: either as contingent, or as containing some element of necessity. For every contingent thing has in it something necessary. For example, that Socrates runs, is in itself contingent; but the relation of running to motion is necessary, for it is necessary that Socrates move if he runs. Now contingency arises from matter, for contingency is a potentiality to be or not to be, and potentiality belongs to matter; whereas necessity results from form, because whatever is

Yet Socrates has some necessary predicates. Over and above his accidental traits, he has necessary traits. Bodies, and Socrates is a body, have characteristic ways of acting. You get apples from an apple tree, bile from the liver, men generate men, and, barring impediment, what goes up comes down. These characteristic ways of acting which bodies have are certainly not accidental, because accidental traits come and go, the bodies which they affect remaining the same in kind; whereas the nonaccidental or necessary traits stick so tight to the bodies they affect that if the nonaccidental trait is suppressed the body is suppressed. Think of a body with no weight, and you have succeeded in thinking of something which is not a body. Think of a body as heavy; you have succeeded in thinking of a natural body. The reason for both statements is that bodies *are* heavy, else they are not bodies. Note well that "heaviness" is not a characteristic of mathematical bodies: a triangle has no weight. "Heaviness" is a characteristic of natural bodies, and it is such a characteristic that you must not only locate it *in* the body, just as you locate a body's accidental traits, but you must also locate "heaviness" in a body as a necessary trait of all physical bodies. If you ask why bodies are heavy, you may indeed never find an answer to your question, but that would not mean that bodies were not necessarily heavy. The reason why bodies are heavy may escape us, but the connection between "bodies" and "heaviness" does not escape us. It is a necessary connection, and "necessary" here means that the trait is necessarily together, or one with a body.

Here we have come across the Aristotelian notion of nature.[5]

---

consequent on form is of necessity in the subject." See also *Sum. Theol.*, I, 82, 1, *Resp.*; *In I Periherm.*, lect. 14; *Contra Gentiles*, I, 67; II, 30; *De Potentia*, V, 3; J. Owens, C.Ss.R., "The Intelligibility of Being," *Gregorianum*, Vol. XXVI, n. 2 (1955), pp. 170-193.

[5] Aristotle speaks of nature in the following ways. *Physics*, II, 1, 192b 8-22: "Of things that exist, some exist by nature, some from other causes. 'By nature' the animals and their parts exist, and the plants and the simple bodies (earth, fire, air, water)—for we say that these and the like exist 'by nature.' All the things mentioned present a feature in which they differ from things which are *not* constituted by nature. Each of them has *within itself* a principle of motion and of stationariness (in respect of place, or of growth and decrease, or by way of alteration). On the other hand, a bed and a coat and anything else of that sort, *qua* receiving these designations—i.e., in so far as they are

There must be a necessary reason why subjects and some of their traits necessarily hold together, because they necessarily do hold together.[6] That reason is Aristotle's nature. Synonyms for "nature" are "essence," "specific kind," even "law," so far forth as law implies a subject which is the source of the recurrent and repetitious actions which law describes. Nature is an islet in the flux of change. Many such islets are so many natures, and the abstract concept of natures is "nature."

---

products of art—have no innate impulse to change. But in so far as they happen to be composed of stone or of earth or of a mixture of the two, they *do* have such an impulse, and just to that extent—which seems to indicate that *nature is a source or cause of being moved and of being at rest in that to which it belongs primarily*, in virtue of a concomitant attribute."

Metaphysics, V (Δ), 4, 1015a 13-19: "From what has been said, then, it is plain that nature in the primary and strict sense is the essence of things which have in themselves, as such, a source of movement; for the matter is called the nature because it is qualified to receive this, and processes of becoming and growing are called nature because they are movements proceeding from this. And nature in this sense is the source of the movement of natural objects, being present in them somehow, either potentially or in complete reality."

Physics, II, 1, 192b 32-34: " 'Nature' then is what has been stated. Things 'have a nature' which have a principle of this kind. Each of them is a substance; for it is a subject, and nature always implies a subject in which it inheres."

Physics, II, 1, 193a 1-8: "*What* nature is, then, and the meaning of the terms 'by nature' and 'according to nature,' has been stated. *That* nature exists, it would be absurd to try to prove; for it is obvious that there are many things of this kind, and to prove what is obvious by what is not is a mark of a man who is unable to distinguish what is self-evident from what is not."

See St. Thomas, *In II Phys.*, lect. 1, nn. 141-148; *In V Metaph.*, lect. 5; *Sum. Theol.*, I, 29, 1, *ad* 4; I–II, 10, 1; 31, 7; 94, 5, *ad* 3.

[6] On the necessary in nature, see Aristotle, *Physics*, II, 9, 200a 30-200b 10: "The necessary in nature, then, is plainly what we call by the name of matter, and the changes in it. Both causes must be stated by the physicist, but especially the end; for that is the cause of the matter, not *vice versa;* and the end is 'that for the sake of which,' and the beginning starts from the definition or essence; as in artificial products, since a house is of such-and-such a kind, certain things must *necessarily* come to be or be there already. Similarly if man is this, then these; if these, then those. Perhaps the necessary is present also in the definition. For if one defines the operation of sawing as being a certain kind of dividing, then this cannot come about unless the saw has teeth of a certain kind; and these cannot be unless it is of iron. For in the definition too there are some parts that are, as it were, its matter." See also *Physics*, II, 8, 198b 10-199a 19; *Metaphysics*, V (Δ), 5; St. Thomas, *In II Phys.*, lect. 15; *In V Metaph.*, lect. 6; *Sum. Theol.*, I, 82, 1, *Resp.*

The Paralogism of Mechanism's Explanation of "Nature"

At this point we must block off a paralogism. Aristotle's nature is a subject with traits which are so necessarily connected with it that the traits are part of the structure of the subject itself. Mechanism commits the paralogism of not thinking so. Mechanism thinks that the traits of an Aristotelian nature stick with the nature, not as parts of the structure of the subject itself, but as imposed upon the subject by a force external to the subject,[7] as the functions of the parts of a watch stick together because a watchmaker puts them together. In answer to this, it may be remarked, *first*, that mechanism's explanation doesn't look right. The laws of nature describe activity which issues apparently from one subject, whereas the activity of a watch quite apparently does not issue from one subject. It issues from the fabricating idea of the watchmaker plus the natures of the parts of the subject, which is the watch. These parts of a watch are an aggregate of natures, and the artistic idea utilizes the natural activity of the parts. Nature may act like a machine, but there's no machine which acts like nature. The activity of nature is in *one* subject of that activity; the activity of a watch is in an *aggregate* of many subjects, and the concert of a watch's activity is concerted by the watchmaker's fabricating idea of a watch. Nature's functions and activity, however, hold together with the subject of activity all by themselves. We have to stand by machines to see that they will run. Nobody has to stand by nature to see that it will run. It runs

[7] Aristotle's criticism of the mechanist position may be found in *Physics*, II, 4, 196a 25–196b 9; II, 8, 198b 10–199a 32; *On Generation and Corruption*, II, 9, 335a 25–336a 14. On modern mechanism, see Descartes, *Le monde*, ch. XVIII, *Traité de l'homme*, in *Oeuvres*; ed. Adam-Tannery, Paris, 1909, Vol. XI, pp. 120 ff. For a criticism of mechanism, see E. Gilson, *The Unity of Philosophical Experience*, N.Y., Scribner's, 1937, pp. 198–220, 271–295; *God and Philosophy*, New Haven, Yale University Press, 1941, pp. 74–144; E. Meyerson, *Identité et realité*, 2nd ed., Paris, Alcan, 1912, pp. 42 ff.; J. Maritain, *The Degrees of Knowledge*, tr. B. Wall and M. Adamson, London, Century Press, 1937, pp. 225–247; Y. Simon, *Prévoir et savoir*. Études sur l'idée de la necessité dans la pensée scientifique et en philosophie, Montreal, Editions de l'Arbre, 1944, pp. 15–34, 54–116, 155–172.

all right by itself. *Second,* besides not looking right, mechanism's explanation is a paralogism. Instead of seeing necessary functions as innate in the subject of activity, where they belong in other words, mechanism sees characteristic activity as caused by something external to the subject. Thus it ousts one nature (whose kind of activity is necessarily part of its structure) only to lug in another nature, viz., an external subject whose activity impinges upon another subject. Mechanism must at least lug in a watchmaker, and he at least is a nature. *Per se* a watchmaker makes watches, even though a man is not *per se* a watchmaker. Just so, according to the paralogism of mechanism, the forces external to nature must be nature, because *they* at least hold steady if their effects do, and the effects do hold steady. Thus mechanism fails to *locate* nature, but it does not fail to acknowledge nature. Besides, forces external to nature must suppose forces *internal* to the parts which the external forces manipulate. Parts must be controllable if they are to be controlled. Parts of a machine must be natures if they are going to yield to the external forces which control them. Why indeed should parts yield to such forces unless the parts be of a *nature* to yield? Indeed sometimes we can't make nature yield: horticulture has more limits than industry. Thus it is that mechanism postulates two natures where Aristotle saw one: mechanism sees a nature in the forces which are external to it; it also sees nature in the forces which an external force can control. In either case you have an exquisitely nonsensical, because paralogistic, explanation of nature: an explanation which proves the precise point which it set out to disprove.

Thus far we are come: the traits of some subjects are necessarily connected with those subjects, not accidentally. The question remains: Are some of those necessary traits quite distinct, as distinct say, as a triangle is distinct from a square? If there are such traits, it follows that there are specifically different kinds of beings, because we have already located those necessary traits *in* the subject. It is they, the subjects, whose structure is one with their necessary traits, and should their traits be as distinct as a triangle is distinct from a square, then it is *they,* the subjects, which are as distinct as a triangle is from a square. The question is, are there specifically distinct traits of some subjects?

The Demonstration of Specific Kinds of Being

There are specifically distinct traits of some subjects for the following reason. Assuming that differences are *in* the differing bodies, assuming, next, that some differences in some bodies are so necessarily connected with those bodies that to suppress those differences is to suppress those bodies, and *vice versa* (this is Aristotle's "nature," a subject and its functional traits, clinging each to the other necessarily), it follows that *such* bodies have in them a necessary *tendency* to keep their traits.[8] The liver necessarily tends to

[8] On tendency in nature, see Aristotle, *Physics*, II, 8, 199a 7-12: "Therefore action for an end is present in things which come to be and are by nature. . . . Now surely as in intelligent action, so in nature; and as in nature, so it is in each action, if nothing interferes. Now intelligent action is for the sake of an end; therefore the nature of things also is so."

St. Thomas, *Contra Gentiles*, III, 2: "Accordingly we must first show that every agent, by its action, intends an end. For in those things which clearly act for an end, we declare the end to be that toward which the movement of the agent tends; for when this is reached, the end is said to be reached, and to fail in this is to fail in the end intended. This may be seen in the physician who aims at health, and in a man who runs toward an appointed goal. Nor does it matter, as to this, whether that which tends to an end be endowed with knowledge or not; for just as the target is the end of the archer, so is it the end of the arrow's flight. Now the movement of every agent tends to something determinate, since it is not from any force that any action proceeds, but heating proceeds from heat, and cooling from cold; and therefore actions are differentiated by their active principles. . . . Were an agent not to act for a definite effect, all effects would be indifferent to it. Now that which is indifferent to many effects does not produce one rather than another. Therefore, from that which is indifferent to either of two effects, no effect results, unless it be determined by something to one of them. Hence it would be impossible for it to act. Therefore every agent tends to some definite effect, which is called its end."

Contra Gentiles, III, 3: "For that every agent acts for an end clearly follows from the fact that every agent tends to something definite. Now that to which an agent tends definitely must needs be befitting to that agent, since the agent would not tend to it save because of some fittingness thereto. But that which is befitting to a thing is good for it. Therefore every agent acts for a good."

See also *Contra Gentiles*, III, 21; *In II Phys.*, lect. 12-14; J. Maritain, *A Preface to Metaphysics*, tr. E. Watkin, N.Y., Scribner's, 1940, pp. 68-74; J. Wild, "Tendency," *The Journal of Philosophy*, Vol. XLIX (1952), pp. 468-472.

secrete bile, even when it doesn't secrete bile. Nitric acid has that about it which necessarily *will*, granted the conditions, burn tissue, even when there is no tissue around to burn; so too, apple trees will grow apples, even before they do grow apples. Certainly they won't grow fish. Now some tendencies are fixed and unchanging. Unchanging, because from induction they are necessary. Fixed, because unfixed or indeterminate necessary tendencies are a contradiction in terms—like tendencies to ride off in all directions at the same time. It can't be done. If a body has necessary tendencies, these tendencies must be determinate. An indeterminate necessary tendency is simply a name for no tendency at all, like the name "nothing." Now, fixed tendency is synonymous with guided tendency, that is, fixed or guided tendency is toward the accomplishment of a definite purpose, e.g., the guided tendency of an apple tree is to produce apples. Just so, the purpose of the ear is for hearing; of the eye, for seeing, etc. To deny this is to admit that one does not know what an apple tree, or an ear, or an eye, is, because one doesn't know what each is for. To one who makes such general denials, as Chesterton remarked, may be addressed the Gospel exhortation in reverse, "he that has ears to hear and does not hear, let him have them cut off." Why not, if ears are not for hearing?

Are the purposes or ends of some tendencies of physical bodies as different as a triangle is different from a square? They are.[9] The

[9] Aristotle discusses the different kinds of tendency in *Physics*, II, 8, 199a 20–33. St. Thomas discusses the different kinds of tendency at length in the following places: *In II Phys.*, lect. 13, nn. 258–259; *De Princ. Nat.*, c. 3, n. 351; *Sum. Theol.*, I, 19, 1, *Resp.*; 59, 1, *Resp.*; 78, 1, *ad* 3; 80, 1, *Resp.*; 81, 2, *Resp.*; 87, 4, *Resp.*; I-II, 1, 2, *Resp.*; 8, 1, *Resp.*; 17, 8, *Resp.*; 26, 1, *Resp.*; *Contra Gentiles*, III, 2; III, 3; III, 16; III, 26; *De Pot.*, III, 15, *Resp.*; *De Malo*, VI, 1, *Resp.*; *De Verit.*, XXV, 1, *Resp.*

See especially *Sum. Theol.*, I, 18, 3, *Resp.*: "Accordingly, there are things that move themselves, not in relation to any form or end naturally inherent in them, but only with relation to the execution of the movement: the form by which they act, and the end of the action are determined for them by their nature. Of this kind are plants, which move themselves according to their inherent nature, with regard only to executing the movements of growth and decay. Other things have self-movement in a higher degree, that is, not only with relation to the execution of the movement, but even with relation to the form which is the principle of movement, which they acquire by themselves. Of this kind are animals, in which the principle of movement is not a naturally implanted form, but one received through sense. . . . Yet although

most obvious case is the difference in purpose between the organic
and the inorganic body. The living body tends to nourish and reproduce itself. The nonliving body does neither. The living body
is therefore different in kind from the nonliving, because the tendency to act as living bodies act is as different from the tendency to
act of the nonliving body as a square is different from a triangle.

Objections to the Demonstration

Any attempt to reduce the living to the nonliving, or *vice versa*,
can only wind up in saying that the living is the nonliving, or *vice
versa*, and so the differences between the living and the nonliving
are not specific, not differences in kind.[10] Now, to say that is not

---

animals of the latter kind receive through sense the form that is the principle
of their movement, nevertheless they cannot of themselves propose to themselves the end of their operation or their movement, for this has been implanted in them by nature; and by natural instinct they are moved to any
action through the form apprehended by sense. Hence such animals as move
themselves in relation to an end that they themselves propose are superior to
these. This can be done only by reason and intellect, whose province it is to
know the proportion between the end and the means to that end, and duly
coordinate them."

[10] On atomism's identification of the living and nonliving, see Aristotle, *On
Generation and Corruption*, I, 2, 315b 6–318b 32, especially 315b 6–8: "Democritus and Leucippus, however, postulate the 'figures,' and make 'alteration' and
coming-to-be result from them. They explain coming-to-be and passing-away
by their 'dissociation' and 'association,' but 'alteration' by their 'grouping' and
'position.' "

Metaphysics, I (A), 4, 985b 2–20: "Leucippus and his associate Democritus
say that the full and the empty are the elements, calling the one being and the
other nonbeing—the full and solid being being, the empty nonbeing, (when
they say being no more is than nonbeing, because the solid no more is than
the empty); and they make these the material causes of things. And as those
who make the underlying substance one generate all other things by its
modifications, in the same way these philosophers say the differences in the
elements are the causes of all other qualities. These differences, they say are
three—shape and order and position. For they say the real is differentiated only
by 'rhythm' and 'intercontact' and 'turning'; and of these rhythm is shape,
intercontact is order, and turning is position; for A differs from N in shape,
AN from NA in order, ⊥ from H in position. The question of movement—
whence or how it is to belong to things—these thinkers, like the others, lazily
neglected."

For a criticism of atomism, see M. Adler, *What Man Has Made of Man*,
N.Y., Longmans, Green, 1937, p. xiv; G. Smith, S.J., *Natural Theology*, pp.
263–265; "Science and Philosophy," *The Biologist*, Vol. XXXV, nn. 2–3 (Dec.-
Feb. 1952–53), pp. 72–79.

only to fly in the face of evidence, a venture which is not always deserving of reproof; it is also to do something much worse. It is to fail to distinguish a tendency to a purpose from the purpose toward which there is tendency. That is sheer intellectual disaster. Clearly the parent (the body tending to reproduce) is not the child (the accomplishment of the parent body's tendency), nor is the tendency to grow, identical with the grown tree. The reason why it is sheer intellectual disaster to think the opposite is this: tendency differs from its accomplishment as "is" differs from "is not." Is hunger identical with nourishment? It is not. Are sexual urges identical with sexual activity? They are not. Is the tendency to live identical with the activity of living? It is not. Not only, therefore, is it gratuitous to suppose that nonliving bodies are really alive, it is impossible that even the tendency to live, which is in living bodies, be identical with the living bodies' life. Tendency to live is part of the structure of living things (nature), but it is not life. Life is the exercise, the act of accomplishment, of the tendencies to live, and these last are not life, not even in living things. Not everything even in living things, is life. Tendency to live is not life, and so, even natures which tend to live are not identical with their act of living. Much less, then, are those bodies alive which do not even have the tendencies to live. Here, in the nonliving, the intellectual disaster of identifying tendency with accomplishment is absolute, because it is contradictory. Here one is saying that the absence of the tendency to live, in nonliving bodies, *is* the tendency to live, in living bodies.

Perhaps the nonliving never achieves the activity of living because the nonliving is hindered or impeded from exercising vital activity by some external force or forces? Perhaps the nonliving would live if only external forces got out of its way? *Then* the nonliving would live. Apparently not. For, external forces must be either guided or unguided tendencies if they are always to get in the way of the nonliving's vital activity. If guided, this is nature once more, lugged back in the guise of *external* guided forces instead of being located where it apparently is, namely, *in* the body itself which either tends, or does not, to live. The old paralogism of mechanism. If unguided, those external forces destroy the notion of the necessary. Certainly there is no necessary reason, in forces which just *happen* to get in

the way, why they always get in the way at all, as they do, if
mechanism is true. And yet, their getting in the way (assuming that
this is the real reason why not all bodies are alive) must be a necessary characteristic of such forces, because their effect is constant:
some bodies never live. In sum, if external forces keep the nonliving
from exercising the activity of living, these forces must do that job
designedly—and this is nature once more; or by accident—and this
will not explain the constancy of their effect.

The Question Which Plurality in Species Raises

We have come a long way in order to arrive at this conclusion:
there are specifically different kinds of beings, viz., the living and
the nonliving. That conclusion is now the starting point of the main
question in this chapter: how is it possible that there be specifically
different kinds of being? Here we are at the level of unity and
multiplicity in the order of specific essence: of unity, because each
kind of being is its *own* specific kind; of multiplicity, because there
are *many* (only two have been adduced here) specific kinds of being.
In Chapter I the question was about unity and multiplicity in the
order of beings which become accidentally, not specifically, different. In this chapter we ask why can there be specifically different
essences in beings?

We should never raise the present question if specifically different
essences in beings stood over against us like dolls on a shelf, each
staying itself. At least we should never know the answer to it. It is
rather because specifically different essences undergo a strange adventure that we raise the question at all. The adventure is this: some
specific essences turn into others. The clearest case of this is that of
the organic turning into the inorganic, when organisms die; and the
inorganic turns into the organic, when the organic eats the inorganic.

Here, as in the phenomenon of becoming, we must face the fact.
The thing happens. By death and nutrition the organic becomes inorganic, and *vice versa*. This fact enables us to discern in different
kinds of being a composite which is over and above the composite of

becoming being, a composite which is the very subject itself of becoming, *before* that subject becomes. That is, besides being a composite of two components, viz., a subject and its becoming, a changing being sometimes "changes" so radically that the very subject itself of change turns into a different kind of being.[11] This phenomenon indicates that the subject of becoming is itself a composite of two components, a composite of potency and act.

The Demonstration of Passive Potency Which Is Prime Matter

The reasons why are as follows. First, the fact: the organic turns into the inorganic, and *vice versa*. Second, the demonstrated dif-

---

[11] Aristotle distinguishes substantial change from other kinds of change in *On Generation and Corruption*, I, 3, 317b 20; II, 4; II, 5; II, 9; I, 4, 319b 32–320a 2: "When the change from contrary to contrary is *in quantity*, it is 'growth and diminution'; when it is *in place*, it is 'motion'; but when nothing persists, of which the resultant is a property (or an 'accident' in any sense of the term), it is 'coming-to-be,' and the converse change is 'passing-away.'"

Physics, V, 1, 225a 1–20: "And since every change is *from* something *to* something—as the word itself *metabole* indicates, implying something 'after' (*meta*) something else, that is to say something earlier and something later—that which changes must change in one of four ways: from subject to subject, from subject to nonsubject, from non-subject to subject, or from nonsubject to nonsubject, where by 'subject' I mean what is affirmatively expressed. So it follows necessarily from what has been said above that there are only three kinds of change, that from subject to subject, that from subject to nonsubject, and that from nonsubject to subject; for the fourth conceivable kind, that from nonsubject to nonsubject, is not change, as in that case there is no opposition either of contraries or of contradictories. Now change from nonsubject to subject, the relation being that of contradiction, is 'coming-to-be'—'unqualified coming to be' when the change takes place in an unqualified way, 'particular coming to be,' when the change is change in a particular character: for instance, a change from notwhite to white is a coming to be of the particular thing, white, while change from unqualified not-being to being is coming to be in an unqualified way, in respect of which we say that a thing 'comes to be' without qualification, not that it 'comes to be' some particular thing. Change from subject to nonsubject is 'perishing'—'unqualified perishing' when the change is from being to not-being, 'particular perishing' when the change is to the opposite negation, the distinction being the same as that made in the case of coming to be."

See *Metaphysics*, X (I), 10, 1058b 36–1059a 9. See also St. Thomas, *In V Phys.*, lect. 1, nn. 639, 643; lect. 2, nn. 654–656; *In VIII Metaph.*, lect. 1, n. 1688; *De Princ. Nat.*, c. 1, n. 338.

ference in kind between the organic and the inorganic. Third, the
following reasoning. (A) There must be *some* factor common to
the organic and inorganic kinds of being. If there were not, one
kind would not turn into the other. Just as in change there must be
a factor common to the stage of the before, the during, and the
after of change, otherwise nothing would be able to change, nothing
would be changing, nothing would have changed, so here: there
must be some factor common to two kinds of being, each of which
kind turns into the other—otherwise the organic would not be *able*
to turn into the inorganic, would not *do* that, would not *have*
turned into the inorganic. The difference between the two cases is
this: a becoming-being becomes accidentally different, whereas the
organic does not *become* the inorganic at all. It can't. In a changing
being there is a time during which a being is changing, and during
that interval the common factor, which is no longer in potency to
change, is not yet so completely actuated as to be changed: there is,
that is, the actuation of a being in potency, which actuated potency
is still in potency to its completion. In one specific kind of being
which turns into another kind, however, there can be no interval
at which the organic is no longer organic and not yet inorganic. If
there were, we should, during the interval, have a being of no particular kind whatsoever, and a being of no particular kind—when
the question is about specific kinds of being—is simply another name
for no being whatsoever, a name for "nothing" in other words.
Now, "nothing" cannot be the factor common to two different
kinds of beings which change, each into the other.

A few new words are needed to express the matter. Do not say:
one kind "becomes" another. As we just saw, this is impossible. Say:
one kind is "generated" from another, and the word "generation"
will then cover the two cases: the case of the living being which is
generated into the nonliving (by death); the case of the nonliving
which is generated into the living (by nutrition).[12] Sometimes the
word "corruption" is used to describe the first case. Sometimes "sub-

---

[12] The case of one living being generating another one is still a case of
generation, but not by way of death or nutrition. All the principles of substantial change, however, still apply to the parent-child relation.

stantial change" is used instead of "generation." The difference between "becoming" and "generation" will be this then: "becoming"
has an interval, even though it be very swift; "generation" is in-
stantaneous, even though the preparation for it be very long; moreover, the becoming being does not differ in kind from itself, but the
living and the nonliving differ in kind, each from the other.

(B) The factor common to both kinds cannot be of either kind,
else it would not be common to both. Here we are at Aristotle's
notion of prime matter.[13] Prime matter is a material potency, of no
kind whatsoever, to be of any body-kind whatsoever. Not immediately of course. It is obvious that there can be intermediate generations between the owl and the baker's daughter. Who cares to
eat an owl? The baker's daughter, however, might eat the fish which
ate the tomcat which ate the owl. Indeed some intermediate generations are necessary; the prime matter of a fish, which prime matter
is to be generated into the man-kind (by nutrition), must first be
generated into the inorganic, even if a man eats his fish alive. Eating
it, kills a live fish, just as cooking it does.

The Main Point Restated

As you see, the main insight is this: a specific kind of being is a
composite of two components: prime matter and its act, substantial
form. Both in "becoming" and in "generation" some factors must

---

[13] On prime matter, see Aristotle, *Metaphysics*, VII (Z), 3, 1029a 20–25: "By
matter I mean that which in itself is neither a particular thing nor of a certain
quantity nor assigned to any other of the categories by which being is determined. For there is something of which each of these is predicated, whose
being is different from that of each of the predicates (for the predicates other
than substance are predicated of substance, while substance is predicated of
matter). Therefore the ultimate substratum is of itself neither a particular
thing nor of a particular quantity nor otherwise positively characterized; nor
yet is it the negations of these, for negations also will belong to it only by
accident."

Physics, I, 5, 188a 18–19: "(For my definition of matter is just this—the
primary substratum of each thing, from which it comes to be without qualification, and which persists in the result.)" See W. Ross, *Aristotle's Physics*,
A Revised Text with Introduction and Commentary, Oxford, Clarendon, 1936,
pp. 22–23. See also St. Thomas, *In I Phys.*, lect. 15, nn. 133, 139; *In VIII
Metaph.*, lect. 1, nn. 1686–1689; *De Princ. Nat.*, c. 1, n. 339.

remain common (unity) to two different termini (multiplicity) of
the same. In "becoming," the permanent factor is a specific kind of
being: the man-kind stays the same whether a man becomes wise or
not, and it stays the *same* in its very becoming wise (although it be
an accidentally different-same or, if you will, a substantially same-
different). In "generation," however, the permanent factor, precisely because it is common to two different kinds, cannot be of any
kind whatsoever. If we name the actuation of a becoming subject
"accident" or "accidental form," then it is natural to name the actuation of prime matter "substantial form." So too, if we name the subject of becoming "substance" or "formed matter," it is natural to
name the subject of generation "formless or unformed matter."
Sometimes "substance" is called "second matter" in distinction to
the subject of generation, which is called "first" or "prime" matter.

Aristotle on Prime Matter

We may now look at Aristotle's description of prime matter. It is
"that which in itself is neither a particular being, nor a certain
quantity, nor assigned to any of the categories by which a being is
determined."[14] There's no objection to poking fun at Aristotle's
description of prime matter provided you see his point. He is saying
that there is a factor in any being of a specific kind which is
thoroughly unintelligible except in its expectancy of substantial
form, and here's the point: to that expectancy, which is prime
matter, answer the most unexpected substantial forms you could
imagine. You have the *queerest* sorts of things in this world. Think
of the giraffe. Almost incredible, even when you see one! Now, if
incongruity is a factor in fun, we have in prime matter the funniest
incongruity there is. God makes even the dust to adore Him. Laugh
if you will at the incongruous ability of what is not even dust (it is
prime matter) to assume a form by which a material composite can
adore God. But don't laugh at the description of that ability (*neque*

---

[14] Aristotle, *Metaphysics*, VII (Z), 3, 1029a 20.

quid, neque quantum, neque quale . . .) as if it were a poor description. Try yourself to describe a formless ability to be of any material kind of being. Your description will either be Aristotle's, or it will be as nonobjective as the child's picture of Pharaoh's army crossing the Red Sea: no sea, because it has receded; no army, because it has passed. A complete blank. In other words, if you don't care to use Aristotle's description of prime matter, you can't say anything intelligible at all about generation and corruption, at least not anything intelligible in terms of kinds of beings.

How Many Kinds of Being Are There?

How many kinds of being there are is a question which metaphysics perhaps cannot settle. Mortimer Adler thinks that they are few: the inanimate, the animate plant, the animate animal, the animate man, and perhaps the "races" of animate animals. Maritain and de Koninck think there are many.[15] The arguments adduced on either side are impressive, and yet the second position seems to have an edge over the first. This much is clear: there *seem* to be many kinds of beings, and there is no peremptory reason as yet why we should not assume that, here, appearances count. The only thing we must not do is to mistake accidentally different appearances of the same kind for the necessarily different appearances of specifically different kinds. There is little danger of this, however, if and when we realize that many subjects of the same necessary tendencies may appear in accidentally different guises: white and black men, e.g., are only accidentally different. At any rate, one clear case of differences in kind, the living and the nonliving, is enough to settle the central issue. The border line cases will have to await solution.

---

[15] On the problem of species, see J. Maritain, "Foreword" in M. Adler, *The Problem of Species*, in *Problems for Thomists*, N.Y., Sheed & Ward, 1940, pp. x–xi, 83–133. For de Koninck's position, see pp. 80–82. Adler's position is given on pp. 51–82.

Summary

In sum, there is passive potency in a subject of change (Chapter II), which we name substance. There is also passive potency in substance itself, which we name prime matter (as in the present chapter). Both potencies are seen in the facts: the fact of becoming, the fact of generation. Each potency compounds with its respective act so as to form different composites: the composite which is a becoming-being, the composite which is a specific kind of being. And it is the distinction between the components of each composite which enables us to see how unity and multiplicity are possible in each sort of being. Peter-becoming-wise is a unit, because it is *he* (potency) who is becoming (act), and he is *not* identically his becoming wise, much less his wisdom. Peter-a-man is a unit, because prime matter (potency) can be a man (act), and prime matter is *not* substantial form, because Peter ceases to be the man he was when he dies.

There remains the final instance of passive potency. That last instance is the subject of the verb predicate "is" (exists).

Suggested Reading

Nature:

Aristotle, *Physics*, II, 1; *Metaphysics*, V (Δ), 4.
St. Thomas Aquinas, *In II Phys.*, lect. 1; *In V Metaph.*, lect. 5; *Sum. Theol.*, I, 29, 1, *ad* 4; I–II, 10, 1; 31, 7; 94, 5, *ad* 3.

Necessity in Nature:

Aristotle, *Physics*, II, 8 and 9; *Metaphysics*, V (Δ), 5.
St. Thomas Aquinas, *In II Phys.*, lect. 15; *In V Metaph.*, lect. 6; *Sum. Theol.*, I, 82, 1.

Tendency in Nature:

Aristotle, *Physics*, II, 8.
St. Thomas Aquinas, *Contra Gentiles*, III, 2; III, 3; III, 21; *In II Phys.*, lects. 12–14.

Maritain, J., *A Preface to Metaphysics*, pp. 68–74.
Wild, J., "Tendency," *The Journal of Philosophy*, Vol. XLIX (1952), pp. 468–472.

Kinds of Tendency:

Aristotle, *Physics*, II, 8.
St. Thomas Aquinas, *In II Phys.*, lect. 13; *De Princ. Nat.*, ch. 3; *Sum. Theol.*, I, 18, 3; 19, 1; 59, 1; 78, 1, *ad* 3; 80, 1; 81, 2; 87, 4; I–II, 1, 2; 8, 1; 17, 8; 26, 1; *Contra Gentiles*, III, 2; III, 3; III, 16; III, 26; *De Pot.*, III, 15; *De Malo*, VI, 1; *De Verit.*, XXV, 1.

Criticism of Mechanism:

Aristotle, *Physics*, II, 4; *On Generation and Corruption*, II, 9.
Gilson, E., *The Unity of Philosophical Experience*, pp. 198–220, 271–295.
——, *God and Philosophy*, pp. 74–144.
Maritain, J., *The Degrees of Knowledge*, pp. 225–247.
Meyerson, E., *Identité et realité*, pp. 42 ff.
Simon, Y., *Prévoir et savoir*, pp. 15–34, 54–116, 155–172.

Criticism of Atomism:

Aristotle, *On Generation and Corruption*, I, 2; *Metaphysics*, I (A), 4.
Adler, M., *What Man Has Made of Man*, p. xiv.
Smith, G., S.J., *Natural Theology*, pp. 263–265.
——, "Science and Philosophy," *The Biologist*, Vol. XXXV, nn. 2–3 (Dec.–Feb., 1952–53), pp. 72–79.

Substantial Change:

Aristotle, *On Generation and Corruption*, I, 3; *Physics*, V, 1; *Metaphysics*, X (I), 10.
St. Thomas Aquinas, *In V Phys.*, lects. 1 and 2; *In VIII Metaph.*, lect. 1; *De Princ. Nat.*, ch. 1.

Prime Matter:

Aristotle, *Physics*, I, 5; *Metaphysics*, VII (Z), 3.
St. Thomas Aquinas, *In I Phys.*, lect. 15; *In VIII Metaph.*, lect. 1; *De Princ. Nat.*, ch. 1.

We must now discern in an experienced existent the final instance of a passive potency which is actuated. This time, passive potency will be the subject itself of existing, and the actuation or act of that potency will be the act of existing itself of that subject.

Our success in reaching that discernment depends largely upon seeing the precise issue, and we shall see that issue better if we refresh our understanding of the two former issues, which are like the present one.

Summary of Passive Potency in Becoming

The attempt to explain change, so far forth as passive potency is an explanation of it, is an attempt to explain how it is possible for an individual of a specific kind, e.g., Peter, who is a man, to stay himself, and nevertheless to be differing the while he is becoming, e.g., when he is moving from here to there.

Many philosophers have answered that question upon the assumption that the becoming of an existent of a specific kind is *given* with such an existent, i.e., upon the assumption that to-be-becoming necessarily pertains to the status of an existent of a specific kind. Upon that assumption, these philosophers must and do explain change thus: Peter *here* is the same Peter *there;* yet to be here is not to-be-there; and so, *here* and *there* are two different modes of an identical Peter. In other words, their explanation is this: the difference in Peter (when here or there or in going from here to there) is identical, because given, with Peter: the same (Peter) *is* different (when here or there or in motion).

It is this very assumption, viz., that *here* and *there* and the *motion* in between *here* and *there* are *necessarily* given with an existent of a specific kind, which we have questioned. Not that becoming is not given. It is given, but not *because* it or its terminus *a quo* and terminus *ad quem* are identical with the status of being a specific kind of existent. Becoming and its termini are not *necessary* features of an *individual* of a specific kind. Specific kinds of individuals do not become specific kinds of individuals. They *are* that to start with; *then* they become; and it is their becoming something accidentally other than their specific kinds, becoming, e.g., fat or lean or here or there, which is in question: and that becoming of theirs is in question because it is not necessary that they become actuated in *those* ways.

No one deserves a medal for seeing that *here* is not *there*, or that Peter stays the same Peter whether here or there or in motion in between here and there. Still less does one deserve a medal for explaining the fact of change by restating it, thus: Peter *here* is the same Peter *there;* only he is different. We need to explain how the fact is possible, precisely because becoming and its termini can't possibly be identified with an individual of a specific kind. For, if becoming and its termini were identically the individual of a kind, then Peter, who is a man, would cease to be himself when in motion, because motion is not Peter. Yet Peter is in motion. Why?

The answer was this: motion was located *in* Peter as an actuation of what an individual of a kind can be; *in him* not only during the interval of his becoming, but also before and after that interval, because Peter can "unbecome" or "unwind," and at any rate he is always becoming in some terms besides the given ones. Thus it is that Peter-becoming is (1) the *same* Peter according to one of his components, and also *different* according to that same component —in the order of potency; and (2) he is *different* according to the second of his components, and also the *same* according to that very same second component—in the order of act. Let us have that again: *in the order of potency*, the one who *can* become is the *same* as the one who *does* become, and when that *same* one becomes, that *same* one is *different; in the order of act*, the one who *does* become is *different* from the one who can become, and when that same one who can become *does* become, that *different* one is the *same*. It is

all very well to see change as a problem of reconciling the same
and the different. So it is. But to effect that reconciliation by making
the same identical with the different is a contradiction in terms. The
reconciliation can be made only by making the same *different* in
actuated potency (and then the different will be the *same*, because
the one who *does* differ is the one who *could* differ); and by making
the different the *same* in actuated *potency* (and then the same will
be different, because the potency is *actuated*).[1]

Summary of Passive Potency in Generation

The situation is similar when there is question of different kinds
of being. We ask, how is it possible that there be different kinds of
being? It won't do to explain the matter by saying that one kind of
being is another kind, e.g., the organic is the inorganic. Nor will it
do to say that there is nothing in common between two different
kinds of being. After all, the organic turns into the inorganic, and
unless we are to revive the days of the Phoenix, springing full blown
and totally new from its ashes, we must acknowledge some factor
common to all kinds of body being. That common factor cannot be
itself a kind of being, because it is common to all kinds. Here, then,
we have another composite of passive potency and act, but this time
the passive potency is of no kind whatsoever, and its act is the reason
why the composite is of a specific kind. As in change, it is the
composite nature of specific kinds which explains the possibility
of there being existents of specific kinds. If you assume that there
are specific kinds of being without discerning the grounds of their
possibility, you must explain the matter by saying that the factor
common to the organic and the inorganic is differentiated in the
organic and inorganic. So it is, but not *because* it is common. If the
common factor were differentiated upon the score that the common
factor is common, it would follow that the common factor would
be the same because it is different. A contradiction in terms. We
must rather say, the common factor is different in the organic and

[1] See Chapter II.

inorganic, not because it's common, but because the common factor has a different actuation in each kind. Then, as in change, the composite nature of a kind of being will be the same and different in relation to a composite of another kind, in both orders of potency and act. The organic kind will have some feature common to the inorganic kind, because prime matter *can* be either kind; and when prime matter is actuated into being one or the other kind, then that which *is* the organic kind will differ from the inorganic kind, because that *is* differing which *can* differ—in the order of potency. Similarly, the organic kind will differ from the inorganic kind because of a different actuation, or act, of prime matter; and when the act of prime matter is present (as it always is), then that which *can* differ (the same) in kind *is* differing in kind—in the order of act.[2]

Summary of Both Passive Potencies

In sum, passive potency is a partial answer to this question: how is it possible that the following facts be given? The facts: there are beings which change; there are beings which are generated one from another. How is that possible? The answer is based upon the following argument. Something simply must be common to the termini of change and generation. To deny it is to deny the facts. Next, that common factor simply cannot differ because it is common. To say so is to state a contradiction in terms. In order to preserve the facts and to escape contradiction, we must say that the common factor or passive potency differs because of a different actualization of it. Once that has been said, it becomes necessary to add that the common factor as *actualized* differs from the common factor as *unactualized;* yet, because it is a *common* factor which is actualized, it is a common factor which persists in the termini of change and generation. In other words, the composite of the common factor and its actualization is both the same and different in each order of potency and act. For, the composite is the *same* as being an actualiza-

[2] See Chapter III.

tion of the *same,* and it is different as being a *different* actualization
of the *same*—in the order of potency. Furthermore, the composite is
different as being a *different* actualization of the same, and it is the
same as being a *different* actualization of the *same*—in the order of
act. As Aristotle remarked, the situation is harder to see than it is to
be.[3] It is also harder, for anyone not an Aristotle, to state than it is
to see. At any rate, the situation in the matter of changing and
generated being is this: such beings are composites of potency and
act.

Passive Potency in Multiple Being

We may now ask how it is possible that different existents enjoy
the same status, viz., of being, each, an existent? The question is
about the possibility of that fact.

It is entirely possible to answer the question without questioning
the possibility of the situation. One can, that is, not only take the
multiplicity and unity of the status of an existent as given (it would
be necessary to do this in any explanation, because each existent
must be itself—unity; and each existent must be like any other
existent, because another existent is also itself—multiplicity), but
one can also take multiplicity and unity as so given that they *must*
be given. Now, whereas an existent must be one existent, it is not at
all apparent why there must be more than one existent. If you assume
that there must be more than one existent, your explanation of
multiplicity must be in the last analysis its identification with unity.
The details of the various stages of such identifications might and
indeed do exhibit the richest sort of intellectuality, but like good
money in the hands of a wastrel the explanation must needs be
wasted. For observe: once you identify multiplicity with unity, you
are saying that two existents *must* be given if one of them is, or

[3] See Aristotle, *Physics,* III, 2, 201b 32–202a 1: "That is why it is hard to
grasp what motion is. It is necessary to class it with privation or with potentiality or with sheer actuality, yet none of these seems possible. There remains,
then, the suggested mode of definition, namely that it is a sort of actuality,
or actuality of the kind described, hard to grasp, but not incapable of existing."

worse still, that absolutely *every* existent must be given if one of them is. This cannot be said, not because it is contradictory to say it, but because it belies the status of an existent as we know that status in experience.

Experience Shows a Difference in Multiple Being Beyond the Differences of Kinds and Accidents

As we experience an existent, its status has something more to it than the features of becoming and of being of a specific kind. That "more" need not be given at all, and if it need not be given in any one case, it obviously need not be given in many cases. (Of course that "more" also affects the features of becoming and of specificity so as to make *them* contingent as well, but their contingency depends upon the contingency of the "more" to be described.) The question, then, is this: What is this "more" in the status of an existent, and how is it related to the status of a specific kind of becoming being?

Let us run a test case. Say, *a man is having his teeth pulled*. The meaning of that statement is quite intelligible without having to know, or to be in, the situation where teeth *are* being pulled. No doubt the meaning of the statement would not be clear unless one had known some similar situation, but that is beside the point. The point is this: it is entirely possible to grasp the meaning of any intelligible statement, indeed it is entirely possible for any intelligible statement to be intelligible, whether one grasps it or not, without knowing whether a situation which is meant, or which is intelligible before it is meant, is also a situation which exists. When you know that a situation meant is also a situation which exists, you know two situations: you know the hang of a situation; you know that a situation which has a certain hang to it exists. No doubt the two situations are situations of the same existent thing, but they are not the same situation, nor are they known as the same. A man who is having his teeth pulled is undergoing a grim adventure, but there is nothing grim about the situation unless he is *in* it. So for our knowledge of the two situations. Get into it, or look at someone in it. There is a difference between knowing what is going on and knowing that what is going on *is* going on.

The point needs emphasis. The status of existing adds nothing whatever to the intelligible contours of what would and does exist if it exists. Yet the status of existing adds something. The status of existing adds nothing to intelligible contours: for, $100 are $100 whether they exist or not. In this Kant was dead right. So also the process of acquiring $100 is a process of acquiring $100, whether you are acquiring $100 or not. Nevertheless, the status of existing adds something to the $100 which you have: it adds the status of *having* $100, and as certainly that added feature is subtracted from the $100 which you do not have. The same holds as between the actual process of acquiring $100 and the meaning of that process. In this Kant was dead wrong. Anyone who ever had, or is acquiring, $100 knows the difference.[4]

What is that difference? We know it is there. We ask, what is there?

Let us, first, name the difference. Let us call $100 as being $100 an *essential* situation. $101 would be a different essential situation. Next, let us name the actual having or the actual acquiring of $100 an *existential* situation. Having or acquiring $101 would be a *different* existential situation. As we saw, there is no *essential* difference between $100 which exist and the same $100 which do not exist. Yet there is an existential difference. How can the existential difference be stated?

The Differences of Multiple Existents Are Existential Differences

The existential situation cannot be stated except in some such way as this: it is an actuation of an essential situation—e.g., one hundred existent dollars are a composite of an essential and an existential situation, a composite of essence ($100) and *esse* (an act

[4] See Kant, *Critique of Pure Reason*, Bk. II, ch. 3, ed. T. M. Greene, pp. 268–269.

of existing). Presently we shall see how this composite character of existents as we know them is the ground of the *possibility* of there being many existents. Right now, however, it is crucial to understand the nature of a composite of essence and *esse*.[5]

What a Composite of Essence and "Esse" Means

First of all, a few terms must be explained. When it is said that an existent as given is a composite of essence and *esse*, what is meant is that *an* existent *in* an essential situation is also *in* an existential one, and that the two situations are not identical, although the existent which is in both situations is one existent. The term essence, therefore, in the expression "a composite of essence and *esse*," might be misleading. It might be taken to mean, not the essential situation

[5] On the nature of the composition of essence and existence, or the identification of essence and existence in Aristotle, see *Metaphysics*, IV (Γ), 2, 1003b 25-35: ". . . for 'one man' and 'man' are the same thing, and so are 'existent man' and 'man,' and the doubling of the words in 'one man and one *existent* man' does not express anything different (it is clear that the two things are not separated either in coming to be or in ceasing to be); and similarly 'one existent man' adds nothing to 'existent man,' so that it is obvious that the addition in these cases means the same thing, and unity is nothing apart from being; and if, further, the substance of each thing is one in no merely accidental way, and similarly is from its very nature something that *is:*—all this being so, there must be exactly as many species of being as of unity." See *Categories*, ch. 5, 2a 11-25; *Posterior Analytics*, II, 7, 92b 5-14.
On the distinction of essence and existence in St. Thomas, mention may be made of the following. *Sum. Theol.*, I, 3, 4, *Resp.:* "First, whatever a thing has besides its essence must be caused either by the constituent principles of that essence (like a proper accident that necessarily accompanies the species—as the faculty of laughing is proper to man—and is caused by the constituent principles of the species), or by some exterior agent,—as heat is caused in water by fire. Therefore, if the being of a thing differs from its essence, this being must be caused either by some exterior agent or by the essential principles of the thing itself. Now it is impossible for a thing's being to be caused only by its essential constituent principles, for nothing can be the sufficient cause of its own being, if its being is caused. Therefore that thing, whose being differs from its essence, must have its being caused by another. . . . Second, being is the actuality of every form or nature; for goodness and humanity are spoken of as actual, only because they are spoken of as being. Therefore, being must be compared to essence, if the latter is distinct from it, as actuality to potentiality."
A parallel text to *Sum. Theol.*, I, 3, 4, *Resp.* is *De Ente et Essentia*, ch. IV;

of *an* existent or *a* being, but an essential situation as essential. This
understanding of such a composite is a complete misunderstanding.
"Essence" in the expression "a composite of essence and *esse*," means
the essential situation of *an* existent: not the *man* situation as *man*,
but the *man* situation of *a* man. The reason is this: essential situations as essential can stay the same *(this man, that man)*, or they can
differ *(man, fish)*, and yet, whether they be the same or different,
·they are essential situations of *distinct* existents. Since essences are
the essential situations of distinct existents, essences are factors in
them, the distinct *existents*. Hence there is no ontological moment
at which there is a *man* situation, another moment at which *esse*
accrues to that *man* situation, and still another at which there is *a*
man. Rather, there is first *a* man, then we discern in *a* man his essential situation, viz., a *man* situation, then we realize that *his* essential situation is the essential situation of *an* existent, and then we see
him as *an existent* which is a composite of essence and *esse*. A composite of essence and *esse* which would not be an *existent* to start
with, would not allow for *many* existents, because the same essence
(this *man*, that *man*) doesn't distinguish many existents, and different essences *(man, fish)* would distinguish many existents only in
their kind. What distinguishes many existents is the *existential* status

Marietti, nn. 27-28. See *Sum. Theol.*, I, 4, 1, *ad* 3; 8, 1, *Resp.*; 44, 1, *Resp.*; 75,
5, *Resp.*; 104, 1, *Resp.*; *In VIII Phys.*, lect. 21; *In IV Metaph.*, lect. 2, n. 558;
De Pot., V, 4, *ad* 3; VII, 2, *ad* 9; *Quodlibet.*, II, q. 2, a. 1, *Resp.*; *De Verit.*,
VIII, 8, *Resp.*; *Contra Gentiles*, I, 22; II, 31; II, 52-54; *In I Sent.*, d. 8, q. 1, a. 1;
De Sub. Sep., c. VI; *De Spir. Creat.*, a. 1, *ad* 9.
A historical exposition of the problem of the distinction between essence
and existence may be found in M. D. Roland-Gosselin, O.P., *Le "De Ente et
Essentia" de St. Thomas d'Aquin*, Paris, Vrin, 1926, pp. 137-205.
On essence and existence, see also E. Gilson, *L'Être et l'essence*, pp. 78-120,
139-183; *Being and Some Philosophers*, pp. 41-73, 74-107; *God and Philosophy*,
pp. 63-73; *Le Thomisme*, 5th ed., *Études de philosophie médiévale*, I, Paris,
Vrin, 1945, pp. 43-68; *The Christian Philosophy of St. Thomas Aquinas*, pp.
29-45; J. Maritain, *Court traité de l'existence et de l'existant*, pp. 42-60; *A
Preface to Metaphysics*, pp. 20-24, 37, n. 13; A. Forest, *La structure métaphysique du concret selon Saint Thomas d'Aquin*, Études de philosophie
médiévale, XIV, Paris, Vrin, 1931, pp. 128-165; G. Smith, S.J., *Natural Theology*, pp. 25-31; W. Walton, "Being, Essence, and Existence," *Review of
Metaphysics*, Vol. III (1950), pp. 339-365; A. Maurer, C.S.B., "Form and Essence in the Philosophy of St. Thomas," *Mediaeval Studies*, Vol. XIII (1951),
pp. 174-176.

of an essence, whether that essence be the same or different. A composite of essence and *esse*, therefore, is *an* existent *in* an essential situation.[6]

Substance

At this point, we need a word to describe the existential status of an existent, no matter what its essential status may be. The word is "substance." "Substance" is the name for the subject of the verb predicate "is" or "exists," as in, e.g., *a man exists*. Substance, that is, names any "clunk" of which you can say "*it* is."[7] When, for example, you say "a man's finger is," or "a man's smile is," you are not pointing to the subject of "is." You are pointing to a qualification, or to a part, of the subject which is. Behind the qualifications or parts of an existent there is always that to which "is" is properly attributed. See it this way: an existent is not made up of little existents, no more than a man is made up of little men, nor is an existent its qualifications.[8] Substance is the name for an existent (no matter

[6] The Aristotelian basis of this doctrine is in *Metaphysics*, IV (Γ), 2, 1003b 25–35; *Categories*, ch. 5, 2a 11–25; *Posterior Analytics*, II, 7, 92b 5–14. See St. Thomas, *In Periherm.*, lect. 5, nn. 70–73; *In II Post. Anal.*, lect. 6; *In IV Metaph.*, lect. 2, nn. 550, 553, 556, 558, and especially n. 550: ". . . est idem dictum, ens homo, vel quod est homo; et non demonstratur aliquid alterum cum secundum dictionem replicamus dicendo, est ens homo, et homo, et unus homo." See also n. 558, in which it is made clear that the man of whom you say that he is signifies the same as the essence of which you can say that it is a man. St. Thomas will (in this passage he is mainly the commentator) make clear that *his* existent involves an act which is *esse*.

[7] Aristotle says that substance is a subject of predicates which is never a predicate, *Metaphysics*, V (Δ), 8, 1017b 10–25: ". . . 'substance' has two senses, (A) the ultimate substratum, which is no longer predicated of anything else, and (B) that which, being a 'this,' is also separable—and of this nature is the shape or form of each thing." *Categories*, ch. 5, 2a 11–25: "Substance, in the truest and primary and most definite sense of the word, is that which is neither predicable of a subject nor present in a subject; for instance, the individual man or horse." See *Metaphysics*, VII (Z), 1, 1028b 2–8; 13, 1038b 15. See also St. Thomas, *De Pot.*, VII, 3, *ad* 4; *In V Metaph.*, lect. 10, n. 902; *In VII Metaph.*, lect. 1, nn. 1246, 1247, 1251; *Contra Gentiles*, I, 25.

[8] See Aristotle, *Physics*, III, 7, 207b 5; *Metaphysics*, VII (Z), 16, 1040b 5–10; X (I), 2, 1053b 16. See also St. Thomas, *Sum. Theol.*, I, 11, 2, *ad* 2: "A *whole* is twofold. In one sense it is homogeneous, composed of dissimilar parts. Now in every homogeneous whole, the whole is made up of parts having the form

of what essence it may be) as being the proper subject of "is." It
is true that such a subject or substance is *in* an essential situation,
but substance is not the name for the essential situation.[9] The name
for the essential situation is "essence." The name for the existent in
an essential situation, so far forth as you mean by the existent the
proper subject of "is," is substance.[10] Thus, it is the fact that an
existent (substance) is always, in our experience, in an essential situation, even though we may not know the essential situation, which
allows us to speak of a composite of essence and *esse;* and it is the
fact that the essential situation is always the situation of an existent

---

of the whole, as, for instance, every part of water is water; and such is the
constitution of a continuous thing made up of its parts. In every heterogeneous
whole, however, every part is wanting in the form belonging to the whole; as,
for instance, no part of a house is a house, nor is any part of man a man. Now
multitude is such a kind of whole. Therefore, inasmuch as its part has not the
form of the multitude, the latter is composed of unities, as a house is composed
of not houses; not, indeed, as if unities constituted multitude so far as they
are undivided, in which way they are opposed to multitude, but so far as
they have being; as also the parts of a house make up the house by the fact
that they are beings, not by the fact that they are not houses."
  [9] On essence and substance, see Aristotle, *Metaphysics*, VII (Z), 3, 1028b 34;
5, 1031a 12; *Metaphysics*, IV (Γ), 8, 1017b 23–25; *Categories*, ch. 5, 2a 11–25;
3b 10–18. See St. Thomas, *Sum. Theol.*, I, 3, 3, *Resp.*: ". . . in things composed
of matter and form, the nature or essence must differ from the *suppositum*,
for the essence or nature includes only what falls within the definition of
man, for it is by this that man is man, and it is this that humanity signifies,
that, namely, whereby man is man. . . . Consequently, humanity and a man
are not wholly identical, but humanity is taken to mean the formal part of a
man, because the principles whereby a thing is defined function as the formal
constituent in relation to individuating matter." *Sum. Theol.*, I, 3, 5, *ad* 1: "The
name *substance* signifies not only what is being of itself—for being cannot of
itself be a genus, . . . but it also signifies an essence to which it belongs to be
in this way, namely, of itself, which being, however, is not its essence." *Sum.
Theol.*, I, 29, 2, *Resp.*: "According to the Philosopher, substance is twofold.
In one sense, it means the *quiddity of a thing*, signified by the definition, and
thus we say that the definition signifies the substance of a thing; in which sense
substance is called by the Greeks *ousia*, which we may call *essence*. In another
sense, substance means a *subject* or *suppositum*, which subsists in the genus of
substance." See also *De Pot.*, IX, 1, *Resp.*; *In V Metaph.*, lect. 10, nn. 902–903.
  [10] See St. Thomas, *De Verit.*, I, 1, *Resp.*: ". . . some predicates may be said to
add to being inasmuch as they express a mode of being not expressed by the
term *being*. This happens in two ways. First, the mode expressed is a certain
special manner of being; for there are different grades of being according to
which we speak when we speak of different levels of existence, and according
to these grades different things are classified. Consequently, *substance* does

(substance) which prohibits us from thinking that essence is the proper subject of "is." Essence is not the proper subject of "is." Substance is the proper subject of "is." Essence is a factor in multiple substances or proper subjects of "is," and because multiple substances are each in an essential situation, that is why essences are components of many existents. Yet it is because existents or substances or the proper subject of "is" are themselves compounded (of the subject of "is" and its "is") that we can speak of a composite of essence and *esse*. The distinction of "is" from each subject of "is" is as between the subject and its own "is"; that is, the distinction is as between an "is" *in* each subject and that subject itself. If you will, the distinction is as between a subject *in esse* and that subject's *esse*. In sum, since essence is the name for the essential situation in which the proper subject of *esse* finds itself, you can say that essence names the same existent as does substance or the proper subject of *esse*, but essence names that same existent in a different way from the way substance names it. In these expressions, a *man*, a being which is a *man*, a *man* who is, the word "man" describes the essential situation of an existent; and substance names that same existent as the proper subject of *esse*, even if the existent were not a man, or even if it were a different man. The problem now is to understand the composite of a proper subject of *esse* (which has an essence) and its *esse*.

---

not add a difference to being by signifying some reality added to it, but *substance* simply expresses a special manner of existing, namely, as being in itself. The same is true of the other classes of existents. . . . We can, however, find nothing that can be predicated of every being affirmatively and, at the same time, absolutely, with the exception of its essence by which the being is said to be. To express this, the term *thing* is used; for, according to Avicenna, thing differs from being because being gets its name from to-be, but thing expresses the quiddity or essence of the being."

St. Thomas will then say that the cause of *ens* causes the causes of individuation and substance to exist, and therefore it causes individuality and substance, *Sum. Theol.*, I, 44, 2, *Resp.; In I Phys.*, lect. 15. See Aristotle, *Metaphysics*, I (A), 3-4, 983b 6-985b 22; II (a), 5, 1002a 8; *Physics*, I, 8, 191a 27; I, 4, 187a 30; 187a 15; I, 5, 188b 34; IV, 6, 213a 29; VIII, 1, 250b 24; *On Generation and Corruption*, II, 9, 335b 24; 336a 4.

A Review of the Composites of Substance and Accidents, and of Prime Matter and Substantial Form

To aid us in understanding that composite, we may recall the nature of the composites of substance and accident, and of prime matter and substantial form.[11] A composite of substance and accidents, as the facts show, is unidentical and identical with itself: Peter's-becoming-wise is *not* Peter, yet it is *he* who is becoming wise. A composite of prime matter is also unidentical and identical with any other such composite: the organic kind of being is not the inorganic kind, yet both kinds are of the same uncharacterizable stuff or prime matter. Now surely, identity and unidentity cannot without contradiction be predicated of the same element. They must therefore be predicated of the composite according to the composite's different components. That predication is possible only if (1) the composite is identical and unidentical according to *each* of its components, and that condition depends (2) on this one, viz., that neither component be the other. Let us recall the meaning of the first condition, which is this: the composite, *besides* being identical with itself according to its potential element, must also be unidentical with itself according to the actualization of that very same *potential* feature. The question is, is this so? Apparently it is, because Peter-becoming-wise is the same old Peter, who could become, that *is* becoming wise: and substantialized prime matter is the same old unspecified stuff, which could be specified, that *is* specified. Moreover (we are still on the first condition), besides being unidentical with itself according to its *actuation*, the composite must also be identical with itself according to the very same *actuation* of its potential element. Is this so? Apparently it is, because Peter's-becoming-wise is not Peter either with or without his becoming, yet it is he all the same who is becoming; and this sort of being is not that sort, yet both sorts are substantialized matter. In sum, actualization so affects the subject of actuation that it is the *actualized* subject which is the *identical* subject, yet *because* actualized, *unidentical;*

[11] See Chapters II and III.

and the subject of actualization is so affected by its actualization as to remain identical, because *it* is actuated; yet not identical, because it *is* actuated.

As to the *second* condition, viz., that neither component is the other, it is perfectly apparent that the components of a composite must be distinct, else there would be no composite, and composite there must be: Peter is not his becoming, yet he becomes; unspecified stuff is not its specification, yet stuff is always specified.

The Composite of Substance (or, Essence) and "Esse"

Having recalled the above we may now better face a similar situation, which is this: a composite of substance and its *esse*, or if you will, the composite of essence and *esse*, must be the *same* as any other such composite, yet *differ* from the other in the very spot in which both composites are the *same*, viz., in their status of being existents. How is this possible?[12]

Notice that our present situation differs from the two preceding ones in this: the status of an existent precedes the status of a changing and a specific kind of being. Before Peter becomes wise, he must first of all exist; and before Peter turns into dust, Peter exists; and before dust turns into Peter, dust exists. In other words, it is not because things change or are generated that they exist; rather, it is because they exist that they change and are generated. Put it this way: it is not because a fish swims that it exists. Upon that hypothesis a fish would not exist unless it swam. Against the fact. Nor is it because a fish is a fish that it exists. Upon that hypothesis, to be an existent would be to be a fish, and so all existents would be fish. Against the fact. Becoming and generation are within the already given framework of the status of an existent.[13] If, therefore, accident is act, and if substantial form is act, the act of existing

[12] On a composite of essence and *esse*, or substance and *esse*, see pp. 63–67 of this chapter.

[13] St. Thomas says that beyond generation and corruption, it is necessary to posit another kind of coming-to-be, viz., creation. See *De Pot.*, III, 5, *Resp.*; *De Sub. Sep.*, ch. VII; *Contra Gentiles*, II, 52; *Sum. Theol.*, I, 44, 2, *Resp.*; I, 45, 1, *ad* 2; I, 104, 1, *Resp.*

(which is also act) must be an act whose function is truly astonishing.

Consider what an act of existing must accomplish. It must (1) add to an essential situation of an existent the feature of existing, and (2) precisely because it accomplishes that, an act of existing must also be the reason why the status of an existent is the status of an existent *essential* situation. Let us paraphrase the functions of *esse* in (1) and (2). (1) It is by *esse* that an essential situation exists. (2) Hence it is by *esse* that an essential situation of an existent is made to *be* essential. For example, it is (1) by his *esse* that a man exists, and so it is by his *esse* that (2) he is a *man*, or a being which is a *man*, or a *man* who exists.[14]

The function of *esse* in (2) looks to be impossible. It is not too hard to see that *esse* adds the feature of existing to an essential situation of an existent, but what on earth has *esse* to do with an essential situation itself? *Esse* certainly cannot bring it about that an essential situation is more or less essential after than it was before it existed. Apparently an essential situation stays the same without any relation to *esse* either in fact or in knowledge, whether it exists or not.

Not so. When we see why, we shall have reached the peak of the metaphysical insight into the present situation. Let us take this matter slowly. Our question is: why can there be many existents? We ask the question because there is no reason in the existents which we know why *they* should be many. For, the multiplicity of the status of an existent cannot be explained by the multiplicity of essence alone. Often enough the essential status is *not* multiple, yet the existential status of the same essence *is* multiple: Peter and Paul are *both* men, yet they are distinct existent *men*. Often enough, too, the accidental status of two existents is or conceivably could be identical, yet identical twins are distinct existents, and at any rate they cannot differ accidentally until they are in existence, and that

---

[14] The pertinent texts are in G. Smith, S.J., "Avicenna and the Possibles," *The New Scholasticism*, Vol. XVII, n. 4 (October 1944), pp. 340–357. Some of these texts are as follows. St. Thomas, *Sum. Theol.*, I, 9, 2, *Resp.; De Pot.*, III, 1, *obj.* 17 and *ad* 17; V, 1, *ad* 1 and *ad* 12; *Quodlibet.*, XII, q. 4, a. 5; *De Verit.*, III, 6, *Resp.* and *ad* 3, 4; III, 3; II, 4.

last situation is a multiplicity in *esse* before it is a multiplicity in an accidental kind of *esse*. Identical twins have to be around first, before they can differ even accidentally. Besides, even unidentical essences, e.g., the organic and the inorganic, if their existential status differs only *because* their essential status does, ought to differ as "is" differs from "is not," because the organic differs from the inorganic as "is" differs from "is not": the organic is *not* the inorganic. Yet both the organic and the inorganic exist and so they don't differ upon the score that one is and the other isn't.

We are on the rack. We are trying to find why it is possible that there be many existents. *Esse* alone cannot be that reason, else this existent would demand that there be that existent, i.e., to be an existent is to be two of them. Nonsense. Nor can essence or an essential situation alone be that reason, not unless to be an essence is identically to be an existent, and this denies the established difference between an essential and an existential situation.

The Position of Idealism Concerning Essence and "Esse"

We could get off the rack by not getting on it. This is the way out which idealism takes. An idealist reduces the essential situation to an existential one: to be of a sort is just a less perfect way of existing than to be of a sort *and* to exist.[15] A realist cannot have that recourse. For a realist, an essential situation is not reducible to an existential one, and *because* it is not, therefore the two situations are hand in glove, not only in the structure of an actual existent, but also in the structure of a possible existent.

[15] Kant undoubtedly does this. See "Der einzig mögliche Beweisgrund zur einer Demonstration des Daseins Gottes," I abth., I betrachtung, *Kant's Schriften*, Berlin, Reimer, 1905, Vol. II, p. 75: "What is added to the essence or to the possible when it is posited as existing is not something *other* than the possible; it's only the possible 'more posited' (mehr gesetzt) than when the possible is posited as possible." Suarez says: ". . . nulla fingi potest conditio, quae constituat esse reale in esse existentiae, quae non reperiatur in esse actualis essentiae. Est ergo hoc [esse actualis essentiae] verum esse existentiae." *Disputationes Metaphysicae*, Disp. XXXI, sec. 4, n. 5; *Opera Omnia*, Paris, Vivès, 1856–77, Vol. XXVI, p. 236.

We may see the realist's position better for having seen the idealist's objection to it. The idealist, then, says to the realist: your supposed components of many existents, namely, essence and *esse*, must
both exist because the composite exists, and to say that one component of an existent composite exists, whereas the other does not
exist, is absurd. Since both components of a composite in *esse* exist,
they must both exist by the same title, viz., by *esse*, for there is no
other title to existence except the act of existing. Existing by the
same title, then, the supposed components must, upon the supposition
of realism, be either (a) themselves composites of essence and *esse*,
or else (b) one component must be identical with the other. The
first alternative leads to an irrelevant and impossible series of composites of essence and *esse;* the second shows that there is no basic
difference between an essential and an existential situation.[16] Thus
idealism.

The Position of Realism Concerning Essence and "Esse"

Realism, in a way, agrees that both components of an existent
exist, yet it maintains that they are two different titles to two different features in an existent. An existent has essential features, and
its title to these is essence. An existent also exists, and its title to
existing is *esse*. And so, it is not quite accurate to say that the components of a composite existent exist. Rather, it is the composite
which exists, and it exists according to two different titles: essence
is the reason why an existent is of a certain sort, whereas its *esse*
is the reason why a sort of existent exists.

Idealism will never admit the above account of the matter, and
for the very reason which causes realism to accept that account.
That reason is as follows. *Esse* cannot make essence to be more es-

[16] Suarez, *Disputationes Metaphysicae*, Disp. XXXI, sec. 4, n. 3, p. 235. See
Disp. XXXI, sec. 1, n. 4, p. 225, where Suarez states the real distinction as a
distinction of *res a re*. See J. Owens, C.Ss.R., "The Number of Terms in the
Suarezian Discussion on Essence and Being," *The Modern Schoolman*, Vol.
XXXIV, n. 3 (March 1957), pp. 147–191; C. Vollert, S. J., *On the Various
Kinds of Distinctions*, Milwaukee, Marquette University Press, 1947.

sential after than it was before it existed: $100 in *esse* are no more or less $100 than before they existed. From that proposition idealism argues: *since* $100 in their preexistential or possible state can exist, even though they don't, this ability to exist is either a feature of their essential structure, or if this ability to exist is not such a feature, at any rate that ability is not needed in order that $100 be $100. Realism denies all that except the "since" clause. Indeed it is that very "since" clause which causes realism to distinguish, and idealism to fail to distinguish, essence from *esse*. The issue between realism and idealism, then, is clearly here: is essence able to exist solely because it is essence? or is essence able to be also because there is an actuation or act which is able to make essence to be? A realist maintains that essence is able to be upon two counts. In other words, just as an existent has two distinct features to it, namely, its essential and its existential feature, so also a possible existent has two distinct features to it, namely, its essential structure and an act which is able to make essence to be. We may put the realist's position figuratively: essence, before it exists, does not float around, unattached or un-related to its prospective *esse;* to that prospective *esse*, essence is related through the medium of a cause which is able, because it exists, to confer the prospective *esse* upon essence.

The Validation of Realism's Position Concerning Essence and "Esse"

We must see this more clearly. An essence which can be, even though it is not, is an answer to the question, *what* is it that can be? just as essence in *esse* is an answer to the question, *what* is it that *is?* Now, the answer to *quid possit* can never be the answer to *an possit*, any more than the answer to *quid sit* can be the answer to *an sit*— not unless you assume that the status of a possible existent is identical with the essential status of that possible existent. The idealist as-sumes the identity of the *existential* situation with the *essential* situa-tion, even in the status of a possible existent. The realist denies that identity. For, the realist argues: if to-be-a-possible-existent is iden-

tically the *essential* features of that possible existent, then no existent
would be possible unless it had those essential features. This cannot
be so, no more than an existential situation can be identically the
essential situation, when both situations are in *esse*. Run a test case
in the order of the actually existent: if to be an existent is to be
$100, there is no other existent except $100. Against the fact. In the
order of the possible existent a realist argues in the same way: if to
be a possible existent is to be $100, there is no possible existent ex-
cept $100. Against the fact, for there *are* actually different existents,
and so there can be. Hence for a realist $100 can exist, before they
do, not solely because they are $100, but also because one hundred
possible dollars are themselves a composite of a subject in an essential
situation ($100) and that subject's prospective *esse*, i.e., its *posse*.

If now we ask how a subject in an essential situation before it
exists is related to its prospective *esse*—i.e., to its *posse*—a realist
answers: Through the medium of a cause, able to make essence to
exist. To illustrate, future children are possible, not only because
children are children, but also because there are generators of children. Without generators, future children are strictly nothing, i.e.,
without generators future children have no status at all as possible
existents. What gives us the illusion that future children are possible
existents apart from the actuality of their generators (which actuality is not the actuality of the act of generating, but the acuality
of generators who can generate) is that we can understand *what*
children are without knowing *that* they are related to their cause.
True, we can. But in so knowing them, we do not know them as
possible existents; we know them only in terms of *what* possible
existents are. Put it this way: whereas actual or possible existents
may be defined without having their relation to their cause involved
in their definition, nevertheless they cannot be known as *many*
actual or possible *existents* without being known as related to a
cause of them, either actually causing them, or able to cause them.[17]
Even in the realm of possible existents, then, a realist discerns two
different titles to the status of an existent, which is one and many:

[17] See St. Thomas, *Sum. Theol.*, I, 44, 1, *ad* 1; *De Pot.*, III, 1, *obj.* 17 and *ad*
17; III, 5, *obj.* 1 and *ad* 1; *De Verit.*, II, 8; III, 3, *ad* 3; III, 6, *Resp.* and *ad* 3, 4;
Sum. Theol., I, 15, 3.

the title of a cause, able to make the possible to exist; the title of the essential situation of the possible existent, which is the reason why the possible existent is of the sort it is.

Summary of Realism's Position on Essence and "Esse"

To pull all this together, the status of an experienced existent has, over and above the multiplicity of its accidental variations, over and above the multiplicity also of the different specific kinds of existents, a multiplicity in the existential status as existential: George is not John (multiplicity), yet both are existents (unity). How is this possible? It is possible only if the *esse* of each existent be not exhausted, so to say, in being united to, or involved in, just one of them. There must, in other words, be enough *esse* to go around or to cover all cases; *esse* cannot expire in being just one existent if there are many of them, and many there are. Now, the only supposition upon which there's enough *esse* left over, so to say, from one existent in order to cover the case of another existent, is that *esse* be not identical with the subject of *esse*. An existent as existent is, therefore, a composite of unidentical components, namely, a subject of *esse*, and the *esse* of which it is the subject. And if the subject of *esse* be in an existential situation, as it is, it is also correct to say that its existential situation is not its essential situation, or that its essence is not its *esse*.

The same goes for the status of a possible existent; only, the possible existent is not a composite of a subject plus its actual *esse*, precisely because it has no actual *esse*. Nevertheless, it is related to its prospective *esse (posse)* through the medium of the *esse* of a cause which is able to make it to be. This shows that the status of a possible existent is still a composite of an essential situation and an existential one. Only, the existential situation of a possible existent is through the medium of the *esse* of its cause.[18]

[18] The essential situation of a possible existent arises from its imitation of the nature of its cause. This proposition, as well as the proposition that possible existents are related to their cause which can produce them, supposes of course the chapters on causality, and so it is advanced here merely for the sake of coherence, not because it is demonstrated.

To see this, ask: which is the better way to state the matter—children can be generated or generators can generate children?[19] The second is incomparably the better way, because to say that children can be generated is to imply that they are waiting around to be generated as subjects of possible *esse*, as if their generators had nothing to do with the possible *esse* by which future children are possible existents. This is nonsense. Apart from generators, future children are strictly nothing as possible existents. What causes us to think that future children as possible existents are something apart from their generators is that we can know *what* they are, viz., children, apart from knowing that there are generators. But this knowledge is not knowledge of future children as possible *existents*. It is knowledge of future children as *kinds* of possible existents, whereas the problem is this: how must future children be known as possible *existents*? They cannot be *known* as possible existents apart from knowing that there is a cause able to generate them, because they cannot *be* possible as possible existents without generators.

There are some shorthand ways of stating the above doctrine. (1) The function of *esse* is to make an existent, actual or possible, of the subject of *esse*. *Esse* fulfills this function both in the order of the actual existent and the possible existent in the manner explained. (2) *Esse* is the principle by which each existent is, or can be, an existent (unity), and also the principle by which no existent is another existent (multiplicity), because *esse*, not being identical with the subject of *esse*, is not used up by any one existent. Thanks to that function of *esse*, the subject of *esse*, which is in an essential situation, is just like any other subject of *esse*, viz., it is an existent

<hr>

[19] See St. Thomas, *De Verit.*, II, 10, *ad contra* 2: "Although in creation there is nothing new except in reference to the creature, the word *creation* implies not only this newness but also something on the part of God; for it signifies a divine action, which is His essence, and connotes an effect in a creature, which is the reception of being from God. So, it does not follow that it is the same to say that God can create something as to say that something can be created by Him. Otherwise, before there was a creature, nothing could be created unless the potency of a creature first existed. This would be positing eternal matter. Therefore, although the potency of a creature does not extend to the existence of actual infinites, this does not exclude ability on the part of God to make actual infinites." See also *De Verit.*, II, 8, *Resp.*; III, 3, *ad* 3; III, 6, *Resp.* and *ad* 3; *Sum. Theol.*, I, 15, 3; I, 22, 1, *ad* 3.

(actual or possible); yet no subject of *esse* is another one. (3) Every subject of *esse* has its own *esse*, and that's why they are all subjects of *esse*, but unless they were different subjects of *esse*, you could not have many beings. (4) *Esse* is the reason why an existent is an existent (actual or possible), and therefore it is the reason why an existent of a sort is distinct from another existent of a sort, whether that other existent be of the same or of a different sort. The *ens-esse* distinction comes first, and upon it are grafted the other distinctions, e.g., essence-*esse*, and substance-accident, and matter-form, etc. (5) Essence causes an existent to be such and such, and the reason why essence does this is because it mimics the essence-*esse* composite of that which can cause an existent to exist.[20] (6) The subject of *esse* and its *esse* are hand in glove in the structure of the status of an existent, because one is *not* the other. The subject of *esse* and its *esse* are not hand in glove because one *is* the other; for then they wouldn't be hand in glove: they would be either the hand or the glove. (7) All multiplicity issues from the multiplicity of the *ens-esse* twoness, not the other way about.

The Answer to Idealism

There is also a short way of meeting the idealists' objection, which is this: *esse* cannot make essence more essential, or, essence is not perfectible by *esse*. Answer: the objection misses the point. Of a surety, *esse* cannot make essence more essential or perfect it in the order of essence. The real question is this: what perfects essence in the order of the status of an existent? Answer: *esse*. Idealism urges: but before essence exists it is nonetheless essence without *esse*. Answer: it is essence without its own actual *esse*, yes; it is essence, as an essential situation of an existent which can be, but without relation to the *esse* of its cause which can make essence to be, no. Nor can it be known as a possible existent unless that relation to its cause be also known. Of course essence can be known as what-it-is which can be, without knowing that causal relation, but this is

[20] See note 18 above. All essences imitate God's essence, which is His *esse*.

not to know the status of a possible existent as existent; still less, i.e., without essence's relation to its cause, is it possible for essence as essence to be a possible existent. Without that relation to its cause, essence is strictly nothing.

Summary of the Chapter

A while back[21] it was said that the *esse* of a subject thereof need not be given at all, and because that is so, there is need to ask why it is given at all? The partial answer to that was: it is *possible* that *esse* be given, because passive potency or a subject of *esse* can exist, and if it can, there is no reason why multiplicity is impossible. Why multiplicity is actual is another question. That multiplicity is possible is clear from the distinction between the subject of *esse* and its *esse*. At this point, and in order to finish off this chapter, we may review the reasons why *esse* need not be given at all. Assume that Caesar crosses the Rubicon. Caesar's crossing the Rubicon need not be given at all unless his crossing and he are identical. Against the fact, for he existed before he crossed. Hence his crossing was not in him under wraps in the sense that his crossing was merely a pulling aside of the wraps and a revelation of him as a Rubicon-crossing-Caesar all the time. To say that his crossing was in Caesar all the while is to deny the reality of change, to deny any real difference between him and his crossing. His crossing, then, was in him potentially. Make the same run for generation and corruption. If you say that the organic turns into the inorganic because the inorganic was under wraps in the inorganic, you are saying that the organic turns into the inorganic because the organic *is* the inorganic. Against the facts. Hence the one is in the other potentially. Now run the crucial test. If you say $100 can exist solely because they are $100, you have said that to be a possible existent is to be $100. Against the fact. There are many other possible existents besides $100. Hence to be 100 possible dollars is to be a subject of *posse*, not solely upon the score that $100 is $100, but also because there is a cause (whose essence

[21] See pp. 61-62 of this chapter.

the possible $100 mimics) able to make $100 to be, and *there* lies the complete *posse* of $100. In all cases of *esse*, whether accidental, specific, or the *esse* of an existent as multiple existent, *esse* need not be given at all. But it can be given, because there are subjects to which it can be given, because there are causes which can give *esse* to these subjects, and this makes all multiplicity possible.

That there are causes is a point which remains to be proved in Chapter VI.

Suggested Reading

Essence and Existence:

St. Thomas Aquinas, *Sum. Theol.*, I, 3, 4, *Resp.*; I, 4, 1, *ad* 3; 8, 1, *Resp.*; 44, 1, *Resp.*; 75, 5, *Resp.*; 104, 1, *Resp.*; *De Ente et Essentia*, ch. IV; *In I Sent.*, d. 8, q. 1, a. 1; *In VIII Phys.*, lect. 21; *In IV Metaph.*, lect. 2, n. 558; *De Pot.*, V, 4, *ad* 3; VII, 2, *ad* 9; *Quodlibet.*, II, q. 2, a. 1, *Resp.*; *De Verit.*, VIII, 8, *Resp.*; *Contra Gentiles*, I, 22; II, 31; II, 52-54; *De Sub. Sep.*, ch. VI; *De Spir. Creat.*, a. 1, *ad* 9.

Forest, A., *La structure métaphysique du concret selon saint Thomas d'Aquin*, pp. 128-165.

Gilson, E., *L'Être et l'essence*, pp. 78-120, 139-183.

———, *Being and Some Philosophers*, pp. 41-107.

———, *God and Philosophy*, pp. 63-73.

———, *Le Thomisme*, pp. 43-68.

———, *The Christian Philosophy of St. Thomas Aquinas*, pp. 29-45.

Maritain, J., *A Preface to Metaphysics*, pp. 20-24, 37, n. 13.

———, *Court traité de l'existence et de l'existant*, pp. 42-60.

Maurer, A., C.S.B., "Form and Essence in the Philosophy of St. Thomas," *Mediaeval Studies*, Vol. XIII (1951), pp. 174-176.

Owens, J., C.Ss.R., "The Number of Terms in the Suarezian Discussion on Essence and Being," *The Modern Schoolman*, Vol. XXXIV, n. 3 (March 1957), pp. 147-191.

Roland-Gosselin, M.D., O.P., *Le "De Ente et Essentia" de St. Thomas d'Aquin*, pp. 137-205.

Smith, G., S.J., *Natural Theology*, pp. 25-31.

———, "Avicenna and the Possibles," *The New Scholasticism*, Vol. XVII, n. 4 (October 1944), pp. 340-357.

Vollert, C., S.J., *On the Various Kinds of Distinctions.*

Walton, W., "Being, Essence and Existence," *Review of Metaphysics*, Vol. III (1950), pp. 339-365.

Substance:

Aristotle, *Metaphysics*, I (A), 3-4; II (a), 5; V (Δ), 8; VII (Z), 1; *Physics*, I, 4; I, 5; I, 8; IV, 6; VIII, 1; *Categories*, ch. V; *On Generation and Corruption*, II, 9.

St. Thomas Aquinas, *De Pot.*, VII, 3, *ad* 4; *In V Metaph.*, lect. 10; *In VII Metaph.*, lect. 1; *Contra Gentiles*, I, 25; *De Verit.*, I, 1, *Resp.*; *Sum. Theol.*, I, 44, 2, *Resp.*; *In I Phys.*, lect. 15.

Essence and Substance:

Aristotle, *Metaphysics*, VII (Z), 3; IV (Γ), 8; *Categories*, ch. 5.

St. Thomas Aquinas, *Sum. Theol.*, I, 3, 3, *Resp.*; I, 3, 5, *ad* 1; I, 29, 2, *Resp.*; *De Pot.*, IX, 1; *In V Metaph.*, lect. 10.

V · SUMMARY OF CHAPTERS I–IV

This chapter will attempt to summarize the preceding ones. The question, then, is this: How is it possible that there be many existents? The question is asked because it is not necessary that there be *many* existents upon the score that to be an existent is to be an existent. Just as we must ask why there are *many* hot things because it is not necessary that there be *any* hot things upon the score that to be a hot thing is to be a hot thing, so we must ask why there are *many* existents because it is not necessary that there be *any* existent upon the score that an existent is an existent. What else indeed could an existent be except an existent, and what else could a hot thing be except hot? But *many* existents, and *many* hot things —that situation is unintelligible upon the supposition that one is many. For, if one existent is many, there is no one existent; conversely, if many existents are one, there aren't many existents.

In order to answer the question, we examined the status of an existent, and we discerned, first, that as given in experience an existent changes, and, next, that there are different specific kinds of existents. Last, we saw that an existent as existent is not another existent, yet another existent is just as much and as truly an existent as the first.

What can possibly account for such a situation? Only this: in each of the three given instances there must be two components— the potential and its actualization. Run through the cases. Without *two* components, a changing being would be both identical and unidentical with itself in a *single* factor: in Peter-becoming-wise, Peter would both be and not be if *he* is the single factor involved, because he would be, since he is Peter, and not be, since he is not his becoming; or else he would both be becoming and not becoming if *becoming* is the single factor involved, because *becoming* is not *not-becoming*.[1] Against the fact, which is this: Peter changes, yet he is not his change. In order to preserve the fact we must say (1) that Peter is *identical* according to his *potential* factor, viz., Peter, and, because that potential factor is becoming *actualized* in his becoming, Peter is not identical according to the actualization of that same *potential* factor; (2) we must say that Peter is unidentical according to his becoming *actualized*, yet because that becoming actualized is *his*, he is identical according as it is *he* who is becoming *actualized*. Make the same run for beings of a specific kind which are generated and corrupted. Without two components, a specific kind of being which is generated or corrupted into another kind would both be identical and unidentical with another kind in a *single* factor.[2] Against the fact, for there is no single factor in the organic which is identically in the inorganic, yet one is generated into the other. In order to preserve the fact, we must say (1) that the organic is identical with the inorganic according to its *potential* factor, viz., prime matter, and, because that potential factor *is* actualized in generation and corruption, that *potential* factor as actualized is not identical with its actualization or with itself as unactualized; (2) we must say that the organic is not identical with the inorganic according to the *actualization* of prime matter, and yet, because that actualization is of common prime matter, the organic and the inorganic are identical according to the prime matter of each, for they are made of the same uncharacterizable stuff. In sum, potency and act are each principles of identity and unidentity in each one's order.

Now run the crucial case. First, see the case. An existent must not only be itself—else *it* would not be; it must also be like any other existent—else another existent would not be either, not being *itself*. Every experienced existent is in the same boat: it must be only itself, yet it must also be like any other existent in order to be itself, because any other existent must also be *itself* in order to be

[1] See Chapter II.
[2] See Chapter III.

an existent. Such being the situation of *many* existents, it follows that the status of any one of them as existent must have two components.[3] For, without two components, an existent would both be like and unlike another one in the identity of an *undifferentiated* status of an existent. Impossible. It would be like saying *x is an existent*, yet, because *x is not another existent*, and because the status of an existent is undifferentiated in both cases, *x is not an existent*. In order to avoid that contradiction we must say, *x is an existent*, and because *x is not y*, although *y also exists*, therefore *x's* status of being an existent is *not* identical with *y's*. Now, the only condition under which it is possible to preserve the facts, viz., that *x* and *y* are both existents, yet existent *x* is not existent *y*, is this: both statuses must be composite statuses. For, we can then say that *x's* status of being an existent is like *y's* according to one component of each composite, and it is unlike *y's* according to the other component of each composite. Having said that much, we must go on to name and describe the function of those components of the status of an existent.

Many existents are given, whether they be the same in essence (this *man*, that *man*) or not (this *man*, this *fish*). Hence the essential situation of an existent cannot of itself account for the multiplicity of existents. For, the essential situation could be the same (this *man*, that *man*), yet two existents are not the same existent. Not even when the essential situations are different could these situations account for the multiplicity of existents. For, two essentially different situations ought then to differ as "is" differs from "is not," because "is fish" differs from "is man" as "is" differs from "is not": man is not a fish. Nevertheless, "is man" and "is fish" do *not* differ as "is" differs from "is not," for both *man* and *fish* exist. How, then, can we state the reason for the possibility of many existents?

We cannot state that reason until we discern that the essential situation of an existent is *not* the existential situation, whether the existent actually exist or be only possible. For, if the essential situation of an existent were the existential situation, all existents would be in the identical essential situation. Against the fact, for

[3] See Chapter IV.

the living is not the nonliving. And even if all existents were in the identical essential situation (some of them are, e.g., George and John are both *men*), they would nevertheless differ as existents, for if they did not, they would be only one existent. Against the fact. Having seen that much, we can now see that an existent as given must be a composite of a subject of "is," which subject is in an essential situation, and that subject's "is," actual or possible. Now we ask two questions: (a) why are many subjects of "is" possible, and (b) whence come their different essential situations? The answers are: (a) they are possible because there are causes which make or are able to make many subjects of "is" to exist; (b) the various *kinds* of the subjects of "is" have their source in the *kinds* their causes are.

Much more, of course, remains to be said, but to say more now would only clutter up the main point.

The main point is this: it is not *because* a subject of "is" is in an essential situation (though it's true it *is* in an essential situation) that it is an existent; rather, it is *because* an essential situation is a situation of a subject of "is" that there *is* an essential situation, actual or possible. It is not because an existent is a fish that it is an existent, else all existents would be fish, and besides, there would be only one fish. It is because being a fish is an essential situation of an existent that there *is* a fish. Keep running examples until you see the point. It's not because George and John are *men* that they are existents, for they don't differ as *men*. It's because the *man* situation of each is a situation of two subjects of *esse* that George and John differ, and thus, therefore, they differ also in the existential *man* situation of each of them. The name of the essential situation of an existent is essence. The name of the *subject* of "is," which subject is in an essential situation, is substance. The actuation or act by which a subject of "is" both exists (actually or possibly) and exists as in an essential situation cannot be named if you mean by "name" a descriptive name. *Esse* cannot be described, and because it cannot, we are led to discern the functions of the components of a given existent. "Is" is the principle of sameness in the order of act, because each existent "is" and "is" is act; and because no existent as existent in an essential situation is another existent (whether their essences be the same or not), "is" is also a principle of unlikeness in the very order in which it is a principle of likeness, viz., in the order of act. On the other hand, essence, whether the same or different, is a principle of unlikeness, because essence is *always* in an existential situation, and that existential situation causes essences to differ in *esse*. Essence is also the principle of likeness, because an existent cannot be such and such without being an existent, and so, in causing an existent to be such and such, essence causes a being to be—in the order of essence, e.g., to be a man.

The above doctrine anticipates somewhat the doctrine on causality. Up to the point of discerning that many existents cannot possibly be unless they are compounded of a subject of "is" which is in an essential situation, and an "is" which, in making the subject of "is" to be a subject of "is," makes the subject's essential situation to be and therefore to be essential, up to that point causality is not involved. However, when we ask why there are or can be many subjects of "is," at that point we must acknowledge a cause of many subjects, actual or possible, of "is."

What gives us the illusion that we need not run an intelligible line to a cause in order to explain the multiplicity of existents is this: multiplicity in kinds or essence is often given (*man*, *fish*), and even when it not given (this *man*, that *man*), we are rightly convinced that there nevertheless is some multiplicity between this and that man. There is indeed. The question is, what sort of multiplicity? Two answers are possible: (1) multiplicity needs no cause if it be given. Now, multiplicity *is* given, even the multiplicity of two identical essences (this *man*, that *man*). Why not say, then, that two identical essences differ as "is" differs from "is not" in this expression, "this essence is not that essence," although each essence is itself? This is Plato's answer, and it is about as good as any if there is no factor in the status of an existent, given in experience, which is extraessential. The only difficulty in Plato's answer is that there cannot *be* an essential situation unless it be the essential situation of an *existent*. Plato, of course, would say to that, "certainly there cannot be an essential situation unless it be the essential situa-

tion of an existent; only you (the realist) think that the veritable
existents are given in experience and are sensible, whereas I, Plato,
do not."[4] (2) Realism answers: if $100 can be, solely upon the score
that $100 is $100, then to-be-able-to-be $100 is to-be-able-to-be
$100; if so, why are $101 also able to be, and what is worse, why are
two $100 bills different? Certainly $100 is not $101, nor are two
$100 possible bills the same. "Of course they're not," argues Platon-
ism, "and that is just what was said: $100 differ from $101 as 'is'
differs from 'is not,' and as to the difference between one possible
$100 bill and another, that too is a difference which is traceable
only to the fact that one essence is not identical with another essence,
because each is itself." A realist adduces again the point which an
essentialist is missing: to be oneself is *not* the only factor in the
status of an existent; rather, an existent first is or can be, and that
is why it is or can be itself. The self-identity of essence is of course
necessary, but what is *not* necessary is the existential status (actual
or possible) of an experienced existent. That existential status is not
necessary, because changing things exist as changing and their changing is not necessary; because kinds of things exist as kinds and their
given kind is not necessary (since one kind turns into another); because any of the many existents, irrespective of its kind, is not
necessary, else the many would be that one. Hence we must have,
according to realism, a reason why multiple existents are multiple,
a reason which is over and above their essential status, and we must
find that reason, if not in them as multiple (that is impossible), then
in something else. The "something else" is a cause which produces
the many, or can produce them. Without a cause, we simply stare at
multiplicity as at an unanswerable problem. With a cause, multiplicity is indeed given, but not *because* it's given (essentialism's
answer), but because a cause gives it or can give it. It is very easy to
avoid causes, because one can think of things in terms of their
essences alone, but if one wishes to think of things as being multiple
existents, one cannot avoid thinking that there is *some* reason for
their multiplicity which cannot be multiplicity itself. That "some
reason" is a cause, and this lands us in the extraordinary position of

[4] See Plato, *Sophistes*, 244a–260d.

saying that x is, because it is solely due to y (a cause) that x is. Contemplate *that* for an instant. The most stupendous proposition possible! x is not y, yet x's status of an existent comes from y's status, which is not x's. Whether or not a realist can make that proposition stick remains to be seen. At any rate, that is the proposition which must needs now be made to stick if there is any such science as metaphysics.

A Restatement of the Reason Why Multiplicity Is Possible

There can be many existents if there can be many subjects of "is." There can be many subjects of "is" if any such subject's "is" is unidentical with that subject. Each subject's "is" is unidentical with each subject if each subject's essential situation is unidentical with its existential situation. Each subject's essential situation is unidentical with its existential situation if multiplicity in the status of an existent is (a) a fact, actual or possible, and (b) if there be a cause of the fact or its possibility. So far we have come.

The Reason Why There Is Multiplicity

We must now posit that last condition in order to have the complete grounds for the multiplicity of the status of an existent. We must see why a cause is necessary in order that there may be many existents, actual or possible.

The Demonstration of a Cause of Multiplicity

A cause is necessary for multiplicity for the following reasons. (1) The potential (which in fact is actualized) cannot, upon the score that it is potential, actuate itself. For, if the potential could actuate itself, it would have to be actual, in order to do the job, whereas, being potential, it is not actual. In short, if the potential alone accounted for its actualization, it would not be potential, but actual. A contradiction in terms.

Run through the cases. If Peter, upon the score that he can get sick, got sick, he would not *become* sick. He would have been sick before he became sick. Against the fact. Again, if the organic, upon the score that it can be corrupted into the inorganic, were corrupted into the inorganic, the organic would have been the inorganic before it was corrupted. Against the fact. Again, if existents, actual or possible, were many solely upon the score that to be an existent is to be many existents, one existent would be many, or many would be one. Against the fact, and impossible.

(2) Granted that the potential cannot actualize itself, granted also that the potential is actualized, we must run an intelligible line from the potential to a surplus or an actual which is not the potential, but which confers upon the potential the potential's actuation. That surplus which confers upon the potential the potential's actuation is a cause. Thus, a cause is necessary in order to explain the multiplicity of the status of an existent in any order of given multiplicity: in the order of change, for without a cause of his becoming, Peter would *be*, he would not *become*, wise; in the order of generation and corruption, for without a cause of either, the organic would *be*, it would not *turn into*, the inorganic; in the order of the status of an existent, for without a cause, one existent would be many, or *vice versa*.

The Notion of a Cause

We must now walk around the notion of a cause.[1] A cause, as we saw, is *not* the potential whose actuation it explains. This feature of a cause is called its "otherness," i.e., a cause is "other" than the potential whose actuation it explains. This is the meaning of "other"

[1] On cause, see Aristotle, *Physics*, II, 3, 194b 23–195a 3; *On Generation and Corruption*, II, 9; *Metaphysics*, I (A), 3, 983a 24-31: "Evidently we have to acquire knowledge of the original causes (for we say we know each thing only when we think we recognize its first cause), and causes are spoken of in

in Aristotle's statement of causality in the order of change: what-ever is moved is moved by the "other."[2]

Furthermore, the cause exists with the actuation which it con-fers upon the potential, e.g., a cause of water-becoming-hot, does not, as cause, become hot; it *is* hot. This feature of a cause is called its "actuality." The cause is *in* the actuation of that by which it will actuate the potential.

Lastly, it will not suffice for a cause to be "other" than its effect, which is the actuation of the potential; nor will it suffice for it to be in the act of that which the potential can be. A cause must *confer* or *bestow* upon the potential that which actuates the potential. This feature of a cause is called its efficiency or the exercise of the cause's causality.[3]

---

four senses. In one of these we mean the substance, i.e., the essence (for the 'why' is reducible finally to the definition, and the ultimate 'why' is a cause and principle); in another the matter or substratum, in a third the source of the change, and in a fourth the cause opposed to this, the purpose and the good (for this is the end of all generation and change)." *Metaphysics*, V (Δ), 2, 1013a 24-35: " 'Cause' means (1) that from which, as immanent material, a thing comes into being, e.g., the bronze is the cause of the statue and the silver of the saucer, and so are the classes which include these. (2) The form or pattern, i.e., the definition of the essence, and the classes which include this (e.g., the ratio 2:1 and number in general are causes of the octave), and the parts included in the definition. (3) That from which the change or the resting from change first begins; e.g., the adviser is a cause of the action, and the father a cause of the child, and in general the maker a cause of the thing made and the change-producing of the changing. (4) The end, i.e., that for the sake of which a thing is; e.g., health is the cause of walking. For "Why does one walk?" we say: "that one may be healthy"; and in speaking thus we think we have given the cause."

See St. Thomas, *In II Phys.*, lects. 5, 6, 10, 11; *In I Metaph.*, lects. 1-3; *De Princ. Nat.*, chs. 3-4; *De Verit.*, VII, 7, ad 1; *Sum. Theol.*, I, 105, 5, Resp.; *Contra Gentiles*, II, 21; *De Pot.*, V, 1, Resp.

See also Chapter II, pp. 12-16; R. Johann, S.J., "A Comment on Secondary Causality," *The Modern Schoolman*, Vol. XXV, n. 1 (1947), pp. 19-25; J. Wild, "A Realistic Defense of Causal Efficiency," *Review of Metaphysics*, Vol. II (1949), pp. 1-14.

[2] See Aristotle, *Physics*, VII, 1, 241b 24-242b 18.

[3] On efficient cause, see Aristotle, *Physics*, II, 3, 194b 30; III, 3, 202a 12-22; *Metaphysics*, V (Δ), 1, 1013a 30-35; 1013b 23; IX (Θ), 8, 1050a 23-1050b 1; XI (K), 9, 1066a 26-34; *On Generation and Corruption*, I, 8; *De Anima*, III, 2, 426a 9; *Posterior Analytics*, II, 8, 93a 5.

See St. Thomas, *In II Phys.*, lect. 3, n. 180; *In III Phys.*, lect. 4, nn. 306, 310-312; lect. 5; *In I Metaph.*, lect. 4, n. 70; *In V Metaph.*, lect. 2, nn. 765, 770, 774, 775; *In VII Metaph.*, lect. 6, n. 1384; *In XI Metaph.*, lect. 9, n. 2312; *De Verit.*,

The Otherness *of a Cause*

A few remarks upon each feature of causality. The "otherness" of the cause means only that the cause is other than the potential. Sometimes this feature of a cause is described by saying the cause is outside of, or extrinsic to, the effect. This is intelligible enough, provided we do not read these expressions as necessarily having a spatial connotation. A cause of sickness may be outside or inside a sick person. At any rate, a cause of sickness is *not* the healthy organism, which can get sick.

Another point: to say that the cause is "other" than the effect is to create the impression that the demonstration of the "otherness" of the cause is the perfect identification or allocation of a cause. On the contrary, we are unable perfectly to identify any cause except the cause of *esse*, God. Short of God, we identify causes only in the sense that we circumscribe the area, so to say, where one or more of them are located. Bad food, e.g., makes one sick, but what is "bad" in bad food? Bacteria, no doubt. But what is bad in *them?* So we go on. Thus, the attempt to answer "whodunit?" is successful only to the extent indicated, but the demonstration that somebody or something within a circumscribed area did the job can be successful, and the demonstration that only God causes multiple existents is the only instance of complete identification of a cause.

The Actuality *of a Cause*

The "actuality" of a cause leaves open the question as to whether the cause's act of being, say, "hot," was caused or not. At any rate, whether caused or not, the actuality of a cause is not being

---

XXVIII, 7, *Resp.; De Pot.,* V, 1, *Resp.; Contra Gentiles,* II, 16; *Sum. Theol.,* I, 2, 3, *Resp.;* I, 3, 4, *Resp.;* I, 104, 1, *Resp.; De Ente et Essentia,* c. IV; *De Princ. Nat.,* c. 4, n. 356; c. 3, n. 350: "Oportet ergo praeter materiam et formam aliquid principium esse quod agat, et hoc dicitur causa efficiens, vel movens, vel agens, vel unde est principium motus." See also Chapter II, pp. 12-19.

understood unless one sees that it is the "being hot" which specifies a cause of something becoming hot. It makes little difference at this point how a cause got hot. That a cause *be* in the act of that which the potential can be, *that* is the notion of the actuality of a cause.

How Efficiency Is Understood

The "efficiency" or exercise of the act of causing means the *causing* of a cause, the reduction, by the cause, of the potential to the actual: the cause's bestowal upon the potential of the potential's actuation. Here, at the point where we come closest to the mystery of causality, we are baffled. We simply don't know *how* causes cause, and because we don't, we are inclined to think that we have accomplished nothing by our demonstration of a cause. True, we have an experience of causality, our own and other things' causality. We have a firm and certain anticipation of the future which *we* cause, the movement of our hand, for example. We also have a firm and certain anticipation sometimes of the future which we do not, but other things do, cause: an eclipse of the sun, for example. The "how" of our anticipative experience of our own future is just as intelligible as the "how" of our anticipative experience of the future of other things, i.e., the "how" is unintelligible in both cases. But "unintelligibility" here does not mean that we don't understand that causes do the job. That much we understand, by proof. It is *how* the job is done that we do not understand. This is only to say that we do not understand *esse*, for it is by existing that a cause causes, and we do not understand "existing" except by asserting it from evidence (John exists), or from proof (because John exists, *his parents existed*). Later, in Chapter VIII, we shall see that within our meagre understanding of "existing" there is also involved our understanding of a final cause.

Efficiency Is Contemporaneous with the Effect

The "efficiency" of a cause in its "causing" implies that causing is contemporaneous with "being effected."[4] When a blacksmith stops beating out a horseshoe, the shoe stops being beaten out. So for all causing. It is simultaneous with its effect.[5] We get the illusion sometimes that a cause causes in the sense that it gives a fillip to the potential, and thereafter the actuated potential takes over and goes on its own. For example, we push a body and it stays in motion, for a while at least, apparently without any further causing on our part; or, we just leave a body alone, and it remains inert. Physicists call this, in much more accurate and sophisticated formulae, of course, the law of inertia, and since our pushing of a body seems to start its motion, which seems to continue thereafter without further effort on our part, some physicists tend to deny the contemporaneity of cause and effect, and so they tend to deny causality.[6] The denial is uncalled for. We simply don't know, yet, all the causes of motion or rest. For that matter, neither do physicists, yet. We do know, however, that a cause is contemporaneous with its effect, as was demonstrated.

[4] Aristotle says that causing is one with being effected, *Physics*, III, 1, 201a 15-17; 201b 10-15; III, 3, 202a 12-202b 23; *Metaphysics*, XI (K), 8, 1050a 23; 9, 1065b 17-1066a 7; 1066a 26-34; *De Anima*, III, 2, 426a 9. St. Thomas says: "Eadem autem actio est eius quod agitur et movetur, et eius quod agit et movet, . . ." *Sum. Theol.*, II–II, 90, 3, *Resp.* See *In III Phys.*, lect. 2, n. 287; *In XI Metaph.*, lect. 9, n. 2297; *Contra Gentiles*, II, 16; *De Princ. Nat.*, c. 5, n. 364. See also Chapter II, pp. 17-22.

[5] Distinguish the duration, or persistence in being, of an effect from the effect as in the process of being effected: e.g., distinguish the metal and the horseshoe from the beating out of the shape of the horseshoe. Once the horseshoe has been beaten out, it continues in being without further effort of the blacksmith. This means that causes as we know them in experience cause only substantial and accidental differences in things whose *esse* they do not cause. *Natural Theology* will make it clear that only God causes *esse*.

[6] For a criticism of some physicists' denial of causality, see Plato, *Phaedo*, 98 ff.; Aristotle, *Physics*, I, 8, 191b ff.; St. Thomas, *De Verit.*, XI, 1, *Resp.* In his denial of causality, Hume says, "all our reasonings concerning causes and effects are derived from nothing but custom," *A Treatise of Human Nature*, Bk. I, Part IV, sec. I; ed. L. Selby-Bigge, p. 183. See also E. Meyerson, *Identité et realité*, p. 42; E. Gilson, *The Unity of Philosophical Experience*, pp. 223-247; *God and Philosophy*, pp. 74-144; G. Smith, S.J., *Natural Theology*, pp. 264-265.

Efficiency Resides in the Effect

One more remark about efficiency. Granted a cause causing, e.g.,
a heater heating, it is apparent that the function of heating is null
unless something be heated by the heating. Of course there can in
some sense be a Bunsen burner burning, or "heating" if you will,
without anything around being heated which *we* see. But that situation is not the situation of a cause causing. A cause causing is always
causing an effect, even when we don't see any effect. We may indeed get the illusion that a cause causing can "go through the
motions," without causing anything. For example, a weaver can go
through the motions of weaving, and a teacher of teaching, and so
on. But precisely, a weaver is not weaving unless something is being
woven, nor is a teacher teaching without someone being taught. If
we are to discern properly the function of efficiency, then, we
must see that causing causes something.[7] There is no weaving without something being woven, no teaching without someone being
taught, and so on. Causing has no meaning unless it means also
that something is being caused: if a heater *is* heating, it is heating
something. We can express this matter by saying that causing is
not precisely an accident of the agent or cause as, say, his color is
the accident of a man. Rather, causing emanates from the agent and
resides in the effect. Thus, the locality of causing is *in* the effect,
and the source of causing is *from* the cause, and the two, causing
and being caused, are the same reality.[8] The exercise of the act of
causing can indeed be described from the viewpoint of the cause,
and in that sense causing seems to be merely the actuation of a
cause, like the accident of *fat* in a fat man; but so to describe causing
is to miss its specificity, because the causing or actuation of a cause

[7] See Aristotle, *Metaphysics*, IX (Θ), 8, 1050a 23. See also pp. 91–93 of this
chapter.
[8] See p. 93 of this chapter. John of St. Thomas says that causing and being
caused are one: causing is *in* the effect, and *from* the cause, *Cursus Philosophicus, Ars Logica*, Pars II, q. 19, a. 2; ed. Reiser, t. I, p. 627b 19; *Phil. Nat.*,
Pars I, q. 14, a. 4; ed. Reiser, t. II, p. 312a 11. On this point, see Y. Simon,
Introduction à l'ontologie du connaître, Paris, Desclée de Brouwer, 1934, pp.
61–68.

is precisely the actuation of the potential, which is not the efficient cause. This, the actuation of the potential is what a cause can accomplish, and when it does accomplish the actuation of the potential, that is what a cause does. In other words, it is upon the potential that a cause is capable of acting, and upon which, when it causes, it does act. Hence there is *one* actuation of a cause, viz., its causing, and that one actuation or causing *is* the effect.[9] Of course, causing must be described differently from the way its effect is described, just as the road from Thebes to Athens must be described differently from the way you describe the road from Athens to Thebes—but it is the same road. Just so, it is the very actuation of the potential which is also the causing of a cause.

Otherness, actuality, efficiency, these integrate the notion of a cause.

Suggested Reading

Cause:

Aristotle, *Physics*, II, 3; *On Generation and Corruption*, II, 9; *Metaphysics*, I (A), 3; V (Δ), 2.

St. Thomas Aquinas, *In II Phys.*, lects. 5, 6, 10, 11; *In I Metaph.*, lects. 1–3; *De Princ. Nat.*, chs. 3–4; *De Verit.*, VII, 7, ad 1; *Sum. Theol.*, I, 105, 5; *Contra Gentiles*, II, 21; *De Pot.*, V, 1.

Johann, R., S.J., "A Comment on Secondary Causality," *The Modern Schoolman*, Vol. XXV, n. 1 (1947), pp. 19–25.

Wild, J., "A Realistic Defense of Causal Efficiency," *Review of Metaphysics*, Vol. II (1949), pp. 1–14.

Efficient Cause:

Aristotle, *Physics*, II, 3; III, 3; *Metaphysics*, V (Δ), 1; IV (Θ), 8; XI (K), 9; *On Generation and Corruption*, I, 8; *De Anima*, III, 2; *Posterior Analytics*, II, 8.

St. Thomas Aquinas, *In II Phys.*, lect. 3; *In III Phys.*, lects. 4–5; *In I Metaph.*, lect. 4; *In V Metaph.*, lect. 2; *In VII Metaph.*, lect. 6; In XI Metaph., lect. 9; *De Verit.*, XXVIII, 7; *De Pot.*, V, 1; *Contra Gentiles*, II, 16; *Sum. Theol.*, I, 2, 3; I, 3, 4; I, 104, 1; *De Ente et Essentia*, ch. IV; *De Princ. Nat.*, chs. 3–4.

[9] See p. 93 of this chapter. See also Aristotle, *Physics*, III, 3, 202a 12–202b 23; *Metaphysics*, XI (K), 9, 1066a 26–34.

VII · THE EXEMPLAR CAUSE

Efficiency itself has integrants. There is, first, its integrant of exemplarity. No thing in existence can be indefinite or of no particular sort. True, our knowledge of being can be indeterminate, e.g., the number of fish in a lake, is it odd or even? We don't know which until we examine, but we do know before examination that the number is odd or even. But the number itself of examined fish, *that* number cannot be odd if it's even, or even if it's odd. An existent being is a definite being; an indefinite being is another word for "nothing." Now, granted that a being is definite, granted that multiple being is caused, we must, therefore, run an intelligible line from an effect of a definite sort to a cause of a definite sort, for unless the cause were of a definite sort, it would be as null as its effect would be if the *effect* were indefinite: that is, an indefinite cause would also be nothing. Against the demonstrated existence of a cause. This likeness or similarity of the cause to the effect is the cause's exemplarity.[1] Besides, then, the efficient cause's function of

---

[1] On the exemplary cause, see Aristotle, *Physics*, II, 3, 194b 30; *Metaphysics*, V (Δ), 2, 1013a 30; VII (Z), 8, 1033b 30–1034a 5: "In some cases indeed it is even obvious that the begetter is of the same kind as the begotten (not, however, the *same* nor one in number, but in form), i.e., in the case of natural products (for man begets man), unless something happens contrary to nature, e.g., the production of a mule by a horse. . . . Obviously, therefore, it is quite unnecessary to set up a Form as a pattern (for we should have looked for Forms in these cases if in any; for these are substances if anything is so); the begetter is adequate to the making of the product and to the causing of the form in the matter."

See St. Thomas, *In II Phys.*, lect. 5, n. 179; *In V Metaph.*, lect. 2, n. 764; *In VII Metaph.*, lect. 7, n. 1428; *Sum. Theol.*, I, 15, 1–3; *De Verit.*, III, 3, *ad* 3; *De Verit.*, III, 1, *Resp.*: "The form of a thing can mean that *according to which* a thing is informed. This is the exemplary form in imitation of which a thing is made. It is in this meaning that *idea* is ordinarily used. Hence, the idea of a

reducing the potential to act, an efficient cause produces an effect like itself, e.g., a heater heating produces heat in the thing heated.

How an Exemplar Is Like Its Effect

A few remarks upon exemplarity. Exemplarity does not mean that the likeness of a cause to its effect is a *visible* likeness. Sometimes indeed there is a visible likeness between the cause and the effect. Babies look human at least, though some mothers do have a fit at the sight of their first baby. Seeds, however, don't look like the parent stock. Yet you can't get cabbages from rabbits, nor can you cure rheumatism by carrying a horse-chestnut. Indeed, the denial of exemplarity is the very source of superstition, which is the persuasion that effects come from antecedents which do not have what it takes (exemplarity) in order to produce the effect. So insistent, in fact, is the human mind's demand for exemplarity in a cause, that superstitious people impose *vi et armis* a likeness to the effects upon the supposed causes of whatever they hope for. Tea leaves must at least *seem* to configurate the "tall dark man" (or woman) whom superstitious people hope to meet. The Roman augurs were more elaborate in their superstitions, yet they were engaged in the same job as their descendants: they tried to wring from the present structure of causes a future which the causes did not exemplarize. A sort of gnosticism which exemplarity denies. Exemplarity is that feature of an efficient cause which explains why its effect is of the sort it is, and it explains the sort the effect is, because the cause itself is of the same sort as the effect. The whitening of a wall, e.g., instead of the blackening of a wall, is traceable to a whitening action, and the whitening action to a whitening agent. This is an efficient cause's

thing is the form which a thing imitates. . . . This therefore seems to constitute the character of an idea: it must be a form which something imitates because of the intention of an agent who antecedently determines the end himself."
On exemplar form, see also John of St. Thomas, *Cursus Philosophicus, Phil. Nat.*, Pars I, q. 11, a. 3; Reiser, t. II, p. 240b 18: ". . . exemplar est formans, quia non est in ipso formato, sed extra, et ideo ad tractatum de causa formali pertinet tractare de exemplari." *Op. cit.*, Pars I, q. 13, a. 1, p. 273b 20; Pars IV, q. 2, a. 3, p. 76b 40; *Ars Logica*, Pars II, q. 21, a. 4; Reiser, t. I, p. 670 ff.

exemplarity: its intelligible contour according to which the effect
will be made.

Intelligible Likeness Is Either in Nature or in Knowledge

When it is said that an efficient cause is of the same sort as the
effect it will produce, what is meant is that the efficient cause
exemplarizes its effects either according to a nature or according to
a knowledge likeness. Cherry trees are like, in nature, to cherries;
rabbits are like, in nature, to rabbits, and so on. Likeness, however,
can be a knowledge likeness. The things an artist makes are not like
his nature; they are like his knowledge of them.[2]

Nature Likeness Presupposes a Knowledge Likeness

Nevertheless, even a likeness in nature presupposes a knowledge
likeness. Without a knowledge likeness over and above the nature
likeness of the acorn to the oak, there would be literally nothing to
which the acorn is like, for the future oak tree does not as yet exist.
To explain: two things, e.g., the present acorn and the future oak,
can be alike only if both acorn and oak exist. If one of them, the oak,
does not exist, then the demonstrated likeness of the acorn to the
oak must be a knowledge likeness, for only knowledge can assure
that the present is like the future. The future exists only in the
knowledge of the future. In whose knowledge? Certainly not the
acorn's knowledge, because it has none. In the knowledge, then,
of the cause of the acorn or nature.

The situation in nature is pretty much as it is in the matter of
artifacts. We deposit our knowledge in the things we make, and so

---

[2] On likeness in nature and knowledge, see Aristotle, *Physics*, II, 1, 193a 28–
193b 18; II, 3, 195a 22–23; *Metaphysics*, VII (Z), 9, 1034a 20–25; 1034a 32–1034b
5; St. Thomas, *In II Phys.*, lect. 5, n. 179; *In VII Metaph.*, lect. 8, nn. 1447,
1449; *Sum. Theol.*, I, 15, 1, *Resp.*
See also Appendix (A) of this chapter.

it is our knowledge which configurates them. Just so, God deposits His knowledge in natures, and so they configurate His knowledge.[3] Of course, there is a great difference between nature and an artifact, but not in the precise point of the comparison we are making. Both nature and artifacts presuppose knowledge, and for exactly the same reason: only knowledge can assure that the inexistent future be like the present cause of the future, because the future can exist only in present *knowledge* of the future. The future cannot exist as present, as it does, except in knowledge. Entirely clear when it is a question of the causality of knowing natures (nothing gets done by a knowing agent unless it knows what it will do), the matter is just as clear when it's a question of nonknowing natures. Only, it needs a bit more discernment to see that nonknowing natures prefigure the future in the knowledge which their causes, not they, have of the future. Certainly, the present must prefigure the future and just as certainly the present can't do that apart from knowledge. Whose knowledge? Not, surely, the knowledge of agents which demonstrably do not know. In the knowledge, therefore, of the cause of nonknowing agents, for their cause is the only source of knowledge left.

The Knowledge-Cause of Nature Causes Nature's Causality

Here it should be noted that the knowledge-cause of nature does not mean a cause whose efficiency by-passes the efficiency of nature as, e.g., the manipulator of marionettes by-passes to some extent

[3] On God and exemplarity, see St. Thomas, *Contra Gentiles*, III, 19; *Sum. Theol.*, I, 15, 2-3; I, 18, 4, *ad* 2: "The thing modeled must be like the exemplar according to the form, not the mode of being. For sometimes the form has being of another kind in the exemplar from that which it has in the thing modeled. Thus the form of a house has immaterial and intelligible being in the mind of the architect; but in the house that exists outside his mind, material and sensible being. Hence the likenesses of these things, which do not have life in themselves, are life in the divine mind, as having a divine being in that mind." *De Verit.*, VIII, 8, *ad* 1: "The divine essence is the archetype of each and every thing in its individuality, because it contains the exemplary ideas of all things."

their natural activity. The gyrations of puppets are not natural movements. They are violent movements. Natural actions issue from within a natural agent, not from a source outside an agent, and it is precisely the cause of natural agents which makes them to act as sources of their own activity. Human art, which makes machines, imitates divine art by utilizing the forces of nature already there. Divine art causes nature and its forces.[4]

Appendix to Chapter VII

APPENDIX (A). Likeness in nature and knowledge.

Aristotle, *Metaphysics*, VII (Z), 9, 1034a 20–25: "And it is clear also from what has been said that in a sense every product of art is produced from a thing which shares its name (as natural products are produced), or from a part of itself which shares its name (e.g., the house is produced from a house, *qua* produced by reason; for the art of building is the form of the house), or from something which contains a part of it—if we exclude things produced by accident; for the cause of the thing's producing the product directly *per se* is the part of the product. . . ."

Aristotle, *Metaphysics*, VII (Z), 9, 1034a 32–1034b 5: "Things which are formed by nature are in the same case as these products of art. For the seed is productive in the same way as the things that work by art; for it has the form potentially, and that from which the seed comes has in a sense the same name as the offspring—only in a sense, for we must not expect parent and offspring always to have exactly the same name, as in the production of 'human being' from 'human being'; for a 'woman' also can be produced by a 'man' —unless the offspring be an imperfect form; which is the reason why the parent of a mule is not a mule."

St. Thomas, *Sum. Theol.*, I, 15, 1, *Resp.*: "In all things not generated by chance, the form must be the end of any generation whatsoever. But an agent does not act for the sake of the form, except

---

[4] In *Sum. Theol.*, I, 105, 5, *Resp.*, St. Thomas shows how the divine art causes nature and its forces. See Appendix (B) of this chapter.

in so far as the likeness of the form is in the agent; which may happen in two ways. For in some agents the form of the thing-to-be-made preexists according to its natural being, as in those that act by their nature; as a man generates a man, or fire generates fire. Whereas in other agents the form of the thing-to-be-made preexists according to intelligible being, as in those that act by the intellect; and thus the likeness of a house preexists in the mind of the builder. And this may be called the idea of the house, since the builder intends to build his house like the form conceived in the mind."

APPENDIX (B). The divine art causes nature and its forces.

St. Thomas, *Sum. Theol.*, I, 105, 5, *Resp.*: "Consequently, just as the matter is for the sake of the form, so the form which is the first act is for the sake of its operation, which is the second act; and thus operation is the end of the creature. We must therefore understand that God works in things in such a manner that things have also their proper operations.

"In order to make this clear, we must observe that of the four causes matter is not a principle of action, but the subject that receives the effect of action. On the other hand, the end, the agent and the form are principles of action, but in a certain order. For the first principle of action is the end which moves the agent, the second is the agent, and the third is the form of that which the agent applies to action (although the agent also acts through its own form). . . .

"Thus then does God work in every agent, according to these three things. First, as an end. For since every operation is for the sake of some good, real or apparent, and since nothing is good, either really or apparently, except in so far as it participates in a likeness to the highest good, which is God, it follows that God Himself is the cause of every operation as its end. Again, it is to be observed that where there are several agents in order, the second always acts in virtue of the first; for the first agent moves the second to act. And thus all agents act in virtue of God Himself; and so, He is the cause of action in every agent. Thirdly, we must observe that God not only moves things to operate, as it were applying their forms and powers to operation, just as the workman applies the axe to cutting (who nevertheless did not himself give the axe its form), but He also gives created agents their forms and preserves them in being. Therefore He is the cause of action not only by giving the form which is the principle of action, as the generator is said to be the cause of movement in things heavy and light, but also as conserving the forms and powers of things; just as the sun is said to be the cause of the manifestation of colors, inasmuch as it gives and conserves the light by which colors are made manifest. And since the form of a thing is within the thing, and all the more so, as it approaches nearer to the first and universal cause; and because in all things God Himself is properly the cause of universal being which is innermost in all things;—it follows that God works intimately in all things."

VIII · THE FINAL CAUSE

We are now at the point of discerning efficiency's most important integrant of all. Not only must an efficient cause prefigure in its nature, which presupposes knowledge, or in its knowledge, the kind which the effect will be, it must also assure that the effect will be. Consider, it has been demonstrated that an efficient cause does the job and that the job it does is the kind which might have been anticipated. There is left this to explain: why does the efficient cause up and do the job at all, rather than do nothing? The question is pertinent, because unless there be located in the efficient cause, *before* it causes, some factor which assures that the efficient cause will cause the effect rather than not, the explanation by a cause falls apart, or rather it was missing its essential piece from the start. For, up to the point where the efficient cause is to act, there is only the exemplarity and actuality of the cause. Now, the resemblance of a cause to its effect and the actuality of a cause will not, alone, get anything done. Some people could write poetry if only they wrote it, or sweep a floor if they would only do it. We must, it is clear, have some reason why efficient causes swing into action rather than sit inert like bumps on a log, as they are entirely capable of doing if exemplarity and actuality are their only features. The only possible way to get a cause off its feet, so to say, and explain its causing, is to locate in it before it causes the tendency to act rather than not.

Tendency[1]

The commonest and oldest illustration of tendency is the push of bodies downwards. (The ancients also thought that light bodies pushed upwards: *gravia deorsum, levia sursum.* They were wrong in the latter illustration, of course, but not in the former; nor were they at all wrong in their insight into the mystery of tendency.) Heft a body in your hand. You can feel its pressure or weight. Let the body go, and it falls. Now, here is the point: before you let the body go, the force or forces according to which it later fell were there all the time; there, in the sense that to be a body is at one and the same time to be something in which those forces reside, i.e., to be a body is also to be heavy. To be "heavy" means to be falling, in some sense, even before the body actually falls, and that sense is this: a body "tends" to fall even before it falls. Tendency, then, is a prefixation of an agent upon operation even before the agent actually operates.

Observe, this prefixation upon acting does not describe the *kind* the operation will be. That sort of prefixation is in the order of exemplary or formal causality; bodies will *fall* if unimpeded, whereas plants will *grow;* such are their natures. The prefixation upon *acting,* however, describes operation in its source, at the period, i.e., where it has not yet begun, but is about to begin. Synonyms for tendency are: urge, bent, desire, appetite, and so on.

No matter what you call it, tendency is the existential status of operation before there is operation. Must we then say that operation exists before it exists? In a way, yes, viz., as in *tendency* to operation. Indeed, this is exactly why the word "nature" (from *nascor,* I am born) was selected to describe the total situation. "Nature" is the name of an agent of a certain sort inasmuch as that kind of agent is about to give birth to, or to issue into, the actual exercise of a kind of operation which corresponds to the kind of agent it is[2] —like a runner on his mark, keyed up and ready to run. The keying

[1] On tendency, see Chapter III, pp. 44–46.
[2] On nature, see Chapter III, pp. 40–41.

up or the readiness of the runner is tendency; thus, the "runner" is the nature plus his keying up, his tendency to run.

We may now analogize the illustration. Something like "heaviness" or "pressure" must reside in every agent whose operation is not identical with the agent. For, if not, we should have to say either that it is not the agent which operates, or else that the agent acts before it acts. Tendency enables us to avoid saying either, because tendency assures us that operation so affects the agent as to make the agent's operation its own, since it tended thereto, yet not so as to identify the agent with its operation, since tendency is not operation.

We now have two prefixations in an agent which may explain its operation: (1) the prefixation of the agent's nature, which describes the kind which the operation will be; (2) the agent's prefixation, by tendency, upon operating rather than not, which explains an agent's operation. Let us call the nature-prefixation an essential determinant of action, and the tendency-prefixation, the existential determinant of action.[3]

Three Stages of Operation

Operation, then, will have three stages, each compounded of an essential and an existential determinant: (1) the stage before operation begins, where the essential determinant is the *kind* of agent in question, and the existential determinant is the agent's *tendency* to act according to the kind it is, (2) the stage of actual operation where there *is operation* of a fixed *kind*, (3) the stage at which by its operation an agent causes a *kind* of effect to *be* or exist.

These stages are not discrete as would be discrete one being after another, like dessert after dinner. Rather, stage (1) must precontain stage (2), and (2) must precontain (3); contrariwise, stage (3) must be precontained in stage (2), and (2), in (1). The present moment of operation, at whatever stage you take operation, must precontain potentially the act of the following moment. Operation, like motion,

---

[3] On nature and tendency prefixation, see Chapter III, pp. 39–41, 44–46. See also *Sum. Theol.*, I–II, 1, 2, *Resp.; Contra Gentiles*, III, 2.

is continuous;[4] its present moment is not separated from its future one; the present moment must be fixed, determined, in relation to the future, just as motion is (*actus existentis in potentia prout in potentia*),[5] else act as act would be potency, or potency as potency would be act. A contradiction in terms. Hence, stage (1) is a metaphysical equivalent to stage (2), and stage (2) is a metaphysical equivalent to stage (3). The three stages are thus different but equivalent metaphysical moments of one operation. In other words, if you ask what it is that assures the continuity from stage (1), through stage (2), to stage (3), the answer depends upon what sort of continuity you mean. If you mean continuity in *kind*, like the continuity of being a *man* throughout the stages of infancy, adolescence, maturity and old age, then the continuity is assured or caused by the essential determinant of operation, namely, the kind of tendency, the kind of operation, the kind of effect in question. If you mean continuity in the *existence* of an operation and its effect, then continuity is caused by the existential determinant of action, namely, tendency, operation, and the *esse* of the effect. Each determinant of action is primary in its own order. So much is clear.

What is not yet clear is this: which stage with its two determinants, (1) or (3), is primary in causality? Our inclination is to say that stage (1) is primary, because stage (1) exists before stage (3), and surely a cause must exist before its effect, i.e., before stage (3). Nevertheless that answer, in its effort to get the horse before the cart, succeeds in doing the exact opposite.

Stage (1) is surely primary to stage (3) in time and as an efficient cause of stage (3). The problem which confronts us is not solved, however, by saying that. We wish to know what causes the efficient cause, whose existence is already assured, to *cause* stage (3). A doctor, for example, is set up in business as one who can cause health in a patient simply by being a doctor. There is no problem there. The problem is here: what causes the doctor to cause the

<hr>

[4] Aristotle says that motion is continuous, *Physics*, III, 1, 200b 16; VI, 1, 231b 15–232a 18. See Chapter II, p. 19.

[5] Motion is the actualization of the potential as potential. See Aristotle, *Physics*, III, 1, 201b 5–7; St. Thomas, *In III Phys.*, lect. 2, n. 285; lect. 3, n. 292. See also Chapter II, pp. 18–22.

patient's health? Surely not the fact that he is a doctor, nor the supposition that sick patients are healthy. It must needs be, then, that it is
the patient's-health-as-intended-by-the-doctor which causes the doctor to cause that health. Here we have isolated that mysterious cause
which causes, not the efficient cause, but the efficient cause's causality. That cause is the end, the health of the patient.[6] The end
causes the doctor to swing into the activity which will make a
patient healthy. The doctor doesn't cause the health of the patient
to be his end. Rather, he causes the end of his operation to exist,
which is to say that he causes the health of the patient. If now we ask
how the end causes operation, it is sufficient at this point to repeat
that the end causes operations by residing in the intention or tendency of the agent or efficient cause, the intention or tendency,
namely, of operating with a view to bringing the end into existence
as an effect. Once in existence as an effect, the end is no longer an
end. It is and is called simply an effect. But before the end exists as
an effect, it exists in the intention of the agent, and it is in the intention of the agent that the end functions causally. And so, stage
(3) as *intended* by the agent is primary to stage (1) in *esse*, the *esse*
namely of intention. Certainly, stage (3) is not primary to stage (1)
as a physical existent. Sick patients are not healthy. Nonetheless,
healthy patients exist in the intention of doctors' operations to make
sick patients healthy. Thus it is stage (3) as *intended* by agents which
is prior, but not in time or efficiency, to stage (2) and (1). This is
to say that the final cause is prior in intention to the causality, stage
(1) and (2), of the efficient cause. Thus a final cause is the very
capstone of efficient causality.

We must see this in another way. If you picture operation as a
journey, then when you come to stage (3) you would stop and
get off because that third stage is the end of the line. Now, the word

---

[6] On the end as a cause, see St. Thomas, *De Princ. Nat.*, c. 4, n. 356: "Finis
etiam non est causa illius quod est efficiens, sed est causa ut efficiens sit efficiens:
sanitas enim non facit medicum esse medicum (et dico de sanitate quae fit
operante medico), sed facit quod medicus sit efficiens. Unde finis est causa
causalitatis efficientis, quia facit efficiens esse efficiens: et similiter facit materiam
esse materiam, et formam esse formam, cum materia non suscipiat formam nisi
propter finem, et formam non perficiat materiam nisi per finem. Unde dicitur
quod finis est causa causarum, quia est causa causalitatis in omnibus causis."

"end," when used as the terminus of operation, means much more than a stopping place. Recall, there are dead ends and stops for gas. These have nothing to do, except incidentally, with the explanation why you packed up and set off on your journey. The stopping place which explains a journey is the one you anticipated before you set out. That stopping place resided anticipatively in the journey which it consummates, and the journey resided anticipatively in your tendency to get going. It is the same with all operations which are not identical with the agent: the ends of those operations exist anticipatively in the operations themselves, and the operations exist anticipatively in the double prefigurement of those operations, which prefigurement is the *kind* of agent in question as well as the *tendency* of an agent to act rather than not, according to the kind of agent it is. This is the reason why *intended* ends come, eventually, to exist, and the point is that they couldn't come to exist unless, before they exist in fact, they were intended to exist by the agents which effect them.

The difficulty in understanding the composites of operation, stages (1) and (2), which presently anticipate the perfection which is conferred upon agent or patient, stage (3), is one with the difficulty of understanding active potency, for this *is* active potency: a power which prefigures by its nature and tendency whatever it accomplishes. That prefigurement is the cause of operation, and that cause of operation is the effect existing in intention before it exists in fact. When the end exists in fact, it is an effect. Hence again, stage (3), as in the *tendency* of nature or of knowledge, stage (1), and as in the operation from which the effect issues, stage (2), is primary in causality to the effect, stage (3).

It remains to refine our notion of active potency. Tendencies can be psychic or apsychic. If psychic, tendencies are to a *known* end, and to the extent that knowledge is caused by the knower, to that extent the ends which reside in knowledge are also caused by the knower. We may express this situation by saying that knowing agents, in the measure in which they elicit or cause their knowledge, elicit or cause their ends. Of course, caused knowledge can be of necessary or non-necessary ends, but even the caused knowledge of necessary ends does not, in perfectly free agents, necessarily cause the exercise of their operation in relation to their necessary ends, though it will necessarily cause this tendency thereto, i.e., it will necessarily cause a free agent's end to be a free agent's end, even though that agent need not accept that end. But this point pertains rather to the philosophy of man and his free choice. . . . If tendencies are apsychic, they are not tendencies to ends caused or fixed or elicited *by* the agents, because they are not known to the agent; rather, they are ends fixed *for* the agent by the agent's nature and, in the last analysis, by the cause of the agent's nature. And so, apsychic tendencies are to ends, but not to ends which are known and therefore elicited or caused by the apsychic agent.[7]

The End Specifies Operation

When it is said that the end specifies operation,[8] we must realize that the end does this in its function of exemplarizing an operation according as the operation is prefigured by the agent's knowledge or nature; in its function of calling forth operation, however, i.e., in its existential function of being the reason why operation exists, an end is not specificative. It is rather the reason for *operation*, not the reason for the *kind* of operation. These two functions of one end had better be named differently. Call the end as specifying operation an *object*. As summoning forth operation, the end has no further name except synonyms: a good, a goal, an objective, etc.[9]

[7] On psychic and apsychic tendencies, see Chapter III, pp. 45–46. See also *Sum. Theol.*, I–II, 1, 2, *Resp.*; I, 18, 3, *Resp.*; *De Princ. Nat.*, c. 3, n. 351.

[8] See St. Thomas, *Sum. Theol.*, I, 15, 1, *Resp.*; II–II, 4, 3, *Resp.*

[9] *Object form* may also be an end, but even when it is, it *specifies* operation, whereas end causes the exercise of operation. See St. Thomas, *Sum. Theol.*, I–II, 18, 2, *ad* 2: "objectum habet quodammodo rationem formae inquantum dat speciem"; *In I Sent.*, d. 1, q. 2, a. 1, *ad* 2: "objectum operationis terminat et perficit speciem et est finis eius."

The best definition of *object* form seems to be in *De Caritate*, a. IV, *Resp.*: ". . . potentia hoc ipsum quod est, dicitur in ordine ad possibile, quod est objectum [the very being of potency lies in its relation to what it can effect; this is the object]."

See St. Thomas, *De Verit.*, XXI, 1, *Resp.* The passage can be paraphrased as follows. The "perfect" may achieve being in two ways: it may achieve

Active potency being the source or cause of a perfection ("perfection" here means only an end or a good: something "new" in
short), and a perfection being either the agent's own or something
else's, there will be two sorts of active potency. One will be the
cause of the agent's own perfection; the second will cause something
else's perfection. One's own health, e.g., or knowledge, or love,
can be the end of some operations; but a house is the end of the
operation of building.[10] The active potency which confers perfection upon the agent is called immanent, because the perfection
caused remains *in* the agent;[11] more precisely, an active potency is
called immanent because the perfection it causes is not extrinsic, as
effects are, to the agent. The active potency which confers perfection upon something other than the agent is called transitive, because the perfection has "gone over" from the agent to the patient.
So for the *operations* and *perfections* of these respective potencies:
operations are *immanent*, or *transitive*, and so are the *perfections*

---

species, or it may achieve according to the *esse* which the "perfect" has in
nature. The first "perfect," achieving species, perfects only in the order of
species. The second "perfect" perfects *not only* according to species but also
makes the perfect species to exist according to the perfection of its species.
This second "perfect" is the perfect known as the *good*. Of course this "second
perfect," in making the "first perfect" to exist, makes the "first perfect" also
to exist as the *first perfect;* but the first perfect doesn't exist upon the score
that it is a first perfect or species; it is a species in the order of formal
causality even if it doesn't exist at all; but the second perfect pulls the first
into the order of existence. See Apendix A of this chapter.
    On object and end, see also *In II de Anima*, lect. 6, n. 305; *Sum. Theol.*,
I, 25, 1, *Resp.*; 57, 1, *Resp.*; 77, 3, *Resp.*; 82, 3, *Resp.*; I–II, 9, 1, *Resp.*; 18, 6,
Resp.; II–II, 117, 3, *Resp.*; 153, 5, *Resp.*; 162, 3; *De Pot.*, VII, 10, *Resp.*; *Contra
Gentiles*, I, 48; II, 98; III, 1; *Quodlibet.*, VIII, q. 9, a. 1, *Resp.*
    See John of St. Thomas, *Cursus Philosophicus, Phil. Nat.*, Pars I, q. 13, a.
1; Reiser, t. II, p. 273b 16; Pars III, q. 2, a. 3, pp. 239–240; Cajetan, *In Sum.
Theol.*, III, q. 2, a. 3.
    See also G. Smith, S.J., "Philosophy and the Unity of Man's Ultimate End,"
Proceedings, Vol. XXVII (1953), 60–83.
    [10] See St. Thomas, *Sum. Theol.*, I, 103, 2, *ad* 1 and 2.
    [11] Immanent action does not "cause" as transitive action does. Immanent
action may have a product (concept, enunciation, syllogism, etc.), or it may
not. If it has, the product is for the sake of the action, not *vice versa;* if it
does not have a product, we have the peak instance of immanence (God's
self-knowledge, for example). In either case, immanent action is for its own
sake. Transitive action always has and is for the sake of the product.

themselves immanent or transitive according to the case. Immanent perfections qualify the agent; transitive, the patient.[12]

Passive and Active Potency Further Contrasted

Passive potency or the power to be acted upon derives all its intelligibility from the cause which reduces passive potency to act: whether or no a football can be kicked, and how far, depends upon the kicker. Active potency, on the other hand, derives all its intelligibility from the end-object. If we wish, in other words, to learn the scope of passive potency, we look to a cause which is able to reduce passive potency to act; if we wish to learn the scope of active potency or cause, we look to the end-object: being *acted upon* is explained by the intention of the *cause* of being acted upon; but acting is explained by the end-object of acting. Both passive and active potency are thus explained by ends: only, the end of passive potency is the end intended by the cause which reduces passive potency to act, whereas the end intended by the cause which reduces potency to act is fixed by a double determinant in the cause,

---

[12] On immanent and transitive action, see Aristotle, *Metaphysics*, V (Δ), 18, 1022b 1-10; IX (Θ), 6, 1048b 28-34; 8, 1050a 23-1050b 1; *De Anima*, I, 3, 407a 32; III, 7, 431a 4-7; *Nicomachean Ethics*, I, 1, 1094a 3; VI, 4, 1140a 1; VI, 5, 1140b 4; VII, 14, 1154b 25-28; St. Thomas, *In I Sent.*, d. 40, q. 1, a. 1, ad 2; *In II Sent.*, d. 12, q. 1, a. 4; *In IX Metaph.*, lect. 8, n. 1865; *Contra Gentiles*, I, 13, 53, 100; II, 1: "There are, however, two sorts of operation, as Aristotle teaches in *Metaphysics* IX: one that remains in the agent and is a perfection of it, as the act of sensing, understanding, and willing; another that passes over into an external thing, and is a perfection of the thing made as a result of that operation, the acts of heating, cutting and building, for example." See also *Contra Gentiles*, II, 22, 23; *De Verit.*, VIII, 1, ad 14; VIII, 6, *Resp.*; XIV, 3, *Resp.*; *De Pot.*, II, 2, *Resp.*; II, 4, *Resp.*; III, 15, *Resp.*; V, 5, *Resp.* and ad 14; *Sum. Theol.*, I, 14, 2, ad 2; 14, 5, ad 1; 18, 1, *Resp.*; 18, 3, *Resp.*; 54, 1, ad 3; 54, 1, ad 3; 54, 2, *Resp.*; 56, 1, *Resp.*; 85, 2, *Resp.*; 87, 3, *Resp.*; I-II, 31, 2, *Resp.*

Cajetan says that St. Thomas denies to immanent action all the attributes of transitive action, *In II de Anima*; ed. Coquelle, 5 B 114b. See John of St. Thomas, *Cursus Philosophicus*, *Phil. Nat.*, Pars I, q. 14, a. 4; Reiser, t. II, pp. 275b, 312a; *Cursus Theologicus*, Pars I, d. 4, a. 6; Vivès, t. III, p. 270; Pars I, d. 11, a. 2, p. 916. See also Y. Simon, *Introduction à l'ontologie du connaître*, pp. 69-72.

viz., by the nature or the knowledge of the cause, and by the cause's existential determinant to act rather than not, its tendency in other words.[13] To the nature or knowledge of the agent corresponds object; to the existential predeterminant of the agent to act rather than not corresponds the end. Thus object and end are two distinct features of the same thing, the cause of operation: the object is prefigured in the agent's nature or knowledge; the end is prefigured in the agent's tendency.[14] Object and end, however, are numerically the same.

Our Knowledge of Ends

To what extent may we know ends when we "look to" them? With absolute certainty so far forth as our knowledge that all operations have ends is concerned. However, our knowledge of what those ends are has degrees of limitation. Ends that are accomplished in matter we know only up to a point, because matter is intelligible only in relation to its actuation, and since we know ends accomplished in matter only universally, that point is the general knowledge we have about them, e.g., the stomach is for digesting food, but who knows perfectly what digestion is? Even artifacts, whose ends we know better than we know the ends of nature, but know well only *after* they are made, we know also only in general terms. Ends which are accomplished in spirits we know perfectly, not of course as we shall know them when we are in possession of those ends, but in the sense that we know perfectly what the end of a spirit is: it is to see God . . .

The complete assurance we have that every operation has an end, and our relatively incomplete assurance—because we know them only in universal terms—as to what those ends are, is beautifully and forever fixed by Aristotle's description of an end: it is that,

[13] The *success* of the active potency in doing what it intends depends also upon factors other than its intentions. A kicker will not kick with a sprained ankle. Nevertheless, even with a sound ankle, he will not kick at all without intending to.

[14] See p. 109 of this chapter.

he says, which each thing for its part seeks.[15] Seeking is the sign
of something being sought (the end), even when we cannot possibly
say why a thing seeks what it does. This definition of an end is by
its sign, e.g., by the seeking for an end. Aristotle also describes an
end thus: that on account of which there is operation.[16] This latter
definition describes end as a cause and it is the explanatory, not
the descriptive, definition of the end.

The End of Operation

Operation can never be its own end, that is, nothing operates just
for the sake of operating. Just as it is impossible that seeing be the
thing seen, so it is impossible that the thing sought be the seeking for it.[17] Some actions indeed *seem* to be for their own sake,
play, e.g., and contemplation, and love. Not so. Indeed, it is harder
to exclude reasons for play than it is to find them. Those reasons
are there all right—like the five reasons for drinking:

> If well upon my theme I think,
> There are five reasons why we drink:
> (1) good health, (2) a friend, (3) because we're dry,
> (4) or maybe will be by and by,
> (5) or any other reason why.

As to knowledge and love, we must realize that the knower and the
lover are perfected in terms of the *known* and the *beloved:* to know
something, not just knowing, and to love *someone*, not just loving,

---

[15] See Aristotle, *Nicomachean Ethics*, I, 1, 1094a 2: ". . . and for this reason
the good has rightly been declared to be that at which all things aim." See
also St. Thomas, *In I Metaph.*, lect. 4, n. 71.

[16] On the end as a final cause, or that on account of which there is operation,
see Aristotle, *Physics*, II, 3, 194b 32–38; II, 8, 199a 20–33; *Metaphysics*, V (Δ),
2, 1013a 32–35. See St. Thomas, *De Princ. Nat.*, c. 3, n. 351; *In II Phys.*, lect.
5, nn. 181, 186; lect. 13; *In I Metaph.*, lect. 4, nn. 70–71; *In V Metaph.*, lect.
2, nn. 771, 773–774, 775; *De Verit.*, III, 1, *Resp.*; XXVIII, 7, *Resp.*; *In Lib. de
Causis*, lect. 1, *ad fin.*; *Contra Gentiles*, III, 2; *Sum. Theol.*, I, 5, 4, *Resp.*;
5, 6, *Resp.*; 6, 2, *ad* 2; 44, 4, *Resp.*; 105, 5, *Resp.*; I–II, 1, 2, *Resp.*; *De
Pot.*, V, 1, *Resp.* See Appendix B of this chapter.

[17] See St. Thomas, *Sum. Theol.*, I–II, 1, 1, *ad* 2.

these are the ends of knowledge and love respectively. Of course, if
one wishes to say that knowledge and love are for their own sake
in the sense that they are for the sake of the perfection they confer
upon the knower and lover (but for his perfection because knowing the *known* and loving the *beloved* perfect him, and not just
because knowing and loving perfect him, for they can't—knowing
is always knowing of something, and so for loving), that is quite
correct. In that sense immanent operations are for their own sake.
As we shall see in *Natural Theology*, there must be but one last
end of all operations.[18]

[18] If all operations be for an end, and if there be any further operation
after one end has been attained, this will mean three things: (1) that the
end attained, although an end, is not the *complete* reason for operation,
for there is *further* operation; (2) that, since there must be a complete
reason for operation, there must be an absolute or ultimate end, one which
explains all operations; (3) that the end which explains all operation must be
single or unique. Consider: in default of a single end which explains all
operation, there must be many ends. This means that many ends *must* be.
Just so, as we saw at length a while back, if many beings must be, they must
all be. A contradiction in both cases. For if many beings must be, then to be
or exist is equivalent to being many. It is the same with ends; if many ends
must be, then to be an end is equivalent to being many ends. Yet, neither
in being nor in ends *must* the many be, else there cannot be many. For, the
word "must" indicates that one being or end cannot be unless they *all* are,
and if that is so, to be one (one nature or one end) is forthwith to be many.
There lies the contradiction, for although in fact there are both many beings
and ends, nevertheless to say that beings and ends *must be* is to say either
that no end is *one* end, or that there are not many ends; for, if to be one
end is to be many of them, there aren't many ends. We must, therefore, say
that natures and ends are many because they are caused to be many. Now,
the cause of the many cannot itself be multiple. Another way of saying
the same thing is this: if ends are necessarily multiple, there must be an
infinite number of them; this is impossible, viz., that there be an infinite number
of anything, for an actually infinite number is a contradiction in terms,
Contra Gentiles, III, 2. See also *Sum. Theol.*, I-II, 1, 4, *Resp.*; I-II, 1, 5, *Resp.*
On the other hand, if ends are indefinite in number, action could never get
started. To illustrate: let *x* be intended for the sake of *y*, *y* for *m*, and so on
indefinitely; there being no end which is intended for its own sake, and not
for another's sake, there is no end at all.
    There is much in the above argument which needs clarification from natural
theology. This much at present is clear. A cause of multiplicity in the status
of an existent cannot itself be multiple. Causes of multiplicity in the states or
kinds of existence—these are multiple, but not the cause of multiplicity in
the status of an existent. To think so is to think that things are many because
they are many—an idle reflection. Now a cause is also an end. There must,
then, be one end for all operations.

Kind of Ends

Sometimes operation, which has one end, attains that end by indirection: you undergo surgery in order to get well. The surgery is a means to health. Here the end (health) resides in the means (surgery), and it resides there only in so far as surgery leads to health. Should surgery *not* lead to health, it obviously would not be a means, and still less an end or good. A means, therefore, is that which is good only because it is related to a good so as by leading to or causing it. It is thus apparent that means are not good in themselves; rather, they are good only as related to the good. Health itself is a good or end. Surgery is a means to a good. Means are called the *useful* good.[19]

The very quantity of useful goods occasions the mistake of thinking that every good is good *because* it is useful. Not at all. If *every* good had to lead to another good, there would not be any *other* good, because it, too, would have to lead to another one, *et sic ad infinitum.* Some goods, then, must lead to nothing else; they are themselves good, health, e.g., friendship, knowledge, and love. Of course one may put those goods in themselves to use, but even

---

[19] On the means as a useful good, see St. Thomas, *Sum. Theol.*, I, 5, 6, *Resp.*: "Thus, in the movement of appetite, the thing desired that terminates the movement of appetite relatively, as a means of tending towards something else, is called the *useful;* that sought after as the last thing absolutely terminating the movement of the appetite, as a thing towards which for its own sake the appetite tends, is called the *befitting,* for the *befitting* is that which is desired for its own sake; but that which terminates the movement of appetite in the form of rest in the thing desired, is called the *pleasant.*"
See also *Sum. Theol.*, I, 82, 1, *Resp.*; 83, 3, *Resp.*; I–II, 8, 2, *Resp.*: "But that which is good and willed in itself is the end. Therefore volition, properly speaking, is of the end itself. On the other hand, the means are good and willed, not in themselves, but as referred to the end. Therefore the will is directed to them only in so far as it is directed to the end; so that what it wills in them, is the end." *Sum. Theol.*, I–II, 8, 3, *sed contra:* "Acts are diversified according to their objects. But the end is a different species of good from the means, which are a useful good." *De Verit.*, V, 1, *Resp.*; XXI, 1, *Resp.*: "First of all and principally, therefore, a being capable of perfecting another after the manner of an end is called good: but secondarily something is called good which leads to an end (as the useful is said to be good), or which naturally follows upon an end (as not only that which has health is called healthy, but also anything which causes, preserves, or signifies health)."

apart from use to which they may be put, *they* are good, whereas
means are not good at all apart from their relation to a good which
leads to no other good—a good in itself. Indeed, some goods in
themselves might be destroyed by use, e.g., to do nothing else but
use a friend, is not to have a friend. In sum, ends always profit the
agent or patient, but some ends do this only as means: these latter
are *useful* goods; but the goods which are "useless," so to say,
profit the agent or patient by a title other than their usefulness,
viz., by the title of being good in themselves.

Psychic Features of Ends

The profit of the end has two factors: the *having* of the end (this
is the existential factor of the end); the *kind* of end which is had
(this is the essential or value factor of the end).[20] Recall that the
having of the end as well as the *kind* of end had has three equivalent
stages. In all but the last, the end resides as intended. In the last
stage, the end resides as actually possessed by the agent, or as
effected by the agent in a patient. As actually possessed, the end
reveals itself in us as satisfaction.[21] We have no notion of what
this satisfaction means in apsychic agents. Certainly it is not a
satisfaction felt. Nevertheless, there must be an apsychic equivalent
to satisfaction in these agents, because they seek ends, and there
would be no seeking unless the sought were worthwhile to the
seeker. In psychic *sensuous* agents, the satisfaction is pleasure. In
psychic sensuous-*rational* agents, the satisfaction is either mainly
sensuous or mainly rational. No human good is wholly one or the
other. Profit, then, is apsychic, or psychic; if psychic, profit is either
primarily sensuous or primarily rational.

Whether primarily sensuous or primarily rational, psychic profit
or satisfaction, then, has two features: the kind of satisfaction had,

[20] See St. Thomas, *Sum. Theol.*, I-II, 11, 3, *ad* 3.
[21] There seems to be some satisfaction even in operation itself at times.
Surgeons like to perform surgery. They get uneasy when their vacations are
long. Nevertheless, operation itself is of a kind, and so it is that *kind* of operation, viz., surgery, which surgeons like, and that kind of operation is ordered
to doing some good to patients.

and the having of it. These two features are inseparable. Both together could be morally good or morally bad.[22] That is another
question. But both are always together. It is a grave error to think
that the moral good is what we do not enjoy, and that moral evil is
what we do enjoy—like the man who thought that what he really
liked was always illegal, immoral, or fattening.[23] No, we enjoy the
moral good, and lawfully; and we enjoy moral evil up to a point,
but unlawfully. The moral good is a special kind of good, the good
for man. The good itself, no matter what be its kind, is always,
when possessed, enjoyed, and so enjoyment is simply a psychic trans-
cription of the good. To try to divorce the two factors of satisfaction, namely, the *kind* of good possessed, and the possessing of it,
can have only two issues, depending upon which factor is emphasized
("emphasized," because the divorce cannot really be effective): if
you emphasize the "having" factor, the metaphysical door is open
to Epicureanism; if you emphasize the "kind" factor, the door is
open to Puritanism. Puritans fear enjoyment. Epicureans fear its loss.
Either position can lead to the psychopathic ward and, when pursued to the limit, it does.

Limited Ends

Goods or ends can be limited. To be healthy, e.g., is not forthwith
to be wise, and *vice versa*. This does not mean that health and
wisdom are not good in themselves. It means that one good is not
the other. Should there be a good which comprises both health and
wisdom and every other good as well, this would be an absolute or
unlimited end or good. Assuming that there is an absolute good,
namely, God, the relation of the limited goods to Him would be that
of limited final causes to an unlimited final cause. Limited goods
would not be means to God, except analogically.

[22] Pyschic rational profit could be derived merely from good ratiocination—
like the profit (ratiocinative) of a neat murder as opposed to a messy one; or
it could be derived from a rational good, e.g., not to commit murder at all,
whether neat or messy.

[23] See G. Smith, S.J., "The Nature and Uses of Liberty," *The New Scholasticism*, Vol. XXVI, n. 3 (July 1952), pp. 321–322.

The analogical situation of all goods, even God Himself, short of the vision of Him, is integrated by the following factors. (1) Limited goods are *in themselves* images of God. They bespeak with their own voice and in their own right the glory of their Creator. (2) Means as means, however, do not themselves bespeak the glory of the end to which they lead. Their voice is the voice of the end speaking in them. They are tagged, so to say, with removable tags. The tags or means are removable, not because the end ceases to be good (the end's tag of being good is not removable) but because, first, the means are not good unless they lead to the end; second, the "good" tag on means is sometimes removable when the means are removable, i.e., when they are multiple. We may also state this in terms of appetite: all goods have a direct, immediate, appeal to appetite; means as means appeal to appetite only because the end to which they lead appeals to appetite. (3) The appeal of limited goods to human appetite, however, is not compelling; not even the good which is God compels us here below. The reason is: all goods, including God, present themselves to our appetite with the same compulsiveness with which they present themselves to our knowledge. Now, *all* goods present themselves to our knowledge as good but not as absolutely necessary for our well-being. A sinner can still manage to get along. At the point, therefore, where goods stand before our appetite, because they so stand before our knowledge, as good but not necessary, at that point goods are *like* means. Means have only the goodness of the end. The limited end or good, however, has its own goodness. Nevertheless, the goodness of any end is not so "all-fired" good in our *knowledge* of it that we cannot take it or leave it, and, because we can take or leave both multiple means and the good which is *known* as limited, in this respect means and end are *alike:* we can take or leave means when they are not unique; whereas we can take or leave ends when they are not *known* as compulsive. The feature common to multiple means and limited goods lies, then, in this: we can pick up both or let both lie. In that we can take or leave the means to an end only because means are sometimes multiple, whereas we can take or leave the end only because no end here below stands in our knowledge as compelling

—in this means and end *differ*. Means can cease to be means when these are multiple, whereas ends cannot cease to be ends even when they are multiple. Of course we may refuse to accept an end, but this refusal does not cause that refused end to cease to be an end, e.g., a doctor who refuses to cure his patient doesn't cause health to cease to be the end of his medical art. To refuse to accept an end is to cause the refused end to cease to be an end for the refuser, but it is, because it *should* be his end all the same, even though he refuses it. In short, the end compels a unique means, but no end *in via* compels at all.[24]

The Instrumental and Principal Cause

The closest approximation to a pure means is an artificial instrument. An artificial instrument prefigures, as do all causes, the *kind* of effect it causes as well as the *causing* of the effect. The first prefigurement comes partly from the nature of the instrument itself (*propria virtus instrumenti*): a saw saws; however, a saw will not prefigure, as a saw, the job of sawing oak instead of pine. The prefigurement, therefore, of sawing oak rather than pine comes from the exemplarity of *another* cause, called the *principal* cause.[25] Moreover, the principal cause is the one which puts the saw to doing the

[24] See St. Thomas, *Sum. Theol.*, I, 82, 2, *Resp.*, and Cajetan's commentary on this text.

[25] On principal and instrumental cause, see Aristotle, *Physics*, II, 5, 196b 28 ff. See St. Thomas, *In IV Sent.*, d. I, q. 1, a. 4, qa. 1: "For a principal agent acts according to the requirements of its own form, and so the active power in it is some form or quality having complete reality according to its own nature. But an instrument acts inasmuch as it is moved by another. Hence, it has a power proportioned to this motion. But motion is not a complete being, but it is a way to being, as it were something between pure potency and pure act, as is said in the third book of the *Physics*. And so the power of an instrument inasmuch as it is an instrument, according as it acts to produce an effect beyond that which is proportioned to it according to its nature, is not a complete reality having a fixed being in its nature, but an incomplete reality (like the power of affecting sight which is in the air inasmuch as it is an instrument moved by an exterior visible thing)."

De Verit., XXVI, 1, *ad* 8: "An instrument performs its instrumental activity inasmuch as it is moved by the principal agent and through this motion shares in some way in the power of the principal agent, but not so that that

particular sort of job it does (*applicatio instrumenti*). The second
prefigurement, the impulse to saw rather than not, comes wholly
from the principal cause.

Even natural instruments, e.g., the twigs with which a bird builds
a nest, are related to natural causes which use them, birds, in the
same way, but with one difference: birds don't make twigs, whereas
we do make tools. Hence the prefigurement of the causality of
instruments in their *natural* principal causes indicates a difference
in *principal* causes, viz., a difference between man and natures. Man
is a principal *responsible* cause, natures are principal causes which are
not responsible. God is. If there weren't twigs around which birds
could use for nests, God would have to supply something else if He
wished to have birds.

Means and Limited Ends

The main difference between instruments and means which are
also ends—intermediary or limited ends they are called, is this.[26]
Instruments are causes in act only when we use them, and they are
that only when we are consciously using them as instruments.
Before their willed use, instruments kick around only as prefiguring
a general sort of use to which they could be put. Means which are
also ends, however, have a full-fledged relation to the end, God,

---

power has its complete existence in the instrument, because motion is an incomplete act."

See also *Contra Gentiles*, II, 21; *Sum. Theol.*, I, 18, 3, *Resp.*; 45, 5, *Resp.*; I–II,
16, 1, *Resp.*; 112, 1, *ad* 1; III, 19, 1, *ad* 2; 62, 1, *ad* 1 and 2; *De Pot.*, III, 4, *Resp.*;
John of St. Thomas, *Cursus Philosophicus, Phil. Nat.*, Pars I, q. 10, a. 2; Reiser, t.
II, pp. 202–204.

[26] On means and instruments, see Aristotle, *Physics*, II, 3, 194b 32–195a 3:
"Again (4) in the sense of end or 'that for the sake of which' a thing is done,
e.g., health is the cause of walking about. ('Why is he walking about?' we
say. 'To be healthy,' and having said that, we think we have assigned the
cause.) The same is true also of all the intermediate steps which are brought
about through the action of something else as means towards the end, e.g.,
reduction of flesh, purging, drugs, or surgical instruments are means towards
health. All these things are 'for the sake of' the end, though they differ from
one another in that some are activities, others instruments." See St. Thomas,
In II Phys., lect. 5, n. 181.

before we use them. Our willing them simply transfers the relation they had before we willed them from their status of being good in themselves, though limited, to a status of being good for us. That *other* intermediary ends could be chosen by us makes no difference in their status of being intermediary ends. Whatever be the intermediary ends chosen, the choice of them endows them only with an *esse volitum*, a status of being good for us, but not with the relation they already had before our choice, namely, of being good in themselves. Thus, to choose means which are also ends is to order by an *esse volitum* that which is already ordered by its *esse naturae*. To choose instruments, however, is to order by an *esse volitum* that which is *not* so ordered except as a *res*, namely, as something which could be an instrument but isn't until it is used. Natural agents use instruments by a nonresponsible *esse volitum*.

Vocabulary of Causes

A fuller vocabulary will now help us to integrate the various causes. Let the passive potency which is the subject of change (substance) and of generation (prime matter) and of *esse* (an existent in an essential situation) be named *matter*. Passive potency is thus a material cause.[27] (1) A *material cause* is thus the subject out of which or in which the actuations of causes occur. "Out of which" distinguishes the material cause *before* its actuation from the material cause plus its actuation, which latter is matter "in which." The actuations of material causes are all called *formal* causes, except that actuation which is *esse*. (2) A *formal cause*[28] is thus that by which matter is what it is, either accidentally (by accidental form), or substantially (by substantial form). *Esse* is not a form at all. We shall return to the last point. We now have two causes: *material and formal.*[29]

[27] On material cause, see Aristotle, *Physics*, II, 3, 194b 23–24; *Metaphysics*, I (A), 3, 983a 30; V (Δ), 2, 1013a 25. See also Chapter II.
[28] On formal cause, see Aristotle, *Physics*, II, 3, 194b 26–28; *Metaphysics*, I (A), 3, 983a 26; V (Δ), 2, 1013a 26–28. See also Chapter II.
[29] Angels have no matter, but they are passive potency or "material" cause with respect to their *esse*.

(3) An *efficient cause*[30] is that which bestows matter's actuation upon matter. Now view an efficient cause according to the essential determinant of its activity, i.e., according to the kind of cause it is. So viewed, an efficient cause is named an *exemplar*. (4) An *exemplar cause*[31] is thus an efficient cause in so far as the efficient cause is like (in its knowledge, or in its nature) its effects. Obviously, this likeness of an efficient cause to its effect is due to the formal cause of the efficient cause, not to the formal cause of the effect: due to the heat of the heater, not to the heat of the thing heated. Thus, there are *two* formal causes: (a) the formal cause of the cause, (b) the formal cause of the effect. The formal cause of the cause is called an *extrinsic* formal cause, because it is extrinsic to the effect. The formal cause of the effect is called an *intrinsic* formal cause, because it is intrinsic to the effect. Thus, an exemplar is also an *extrinsic formal cause*.[32] The *formal intrinsic cause* is usually called a formal cause without further specification.

Now look at our efficient cause according to its existential determinant, its tendency or impulse to reduce potency to act. This tendency is the effect intended or tended toward. Since the effect as intended is the cause, eventually—operation must intervene—of the effect as accomplished in the agent or patient, we must name the intended effect by a special cause name. Its name is *final cause*.[33] (5) Thus, a final cause is that cause which causes the tendency of active potency to reduce passive potency to act, and it also causes the reductive operation of active potency itself, or, as Aristotle remarks, the final cause is that on account of which something is done.[34] You may also define final cause by its sign, which is the seeking

[30] On efficient cause, see Aristotle, *Physics*, II, 3, 194b 30-32; *Metaphysics*, I (A), 3, 983a 30; V (Δ), 2, 1013a 29-32. See also Chapter IV.

[31] On exemplar cause, see Aristotle, *Metaphysics*, VII (Z), 8, 1033b 30-1034a 5. See also Chapter VII.

[32] On the exemplar as an extrinsic formal cause, see St. Thomas, *In V Metaph.*, lect. 2, n. 764. See also Chapter VII.

[33] On final cause, see Aristotle, *Physics*, II, 3, 194b 32-195a 2; *Metaphysics*, I (A), 3, 983a 31; V (Δ), 2, 1013a 32-35. See also Chapter VIII, pp. 106-109.

[34] On the end as a cause, see Aristotle, *Physics*, II, 3, 194b 32; *Metaphysics*, I (A), 3, 983a 31; V (Δ), 2, 1013a 32. See also Chapter VIII, pp. 109-113.

of things. Then a final cause is that which each thing seeks.[35] We may note here again that the end intended has two features to it: the feature which is essential, and the feature which is existential. Both features exist only as intended, of course, but the point is that there are two features to an end. The essential determinant of an end is called an *object;* the existential feature of an end has no further name: it is the end as end.[36] For example, that it be apples and not pears which an apple tree tends to produce is due not only to the exemplarity of the apple tree, but also, by the very nature of *that* exemplarity, to the exemplarity of the intended apples.[37] The end intended as having its *own* specific features is called an *object.* An *object* is an end intended as being of a specific kind. An end as end, however, is the cause of operation. Thus, object and end are identical *in re,* but our understanding of object is not our understanding of end. Our understanding of end as end is the understanding of a summons to which the answer is tendency and operation. Our understanding of object is the understanding of the kind which the summons is, to which the answer is the kind which the nature and its tendency and its operation is.

Appendix to Chapter VIII

APPENDIX (A). The "perfect" may achieve being in two ways.

St. Thomas, *De Verit.,* XXI, 1, *Resp.:* ". . . in any being there are two aspects to be considered, the formal character of its species and the act of being by which it subsists in that species. And so a being can be perfective in two ways. (1) It can be so just according to its specific character. In this way the intellect is perfected by a being, for it perceives the formal character of the being. But the

[35] That the final cause is that which all things seek, see Aristotle, *Nicomachean Ethics,* I, 1, 1094a 2; St. Thomas, *In I Metaph.,* lect. 4, n. 71. See also Chapter VIII, pp. 112–113.
[36] On object and end, see Chapter VIII, p. 109.
[37] This last sort of exemplarity, viz., of the apples, is not primary exemplarity. The exemplarity of the apple tree is primary. The exemplarity of the apples is, as in the text, named "object."

being is still not in it according to its natural existence. It is this mode of perfecting which the true adds to being. For the true is in the mind, as the Philosopher says, and every being is called true inasmuch as it is conformed or conformable to intellect. For this reason all who correctly define *true* put intellect in its definition. (2) A being is perfective of another not only according to its specific character but also according to the existence which it has in reality. In this fashion the good is perfective; for the good is in things, as the Philosopher says. Inasmuch as one being by reason of its act of existing is such as to perfect and complete another, it stands to that other as an end. And hence it is that all who rightly define *good* put in its notion something about its status as an end. The Philosopher accordingly says that they excellently defined good who said that it is 'that which all things desire.' First of all and principally, therefore, a being capable of perfecting another after the manner of an end is called good; but secondarily something is called good which leads to an end (as the useful is said to be good), or which naturally follows upon an end (as not only that which has health is called healthy, but also anything which causes, preserves, or signifies health)."

APPENDIX (B). The end as a final cause.

St. Thomas, *In V Metaph.*, lect. 2, n. 771: "The fourth kind of cause is the end. This is that for the sake of which something happens, as health is the cause of walking. Because it is less evident that the end is a cause, since it is the last to come to be, therefore it was also omitted from consideration by earlier philosophers, as is noted in the first book. Hence Aristotle proves in a special manner that the end is a cause. For the question, 'why?' or 'on what account?' is a question about a cause. For when someone asks us, 'why, or for what reason,' is someone walking? we give a suitable answer when we say, 'for his health.' And in answering this way, we think we are giving the cause. Hence it is clear that the end is a cause. Not only the ultimate end for which the agent acts is a cause with regard to those things which precede it, but all the intermediate steps between the first agent and the ultimate end are called ends with regard to what precedes them. In the same way, the intermediaries are called the agent cause and source of motion with regard to what follows them."

St. Thomas, *In V Metaph.*, lect. 2, n. 775: "We ought to understand that of the four kinds of causes previously mentioned, two of them correspond to each other, and the other two also. For the efficient cause and the end correspond to each other, in that the efficient cause is the principle of change, and the end is its term. Similarly, matter and form correspond to each other, for the form gives *esse*, but the matter receives it. Therefore, the efficient cause is the cause of the end, and the end is the cause of the efficient cause. The efficient cause is the cause of the end, inasmuch as it makes it to be, because by bringing about change, the efficient cause makes the end exist. But the end is a cause of the efficient cause, not indeed of its being, but with regard to its causality. For, the efficient cause is a cause inasmuch as it acts, and it does not act except for the sake of an end. Therefore the efficient cause has its causality from the end."

Suggested Reading

Final Cause:

Aristotle, *Nicomachean Ethics*, I, 1; *Physics*, II, 3 and 8; *Metaphysics*, V (Δ), 2.

St. Thomas Aquinas, *In I Metaph.*, lect. 4, nn. 70–71; *In V Metaph.*, lect. 2, nn. 771–775; *De Princ. Nat.*, ch. 3; *In II Phys.*, lect. 5, nn. 181, 186; lect. 13; *De Verit.*, III, 1, *Resp.*; XXVIII, 7, *Resp.*; *In Lib. de Causis*, lect. 1, *ad fin.*; *Contra Gentiles*, III, 2; *Sum. Theol.*, I, 5, 4, *Resp.*; 5, 6, *Resp.*; 6, 2, *ad* 2; 44, 4, *Resp.*; 105, 5, *Resp.*; I–II, 1, 2, *Resp.*; *De Pot.*, V, 1, *Resp.*

Principal and Instrumental Cause:

Aristotle, *Physics*, II, 5.

St. Thomas Aquinas, *In IV Sent.*, d. 1, q. 1, a. 4, qa. 1; *Sum. Theol.*, I, 18, 3; 45, 5; I–II, 16, 1; 112, 1, *ad* 1; III, 19, *ad* 2; 62, 1, *ad* 1 and 2; *De Pot.*, III, 4, *Resp.*; *Contra Gentiles*, II, 21.

John of St. Thomas, *Phil. Nat.*, Pars I, q. 10, a. 2.

Object and End:

St. Thomas Aquinas, *De Princ. Nat.*, chs. 3 and 4; *In I Sent.*, d. 1, q. 2,
  a. 1, *ad* 2; *Sum. Theol.*, I, 25, 1; 57, 1; 77, 3; 82, 3; I–II, 1, 2; 9, 1;
  18, 2, *ad* 2; 18, 3; 18, 6; II–II, 117, 3; 153, 5; 162, 3; *De Pot.*, VII,
  10; *Contra Gentiles*, I, 48; II, 98; III, 1; *Quodlibet.*, VIII, q. 9, a.
  1, *Resp.*; *De Carit.*, a. IV, *Resp.*; *De Verit.*, XXI, 1, *Resp.*; *In II de
  Anima*, lect. 6, n. 305.
Cajetan, *In Sum. Theol.*, III, q. 2, a. 3.
John of St. Thomas, *Phil. Nat.*, Pars I, q. 13, a. 1.

The Means as a Useful Good:

Aristotle, *Physics*, II, 3.
St. Thomas Aquinas, *Sum. Theol.*, I, 5, 6; 82, 1; 83, 3; I–II, 8, 2; 8, 3,
  sed contra; De Verit., V, 1, *Resp.*; XXI, 1, *Resp.*; *In II Phys.*, lect.
  5, n. 181.

Immanent and Transitive Act:

Aristotle, *Metaphysics*, V (Δ), 18; IX (Θ), 6; *De Anima*, I, 3; III, 7;
  Nicomachean Ethics, I, 1.
St. Thomas Aquinas, *In I Sent.*, d. 40, q. 1, a. 1, *ad* 2; *In II Sent.*, d. 12, q. 1,
  a. 4; *In IX Metaph.*, lect. 8, n. 1865; *Contra Gentiles*, I, 13, 53, 100;
  II, 1, 22, 23; *De Verit.*, VIII, 1, *ad* 14; VIII, 6, *Resp.*; XIV, 3, *Resp.*;
  De Pot., II, 2, *Resp.*; II, 4, *Resp.*; III, 15, *Resp.*; V, 5, *Resp.*; and *ad* 14;
  Sum. Theol., I, 14, 2, *ad* 2; 14, 5, *ad* 1; 18, 1, *Resp.*; 18, 3, *Resp.*; 54, 1,
  ad 3; 52, 2, *Resp.*; 56, 1, *Resp.*; 85, 2, *Resp.*; 87, 3, *Resp.*; I–II, 31, 2,
  Resp.
Cajetan, *In De Anima*, II, 5B 114b.
John of St. Thomas, *Phil. Nat.*, Pars I, q. 14, a. 4; *Curs. Theol.*, Pars I,
  d. 4, a. 6.
Simon, Y., *Introduction à l'ontologie du connaître*, pp. 69–72.

IX · THE DIFFERENT DESIROUS "ESSE'S"

Summary of Chapter VIII

We may now view more closely the end as end, but before we do, we should recall what precisely it means to speak of the end as end or cause. It means that the end as end is intended, striven for by the operation of the agent and, sometimes, possessed by the agent, or accomplished by the agent in a patient.

Assume a nature: a kind of agent plus its kind of tendency, e.g., an apple tree, tending to grow apples. Assume, next, an operation of nature: an apple tree growing apples. Assume, lastly, the accomplished result of nature's operation: apples. Apples as the *product* which is intended by nature and its operations do not as yet exist in nature or its operations. When apples do exist they are effected; they are not intended any more. And yet, if the intended apples are to be a cause, as they are, of nature and its operations, they simply must exist. Now, to say that the cause of apples is the apple tree is true enough in the order of efficient causality, but to say only this is to miss the insight that the apple tree is *not* the apples; and to miss that insight is to miss this one: since the cause, viz., the apple tree, is not in the *esse* of the effect, viz., the *esse* of apples, as every cause must be, it is absolutely impossible that apples, which exist by their own *esse*, be the cause of themselves as they would have to be if they existed in the tree before they existed in themselves. Clearly then, if apples cannot be a cause by the title of their *own* esse, and if they are nevertheless a cause, they must exist and be a cause by the title of an *esse* which is other than their *own*. That

127

esse which is other than their own is their sought-for-*esse*, a tended-towards-*esse*. By whose or what's seeking or tendency? By the tree's, of course. Apart from their tended-toward-(or intended) *esse*, apples have no status as a final cause in act. It is in that desirous *esse* of the tree's, a tending-toward-growing-apples-*esse*, that apples reside as a final cause: the end intended.

In the intended *esse* of apples, intended by the tree's tendency and operations of course, there are, as we saw, two features: the feature of the *kind* of nature intending, e.g., an apple tree, not a pear tree; the feature of tendency and operation themselves. The first feature is assured, because the kind of thing-tended-toward is invriscerated within the kind of thing-tending-toward. The second feature is assured by the existential status of tendency and operation themselves.

A final cause is thus a juncture or a joining of the end as a *kind* of thing intended (this is the end as *object*) with the agent's *tending* toward and *operating in view of* the production in *esse* of that kind of thing. Thus, the final cause, apples, is apples which are being-sought-for-by-appetite (*esse appetitus*). As St. Thomas remarks, the actuation of what can be sought for (*esse appetibilis*) is the very act of seeking that which can be sought for (*est actu appeti*).[1]

And so, final cause is the capstone of efficient causation.[2] The need and nature of efficient causation is built up this way: the po-

---

[1] See St. Thomas, *De Verit.*, XXII, 1, *Resp.*: "To desire or have appetency [*appetere*] is nothing else but to strive for something [*ad aliquid petere*], stretching, as it were, toward something which is destined for oneself." See also *Sum. Theol.*, I, 16, 1, *Resp.*; 80, 2, *Resp.*; I–II, 8, 1, *Resp.*; 50, 5, *ad* 1.

[2] On final and efficient causation, see St. Thomas, *De Princ. Nat.*, c. 4, n. 356; *In V Metaph.*, lect. 2, n. 775: "The efficient cause is a cause inasmuch as it acts, and it does not act except for the sake of an end. Therefore the efficient cause has its causality from the end." *De Verit.*, XXVIII, 7, *Resp.*: "What must be called simply prior in the order of nature, however, is that which is prior in the line of that cause which is prior in the very character of causality. The outstanding example of this is the end, which is called the cause of causes because all the other causes receive from the final cause their status as causes; for the efficient cause does not act except for the sake of the end, and by reason of the action of the efficient cause the form perfects the matter and the matter supports the form." *Sum. Theol.*, I, 5, 4, *Resp.*: "Now in causing, first comes goodness and the end, moving the agent to act; second, the action of the agent moving to the form; third comes the form. *De Pot.*, V, 1, *Resp.*: "The end is a cause only inasmuch as it moves the efficient cause to act, since it comes first not in existence but only in intention."

tential as potential cannot actuate itself; else, as potential, it would have to be actual in order to actualize itself. A contradiction in terms. Yet the potential is actualized. Given. It follows that the actualization of the potential must come from another "actual," namely, the efficient cause. So far, good. But we must see farther. We must not only see that the "actual," which is the efficient cause, is the reason for the reduction of the potential to the potential's own actuation; we must also see that the "actual," which is the efficient cause, is a "seeking-actual," a desirous *esse*, desirous, that is, of the term or end of its operation. This, the *desirous* feature of the *esse* of an efficient cause, is the last block in the structure of a cause, for by that block the structure stands complete: an efficient cause's *causing* is at last accounted for by the cause of causes, the end.

In sum, efficient causes bestow actuation upon the potential or patient, whereas final causes are the actuation of efficient causes themselves. Nor must that actuation of efficient causes by final causes be thought of as if final causes actuated efficient causes by a desire for themselves (the final cause) which desire was *not* there all along, a sort of afterthought, so to say. No, final causes reveal that the *esse* of efficient causes was a desirous *esse* all the time. Agents desire ends because agents exist; it's not because they desire ends that agents exist. The *esse* of all agents is a desirous *esse*.

The Feature Which Is Common to All Desirous "Esse's"

Once the basic insight into the nature and need of final causes is possessed, we may better see the various situations of desirous *esse*. All the situations of desirous *esse* have this in common: desirous *esse* is always desirous of something desirable. In other words, to the essential and existential components of desire, there correspond the essential and existential components of the thing desired: to the "object" feature of the end, there corresponds the nature of the agent, and to the "end" feature of the object, there corresponds appetite in the agent. Desire in act is the desirable thing in the act of being desired. Briefly, the end as cause is always a juncture of a kind of thing desired (object) with the desiring of that kind of thing. The question now is this: how is that juncture or intention caused, or, how do the agents' desire and their corresponding end-objects come into act? In different ways, and these different ways are the different situations of a desirous *esse*.[3]

Differentiating Features of Desirous "Esse's" *The Desirous "Esse" of the Inanimate*

First, the desires and end-objects of some agents are in act once such agents are given. Nitric acid, e.g., will "do its stuff," because "doing its stuff" is given with the agent. Of course there has to be a patient around for nitric acid to go to work on, but given the acid and the patient, the acid will go to work without further actuation. We may express this situation in several ways. With some natures, tendency, performance, and effect, barring chance, are given. Or, we may express the matter thus: some agents are always completely actuated as agents by the efficient cause of these agents. The only way to avoid the effects of such agents is to get out of their way or to bottle them up. We may, of course, *guide* the activity of such agents, and in the measure that we do, we shall dominate nature. Or, we may state the matter thus: some agents do not cause their desirous *esse*, which desirous *esse* is one with their *esse*, and causes effects, and so they do not cause the end-object of that desirous *esse*; for, desirous *esse* and its end-object are the same thing in different relations. Such agents are named "natures" in the strong sense of the word.

---

[3] See Aristotle, *Physics*, II, 8, 199a 20–33; St. Thomas, *Sum. Theol.*, I, 18, 1–3; 19, 1, *Resp.*; 59, 1, *Resp.*; 60, 1, *Resp.*; 78, 1, *ad* 3; 79, 1, *Resp.*; 80, 1, *Resp.*; 81, 2, *Resp.*; 82, 1, *Resp.*; 87, 4, *Resp.*; I–II, 1, 2, *Resp.*; 3, 4, *Resp.*; 8, 1, *Resp.*; 17, 8, *Resp.*; 26, 1, *Resp.*; 30, 4, *Resp.*; *Contra Gentiles*, III, 2–3; III, 16; *De Pot.*, I, 3, *Resp.*; III, 15, *Resp.*; *De Malo*, VI, 1, *Resp.*; *De Verit.*, XXV, 1, *Resp.*; *De Princ. Nat.*, c. 3, n. 351.

The Desirous "Esse" of Plants

Second, some agents have a margin of unfixation in their desires and the end-objects of those desires. The sign that they have is this: they do many different sorts of things: they grow, e.g., reproduce, and nourish themselves. Now, if nourishment is not reproduction, and if neither is growth, such agents must have within their causal resources at least the feature of performance or execution of their actions. If at least performance were not caused by such agents, there would be no reason in them why they *did* one sort of thing instead of another. Their *doing* of this rather than that must, therefore, lie within their own causality. Of course, this "doing" of theirs is necessary, but it is more *their* doing than, as in inanimate "nature" (the strong sense of the word), it is the "doing" of their cause.[4] Nature in the strong sense causes only effects, not the performance which causes effects. Plants cause effects and also their own performance which causes effects.

The Desirous "Esse" of Animals

Third, there is the desirous *esse* of animals. Here the desirous *esse* and its end-object is not only multiple, as in plants. There is also a multiplicity within each sort of thing which an animal accomplishes. Animals can feel only the sensible: for example, they can hear only sound, touch only the resistent, see only the colored, and so on. Let us call such objects "proper sensibles"; sensibles, that is, which are proper to each sense. Observe now that within the proper sensible there is still a margin of unfixation. Though an animal will necessarily hear sound if it hears anything, it will not necessarily hear A flat unless A flat is sounding. So for the other sensibles, e.g., an animal will necessarily see color, but which color? That depends in part upon which color is kicking around to be seen, and in part upon

---

[4] Natures in the strong sense of the word *potius aguntur quam agunt*. They don't cause the causality of their effects; that is caused for them (*aguntur*). They cause their *effects*. See *Sum. Theol.*, I, 18, 1–3.

the animal's sensorium. Let us call the sensible which an animal actually senses a particular sensible. In this area of particular sensibles, an animal is a co-cause of its sensation *and* of the object of its sensations. Hence, animals are a part cause of the particular objects of their sensation. A horse will eat grass if he sees or smells it, but he need not see grass, and so need not eat grass; when he does see grass, he will be a co-cause of his seeing; and the grass another co-cause.

The Desirous "Esse" of Man

Fourthly, there is the desirous *esse* of man. Like an animal's or plant's, a man's end-object has a phase of fixation, a moment of necessity. That phase or moment is in the area of "the good."

Man's Desirous "Esse" Is in Part Necessitated

"The good" is not of itself limited to being a particular kind of good. This is to say that it is not solely *because* a good is of a particular kind that it is good; rather, it is because a particular kind of good is good that we desire it.[5] For example, it is not *wholly* because a good turns up as *Veuve Cliquot* that it is good; rather, it is because *Veuve Cliquot* turns up as a good—*that* is the reason why we like it. The good is like "being": it's not because a being is a fish that it exists, else there would be no being but a fish; it is rather because

[5] On the necessity in man's desirous *esse*, see St. Thomas, *Sum. Theol.*, I, 6, 2, *ad* 2; 82, 1, *Resp.*; I–II, 2, 8, *Resp.*; 8, 1, *Resp.*; 10, 1, *Resp.*; *Contra Gentiles*, I, 81; *De Verit.*, XXII, 1 and 5; *De Malo*, VI, 1, *Resp.*; *De Pot.*, III, 15, *Resp.*; *De Princ. Nat.*, c. 3, n. 351. See Appendix A of this chapter.

See also G. Smith, S.J., "Intelligence and Liberty," *The New Scholasticism*, Vol. XV, n. 1 (January 1941), pp. 1–17; A. C. Pegis, "Necessity and Liberty: An Historical Note on St. Thomas Aquinas," *The New Scholasticism*, Vol. XV, n. 1 (January 1941), pp. 18–45; Y. Simon, *Traité du libre arbitre*, Liège, Sciences et Lettres, 1951, pp. 38–53; E. Salmon, *The Good in Existential Metaphysics*, Milwaukee, Marquette University Press, 1953, pp. 1–76; J. Maritain, *Neuf leçons sur les notions premières de la philosophie morale*, Paris, Téqui, 1949, pp. 25–42, 77–83.

a fish is a being that it exists. So for "the good." It is not because a good is necessarily *Veuve Cliquot* that we desire it; it is because *Veuve Cliquot* is a good that we desire it. See it this way: in order to be good, no being has to be limited, else there would be no good except it have the given limitation. Against the fact: there are many goods.

We may express this metaphysical situation in psychological terms. If there were no good to satisfy man's food hunger except meat, a man would have no food desire except for meat. He would be exclusively a carnivore. Against the fact. Contrast this area of man's fixation of his appetite with an animal's. It *is* solely because a good is sensible that an animal desires it. As Joad says, the principle of a dog's life might be stated thus: whatever is, smells; whatever smells not, is not.[6] Man, however, likes the sensible and the non-sensible goods, justice, for instance. This shows that his desires are not fixed merely upon the score that their end-objects are of a given kind of good. Yet his likes and even dislikes *are* fixed upon the score that whatever he likes or dislikes is liked or disliked because it is or seems good to him. About that *reason* why he likes or dislikes anything, a man has nothing to say or do: he must, whatever object he chooses, choose that object because he thinks it good.[7] A most mysterious creature, man. He must like whatever he does like because he thinks it good to do so. Yet there is no compulsion in his desire for a particular good, and this is so precisely because a particular good is known as particular.

[6] C. E. M. Joad, *Return to Philosophy*, N.Y., Dutton, 1936, pp. 189–190.
[7] See St. Thomas, *Sum. Theol.*, I–II, 8, 1, *Resp.*: "Now every appetite is only of something good. The reason for this is that the appetite is nothing else than the inclination of a being desirous of a thing towards that thing. Now every inclination is to something like and suitable to the thing inclined. Since, therefore, everything, inasmuch as it is being and substance, is a good, it must needs be that every inclination is to something good. And hence it is that the Philosopher says that *the good is that which all desire.* . . . Therefore, just as the natural appetite tends to good existing in a thing, so the animal or the voluntary appetite tends to the apprehended good. Consequently, in order that the will tend to anything, it is requisite, not that this be good in very truth, but that it be apprehended as good. Therefore the Philosopher says that *the end is a good, or an apparent good.*"

Man's Desirous "Esse" Is in Part Free

This leads to the consideration of man's desirous *esse* in relation
to a particular end-object. And first let us locate the desirous *esse*
we are talking about. It is *not* man's desirous *esse* in the stage where
it is tendency. It is *not* his desirous *esse* in the stage where it is
operation, not at least where operation means the execution of his
desires. It *is* his desirous *esse* which is his internal act of choice.[8]
Tendency precedes choice, and execution follows it. At the peak of
man's desirous *esse* which is his choice, a man may choose among
alternatives; indeed, he may choose none of the alternatives, for that
too is an alternative, viz., not to choose as opposed to choosing.
Why? Precisely because there *are* alternatives. Why are there? Precisely because "the good" always stands in that knowledge of it
which confronts a man's choice as good-but-not-necessary. Were
man's knowledge of the good which confronts his choice a knowledge of a-good-and-necessary, he would have to choose it. But the
knowledge of the good which confronts man's choice is knowledge
of the good-but-not-necessary. Contrast this situation with the animal's situation *vis-à-vis* sensible goods. An animal *must* "choose"
whatever it does, precisely because the animal doesn't *know* the
limited good as limited, though it is. Man *knows* the limited good as
limited (good-but-not-necessary), and so man's choice of the limited
good is not compelled by that good. The good, known as limited,
is never so "all fired" good as to compel man's choice of it.[9]

[8] On the freedom in man's desirous *esse*, see St. Thomas, *De Verit.*, XX,
6, *Resp.*; *Sum. Theol.*, I-II, 13, 6, *Resp.*; I, 59, 3, *Resp.*: "Only an agent endowed
with an intellect can act with a judgment which is free, in so far as it knows
the universal nature of goodness, from which it can judge this or the other
thing to be good. Consequently, wherever there is intellect, there is free
choice." See Appendix B of this chapter.

See also *Sum. Theol.*, I, 83, 1, *Resp.*; I-II, 10, 2, *Resp.*; *De Verit.*, XXIV, 1,
Resp.; *De Malo*, VI, 1, *Resp.*

In addition to the secondary sources cited in note 5 above, see especially Y.
Simon, *Traité du libre arbitre*, pp. 71–111, 117–122; "On the Foreseeability of
Free Acts," *The New Scholasticism*, Vol. XXII, n. 4 (October 1948), pp. 357–
370; J. Maritain, *Du Régime temporel et de la liberté*, première partie: *Une
philosophie de la liberté*, Paris, Desclée de Brouwer, 2e ed., 1933.

[9] There is much philosophy of nature being presupposed here, but even if
we know very little about animals, it is quite clear that man's choice is always

Now, since man does choose limited goods, this must be because he endows them with what they need in order to make them effectively his end-objects. This endowment is his wish that limited goods be good for him. And this wish is the spot at which man's desirous *esse* is responsible, an act caused by himself, a desire of his own making, his free choice.

Summary of the Differences in Desirous "Esse's"

In sum, all desire is fixed by the end-object. Sometimes only the cause of the agent, God, does that fixing. This is the situation of inanimate natures. Inanimate natures cause only their effects, not their causality which causes their effects. Sometimes God and the agent itself do that fixing, but up to different points. Plants fix or cause only the performance or execution of the operations, which involve their end-objects. They do not cause their end-objects to be their end-objects. Plants, under God, cause only the executive feature of their causality. Inanimate natures don't do even that much. Animals cause the performance of their operations *and* are also co-causes of the *kind* their operations will be: seeing, tasting, etc. Men cause all that plants and animals do, and besides, they are the full causes, under God, of the very end-objects of their operations. This is to say that men are the causes of the predeterminants of their operations: they are causes of the predeterminant of what kind of thing they choose, because they are causes of the very choosing of that kind of thing: they are causes of their choice, in other words. Thus the end is always a juncture of formal causality (the exemplar in nature or in knowledge) with final causality (the exemplar's *desire*), a juncture of the essential and existential determinants

---

of a good which twinkles, so to say: it flashes as good; then the light goes out or is dimmed: no good is known as necessitating choice. If we wish to keep the light on, we must hold it on. This is choice. The luminosity is "the good"; the twinkling of the light is the good known as limited; choice is the keeping of the light on or off. See Y. Simon, *Traité du libre arbitre*, pp. 75-76. See also St. Thomas, *Sum. Theol.*, I-II, 10, 2.

of operation.[10] Sometimes that juncture is made *for* agents, not *by*
them, by their cause: inanimate nature. Sometimes the agent itself
makes that juncture. If the agent does not make that juncture responsibly, but makes it nevertheless, the agent is a plant or an animal.
If the agent makes that juncture responsibly in the sense that he
could, had he wished, not have made it, the agent is a free agent.

Final Causes in Practical and Speculative Sciences

Some things cannot be made, because they already are in *esse*,
their own or their causes'. These things are called the "inoperables."
Since the inoperables' *esse* is none of our doing, *they* cause our
knowledge about them; our knowledge doesn't cause *them* to exist
or to be of a kind. Such knowledge, viz., of the inoperables, is called
speculative knowledge, from *speculor*, I look at; because, in effect,
speculative knowledge can do nothing but look at inoperables. Rep-
licating in a knowledge mode the *esse* which the inoperable already
has in its own right, speculative knowledge can only record, so to
say, what is there to be recorded; it can't make the inoperable to be,
because the inoperable already is, actually or possibly.

On the other hand, some things can be made by us, and the question
is, how do we know these "operables"? We know them by a knowledge which is the cause of them. Such knowledge is called practical
knowledge (from πράττω, I make; πρᾶξις, a work).[11]

---

[10] On the end as a juncture of formal and final causality, see St. Thomas,
De Verit., XXVIII, 7, *Resp.*: "The outstanding example of this is the end,
which is called the cause of causes because all the other causes receive from
the final cause their status as causes; for the efficient cause does not act except
for the sake of the end, and by reason of the action of the efficient cause the
form perfects the matter and the matter supports the form." *Sum. Theol.*, I, 5,
4, *Resp.*: "Now in causing, first comes goodness and the end, moving the agent
to act; second the action of the agent moving to the form; third comes the
form."

[11] On speculative and practical knowledge, see Aristotle, *Nicomachean Ethics*,
VI, 2, 1139a 16–1139b 13; *De Anima*, III, 10, 433a 13–18; *Metaphysics*, II (a),
1, 993b 20–22. See St. Thomas, *In III Sent.*, d. 23, q. 2, a. 3, *sol.* 3, *ad* 3; *In I
Ethic.*, lect. 1 and 3; *In Boet. de Trin.*, V, 1, *Resp.* and *ad* 4; *In VI Ethic.*, lect.
2, nn. 1132, 1136; *In III de Anima*, lect. 12, n. 780; lect. 15, n. 820; *Contra Gentiles*, III, 75; *De Verit.*, II, 8, *Resp.*; III, 3, *Resp.*; XXII, 10, *Resp.*; *Sum. Theol.*,

Perhaps the first remark to be made about practical knowledge is this: the operable is not known as we know the possible. We know the possible when we know that it has a cause, e.g., we know children as possible when we know there are generators of children. Yet, whereas the operable is indeed possible, we do not know the operable by knowing that it has a cause. Rather, we know the operable by a knowledge which *is* a cause of the operable. For example, we know the prospective movement of our hand by a knowledge which anticipates that movement, because it causes that movement. The movement of the planets, on the other hand, we can know by a knowledge which anticipates indeed, but does not cause, their movement, because such knowledge is only about a cause of their movement; it is not the cause of their movement. Thus, whereas speculative knowledge is about a cause or effect, practical knowledge is a cause. A most mysterious knowledge, practical knowledge —like summoning spirits and the works of spirits from the vasty deep, and in this instance they will come. Speculative knowledge summons nothing into *esse*, but practical knowledge does: it summons into *esse* all the works of man, including the work which is himself, a good man, a bad man, a doctor, lawyer, merchant, etc.

The second remark to be made about practical knowledge is this: practical knowledge is causative knowledge because it is willed knowledge. Of course all knowledge is willed in the sense that one will never know unless one wishes to know: one must always will, that is, to exercise any act of knowledge. Yet it is not because we wish the sum of these units, 1, 1, 1, 1, to be 4 that the sum is 4. That sum is not caused by our willing it; only our act of knowing that sum is caused by willing it. However, our knowledge that we will purchase or not purchase four apples, or that we will purchase four apples instead of four bananas—that knowledge is not only

---

I, 1, 4, *Resp.;* 14, 16, *Resp.;* 79, 11, *Resp.* and *ad* 2, and Cajetan's commentary on this text.

See John of St. Thomas, *Cursus Philosophicus, Ars Logica,* Pars II, q. 1, a. 4; Reiser, t. I, pp. 269a–277b; *Cursus Theologicus,* Pars I, q. 1, d. 2, a. 10; Solesmes, t. I, nn. 4–5, pp. 395–396.

See also J. Maritain, *Distinguer pour unir, ou les degrés du savoir,* pp. 618–625, 879–896; Y. Simon, *Critique de la connaissance morale,* Paris, Labergerie, 1934, pp. 7–19.

brought into exercise by our will, it is also, by being willed to be true, a cause of our purchase. The distinctive feature of practical knowledge, then, is not that it is brought into the *esse cognitum* by a will act (any knowledge is so brought into *esse*), but that the will act endows the specificative features of an *esse cognitum* with an *esse volitum:* we know what we shall do, because we will to do it. In short, practical knowledge, e.g., I shall buy four apples, is true because we wish it to be true, whereas speculative knowledge is true because it squares with things as they are.

Be sure you do not view the will act's point of impact upon the intellect in practical knowledge in this way: first, we know the operables speculatively, as the prospective object of our desire; next, we tag the operable with our desire for it, and lastly we know the operable as so tagged with our desire to make or do it. No. Such an account of the matter does not, though it seems to, make sense. For, there is no subject of the *esse cognitum*, no specificative features, that is, in anything we know, unless that subject's appropriate *esse* be also known either in exercised or signified act: those acts are the *esse* of nature, e.g., (known by first intention), or the *esse* of knowledge (known by second intention), or the *esse volitum* (known by wishing something to be true). Now, there *is* no subject of an *esse volitum* unless, by being willed, it is made to be such a subject: we *know* what we will do or make because we *wish* to do or make what we know. Here, then, lies the mystery of practical knowledge: it is knowledge whose specificative features, viz., the *kind* of thing we wish to do or make, which is included within our wish to act, are caused to be actually specificative of what we will do, because we wish them to be.

It may help to see this point from several directions. To know that you will buy apples is surely knowledge which is causative of your purchase. Now, it is incidental to the cause of the purchase that you wish to buy apples for this or that reason (*finis operantis*), because any old reason would suffice to get the apples bought. But what is not incidental but essential to causing the transaction is that there *be* a purpose, no matter what, which will get the job done (*finis operis*).[12] In other words, you must *wish* to buy apples, no matter for what reason, if you are going to *know* that you will buy them. Thus, the knowledge that you will buy apples, which knowledge is the cause of your purchase, can only be willed knowledge. Knowledge about apples is not willed, except in the sense that you wish to know about apples. But the purpose or end of the job of buying apples (*finis operis*) is to buy them; it is not just the purpose of knowing about apples, about where they can be bought, etc. To repeat, the purpose or end of the job (*finis operis*) of knowing all about apples is simply to know all about apples; but the *finis operis* of practical knowledge is the *opus* of making or doing something, which *opus* is over and above knowing something. In sum, the inoperable cannot be willed to be, it can only be known to be; the operable cannot be known unless it is willed, because it cannot be operable unless it be willed.

We may also see the matter this way. Let us name the total object of knowledge the *material object*. The material object will, then, have many, many unknown features in it—like a topic or subject of discourse about which one can say something but not everything. Let us name the known or knowable features of a material object, together with the way those known or knowable features are related to knowledge, the *formal object* of knowledge. For example, a tree is a material object of knowledge; the rustling of its leaves, known as *heard*, is *sound*, a formal object; the green of the leaves, known as *seen*, is *color*, another formal object; the tree's size or dimensions, known as *quantified stuff*, is still another formal object. Formal objects will, then, be distinguished according to the job (*opus*) which the act of knowing them accomplishes: the job of hearing *sound*, of seeing *color*, of knowing *quantity*, etc. This is called the *finis*

---

[12] See St. Thomas, *De Verit.*, XXI, 1, *Resp.*: ". . . in any being there are two aspects to be considered, the formal character of its species and the act of being by which it subsists in the species." See *In II de Anima*, lect. 6, n. 305; *Sum. Theol.*, I, 25, 1, *Resp.*; 57, 1, *Resp.*; 77, 3, *Resp.*; 82, 3, *Resp.*; I-II, 9, 1, *Resp.*; 18, 6, *Resp.*; II-II, 117, 3, *Resp.*; 153, 5, *Resp.*; 162, 3, *Resp.*; *De Pot.*, VII, 10, *Resp.*; *Contra Gentiles*, I, 48; II, 98; III, 1; *Quodlibet.*, VIII, q. 9, a. 1, *Resp.* See also John of St. Thomas, *Cursus Philosophicus*, Phil. Nat., Pars I, q. 13, a. 1; Reiser, t. II, p. 273b 16; Pars III, q. 2, a. 3, pp. 239–240; Cajetan, *In Sum. Theol.*, III, q. 2, a. 3. Cf. Chapter VIII, n. 9.

operis, the purpose of an operation of knowing as distinguished from
the purpose of the operant, *finis operantis*. A man might eat in order
to stuff himself (*finis operantis*), but eating food will nourish him
all the same (*finis operis*). Now, if the *finis operis* of knowing accomplishes nothing more than knowing, the formal object of knowing is the inoperable, and the knowledge is speculative. On the other
hand, if the job of knowing (*finis operis*) will accomplish something
other than knowing—the job of knowing you will buy apples, e.g.,
will accomplish their purchase as well—the formal object of knowing is the operable, and such knowledge is practical. The *operant's*
purpose in knowing anything does not change the operable into the
inoperable, or *vice versa;* only the *operation's* purpose does that.
Thus, to study geometry in order to get a degree (*finis operantis*)
does not make geometry a practical science. Geometry is a speculative science, because the job of knowing geometry is achieved by
knowing geometry, whether one gets a degree or not. Nor is the
knowledge of the formulae of the stresses, angles, size, and so on,
of a house a practical science, because the knowledge of those
formulae doesn't issue into anything else except the knowledge of
them. Should you know that you will make a house according to
those formulae, then you have a practical science. In sum, when
the end of knowing is just knowing, the knowledge is speculative,
whether the material object be makeable (a house) or not (God);
when the end of knowing is productive of something other than
knowing, the knowledge is practical, even though there may be
speculative features in it.[13]

We may now view the matter this way. Both speculative and
practical knowledge have an end or purpose (*finis operis*). The end

[13] In the famous *Sum. Theol.*, I, 14, 16 text, there are only two *per se* members of the division: practical knowledge (*ex fine operis*) and speculative (*ex
fine operis*). The two other members of the division are accidental: speculative
knowledge acquired for an ulterior practical purpose (*finis operantis*) is *still*
speculative, though it may be called practical *ex fine operantis*, which is accidental to knowing speculatively; and speculative knowledge about something
which can be made, e.g., a house, is also speculative, though it can be called
practical *ex objecto* (*materiali*, scil., *ex re scita*). The beginner had better forget these two accidental members of the division: geometry is *not* a practical
science *ex fine operantis*, although that *finis* may be practical; and architecture
is *not* practical *ex objecto materiali*, though an architect's knowledge is about
things which can be made.
See *De Verit.*, III, 1, where the above point is made quite clear.

accomplished by speculative knowledge is the good of knowing the truth; the good accomplished by practical knowledge is the good of making or doing something.[14] In speculative knowledge, the job of knowing profits the knower; in practical knowledge, the job of knowing profits the knower, indeed, but only incidentally—no small profit, but incidental nevertheless. Workers or makers are more content when at work than they are when they are layed off. Nevertheless, the profit of "making" knowledge *per se* is for the thing which such knowledge makes; there is no profit in making, except incidentally, for the maker. Thus, speculative knowledge is achieved by knowing the truth; practical knowledge is achieved by its product, the artifact.

Not that there is not truth in practical knowledge. There is. But the truth of practical knowledge is caused by being willed, whereas the truth of speculative knowledge is not. You don't, by willing it, make it true that 2 plus 2 equals 4; you do, by willing it, make it true that you will buy four apples, or plant four apple trees. The truth of speculative knowledge, then, lies in its conformity with things; the truth of practical knowledge lies in its conformity with your will: it is true, e.g., that you will do this or that, or not do this or that, when and if you will to do this or that.

We may now ask, and this is still another way of viewing the matter, which is better knowledge, speculative or practical? If you mean, which is better for the knower, the answer is obvious, because only speculative knowledge *per se* profits the knower. Practical knowledge is obviously better for making things if only because it is the only knowledge which makes things.

Practical Moral Knowledge

There is a much more mysterious practical knowledge than the artist's. The artist's practical knowledge causes an artifact, something

[14] See Aristotle, *De Anima*, III, 10, 433a 14; St. Thomas, *In III Sent.*, d. 23, q. 2, a. 3, *sol.* 2, *ad* 3; *De Verit.* III, 3, *Resp.*: "As is said in *The Soul:* 'Practical knowledge differs from speculative knowledge in its end.' For the end of speculative knowledge is simply truth, but the end of practical knowledge, . . . is action."

distinct from his knowledge, whereas a morally good man's practical knowledge causes *him* to be good.[15]

The difference between the two sorts of practical knowledge might be seen in this way. The relation of the artist's causal knowledge to his artifact is such that if there be any defect in the artist's knowledge—sometimes artistic knowledge is creative enough, but scarcely worth creating—or any defect in his skill, tools, or material, the artifact will suffer: for lack of powder there will be no shooting. The good man's practical knowledge, however, might be mistaken knowledge, invincibly mistaken, that is. For example, a man might mistakenly think he is giving alms whereas he is giving a bribe. Clearly, what is wrong here is the *finis operis*, which is bribery, for *that* in effect is what a good man's external act is accomplishing, though he doesn't and, by hypothesis, can't know it. The mistake lies, therefore, in the external or executive action of giving what in fact is a bribe. Yet the man's intention, let us suppose, is good: he thinks he is giving alms. The external act is mistaken, but not the internal act, the man's good intention.[16] That internal act (I will to give alms) is not only true upon the score that it is in accord

[15] See Aristotle, *Nicomachean Ethics*, VI, 5, 1140b 20–25: "Practical wisdom, then, must be a reasoned and true state of a capacity to act with regard to human goods. But further, while there is such a thing as excellence in art, there is no such thing as excellence in practical wisdom; and in art he who errs willingly is preferable, but in practical wisdom, as in the virtues, he is the reverse."

St. Thomas, *Sum. Theol.*, I–II, 57, 4, *Resp.*: "Consequently, it is requisite for prudence, which is right reason about things to be done, that man be well disposed with regard to ends; and this depends on the rectitude of his appetite. Therefore, for prudence there is need of moral virtue, which rectifies the appetite. On the other hand, the good of things made by art is not the good of man's appetite, but the good of the artificial things themselves, and hence art does not presuppose rectitude of the appetite. The consequence is that more praise is given to a craftsman who is at fault willingly, than to the one who is unwillingly; whereas it is more contrary to prudence to sin willingly than unwillingly, since rectitude of the will is essential to prudence, but not to art."

See also Cajetan, *In Sum. Theol.*, I–II, q. 57, a. 5, *ad* 3; J. Maritain, *Creative Intuition in Art and Poetry*, N.Y., Meridian, 1957, pp. 36–38; Y. Simon, *Critique de la connaissance morale*, pp. 36–37.

[16] On goodness in the internal and external act of the will, see St. Thomas, *Sum. Theol.*, I–II, 20, 1–4. On truth in speculative and practical matters, see St. Thomas, *Sum. Theol.*, I–II, 57, 5, *ad* 3; Y. Simon, *Critique de la connaissance morale*, pp. 26–37.

with his will (all internal acts or intentions are in accord with the
intender's will, even morally bad acts, for, it is true that one wills
to give alms or a bribe only when and if one wills either); it is also
true upon the score that it is in accord with his *good* will. To bring
out the point clearly, if one decides against doing what he knows he
should do, it is clear that this decision is in accord with his act of
willing, but the act of willing is bad. If one decides in favor of doing
what he should do, that decision is both in accord with his will and
with his *good* will. Here, then, is a practical knowledge whose truth
lies in the conformity between what one thinks one *should* do and
with what one actually wishes to do, and not merely in the conformity between what one thinks of doing with his wishing to do
it. What, then, is the mysterious relation of the *finis operantis*, which
is good, to the *finis operis*, on the hypothesis that the latter is bad
but not known to be bad? Apparently, the *finis operis* here wears
the disguise of the good, and as so disguised, it is willed. The question is, why will an artist's mistake be fatal, sometimes wholly so,
to his artifact, whereas the good man's honest mistake cannot be
wholly fatal to his goodness? The answer can be given, but its
demonstration will have to wait for natural theology.

The end of man is to see God. This a man cannot do unless he
wishes to. Moreover, the wish alone to see God cannot accomplish
the operation of seeing Him; just so, a man cannot know anything
without wishing to, and yet it is not his wishing which is his
knowing.

The wish to see God is accomplished on earth by accepting the
moral good; the refusal to accept the moral good is the rejection of
God.[17]

The acceptance of the moral good, or its rejection, is fully within
our power: "nothing is so within our power as our will."[18] That a
man can reject the moral good is of course a miserable possibility,

---

[17] On the acceptance of the moral good, see G. Smith, S.J., *The Truth That
Frees*, pp. 55-60; J. Maritain, *Neuf leçons sur les notions premières de la
philosophie morale*, pp. 31-33, 36-40, 84-86; *Court traité de l'existence et de
l'existant*, pp. 84-101.
[18] See St. Augustine, *De Libero Arbitrio*, III, 3, 7; PL 32, 1274: ". . . nihil tam
in nostra potestate, quam ipsa voluntas est."

a precarious freedom not yet fixed in the possession of the good. Concerning the causality of moral evil, something will be said later,[19] but right now let us fix our attention upon our glorious power of choosing a moral good, and in it God.

This is an act which is totally exempt from interfering lines of secondary creaturely causality. True, the execution of our wishes for goods which are, or are involved in, matter is more or less subject to interfering causes: there's many a slip 'twixt the cup and the lip. But though one may be forced to do many things one does not wish, one cannot be forced to wish to do these things. The act of wishing to do the right thing is totally ours. Indeed, no act is so stamped with the seal, "mine," as this wish.

The reason why that is so is because no act is so stamped with the seal, "God's." It is *because* our wishing for the moral good is so wholly His that it is so wholly ours. The causality of physical natures, on the other hand, is not wholly theirs. No physical nature is the cause of the predeterminants of its activity; the cause of the predeterminants of the operations of physical natures causes physical natures and their operations; the operations of physical natures cause effects. Thus, natural causes are only more or less possessive of their causality, because they only more or less possess themselves. Man's causality, however, is fully his, because he causes the predeterminants of his causality, because God causes man to do this. In physical natures, God does something which they do not do: He causes the predeterminants of their causality. In human natures, God's causality of their human acts causes human natures to cause those acts.

This being so, since it is inconceivable that the first efficient cause be not also the first final cause, it is also inconceivable, and for exactly the same reason, that the acceptance of the moral good by a man's wish to accept that good be not the same, exactly, as his reception of the moral good. To say that God gives is the same as to say that man receives. If, then, there be a mistake here, that mistake cannot lie in a discrepancy between what is given (man's acceptance) and what is received (the goodness of the man who accepts). The mistake must lie in an external act, not in the internal

[19] On the causality of moral evil, see G. Smith, S.J., *Natural Theology*, pp. 255-256; J. Maritain, *St. Thomas and the Problem of Evil*, Milwaukee, Marquette University Press, 1942, pp. 20-29.

one. In short, the *finis operis* here *is* the *finis operantis*:[20] the good man is made good by his good intention. The mistake in the *opus* which is external to, or executive of, his intention is no doubt deplorable, but he is not deplorable. He needs instruction about what is good, not an exhortation to accept it.

We may now recur to our question, why can an artist's mistake be fatal to his artifact, whereas a good man's honest mistake cannot be fatal to his goodness? It is because there is something within the artist's causality which is not wholly his, his original endowment of talent, e.g., his skill, his tools, his material, etc. All these or any part of them, if defective, can ruin his work. A good man's causality, however, cannot totally ruin *his* work, because a good man causes the predeterminants of his causality of goodness. An artist is not wholly dominant over his work; a good man is.

Appendix to Chapter IX

APPENDIX (A). The necessity in man's desirous *esse.*

St. Thomas, *Sum. Theol.*, I–II, 10, 1, *Resp.:* ". . . the principle of voluntary movements must be something naturally willed. Now this is the good in general, namely, that to which the will tends naturally, in the same way as each power tends to its object; and again it is the last end, which stands in the same relation to things appetible, as the first principles of demonstration to things intelligible; and, speaking generally, it is all those things which belong to the one willing according to his nature. For it is not only things pertaining to the will that the will desires, but also that which pertains to each power, and to the entire man. Therefore man wills naturally not only the object of the will, but also other things that are appropriate to the other powers, such as the knowledge of truth, which befits the intellect, and to be and to live and other like things which regard his natural well-being—all of which are included in the object of the will as so many particular goods."

---

[20] St. Thomas, *In II Sent.*, d. 1, q. 1, a. 1, *Sol.:* ". . . finis operis semper reducitur in finem operantis. . . ."

APPENDIX (B). The freedom in man's desirous *esse*.

St. Thomas, *Sum. Theol.*, I–II, 13, 6, *Resp.*: "Man does not choose of necessity. And this is because that which is possible not to be, is not of necessity. Now the reason why it is possible not to choose, or to choose, may be gathered from a twofold power in man. For man can will and not will, act and not act; and again, he can will this or that, and do this or that. The reason for this is to be found in the very power of reason. For the will can tend to whatever the reason can apprehend as good. Now the reason can apprehend as good not only this, viz., *to will* or *to act*, but also this, viz., *not to will* and *not to act*. Again, in all particular goods, the reason can consider the nature of some good, and the lack of some good, which has the nature of an evil; and in this way, it can apprehend any single one of such goods as to be chosen or to be avoided. The perfect good alone, which is happiness, cannot be apprehended by the reason as an evil, or as lacking in any way. Consequently, man wills happiness of necessity, nor can he will not to be happy, or to be unhappy. Now since choice is not of the end, but of the means, as was stated above, it is not of the perfect good, which is happiness, but of other and particular goods. Therefore man chooses, not of necessity, but freely."

St. Thomas, *De Verit.*, XX, 6, *Resp.*: "Since the will is said to be free inasmuch as it is not necessitated, the freedom of the will can be viewed in three respects; (1) as regards its act, inasmuch as it can will or not will; (2) as regards its object, inasmuch as it can will this or that, even if one is the opposite of the other; and (3) as regards its ordination to the end, inasmuch as it can will good or evil."

Suggested Reading

Final and Efficient Cause:

St. Thomas Aquinas, *De Verit.*, XXII, 1, *Resp.*; XXVIII, 7, *Resp.*; *Sum. Theol.*, I, 5, 4; 16, 1, *Resp.*; 80, 2, *Resp.*; I–II, 8, 1, *Resp.*; 50, 5, *ad* 1; *In V Metaph.*, lect. 2; *De Princ. Nat.*, ch. 4.

Desirous "ESSE":

Aristotle, *Physics*, II, 8.
St. Thomas Aquinas, *Sum. Theol.*, I, 18, 1–3; 19, 1; 59, 1; 60, 1; 78, 1, *ad* 3; 79, 1; 80, 1; 81, 2; 82, 1; 87, 4; I–II, 1, 2; 3, 4; 8, 1; 17, 8; 26, 1; 30, 4; *Contra Gentiles*, III, 2–3; III, 16; *De Pot.*, I, 3, *Resp.*; III, 15, *Resp.*; *De Malo*, VI, 1, *Resp.*; *De Verit.*, XXV, 1, *Resp.*; *De Princ. Nat.*, ch. 3.

Desirous "ESSE" *in Man:*

St. Thomas Aquinas, *Sum. Theol.*, I, 6, 2, *ad* 2; 59, 3, *Resp.*; 82, 1; 83, 1; I–II, 2, 8, *Resp.*; 8, 1, *Resp.*; 10, 1–2; 13, 6, *Resp.*; *Contra Gentiles*, I, 81; *De Verit.*, XX, 6, *Resp.*; XXII, 1 and 5; XXIV, 1, *Resp.*; *De Malo*, VI, 1, *Resp.*; *De Pot.*, III, 15, *Resp.*; *De Princ. Nat.*, ch. 3.
Maritain, J., *Neuf leçons sur les notions premières de la philosophie morale*, pp. 77–83.
——, *Du Régime temporel et de la liberté*, première partie: *Une philosophie de la liberté.*
Pegis, A., "Necessity and Liberty: An Historical Note on St. Thomas Aquinas," *The New Scholasticism*, Vol. XV, n. 1 (January 1941), pp. 18–45.
Salmon, E., *The Good in Existential Metaphysics*, pp. 1–76.
Simon, Y., *Traité du libre arbitre*, pp. 38–53.
——, "On the Foreseeability of Free Acts," *The New Scholasticism*, Vol. XXII, n. 4 (October 1948), pp. 357–370.
Smith, G., S.J., "Intelligence and Liberty," *The New Scholasticism*, Vol. XV, n. 1 (January 1941), pp. 1–17.

Speculative and Practical Knowledge:

Aristotle, *Nicomachean Ethics*, VI, 2; *De Anima*, III, 10; *Metaphysics*, II (a), 1.
St. Thomas Aquinas, *In III Sent.*, d. 23, q. 2, a. 3; *In I Ethic.*, lects. 1 and 3; *In VI Ethic.*, lect. 2, nn. 1132, 1136; *In Boet. de Trin.*, VI, 1, *Resp.* and *ad* 4; *In III de Anima*, lect. 12, n. 780; lect. 15, n. 820; *Contra Gentiles*, III, 75; *De Verit.*, II, 8, *Resp.*; III, 3, *Resp.*; XXII, 10, *Resp.*; *Sum. Theol.*, I, 1, 4, *Resp.*; 14, 16, *Resp.*; 79, 11, *Resp.* and *ad* 2.
Cajetan, *In Sum. Theol.*, I, 79, 11.
John of St. Thomas, *Ars Logica*, Pars II, q. 1, a. 4; *Curs. Theol.*, Pars I, q. 1, d. 2, a. 10.
Maritain, J., *Distinguer pour unir, ou les degrés du savoir*, pp. 618–625.
Simon, Y., *Critique de la connaissance morale*, pp. 7–19.

Practical Moral Knowledge:

Aristotle, *Nicomachean Ethics*, VI, 5.
St. Thomas Aquinas, *Sum. Theol.*, I–II, 20, 1–4; 57, 4, *Resp.*; 57, 5.
Maritain, J., *Creative Intuition in Art and Poetry*, pp. 36–38.
——, *Neuf leçons sur les notions premières de la philosophie morale*, pp. 31–33, 36–40, 84–86.
——, *Court traité de l'existence et de l'existant*, pp. 84–101.
Simon, Y., *Critique de la connaissance morale*, pp. 36–37.
Smith, G., S.J., *The Truth That Frees*, pp. 55–60.

The State of the Question

The question why being is multiple is now pretty much absolved. Being is multiple, because (1) multiple being at various levels is a composite of potency and act, and so being can be multiple; (2) at the various levels of its multiplicity, being is caused to be multiple.

There remains the question about how being, which is one and many in itself, is also one and many in our knowledge of it. Obviously, by answering the first question, one has assumed that the answer to the second question is like the answer to the first. For, if being did not stand in our knowledge of the one and many, quite as the one and many stand in themselves, apart from our knowledge, neither answer could be valid. We must ask, therefore, not if we know being as one and many, but how we do. This leads us into an inquiry about the nature of our knowledge about being.

Some Descriptions of Knowledge

An agent is always the subject of its operation: a runner runs; running doesn't run. Just so, I think; my "thinking" doesn't think. I am always the subject of my act of knowing, just as I am always the subject of my act of existing. I am the one who knows, quite as I am the one who exists.

Yet the act of knowing is not only a qualification of the knower, quite as any accident qualifies a substance. The act of knowing also has this feature peculiar to it: it is a qualification of the knower in

terms of the known.[1] This distinctive feature of the act of knowing
is not the easiest thing in the world to grasp. We must have several
go's at it.

To know, say, "green" quite obviously causes a knower-of-green
to be a knower-of-green, quite as "to run" causes a runner to run.
Observe however, that "to run" is an accident of the runner which
qualifies the runner as form qualifies matter. Now, although "knowing green" is also related to the knower as form is related to matter,
it is not *upon that score* an act of knowledge. If it were, knowers-
of-green would *be* green, and green things would *know* they were
green. Against the facts. The facts are that green things don't *know*
they are green upon the score that they *are* green, nor *are* knowers-
of-green green because they *know* green. This means that the two
accidents, viz., knowing-green and being green differ in that knowing-green is specified by something which is not the knower nor his
act of knowledge, whereas being-green specifies only the thing
which is green. Thus, knowing-green not only specifies the knower,
it is also an act which *is* specified by something which is neither the
knower nor his act of knowledge. That "something" is "the other,"
viz., a green thing, "as other."

[1] On the act of knowing as a qualification of the knower in terms of the
known, see Aristotle, *De Anima*, III, 8, 431b 20–432a 2; St. Thomas, *In II de
Anima*, lect. 5; *In III de Anima*, lect. 13, n. 787; *Contra Gentiles*, II, 98; IV, 11;
De Verit., I, 1, *Resp.*; II, 2, *Resp.*; II, 3, *Resp.* and *ad* 1; II, 14, *Resp.*; *Sum.
Theol.*, I, 14, 1, *Resp.*; 84, 2, *Resp.*; *In I Sent.*, d. 19, q. 5, a. 1; *De Pot.*, IX, 5,
Resp.; *Quodlibet.*, VII, q. 1, a. 4, *Resp.* See Appendix A of this chapter.
  For a bibliography on the Thomistic doctrine of knowledge, see G. Kluber-
tanz, S.J., *The Discursive Power. Sources and Doctrine of the Vis Cogitativa
According to St. Thomas Aquinas*, St. Louis, 1952, pp. 331–346.
  See also J. Maritain, *Distinguer pour unir, ou les degrés du savoir*, cc. III–
IV; *Réflexions sur l'intelligence et sur sa vie propre*, 2 ed., Paris, Nouvelle
Libraire Nationale, 1926, cc. I, II, IX; E. Gilson, *L'Être et l'essence*, pp. 248–
328; *Being and Some Philosophers*, pp. 190–215; *Le Thomisme*, pp. 290–331;
The Christian Philosophy of St. Thomas Aquinas, pp. 207–222; G. Phelan,
"Verum Sequitur Esse Rerum," *Mediaeval Studies*, Vol. I (1939), pp. 11–22;
J. de Tonquédec, S.J., *La critique de la connaissance*, Paris, Beauchesne, 1929,
cc. I, IV, VI, VII, Appendix, II, VII; J. Maréchal, S.J., *Le point de départ de
la métaphysique*, 3 ed., Vol. V, Paris, Desclée de Brouwer, 1944, Bk. I, cc. I,
II; Bk. II, Sec. I, II, III; Y. Simon, *Introduction à l'ontologie du connaître*, cc.
I, II, III; *Prévoir et savoir*, cc. V, VI; J. Peghaire, C.S.Sp., *Regards surs le
connaître*, Montreal, Fides, 1948; P. Rousselot, S.J., *The Intellectualism of
Saint Thomas*, N.Y., Sheed & Ward, 1935, pp. 17–60; J. Wild, *Introduction
to Realistic Philosophy*, N.Y., Harper, 1948, pp. 436–439, 448–462.

"The other" means the thing known in contrast to the knower and to his act of knowledge. "As other" is a reduplicative emphasis which insists that it is not *because* the knower is "other" than or different from what he was when he was a non-knower (though he *is* different) that he is a knower; nor is it *because* "the other," which is the known, is different from what it was before it was known (for it isn't) that it is known; it is rather because a knower is, by knowledge, something other than himself that he is a knower. One might say that to be, by knowledge, "the other as other" is to be by knowledge the not-self as not-self; for, knowledge speaks to me of something which is "not-me," even when it speaks to me of me. To know oneself is surely not to be oneself, because knowers sometimes are not in the knowing state at all. Yet they exist when they know nothing.

Another description of the matter may help. If we agree to call the act of knowing a "form" (accident) of the knower, then the "form" of knowledge, besides being the form of the knower, is also the form of the known. Thus, the act of knowledge is a form as qualifying the knower. This is a matter-form relation; and it is also a form *in* the knower *of* the known. That relation of the knower to the known is not a matter-form relation at all. It is the latter sense of the word "form" which is distinctive of knowledge. It is not that knowers have other "forms" (though they do) that they know; it is because the forms they have are the forms of *other things* that they are knowers. The form of the other is the form of knowledge.[2]

---

[2] See Aristotle, *De Anima*, II, 12, 424a 17–23: "By a 'sense' is meant what has the power of receiving into itself the sensible forms of things without the matter. This must be conceived of as taking place in the way in which a piece of wax takes on the impress of a signet-ring without the iron or gold; we say that what produces the impression is a signet of bronze or gold, but its particular metallic constitution makes no difference: in a similar way the sense is affected by what is colored or flavored or sounding, but it is indifferent what in each case the *substance* is; what alone matters is what *quality* it has, i.e., in what *ratio* its constituents are combined."

See also St. Thomas, *In II de Anima*, lect. 24, nn. 551, 553; *Sum. Theol.*, I, 84, 2, *Resp.*; *De Verit.*, II, 2, *Resp.*: "The perfection of one thing cannot be in another according to the determined act of existence which it has in the thing itself. Hence, if we wish to consider it in so far as it can be in another, we must consider it apart from those things which determine it by their very nature. Now, since forms and perfections of things are made determinate by

Still another description. The act of existing causes the subjects of that act to exist. Thus, it is by his act of existing that John exists. And modes of the act of existing cause the subject to exist in these modes. Thus, for John to be fat is for John to exist as fat. The act of knowing, however, does not cause the subject of that act either to exist as the things which are known exist, or to exist in any of the physical modes in which things known exist. To know green is neither to exist as knowers of green exist in their natural being, nor as green things exist in their natural being. Rather, to know green is to exist in a way totally different from the way subjects of existence and their modes exist: to know is to exist, but not as subjects of existence exist. Positively, to know green is to exist in a cognitive way of being green. The act of knowing is a cognitive or intentional way of being, not a physical way of being.[3]

"To be the other as other," "to have the forms of other things," "to exist, but not as subjects of being exist," "to be in an intentional, not a physical, way the thing known," all these descriptions of knowledge are demonstrated descriptions which are drawn from two premises: (1) we know things (evident); (2) it could not be things which we know, unless we know them according to the ways described. The difference in the descriptions of knowledge is merely

---

matter, a thing is knowable in so far as it is separated from matter. . . . Hence, those ancient philosophers erred who asserted that like is known by like, meaning by this that the soul, which knows all things, is materially constituted of all things: . . ."

[3] On knowledge as intentional existence, see Aristotle, *De Anima*, II, 5, 417b 2–7; III, 8, 431b 20–432a 2. See also St. Thomas, *In I de Anima*, lect. 4, n. 43; *In II de Anima*, lect. 5, nn. 282–284; lect. 12, n. 377; lect. 24, n. 551; *In III de Anima*, lect. 13, nn. 787–791; *De Verit.*, II, 2, *Resp.*; VIII, 6, *Resp.*; VIII, 8, *Resp.*; *Q.D. de Anima*, a. 20; *De Pot.*, IX, 5, *Resp.*; *In VI Metaph.*, lect. 4, n. 1234; *Quodlibet.*, VII, q. 1, a. 2, *Resp.*; VII, q. 1, a. 4, *Resp.*; *Contra Gentiles*, I, 53: ". . . an external thing understood by us does not exist in our intellect according to its own nature; rather, it is necessary that its species be in our intellect, and through this species the intellect comes to be in act." *Sum. Theol.*, I, 84, 2, *Resp.*: ". . . material things known must needs exist in the knower, not materially, but rather immaterially."

See John of St. Thomas, *Cursus Philosophicus, Ars Logica*, Pars II, q. 21, a. 4; Reiser, t. I, pp. 676b 44–677a 20; Cajetan, *In II de Anima*, 6 B 133b; *In Sum. Theol.*, I, 55, 3; 79, 2. See also J. Maritain, *Distinguer pour unir, ou les degrés du savoir*, c. III and Annexe I; Y. Simon, *Introduction à l'ontologie du connaître*, pp. 13–39.

a difference of viewpoints, and the elaboration of the minor premise can be seen in epistemology.

Intentional "Esse"

The point to the demonstration that any of the above descriptions of knowledge is true will be wholly missed if one fails to see that the way things exist in knowing is an *intentionally* existential way, that is, the thing known exists in knowledge by an act of existing which is neither the knower's physical act of existing nor the known thing's physical act of existing. To explain again, assume a knower. Assume that the knower knows, say, that *John is*. The way the known (John) exists in knowledge is not by reason of the "is" which is John's or the knower's. It is by a new "is," the "is" of "is known" —a cognitive or an intentional "is." Thus, the intentional being, which is the way things have of being known, is not the content of knowledge; it is the actuation of that content, which actuation is precisely the content's "is known," not the "is" of John nor the "is" of the knower of John. Content is common both to knowledge and to things. To think that the content of knowledge is identical with the way that content exists in knowledge, viz., by an intentional act of existing, is to revive one or other form of idealism.

We may name the being of knowledge *intentional* being. We may name the content of knowledge the *object* of knowledge.

The Objects of Intentional "Esse"

Intentional being may function in two ways: first, so as by making known the things which do or can exist *outside* of the act of knowledge; secondly, so as by making known the things which exist only *within* the act of knowledge. Thus, we have *two* viewpoints of things which are known, and since these things are called *objects*, we have *two* objects of knowledge. The object which exists or can exist outside of knowledge is an object of first intention, or simply, a first intention; the object which can exist only within knowledge is an object of second intention, or simply, a second intention.[4]

To illustrate. When we know that a man exists or can exist, or how he exists or can exist, we have knowledge of an object which exists or can exist outside of knowledge: a first intention. Obviously, the man whom we know in that way, exists or can exist in all his own physical splendor, with his ears layed back, say, eating corn off the cob, and washing it all down with a highball as long as his leg. He is not intentional being, but the *knowledge* of him is, and that knowledge about him is first intentional being. But that is not the whole story. Not only do we know, by first intentions, physically existent objects; we also know, by second intentions, mentally existent objects, objects, that is, which exist only in the mind. For example, we know that the *man* in the proposition, *man is a species,* exists as related to many individuals of the same kind: for, *man* is what any individual of the man kind is. Now, as being affected by that relation, the relation, namely, of being a species (*esse speciem*), that man *is* a species, quite as the *man* in the proposition, *a man exists, does* exist. But the *man* in the proposition, *man is a species,* exists in a way of existing which not only is not, but also *cannot* be (*there* is the point) a physical way of existing at all. The knowledge of *man* in the proposition, *man is a species,* is knowledge of an object which can exist only in knowledge, because that man has universality; and since that universality of his can exist only in knowledge, so can *he* who has universality exist only in knowledge. On the other hand, the knowledge of *man* in the proposition, *a man exists,* is knowledge of an object which exists both in and outside of knowledge.[5]

[4] On first and second intentions, see Aristotle, *Topics,* I, cc. 5–6; *Categories,* ch. 5, 2a 14; St. Thomas, *In I Post. Anal.,* lect. 20, n. 5; *De Pot.,* VII, 6, *Resp.;* VII, 9, *Resp.; In IV Metaph.,* lect. 4, n. 574; *Sum. Theol.,* I, 28, 1, *Resp.* See Appendix (B) of this chapter.
See also Cajetan, *In Sum. Theol.,* I, 28, 1; John of St. Thomas, *Cursus Philosophicus, Ars Logica,* Pars II, q. 1, a. 3; Reiser, t. I, pp. 259b–269a; Pars II, q. 2, a. 1, pp. 285b–290b; Pars II, q. 2, a. 2, pp. 290b–293b.
[5] There are many second intentional ways of existing: as being a species, a genus, a difference, an accidental predicate, a property, a subject of a

The plaguing difficulty about discerning first from second intentions centers about the following points. (1) First and second intentions are names for the contents or objects of knowledge, whereas intentional being is the name for the actuation of those contents of knowledge, the actuation which is their "is known" or "the knowing of them." Thus, the word "intentional" could be an adjective qualifying *esse*, and it could also be an adjective qualifying "object." As qualifying *esse*, "intentional" distinguishes objects as existing in an act of knowledge from those same objects which also can or do exist in their own right as well. Objects existing in their own right have physical *esse* or an *esse naturae*. Thus, in the knowledge that *John exists*, John is in intentional *esse*, and yet John exists also apart from his intentional or being-known-*esse*. As qualifying "object," "intentional" distinguishes within the intentional *esse* *two* intentional objects: objects which do or can exist outside the act of knowledge (first intentions) from objects which cannot exist outside the act of knowledge (second intentions). Thus, in the knowledge that *man is a species*, the man who is known as a species exists only in knowledge. For, the man whose whole being lies in being known as a species cannot exist outside the status of being known as a species, because there are no mental species existing by the title of a physical *esse*. Only the *individuals* of a species exist by physical *esse*. (2) "Is known" or "knowing" reveals nothing upon the score of "being known" about *what* it is that is known. Now, reflection reveals that

judgment, a predicate, as being *a priori*, as being a consequence, etc. There are also negations, e.g., *Peter is not an ass*, because Peter is Peter (and an ass is an ass), *not* because a not-being-an-ass is Peter. There are many non-asses which are not Peter. Peter is not an ass mainly upon the score that he is Peter. *We* put the negation into the proposition. For, beings are not negations of being, and yet we would never know beings unless, when the occasion is appropriate, we denied one being of the other; and so negations, along with relations of reason like those already named, are second intentions. The relations of reason are the field of logic. There is no especial science of negations. If one did not negate one being of another when the occasion is appropriate, it would not be so much that one was wrong as that one had no mind at all. See St. Thomas, *In IV Metaph.*, lect. 1, n. 540; *De Ente et Essentia*, c. I; Cajetan, *In De Ente et Essentia*, c. 1; ed. Laurent, n. 9: "Negations and privations of this kind are not beings except objectively in the soul: thus, their being is nothing else than *to be known*, in the manner in which all beings of reason have being."

some objects are known to exist with their own *esse* or in the *esse* of their cause; and reflection also reveals that some objects are not known, or, positively, are known not to exist with any physical *esse* at all, either their own or the *esse* of their cause, which latter's *esse* is their *posse*. The latter are the objects of second intention. Whence come those second objects, those second intentions: *esse speciem, esse predicatum, esse modum ponentem, modum tollentem, esse consequentiam,* etc.? They cannot come from *esse intentionale* as if *that* actuation were the stuff out of which *they* are made. To think so is to reduce logic and metaphysics to psychology and, eventually, to some form of nominalism. Nor can they come from the content or objects of knowledge, cannot come, that is, from that which has those relations—as if those objects had those relations apart from the intentional *esse* by which alone they have those relations. The man who is a species, as we just saw, is not a species apart from his being known to be a species. (The man who is known to exist, however, *has* a relation to his physical *esse*, even if he were not known to exist.) To think that there exists the *man* who is species apart from the status he has of being known to be a species is to reduce metaphysics to logic, and, eventually, to some form of *idealism.* It remains that the *esse speciem,* etc., is an item of information about man when man is in a state of being known to be known (second intention), not in a state of being known to be (first intention). (3) The whole being of the *man* who is known as a species lies precisely in his being known as a species, whereas the whole being of a man who is known to exist does not. The man who is known to exist has a leg in two states of existence: his own state of existence, and his state of being known. The man who is known as a species, however, has a leg in only one state of existing: his state of being known to be a species. One might say that any second intention is the sole instance where *esse est percipi* (to be is to be known). But the reason why, here, *speciem esse est speciem percipi* (why the knowing of the species is the being of the species) is because of another object (a first intention) whose whole being does *not* lie in its being perceived; rather, that latter object's being lies also here: though perceived, it does or can exist whether perceived or not.[6] The second intention, however, cannot exist except in its being known, not to exist, but in its being known to be known. In order to be a second intention, then, an object must (a) not only be *in* knowledge, just like any object of knowledge, it must also (b) be knowledge *alone*. (4) "To be knowledge alone" does not mean to be the knowledge of a *man as man* either in this proposition, *a man exists*, or in this, *man is a species*. The knowledge of both those men has the same intelligible content; and both those men are the same specifications of their predicates. It is not upon that score that first intentions differ from second. Nor do the knowledges of those two men differ upon the score that *man* in *a man exists* is outside of knowledge (though, physically, he is or can be), whereas *man* in *man is a species* is not outside knowledge (though he is not). Both men are in knowledge. The two knowledges of the two men differ in this: the way the man, who is known to exist, "is knowledge" is as knowledge of him, whereas the way the man, who is known as a species, "is knowledge alone" is as knowledge of his specific *universality*. Knowledge of *him* is knowledge of an object which can exist apart from knowledge; but knowledge of him in his specific universality is knowledge of an object which cannot exist apart from knowledge, because there *is* no universality apart from knowledge. There are no universals on the loose in things. Universals are only in the realm of the spirit or soul of man. The same thing can be said of any second intention.

To sum up: (1) a second intention is the object of knowledge which cannot exist except in knowledge; (2) this means that a second intention is in and is known to be in knowledge alone; (3) to be, and to be known to be, in knowledge alone is an instance where *esse est percipi*; (4) that *esse* which is *percipi* is a relation of reason,

---

[6] Though there is a difference between *percipi* and *intelligi*, that difference is not to the point here. In any case, Berkeley is partly wrong: he doesn't allow for an object of a *percipi* whose *esse* is *not* wholly a *percipi*, viz., a first intention. He is also partly right: there is an object whose *esse* is wholly a *percipi*, viz., a second intention; but the second intention depends upon the first intention. Indeed, one might say that the purely mental existence of second intentions is the best guarantee of the physical existence of the object of first intentions. For Berkeley's position, see *A Treatise Concerning the Principles of Human Knowledge*, nn. 33, 24, 3; ed. A. Fraser, *Berkeley's Complete Works*, Oxford, Clarendon, 1901, Vol. I, pp. 275, 258–259.

a relation which reason makes because that relation *is* the *percipi;* whereas the relation which reason makes, as it does in knowing that John exists, is made as one remakes in intentional *esse* what one has discerned to have already been made in physical *esse.*

The Division of the Objects of Knowledge

Dividing, now, the objects of knowledge *according to what knowledge is of,* we have (1) knowledge of things—first intention; (2) we have knowledge of knowledge of things (relations of reason) —second intentions. Dividing objects of knowledge *according to what knowledge is,* we have (1) knowledge which is viewed as an accident, like the running of a runner. About knowledge viewed as an accident, there's nothing distinctively metaphysical to say. It is simply an accident whose name is "formal or subjective concept." (2) Viewed as a quality of the knower which, besides specifying him as a knower, specifies him also in terms of the known, the object of knowledge is distinctively metaphysical. For, here we have an object which is *not* the knower, nor his knowing, but is the *thing known.* Here, knowing green and knowing red, though they do not differ as qualifications of the knower as knower (as formal concepts), nevertheless do differ as qualifications of the knower in terms of different knowns. These knowns are named objective concepts or the formal object of concepts.[7] Sometimes those knowns are (a)

---

[7] On the objective concept, see St. Thomas, *De Pot.,* VII, 9, *Resp.;* VIII, 1, *Resp.; Quodlibet.,* V, q. 5, a. 2, *ad* 1; *Sum. Theol.,* I, 34, 1, *ad* 2 and Cajetan's commentary on this text; *Contra Gentiles,* I, 53; IV, 11. See Appendix (C) of this chapter.

See Cajetan, *In De Ente et Essentia,* q. 2, n. 14: "The concept is twofold: formal and objective. A formal concept is a kind of representation which the possible intellect forms in itself, and is objectively representative of the thing grasped; which representation is referred to by philosophers as an intention or a concept, by theologians as a word. An objective concept is that which, represented by the formal concept, terminates the act of knowing; for example, the formal concept of lion is that representation which the possible intellect forms of a leonine quiddity when we want to know it; the objective concept of the same thing is the leonine nature itself, represented and known. Nor must we think that, when a name is said to signify a concept, it signifies only one: for the name of lion signifies both concepts, though it does so in

in things, and in the mind too of course, and then they are first intentions; (b) sometimes they are not in things, but only in the mind, and then they are second intentions. Dividing the objects of knowledge *according as they are means by which we know things,* as lungs are means by which *we* yell, we are (1) speaking of subjective concepts. Subjective concepts are not in things except as accidents of the knower, and as accidents of the knower they are not particularly significative of knowledge, no more than a Ph.D. degree is particularly revelatory of what a Doctor of Philosophy knows. (2) If, however, we speak of the "means" by which we know *things,* then those means are (a) sometimes "in things," as the known *fat* is in fat man, somewhat as the tail of the dog, by which we grab the dog, is in the dog (first intention); (b) sometimes they are not in things, but only in us. "In us," not as a physical part of us (lungs), nor as an accident (though second intentions *are* accidents), but as a relation of universality (second intention) which we bestow upon "means" (1) in order to, or as a means by which we may, understand our first intentional knowledge of things.[8] We could, e.g., never understand *fat man* if we didn't understand *fat* as accidental to *man.*

The Finality of Intentions

Why do we make first and second intentions? To answer: "for exactly the same reason that roosters crow" is true enough, but not particularly significant. To answer: "we make first intentions in

---

diverse ways: it is the sign of the formal concept as a medium or a *quo,* and of the objective concept as the term or the *quod.* Whence, to speak of the concept of being and its signification is one and the same thing."

See also John of St. Thomas, *Cursus Philosophicus, De Anima,* Pars IV, q. 11, a. 2; Reiser, t. III, pp. 358b 37–359a 16; *Ars Logica,* Pars II, q. 2, a. 2; Reiser, t. I, p. 291a 5–25; J. Maritain, *An Introduction to Logic,* N.Y., Sheed & Ward, 1937, pp. 17–19; *Réflexions sur l'intelligence et sur sa vie propre,* pp. 9–77; J. Peghaire, C.S.Sp., *Intellectus et Ratio selon S. Thomas d'Aquin,* Paris, 1936, pp. 14 ff.; B. Lonergan, S.J., "The Concept of Verbum in the Writings of St. Thomas Aquinas," *Theological Studies,* Vol. VII (1946), pp. 349–392; Vol. VIII (1947), pp. 35–79, 404–444; Vol. X (1949), pp. 3–40, 359–393.

[8] A material concept or the material object of a concept is an object in all its unknown residue of intelligibility.

order to understand things, and we make second intentions in order to understand our understanding of things" is true and distinctively significant, metaphysically, provided the answer be evolved.

To know means, first, to be aware that things exist and, secondly, to see connections among them. It is mainly because of the second of these two features about "knowing things" that we call a man wise or stupid. A stupid man sees few connections among things; a wise man, many. The more connections, and especially the more significant or necessary the connections which a man sees among things, the wiser man he. Of course, in being aware that things exist and are somewhat connected, both the wise and the stupid man start even. Everyone, wise or stupid, knows that things exist. Moreover, both the wise and stupid man start even in being aware of a certain unity and multiplicity in being and in their knowledge of being. Everyone who lives under the sky knows that John-shaving is a unit, because he *is* shaving, and a plurality, because John is *not* identically his shaving. Likewise, everyone knows that a fish and a fishhook are both bodies (unity), but not the same kind of bodies (plurality). Lastly, everyone knows that John and George are both existents (unity), yet John is not George (plurality). It is not because a man knows these things that he is wise. Anyone can see some connections (unity) among different things (plurality), and if he didn't, it would not be so much that he was wrong, as that he had little or no mind at all. A wise man, however, sees in what those connections among things lie, and, because in seeing in what those connections lie, he eventually discovers the many of the kingpin connections (connections of increasing necessity)—upon that score is he wise.[9]

We must go into this more fully. Connections are given and are known as given. This is as much as to say that there is unity (connections) in plurality. Everyone knows this. What are those connections in our knowledge of them?

<hr />

[9] On connections and identities, see E. Meyerson, *Identité et realité*, pp. 399 ff.; Y. Simon, *Traité du libre arbitre*, p. 32; G. Smith, S.J., "Philosophy and the Unity of Man's Ultimate End," *Proceedings of the American Catholic Philosophical Association*, Vol. XXVII (April 1953), p. 69.

The Problem of First Intentional Knowledge of a Changing Being

There is, first, the connection between a subject of qualifications and the subject's qualifications. For example, John (subject) is shaving (qualification of subject), babies cry, etc. This connection must be understood thus: though other than or different from the subject of them (John), the qualifications are nevertheless the subject's qualifications. Men *do* shave, and we might as well say so; yet to be a man is not necessarily or identically to be shaving, and we might as well say that too. We say both when we say that a man is shaving.

The familiarity of such statements and the ease with which we make them conceal a truly stupendous state of affairs: something or some feature (shaving) which is *not* the subject (a man) is *said* to be connected with the subject: a man is *not* his shaving, yet *he* shaves all the same. No wonder Aristotle thought that the situation is very difficult to explain, though very easy to be.[10] Easy to be! Not at all. Aristotle means that the familiarity of the situation makes it seem easy to be, like a father's love for his children. Nevertheless, the situation is doubly astounding. It is as difficult to explain as it is to be. Whether we view it in itself or in its involvement in our knowledge, there is a mysterious connection between two unidentical factors: something which is *not* the subject is, and is said to be, true of the subject. What *is* the connection between shaving and a shaver in itself and in our knowledge of it? An attempt has already been made to answer the first part of the question. The second question, why do we *assert* or *say* that two unidentical factors (John, shaving) are the same *in re?* is our present question.

The Problem of First Intentional Knowledge of Kinds of Being

Before answering the question, let us advert to another, similar and similarly astounding situation. Not only do we know John

[10] See Aristotle, *Physics*, III, 2, 201b 32–202a 1.

shaves, we also know that he argues, cooks his food, falls in love in and out of season, laughs, is a featherless biped, has prehensile thumbs, etc. As we saw, none of these predicates, singly or in combination is, in our knowledge of them, identically our knowledge of John; yet we know he *is* those predicates, singly and sometimes in combination. See now this: (1) those predicates are not only our knowledge of John, they are also our knowledge of anyone-like-John; (2) those predicates are not even identically our knowledge of anyone-like-John. Anyone-like-John is an ontological constant, a "clunk" which is not identically the predicates themselves—like something in a sack, a sack of predicates. Off we walk with the sack, confident that what is in it (anything-like-John) will stay there, and that nothing else will get into that sack. Here, then, is a wondrous situation: (1) anyone-like-John is now in a sack of predicates, and (2) not even that "anyone" is identically its predicates. What is in the sack? As we saw, an ontological x is there. This we know. But the reason why it's there cannot be because we identify that x with any one or all of its predicates. To show this, make this test. Say that the x is identically one who laughs, etc. You have said that one who laughs is one who laughs. Like saying "laughs" twice over, a brace of singularly unintelligent phonisms. To avoid psittacism, we must recognize that the x is an ontological constant, present to the mind, at the center of the predicates we observe.[11] The name of that constant is substance, and substance is thus the known territory upon which the known hailstones of its predicates are falling, on pain of falling on nothing known—on no known territory whatsoever. It was one of Aristotle's glories to have seen the point: substance is the subject of predicates, but never itself a predicate.[12] Substance, then, is that of which one must say *it* is, and also that of which we say it is whatever else we can truthfully name it. Nevertheless, you cannot say that the "it" is identically any one or all of its predicates; because as we saw, if you do, you're saying the same thing (the subject) twice over.

[11] See Y. Simon, *Traité du libre arbitre*, pp. 35-36; J. Maritain, *Distinguer pour unir, ou les degrés du savoir*, pp. 399 ff.
[12] See Aristotle, *Categories*, ch. 5, 2a 11-2b 14.

We now have, within our knowledge, substance: the knowledge of a unit, which knowledge, we know, is not identically the knowledge of any of its components (predicates), either singly or in combination. Why, then, do we connect that unit with its predicates, as we do, whereas we know it is not identical with its predicates? We say a man—any man, that is, not just John—laughs, argues, etc.; yet to know a man or any man is not necessarily to know to-be-laughing or to-be-arguing, and so on.

The Problem of First Intentional Knowledge of Being

Perhaps, and we are now approaching the third and last astounding instance of our connecting in knowledge certain factors which are not identified in knowledge, perhaps we could resolve the antinomy by discovering the predicate of anyone-like-John which is self-explanatory of all which anyone-like-John does and is. As we know, that predicate is a definition of the subject, e.g., *man is a rational animal.* Thus, the definition of man would seem to be what we want, viz., a connection of identity in our knowledge, an identity of knowing the subject with knowing the predicate. Surely, the identity of subject with predicate in our knowledge of the definition of the subject would seem to answer the question, why do we *know* being as one and many? The reason might seem to be this: the knowledge connections we have been making all along, viz., of John with his shaving; of anyone-like-John with his constellation of necessary predicates, are now seen to have been based all along upon a connection of identity between a subject and its definition. Surely, to know *man* in his definition (rational animal) is to know *fully* the nature of man; for, fully to think the subject in terms of its definition is fully to think the predicate; it is knowledge of the subject which is identically knowledge of the predicate. In other words, if it were true that things are identically the definitions of them, we should have hit upon the reason why our knowledge items are connected, loosely at first in perinoetic knowledge; then more necessarily in dianoetic knowledge; then absolutely in their definitions.[18] And because we seem now to know that things are identically their definitions (that our success in reaching a thing's definition is infrequent is beside the point), we now apparently know that our knowing of being is our knowledge of the definition of a being.

It is not so, and that on two counts. First, because to know the definition of a thing is not to know whether the thing defined exists or not, and only to know an existent, actual or possible, is to know a being. Second, because even if we were to suppose it true that our knowledge of a thing's definition were identically the knowledge that that thing exists, we should still have to face these facts; many different beings have the *same* definition, and *different* definitions are nevertheless of things which are known to be the *same* in being existents. These facts we cannot face if we say that to know the definition of a thing is to know that it exists. No doubt, in discovering definitions we discover a knowledge unit of two factors (S and P) which are now seen to differ only as undeveloped knowledge (knowledge of the S) differs from the same knowledge fully developed (knowledge of the P), but this discovery does not disclose a knowledge unit which is knowledge *both* of a thing's definition *and* its status of being an existent.

And so, we are now at a third astounding connection which our knowledge makes between unidentical factors. As we saw, the first connection is as between, e.g., our knowing "shaving" and "John." We know John is not his shaving; yet we know he is shaving all the same. The second connection is this: we connect our knowledge of anyone-like-John with the constellation of anyone-like-John's necessary predicates, although we also know that anyone-like-John is not identically any one of those predicates, either singly or in combination. Thirdly, although we define anyone-like-John as a rational animal, and so we connect our knowledge of rational animal with our knowledge of that which (rational animal) exists or can exist, yet we know that our knowledge of definitions is not forthwith knowledge that the things defined exist or can exist. This,

[18] On perinoetic and dianoetic knowledge, see J. Maritain, *Distinguer pour unir, ou les degrés du savoir*, pp. 399 ff.

then, is a third amazing situation. Why do we sometimes say that the thing defined exists or can exist, whereas we know that there is no necessary connection between definitions and the existence of the thing defined?

Perhaps the three above examples can be brought to their peak in this one: we know that Caesar, who crossed the Rubicon, cannot *now* have *not* crossed the Rubicon; yet there's no knowledge identity between Caesar and his crossing *before* the event. Why do we make that knowledge connection of Caesar and his crossing *now*, and absolutely, but not *before* the event?[14]

It begins to look suspiciously as though there is a connecting knowledge rod between unidentical factors in our knowledge; only, that rod cannot, it seems, quite make the connection. That the rod is there is apparent: we know that John *does* shave, that a subject *is* its necessary predicates, that a man *is* a rational animal which exists or can exist; we know that Caesar *is* the one who crossed the Rubicon. That the rod does not seem quite to make the connection is also apparent: we know that John is not identically his shaving, that a subject is not identically its necessary predicates, and that a rational animal is not identically that which exists or can exist; we know, lastly, that to know Caesar is not necessarily to know the one who crossed the Rubicon until after we know he did cross. What is that rod which always connects our knowledge of two unidentical factors so as to make them one, loosely one at first (in our knowledge that John is shaving), then more tightly (in our knowledge that anyone-like-John is all his necessary predicates), then tighter still (in our knowledge that the *definiendum* is its definition), then so tightly that nothing, absolutely nothing, can split those factors (in our knowledge that the one who crossed the Rubicon cannot *now* not have crossed)?

---

[14] On the necessary and contingent event, see St. Thomas, *Sum. Theol.*, I, 86, 3, *Resp.*; 19, 3, *Resp.*; 82, 1, *Resp.*; *In I Periherm.*, lect. 14; *Contra Gentiles*, I, 67; II, 30; *De Pot.*, V, 3; J. Owens, C.Ss.R., "The Intelligibility of Being," *Gregorianum*, Vol. XXVI, n. 2 (1955), pp. 170–193.

Appendix to Chapter X

APPENDIX (A). The act of knowing is a qualification of the knower in terms of the known.

St. Thomas, *De Verit.*, II, 2, *Resp.:* "The perfection of each individual thing considered in itself is imperfect, being a part of the perfection of the entire universe, which arises from the sum total of the perfections of all individual things. In order that there might be some remedy for this imperfection, another kind of perfection is to be found in created things. It consists in this, that the perfection belonging to one thing is found in another. This is the perfection of a knower in so far as he knows; for something is known by a knower by reason of the fact that the thing known is, in some fashion, in the possession of the knower. Hence it is said in *The Soul* that the soul is, 'in some manner, all things,' since its nature is such that it can know all things."

St. Thomas, *Sum. Theol.*, I, 14, 1, *Resp.:* ". . . knowing beings are distinguished from nonknowing beings in that the latter possess only their own form; whereas the knowing being is naturally adapted to have also the form of some other thing, for the species of the thing known is in the knower. Hence it is manifest that the nature of a nonknowing being is more contracted and limited; whereas the nature of knowing beings has a greater amplitude and extension. That is why the Philosopher says that *the soul is in a sense all things.*"

APPENDIX (B). First and second intentions.

St. Thomas, *Sum. Theol.*, I, 28, 1, *Resp.:* ". . . in relations alone is there found something which is only in the apprehension and not in reality. This is not found in any other genus, since other genera as quantity and quality, in their strict and proper meaning, signify something inherent in a subject. But relation in its own proper meaning signifies only what refers to another. Such relation to another exists sometimes in the nature of things, as in those things which by their own very nature are ordered to each other and

have a mutual inclination. Such relations are necessarily real relations, as in a heavy body is found an inclination and order to the
center of the universe; and hence there exists in the heavy body a
certain relation in regard to the center, and the same applies to
other things. Sometimes, however, this reference to another, signified by relation, is to be found only in the apprehension of the
reason comparing one thing to another, and this is a logical relation
only; as, for instance, when reason compares man to animal as the
species to the genus. But when something proceeds from a principle
of the same nature, then both the one proceeding and the source
of procession communicate in the same order; and then they have
real relations to each other."

APPENDIX (C). The objective concept.

St. Thomas, *Contra Gentiles*, I, 53: "Understanding remains in
the one understanding, but it is related to the thing understood
because the abovementioned species, which is a principle of intellectual operation as a form, is the likeness of the thing understood.
We must further consider that the intellect, having been informed
by the species of the thing, by an act of understanding forms within
itself a certain intention of the thing understood, that is to say,
its notion, which the definition signifies. . . . Now, since the understood intention is, as it were, a terminus of intelligible operation,
it is distinct from the intelligible species that actualizes the intellect,
and that we must consider the principle of intellectual operation,
though both are a likeness of the thing understood. For, by the fact
that the intelligible species, which is the form of the intellect and the
principle of understanding, is the likeness of the external thing, it
follows that the intellect forms an intention like that thing, since
such as a thing is, such are its works. And because the understood
intention is like some thing, it follows that the intellect, by forming
such an intention, knows that thing."

St. Thomas, *Contra Gentiles*, IV, 11: "Now, I mean by the 'intention understood' what the intellect conceives in itself of the thing
understood. To be sure, in us this is neither the thing which is
understood nor is it the very substance of the intellect. But it is a

certain likeness of the thing understood conceived in the intellect, and which the exterior words signify. So, the intention itself is named the 'interior word' which is signified by the exterior word. Indeed, that the intention aforesaid is not within us the thing understood is clear from this: it is one thing to understand a thing, and another to understand the intention itself, yet the intellect does so when it reflects on its own work; accordingly, some sciences are about things, and others are about intentions understood. Now, that the intention understood is not the very intellect within us is clear from this: the act of being of the intention understood consists in its very being understood; the being of our intellect does not so consist; its being is not its act of understanding."

Suggested Reading

Knowledge as a Qualification of the Knower:

Aristotle, *De Anima*, II, 12; III, 8.
St. Thomas Aquinas, *In II de Anima*, lect. 5; *In II de Anima*, lect. 24, nn. 551, 553; *In III de Anima*, lect. 13, n. 787; *Contra Gentiles*, II, 98; IV, 11; *De Verit.*, I, 1; II, 2, 3, 14; *Sum. Theol.*, I, 14, 1; 84, 2; *In I Sent.*, d. 19, q. 5, a. 1; *De Pot.*, IX, 5; *Quodlibet.*, VII, q. 1, a. 4.
Gilson, E., *L'Être et l'essence*, pp. 248–328.
———, *Being and Some Philosophers*, pp. 190–215.
———, *Le Thomisme*, pp. 290–331.
———, *The Christian Philosophy of St. Thomas Aquinas*, pp. 207–222.
Klubertanz, G., S.J., *The Discursive Power. Sources and Doctrine of the Vis Cogitativa According to St. Thomas Aquinas*, pp. 331–346.
Maréchal, J., S.J., *Le point de départ de la métaphysique*, Vol. V, Bk. I, chs. I and II; Bk. II, Sec. I, II, III.
Maritain, J., *Distinguer pour unir, ou les degrés du savoir*, chs. III and IV.
———, *Réflexions sur l'intelligence et sur sa vie propre*, chs. I, II, and IX.
Peghaire, J., C.S.Sp., *Regards sur le connaître*.
Phelan, G., "Verum Sequitur Esse Rerum," *Mediaeval Studies*, Vol. I (1939), pp. 11–22.
Rousselot, P., S.J., *The Intellectualism of St. Thomas*, pp. 17–60.
Simon, Y., *Introduction à l'ontologie du connaître*, chs. I, II and III.
———, *Prévoir et savoir*, chs. V and VI.

Tonquédec de, J., S.J., *La critique de la connaissance*, chs. I, IV, VI, VII; Appendix, II, VII.
Wild, J., *Introduction to Realistic Philosophy*, pp. 436–439, 448–462.

Knowledge as Intentional Existence:

Aristotle, *De Anima*, II, 5; III, 8.
St. Thomas Aquinas, *In I de Anima*, lect. 4, n. 43; *In II de Anima*, lect. 5, nn. 282–284; lect. 12, n. 377; lect. 24, n. 551; *In III de Anima*, lect. 13, nn. 787–791; *De Verit.*, II, 2; VIII, 6, 8; *Q.D. de Anima*, a. 20; *De Pot.*, IX, 5; *In VI Metaph.*, lect. 4, n. 1234; *Quodlibet.*, VII, q. 1, a. 2; VII, q. 1, a. 4; *Contra Gentiles*, I, 53; *Sum. Theol.*, I, 84, 2.
John of St. Thomas, *Ars Logica*, Pars II, q. 21, a. 4.
Cajetan, *In II de Anima*, 6, B 133b; *In Sum. Theol.*, I, 55, 3; 79, 2.
Maritain, J., *Distinguer pour unir, ou les degrés du savoir*, ch. III and Annexe I.
Simon, Y., *Introduction à l'ontologie du connaître*, pp. 13–39.

First and Second Intentions:

Aristotle, *Topics*, I, chs. 5–6; *Categories*, ch. 5.
St. Thomas Aquinas, *In I Post. Anal.*, lect. 20, n. 5; *De Pot.*, VII, 6, 9; *In IV Metaph.*, lect. 1, n. 540; lect. 4, n. 574; *De Ente et Essentia*, ch. I.
Cajetan, *In Sum. Theol.*, I, 28, 1.
John of St. Thomas, *Ars Logica*, Pars II, q. 1, a. 3; Pars II, q. 2, a. 1 and a. 2.

Objective Concept:

St. Thomas Aquinas, *De Pot.*, VII, 9; VIII, 1; *Quodlibet.*, V, q. 5, a. 2; *Sum. Theol.*, I, 34, 1, ad 2; *Contra Gentiles*, I, 53; IV, 11.
Cajetan, *In Sum. Theol.*, I, 34, 1, ad 2; *In De Ente et Essentia*, c. I, q. 2.
John of St. Thomas, *De Anima*, Pars IV, q. 11, a. 2; *Ars Logica*, Pars II, q. 2, a. 2.
Lonergan, B., S.J., "The Concept of Verbum in the Writings of St. Thomas Aquinas," *Theological Studies*, Vol. VII (1946), pp. 349–392; Vol. VIII (1947), pp. 35–79, 404–444; Vol. X (1949), pp. 3–40, 359–393.
Maritain, J., *An Introduction to Logic*, pp. 17–19.
———, *Réflexions sur l'intelligence et sur sa vie propre*, pp. 9–77.
Peghaire, J., C.S.Sp., *Intellectus et Ratio selon S. Thomas d'Aquin*, pp. 14 ff.

Our Knowledge of Contingent Being

Perhaps the questions posed in the last chapter may be better answered if the answers are given in the reverse order to the questions.

We ask then, first, why our knowledge that Caesar crossed the Rubicon is as hard a knowledge unit now as is the fact itself—now? How explain that the most contingent feature in the history of being, namely, being's history and our knowledge of its history, are both necessary once history is in being, but not before?

This much is clear to start with: both history and our knowledge of history are irreversible, necessary; yet nothing in history or in our knowledge of history need have been. Caesar need not have crossed the river, and if he had not, we need not have known it.[1] Observe, secondly, that there is no need to ask our question at all, provided we are content to stay upon a certain level of being and of our knowledge thereof, quite as there is no need to ask why we

---

[1] Events which occur by the necessities of nature are not historical events. Thus, that water boils at 212° sea level (by a necessity of nature) is not an historical event, the actual boiling of the water. The enumeration that this water, and that, and that, etc., boiled at 212° sea level is indeed a kind of history, but it would be a repetitious and boring history. An historian at least tries to find the necessary causes of water boiling, and even if he cannot quite succeed, because the causes of the event are not all determinate, he is nonetheless engaged in a laudable task which will find its full confirmation in prophecy or revelation and in the beatific vision. See B. Muller-Thym, "Of History as a Calculus Whose Term is Science," *The Modern Schoolman*, Vol. XIX, n. 3 (March 1942), pp. 41–47; Vol. XIX, n. 4 (May 1942), pp. 73–76.

digest our dinner, provided we are content with digesting it. Any life, including the life of science, can be led without any direct help or hindrance from metaphysics. However, once the question is asked about the source of necessities in being, only metaphysics can answer the question, and when metaphysics does, the scientist if not his science will benefit immensely from the answer. Just so, we sometimes need doctors in order to keep our digestive system a going concern.

Two answers, clearly, are unsatisfactory, the first of which is the following. The contingent in being, viz., that which can be and also can not-be, is really if we only knew better, necessary, viz., that which must be. Thus, if we only knew Caesar fully, we should have known him for the Rubicon crossing chap he was all along, even before he crossed the river. Though espoused by some of the greatest names in philosophy, this answer won't work,[2] because we know that history is not science. Nothing in science will assure that there is, e.g., water, at sea level, over a fire, boiling. Science simply states that if the conditions are present, water will boil at $212°$ sea level. That the conditions be present is a matter of history, not a

---

[2] On the identification of contingent and necessary being in Greek thought, see Parmenides, *On Truth*, in M. C. Nahm, *Selections from Early Greek Philosophy*, N.Y., Crofts, 1941, pp. 113-117. Plato's development of this point may be found in *Phaedo*, 65a-66e, 76a-77c, 101c-e; *Phaedrus*, 247c; *Republic*, IX, 585a-d; *Philebus*, 15a ff.; *Sophistes*, 254b-257c; *Parmenides*, 132a-d.

For St. Thomas' criticism of Plato in identifying the way of understanding and the way of existing, see *De Spir. Creat.*, a. 3, *Resp.*; a. 9, *ad 6*; *Sum. Theol.*, I, 84, 1, *Resp.*; 85, 3, *ad 4*; *In I Metaph.*, lect. 10, n. 158.

On the identification of thought and being in modern thought, see Descartes, *Reply to Objections* II, prop. 1 and defin. 9; ed. Haldane and Ross, Vol. II, pp. 57, 53; *Discours de la méthode*; ed. Adam-Tannery, *Oeuvres complètes*, Vol. VII, Pt. II, p. 359.

See also Berkeley, *A Treatise Concerning the Principles of Human Understanding*, nn. 33, 24, 3; ed. A. Fraser, Vol. I, pp. 275, 258-259; Leibniz, *The Monadology*, nn. 7, 80; in *The Monadology and Other Philosophical Writings*, tr. R. Latta, London, Oxford University Press, 1925, pp. 219, 263-264; Spinoza, *Ethics*, Pt. I, prop. 11; Pt. II, props. 1-3; tr. W. White and A. Stirling, Edinburgh, Oxford University Press, 1927, pp. 9-12, 47-48; Kant, *Critique of Pure Reason*; in T. M. Greene, *Kant Selections*, N.Y., Scribners, 1929, p. 2; *Prolegomena to any Future Metaphysics*; tr. P. Lucas, Manchester, University Press, 1953, pp. 9-10; Hegel, *The History of Philosophy*; tr. E. Haldane, *Hegel's Lectures on the History of Philosophy*, London, Routledge and Kegan Paul, 1955, Vol. I, pp. 19-20.

matter of science. The second unsatisfactory answer is this: there is nothing necessary in history even after it has occurred. This answer won't work because it puts a surd, or better, an absurd into our thinking. It denies the existence of science. Now, we *know* there is science about contingent beings: water *does* boil at 212° sea level, cattle *are* ruminants, and so on. No wonder the modern existentialists,[3] who proffer this second explanation, are themselves so nauseated by it. Any serious attempt to get along without necessities in contingent beings is a kind of metaphysical foretaste of hell.

Hypothetical Solution of the Problem

Our question can be answered if two conditions can be posited. The first condition is this: if the existential status *(esse naturae)* of history and of our knowledge of history *(esse intentionale)* are quite distinct from any and every quidditative factor in history and

[3] See J.-P. Sartre, *La nausée*, Paris, Gallimard, 1938. See also Sartre's *Being and Nothingness*; tr. H. Barnes, N.Y., Philosophical Library, 1956, p. 1: "Being will be disclosed to us by some kind of immediate access—boredom, nausea, etc., and ontology will be the description of the phenomenon of being as it manifests itself; that is, without intermediacy." P. lxviii: "An existent phenomenon can never be derived from another existent *qua* existent. This is what we shall call the contingency of being-in-itself. . . . Being-in-itself is never either possible or impossible. It is." P. 619: "We, indeed apply the term 'metaphysical' to the study of individual processes which have given birth to this world as a concrete and particular totality." See *Existentialism*; tr. B. Frechtman, N.Y., Philosophical Library, 1947, pp. 25-27: "When we speak of forlornness, a term Heidegger was fond of, we mean only that God does not exist and that we have to face all the consequences of this. . . . The existentialist, on the contrary, thinks it very distressing that God does not exist, because all possibility of finding values in a heaven of ideas disappears along with Him; there can no longer be an *a priori* Good, since there is no infinite and perfect consciousness to think it. Nowhere is it written that the Good exists, that we must be honest, that we must not lie; because the fact is we are on a plane where there are only men. Dostoievsky said, 'If God didn't exist, everything would be possible.' That is the very starting point of existentialism. Indeed, everything is permissible if God does not exist, and as a result man is forlorn, because neither within him nor without does he find anything to cling to."
See also S. Kierkegaard, *The Sickness unto Death*; tr. W. Lowrie, Princeton, Princeton University Press, 1946, pp. 32-42; *The Concept of Dread*; tr. W. Lowrie, Princeton, Princeton University Press, 1944, pp. 50-56, 83-98; M. Heidegger, the chapter entitled "What is Metaphysics?" in *Existence and Being*, tr. R. F. C. Hull and A. Crick, ed. W. Brock, Chicago, Regnery, 1949.

our knowledge of history; or, to put it in another way, if there *are* no quidditative factors in history or in our knowledge of history, unless they are and we know them to be in *esse*, real or intentional. The first condition depends upon this second one: if the *esse* of history *(esse naturae)* and of our knowledge of history *(esse intentionale)* derive from an uncaused cause of both "*esse*'s." The first condition is related to the second as that which, posited in any case as given, must be posited as proved when it is proved that there is an *esse* which is not involved in being a quidditative nature at all, but which is the cause of the *esse* by which quidditative natures exist. In order to solve our problem, then, we need to know, not that history exists, nor that, once in existence, history is necessary. These points are both given. We need to know, rather, that the *esse* of history derives from an uncaused cause of history. Once that uncaused cause of history is proved, our problem is solved.

The reader's reaction to such a claim will doubtless be this: "It *is!* Why?" It is solved because it is the explanation of history, and none other is. The only other attempted explanations are the ones already mentioned: history is necessary in its causes, or, history is not necessary even when there is history. Neither of those two explanations works, for the first denies contingency, the second necessity. Nor will it do to state the problem and then walk away from it.[4] That the explanation suggested explains must now be established.

We need to know why an event, identical with itself, is not identical with the *esse* by which it *is* itself. The first point, namely, that an event is identical with itself, is given in the self-identity of a being. The second point, that an historical event is not identical with the *esse* by which it is itself, is also given so far forth as we all see that if *esse* were identical with or absorbed by a given "self," there could not be another given "self." Against the fact, for there are many beings. Both of these points are the first condition, mentioned a while back, for there being a solution. That first condition, then, is the accidentality of the relation of an event in

---

[4] Plato knew the problem, and he had his answer to it: The Greek God *mixed* the contingent and the necessary. See *Timaeus,* 53b–c. This is very good, but loose talk.

esse with the *esse* by which that event exists, and we are here merely noting or acknowledging that accidental or non-necessary relation of an event in *esse* to its *esse*. This of course leaves that accidental *esse* of an historical event unexplained. Now comes the second condition which, if validated, would explain the event: if the event's *esse*, accidentally related to the event, is necessarily related to a cause of the event's *esse*. This necessary relation of an event's *esse* to its cause would explain the event's existence, and once that is explained, then *ipso facto* that event in *esse* must necessarily be in *esse*.[5] This explanation of course leaves unexplained the uncaused cause of *esse*, but whoever tried to or can explain that? What we are trying to explain is the *esse* of an event which need not be, but which, once it is, must be.

The Solution to the Problem of Our Knowledge of Contingent Being

It remains to posit the second hypothesis: the contingent is caused to be.

[5] On the necessary relation between the *esse* of a being and its cause, see St. Thomas, *Sum. Theol.*, I, 2, 3, *Resp.*; 3, 4, *Resp.*; 44, 1, *Resp.* and *ad* 1; *Contra Gentiles*, I, 22; II, 15. See especially *Contra Gentiles*, I, 15: "We find in the world, furthermore, certain beings, those namely that are subject to generation and corruption, which can be and not-be. But what can be has a cause because, since it is equally related to two contraries, namely, being and non-being, it must be owing to some cause that being accrues to it. Now, as we have proved by the reasoning of Aristotle, one cannot proceed to infinity among causes. We must therefore posit something that is a necessary being. Every necessary being, however, either has the cause of its necessity in an outside source or, if it does not, it is necessary through itself. But one cannot proceed to infinity among necessary beings the cause of whose necessity lies in an outside source. We must therefore posit a first necessary being, which is necessary through itself."

De Ente et Essentia, c. IV; Marietti, n. 27: "Everything, then, which is such that its act of existing is other than its nature must needs have its act of existing from something else. And since every being which exists through another is reduced, as to its first cause, to one existing in virtue of itself, there must be some being which is the cause of the existing of all things because it itself is the act of existing alone. If that were not so, we would proceed to infinity among causes, since, as we have said, every being which is not the act of existing alone has a cause of its existence. . . . This is the First Cause, God."

The meaning of the proposition must be made more explicit. "The contingent" means that which can be and can also not-be; or, if one prefers, "the contingent" means that which is, but can not-be; or, that which is not, but can-be. We derive the notion of the contingent from the fact that some things were, but are not now—*fuit Ilyium, fuit Troia . . .*; and so some things *can* not-be, because they *are* not any more. We can also derive the notion of the contingent from the fact that some things are not now, but will be, e.g., of two contradictories before the event, one of them *must* be, and so it *can* be. To recur to our example, before the event this disjunction was true: *erit Ilyium vel non erit*, and so one of those contradictories *can* be, because one of them *must* be. Now the predicate, "is caused" is not true of the contingent event upon the score that the contingent event is contingent. Certainly, that which is not but can be, is not caused until it exists, and so of the contingent which is not but can-be, one cannot say that "is caused" is a predicate of that event until it *is* caused. Nor, even when the contingent *is* caused or exists, can one say that the predicate "is caused" is true of that contingent, which is, but can not-be, upon the score that the event must be caused, because then the contingent, being necessarily caused, necessarily exists. To say this is to say that the event cannot not be. Against the fact. In sum, there is no formal identity between the subject, "contingent," and the predicate "is caused." The contingent is not caused because it is contingent; rather, because the contingent's *esse* is not necessary, therefore it is caused to be. Why?

For this reason: either there is no being which simply happens to be in *esse* or there is a cause of that being; but there is a being which simply happens to be in *esse;* therefore there is a cause of it. Concerning the major premise, the disjunction is valid only if there is a necessary relation, not between "what happens to be in *esse*" and its *esse,* but between the accidental *esse* of a being in *esse* and a cause of that being. For, if a being is posited which exists only because it is caused to exist, you must posit that cause.[6] Such is the

6 See St. Thomas, *Sum. Theol.,* I, 44, 1, *ad* 2: "The reason why an efficient cause is required is not merely because the effect can not-be, but because the effect would not be if the cause were not." *Contra Gentiles,* II, 52: "To be caused by another does not appertain to a being inasmuch as it is being;

case of an experienced being: it is a being which exists only because it is caused to exist. We are now at the heart of the matter: why is an experienced being caused to be? See well that the question is not, why *must* an experienced being be? It need not be at all. Nor is the question this: why *must* the experienced being be caused to be? It need not be caused to be at all. The question is: why *is* an experienced being caused to be? The answer is, it is caused to be, precisely because its own *esse* is not necessary, and it does exist. It is existential act which is in question, and since existential act *(esse)* as such is not *per se* caused or uncaused, contingent or necessary,[7] the question whether that act is caused or uncaused is alone pertinent. *When* is that act caused? In reply, once more, that act is caused to be when it may or may not be in the subject of that act, and nevertheless *is* in that subject. In other words, *because* there

---

otherwise, every being would be caused by another, so that we should have to proceed to infinity in causes—an impossibility, as was shown in Book I of this work. Therefore, that being which is subsisting must be uncaused. Therefore, no caused being is its own being."

[7] On existential act, see St. Thomas, *In I Sent.*, d. 8, q. 4, a. 1, *ad* 1; In *IV Metaph.*, lect. 5, n. 593; *In V Metaph.*, lect. 9, n. 889; *In Boet. de Trin.*, V, 3, *Resp.*; *Q.D. de Anima*, a. 9, *Resp.*; *De Sub. Sep.*, c. VI, in *Opuscula Philosophica*; ed. Marietti, n. 71; *Contra Gentiles*, I, 25-26; II, 52; *Sum. Theol.*, I, 3, 4, *ad* 1; 8, 1, *Resp.* See especially *De Ente et Essentia*, ch. V; Marietti, n. 30: "But just as existing-in-general [*esse commune*] does not include in its notion any addition, so neither does it imply any exclusion of addition; otherwise, nothing could be understood to exist in which something would be added over and above the act of existing." *De Pot.*, VII, 2, *ad* 9: "Nothing that is outside the range of being can be added to *being;* for nothing is outside its range except *nonbeing*, which can be neither form nor matter." *De Verit.*, I, 1, *Resp.*: ". . . nothing can be added to being as though it were something not included in being—in a way that a difference is added to a genus or an accident to a subject—for every reality is essentially a being. . . . Some predicates may be said to add to being inasmuch as they express a mode of being not expressed by the term *being.*" *In I Periherm.*, lect. 5, n. 73: ". . . hoc verbum est consignificat compositionem, quia non eam principaliter significat, sed ex consequenti; significat enim primo illud quod cadit in intellectu per modum actualitatis absolute: nam est, simpliciter dictum, significat in actu esse; et ideo significat per modum verbi. Quia vero actualitas, quam principaliter significat hoc verbum est, est communiter actualitas omnis formae, vel actus substantialis vel accidentalis, inde est quod cum volumus significare quamcumque formam vel actum actualiter inesse alicui subiecto, significamus illud per hoc verbum est, vel simpliciter vel secundum quid: simpliciter quidem secundum praesens tempus; secundum quid autem secundum alia tempora. Et ideo ex consequenti hoc verbum est significat compositionem."

is no absolutely necessary connection between Caesar's crossing and the existence of that crossing, and *because* nevertheless there *is* a connection, you must posit a "connector" or cause of the existence of that crossing, God, the only cause of *esse*.[8]

Why only God? The question is asked because, at this point, the demonstration does not determine whether the cause, though necessary in order to explain the existence of the contingent event, has the same sort of necessity as the event itself, viz., a factual necessity. The answer is, only God or God alone is the cause of the contingent because, being *only esse*, He *alone* is *esse*.

If God were not only *esse*, there would be an accidental relation of Him to His *esse*, just as there is in the contingent; this act of God's in turn would then have to be caused to be, just as the contingent's existential act is caused to be; and so He would not be the cause of *esse*, as He was proved to be. So, there is no subject factor in Him which is not His *esse*, He is only *esse*. Now, one who is only *esse* is alone *esse*,[9] because otherwise there would be two, at least, "only *esse*'s" or causes of *esse*. A contradiction in terms, one cause of *esse*, precisely because it *is* the cause of *esse*, being the cause of the other's *esse*, which other's *esse* is and is not a cause of *esse* if its own *esse* is caused and uncaused.

Last, the demonstration indicates that the cause of *esse* causes

[8] See H. Schwartz, "Plato, Aristotle, St. Thomas and Univocity," *The New Scholasticism*, Vol. XXVII, n. 4 (October 1953), p. 381. Another argument for the existence of God could also be constructed from the possible (the contingent which is not but can be), thus: the possibility of existing lies in a cause-able-to-create, even though the cause does not create. See Chapter IV, pp. 72-78. See also St. Thomas, *Sum. Theol.*, I, 44, 1, *ad* 1; *De Pot.*, III, 1, *obj.* 17 and *ad* 17; III, 5, *obj.* 1 and *ad* 1; *De Verit.*, II, 8, *Resp.*; III, 3, *ad* 3; III, 6, *Resp.* and *ad* 3; *Sum. Theol.*, I, 15, 3, *Resp.*

[9] Being only *esse*, God alone is *esse*. See St. Thomas, *De Ente et Essentia*, c. IV; Marietti, n. 26: "The act of existing is other than essence or quiddity, unless, perhaps, there is a being whose quiddity is its very act of existing. And there can be only one such being, the First Being. . . . But, should there exist some being which is simply the act of existing, so that the act of existing be itself subsistent, a difference cannot be added to this act of existing. Otherwise, it would not be purely and simply the act of existing, but the act of existing plus a certain form." *De Ente et Essentia*, ch. V, n. 30: "God is purely and simply the act of existing, . . . The act of existing which is God is such that no addition can be made to it. . . . the First Cause, being purely and simply the act of existing, is individualized by its unalloyed perfection."

freely,[10] for if there were coercion in the cause of *esse* to cause,
that coercive factor, compelling the cause of *esse* to cause, would
make the contingent's *esse* necessary. Against the fact, for the
contingent's *esse* is not necessary. One may also see the point from
the aspect of God's *esse*. If God had to create, He would not be
only *esse*, as was proved; He would also be *esse* together with a hav-
ing-to-create-feature in His *esse*, whereas there is no feature except
esse in Him Who is only *esse*.

And so, God is a necessary being, because He is; not the other
way about, viz., He is, because He is necessary. And again, God is
known to exist and to be a necessary being because He is known to
cause contingent being; but that "because" clause is merely the
reason why we *know* God exists and is necessary and causes; it is not
the reason why He is, is necessary, or why He causes. So too, one
might add, for contingents: they neither exist nor are they contingents because we *know* they exist and are contingents; rather,
they are known to exist and to be contingent because they exist so as
not to have their *esse* identical with them, since they can be and
also not-be. Now, that existential act of theirs cannot be located
as in a source either in them or in our knowledge of them, but only
in a cause of their existential act and in our knowledge that there
is such a cause. In sum, contingency is a way of existing, and, pretty
much like any other way of existing, it cannot be explained upon
the score that existential act is identical with that way of existing,
for then there would be literally no two ways of existing, not even
the contingent ways, because the identification of "is" with the contingent way of existing would force the contingent way of existing
to be necessary. Certainly, if to exist is to exist contingently, and if
there *is* an existent, it follows that contingents must exist. Against
the fact. No, there are contingents because their existential act is

[10] See St. Thomas, *Sum. Theol.*, I, 19, 3–4; *De Pot.*, I, 5, *Resp.*; III, 15, *Resp.*;
Contra Gentiles, II, 22: "God's power is through itself the cause of being, and
the act of being is His proper effect, . . . Hence, His power reaches out to
all things with which the notion of being is not incompatible; for, if God's
power were limited to some particular effect, He would not be through Himself the cause of a being as such, but of this particular being." *Contra Gentiles*,
II, 23: "The power of God, however, is supreme over all things. It therefore
acts on all things by will, not by natural necessity."

caused, and when we know them as caused, we know the source, or have the explanation, of the contingency and necessity which we knew all along. Thus, we know that contingents are contingents pretty much as we know that God exists, viz., by a demonstration which at one and the same time shows that *that* is caused which has an uncaused cause. Before the demonstration, we know only that beings exist with an existential act related to them accidentally. After the demonstration, we know that things exist as contingents which are dependent upon God.

Suggested Reading

The Necessary and Contingent Event:

St. Thomas Aquinas, *Sum. Theol.*, I, 86, 3; 19, 3; 82, 1; *In I Periherm.*, lect. 14; *Contra Gentiles*, I, 67; II, 30; *De Pot.*, V, 3.

Muller-Thym, B., "Of History as a Calculus Whose Term is Science," *The Modern Schoolman*, Vol. XIX, n. 3 (March 1942), pp. 41-47; Vol. XIX, n. 4 (May 1942), pp. 73-76.

Owens, J., C.Ss.R., "The Intelligibility of Being," *Gregorianum*, Vol. XXVI, n. 2 (1955), pp. 170-193.

The Necessary Relation Between the "ESSE" of a Being and Its Cause:

St. Thomas Aquinas, *Sum. Theol.*, I, 2, 3; 3, 4; 15, 3; 19, 3-4; 44, 1; *Contra Gentiles*, I, 15 and 22; II, 15; II, 22-23; II, 52; *De Ente et Essentia*, ch. IV and V; *De Pot.*, I, 5; III, 1 and 5; III, 15; *De Verit.*, II, 8; III, 3 and 6.

Schwartz, H., "Plato, Aristotle, St. Thomas and Univocity," *The New Scholasticism*, Vol. XXVII, n. 4 (October 1953), pp. 373-403.

Existential Act:

St. Thomas Aquinas, *In I Sent.*, d. 8, q. 4, a. 1, *ad* 1; *In I Periherm.*, lect. 5, n. 73; *In IV Metaph.*, lect. 5, n. 593; *In V Metaph.*, lect. 9, n. 889; *In Boet. de Trin.*, V, 3, *Resp.*; *Q.D. de Anima*, a. 9, *Resp.*; *De Sub. Sep.*, c. VI; *Contra Gentiles*, I, 25-26; II, 52; *Sum. Theol.*, I, 3, 4, *ad* 1; 8, 1, *Resp.*; *De Ente et Essentia*, ch. V; *De Pot.*, VII, 2, *ad* 9; *De Verit.*, I, 1, *Resp.*

XII · ANALOGY

The Analogue

We now seem to have left far behind our original question, how does being stand in our knowledge of being? Not for a moment. We know now that being is known to be whatever exists *and*, when God is demonstrated, also a cause of whatever exists.

Suppose, though, that one does not know or is not thinking of the cause of being, how does being stand in one's knowledge of being *then?* It stands as knowledge of an analogue.

An analogue is known existential act, whether that act be later known as caused or uncaused, contingent or necessary, of a kind or not of a kind, the existential act of this, that, or the other being. This knowledge of existential act is like a reception committee awaiting the advent of the knowledge of any and all beings. There is no other reception committee. To change the figure, our knowledge of existential act is like a biological medium in which alone would thrive all living cultures; only, the medium here is immaterial and the cultures are absolutely everything there is. Thus, if we ask, is God known in that knowledge medium before He is proved to exist? the answer is yes, He is known as a cause is known before it is known that there *is* a cause, or, as a cause is known in its effect before we know that the effect *is* an effect. One may see the matter this way: one's future and as yet unknown wife or husband, and children of course, are already known when one knows existential act. Certainly, one's as yet unknown wife or husband, and children,

will not fall short, when they are known, of being known as beings
—let us hope. Recall the remark of the flustered nurse to the new,
anxious and expectant father, "congratulations, it's a baby." Of
course. What else? Just so, presently unknown beings are presently
known in the knowledge of existential act, because if they were not,
they wouldn't be recognized as beings when they came along. And
yet, not quite "just so." Our expectant knowledge of unknown
beings would not be belied or excessively astonished no matter what
turned up, a stone baby for example, for a stone baby is also a being.

Obviously, so to know one's future wife or husband or God for
that matter, is pretty thin knowledge of them. Certainly. Expectancy
is not as rich as fulfillment. The promise is not the gift. And yet
the gift here never belies the promise. Absolutely everything will
fit into that expectant knowledge, or else it won't be a being, and
so it won't be known at all. As compared, then, with its fulfillment,
our knowledge of existential act is unspeakably poor; as a medium
into which will fit, or not at all, absolutely everything, our knowledge of existential act is unspeakably rich. The capital, which is our
knowledge of existential act, is literally infinite in its resources; the
checks we draw against that capital are piddling, even when we
demonstrate God.

The Analogue and the Analogy of Being

The knowledge of existential act is knowledge of an analogue, a
knowledge which anticipates the knowledge of absolutely everything which can be known: caused or uncaused being, contingent or
necessary being, being of any and all kinds, real or intentional being.[1]

[1] On the anticipative knowledge of existential act, see Aristotle, De Anima,
III, 8, 431b 21: "Because the understanding of being is primary for the intellect,
the intellect is able to know all that is included in being, and therefore the
soul is in a way all existing things." See also St. Thomas, De Verit., I, 1, Resp.;
II, 2, Resp.; De Ente et Essentia, Introd. and c. I; Sum. Theol., I, 5, 2, Resp.;
14, 1, Resp.; Contra Gentiles, II, 21: "The act of being is the first effect, and
this is evident by reason of the universal presence of this act. It follows that
the proper cause of the act of being is the first and universal agent, namely,
God." Sum. Theol., I-II, 94, 2, Resp.: "A certain order is to be found in those

When from evidence or proof the knowledge of definite, particular beings answers the (anticipatory) knowledge of the analogue, then we have the analogy of being. The analogy of being is a known similar and dissimilar relation of each known being or analogate to its analogue.[2] Thus, the way x-analogate is related to its *own esse*,

---

things that are apprehended by men. For that which first falls under apprehension is *being*, the understanding of which is included in all things whatsoever a man apprehends."

This knowledge of existential act may be compared to the knowledge of first principles from which all other knowledge is derived. See *De Verit.*, XVI, 1, *Resp.*

[2] Aristotle discusses the analogy of being in *Metaphysics*, IV (Γ), 2, 1003a 32–1003b 15; XI (K), 3, 1060b 31–1061a 17. See Appendix A of this chapter. For St. Thomas' treatment of the analogy of being, see *In IV Metaph.*, lect. 1, n. 535; *In V Metaph.*, lect. 8, n. 879; *In XI Metaph.*, lect. 3, n. 2197; *In I Sent.*, d. 35, q. 1, a. 4, *Sol.*; *De Pot.*, III, 4, *ad* 9; VII, 7, *Resp.*; *Contra Gentiles*, I, 32–33; II, 15; *Sum. Theol.*, I, 12, 1, *ad* 4; *De Princ. Nat.*, c. 6, nn. 365–367.

St. Thomas lists three kinds of analogy in *In I Sent.*, d. 19, q. 5, a. 2, *ad* 1: "Ad primum igitur dicendum quod aliquid dicitur secundum analogiam tripliciter vel *secundum intentionem tantum, et non secundum esse;* et hoc est quando una intentio refertur ad plura per prius et posterius, quae tamen non habet esse nisi in uno; sicut intentio sanitatis refertur ad animal, urinam et dietam diversimode, secundum prius et posterius; non tamen secundum diversum esse, quia esse sanitatis non est nisi in animali. *Vel secundum esse et non secundum intentionem;* et hoc contingit quando plura parificantur in intentione alicuius communis, sed illud commune non habet esse unius rationis in omnibus, sicut omnia corpora parificantur in intentione corporeitatis. . . . *Vel secundum intentionem et secundum esse;* et hoc est quando neque parificatur in intentione communi neque in esse; sicut ens dicitur de substantia et accidente; et de talibus oportet quod natura communis habeat aliquod esse in unoquoque eorum de quibus dicitur, sed differens secundum rationem majoris vel minoris perfectionis. Et similiter dico, quod veritas, et bonitas, et omnia huiusmodi dicuntur analogice de Deo et creaturis. Unde oportet quod secundum suum esse omnia haec in Deo sint, et in creaturis secundum rationem majoris perfectionis et minoris; . . ."

For an interpretation of the above kinds of analogy, see John of St. Thomas, *Cursus Philosophicus, Ars Logica*, Pars II, q. 13, a. 3; Reiser, t. I, pp. 482–484; Cajetan, *In De Ente et Essentia*, q. 3, nn. 18, 21; *De Nominum Analogia. De Conceptu Entis;* ed. P. N. Zammit, O.P., Romae, Institutum "Angelicum," 1934, especially c. I, n. 6; c. II, nn. 19–20; c. III, n. 23. Cajetan calls analogy *secundum intentionem tantum et non secundum esse* the analogy of attribution; analogy *secundum esse et non secundum intentionem* the analogy of inequality; analogy *secundum intentionem et secundum esse* the analogy of proportionality. For a criticism of Cajetan's notion of *esse*, see E. Gilson. "Cajétan et l'existence," *Tijdschrift voor Philosophie*, Vol. XV (1953), pp. 267–287; A. Maurer, C.S.B., "St. Thomas and the Analogy of Genus," *The New Scholasticism*, Vol. XXIX, n. 2 (April, 1955), pp. 127–144.

St. Thomas discusses the analogy of cause to effect in *De Verit.*, II, 11, *Resp.*; XXIII, 7, *ad* 9. See Appendix (B) of this chapter. For St. Thomas' distinction between univocal, equivocal and analogous predication, see *Contra Gentiles*, I,

viz., by being the x-subject of that *esse*, is like the way y-analogate is related to *its* own *esse*, viz., by being the y-analogate of that *esse;* yet, because x's *esse* is not y's, those relations are unidentical, dissimilar, unlike.[3]

The Source of Our Knowledge of the Analogue and of Its Analogy

We may now ask in a different context the same question we asked a while back. A while back we asked what was the source of our knowledge of the contingent and necessary. We may now ask the same question in a different context: what is the source of our knowledge of the analogue and of its analogy? The answer is: that source is our knowledge that there are many beings, and that they are caused to be. It is as pertinent now as then to remark that the knowledge of the analogue and of its analogy is a knowledge with which we are all endowed and which we all use, even without having to account for the matter—like our knowledge of the necessity and contingency of history, or like M. Jourdain's prose, which he always spoke without knowing it was prose. Nevertheless, it may not be useless to redescribe in the context of analogy the source of our analogous knowledge. It is that source which assures us that the *esse* which we all know as analogal *must* be analogal.

34; *De Pot.*, VII, 7, *Resp.*; *Sum. Theol.*, I, 13, 5, *Resp.* See Appendix (C) of this chapter.

St. Thomas' notion of the analogy of being is discussed in the following works. M.T.-L. Penido, *Le rôle de l'analogie en théologie dogmatique*, Paris, Vrin, 1931, pp. 11–78, 85–87, 96, 134 ff.; G. B. Phelan, *St. Thomas and Analogy*, Milwaukee, Marquette University Press, 1941; E. L. Mascall, *Existence and Analogy*, N. Y., Longmans, Green, 1949, ch. V; H. Lyttkens, *The Analogy between God and the World*, Uppsala, Almquist & Wiksells, 1952, pp. 18–58, 164–175; J. F. Anderson, *The Bond of Being*, St. Louis, Herder, 1949, chs. I, VIII, XIII, XVII, XXII; J. Maritain, *Distinguer pour unir, ou les degrés du savoir*, pp. 821–826; E. Gilson, *Le Thomisme*, pp. 150–160; *The Christian Philosophy of St. Thomas Aquinas*, pp. 105, 360–361; R. Arnou, S.J., *Metaphysica Generalis*, pp. 95–109; L.-B. Geiger, O.P., *La participation dans la philosophie de s. Thomas d'Aquin*, pp. 77–84, 156–217, 238–258, 365–398.

[3] In mathematics, the relations of a half, e.g., to its double, whether in arithmetic or in geometry, are identical relations, not analogical—except by a loose usage of the term.

The Analogue and Analogy in Knowledge
Before the Demonstration

Our knowledge of the analogue and of its analogy before the demonstration of a cause of the analogue arises as follows. Assume a true assertion, *x is or exists*. Ask now, is *x* known as an existent *because* it is known as *x?* The answer must be no, and for this reason: if to be known as an existent is to-be-known-as-*x*, no other existent but *x* could be known. Against the fact, for we know there is *y*. Thus the known status of being an existent is knowledge which is not confined to, or exhausted by, the knowledge of any existent given to our knowledge. This knowledge is the knowledge of the analogue or the transcendental.

Having thus separated[4] our knowledge of existential act from any one of its possessors so as to have that knowledge anticipatively true of any, as yet unknown, possessor, we can understand that when we predicate the verb "exists" of any existent, the "exists" is so affected by the subject of our verb that the subject is like and unlike the way any other subject of "exists" affects the same "exists." "Like," because all subjects of the verb "exists" exist, actually or possibly; "unlike," because each subject of the verb "exists" exists in a way proper to each subject: a dog exists in a doggish way, his owner in his owner's way, and God in a Goddish way. This is the analogy of being, the known likeness and unlikeness, similarity and dissimilarity, of the relations which each subject bears to its existential act: just as it is a dog which is the proper subject of the situation described in the proposition, *a dog exists,* so it is God Who is the proper subject of the situation described in the proposition, *God exists*—thus the relations are alike; yet a dog is not God, because the situation described by the verb "exists" is affected by a way of existing which is proper to each subject—thus the relations are dissimilar.

As was often remarked, it is not necessary in order to know an analogue and its analogy to be able to account for, that is

---

[4] See Chapter XI, p. 176; Chapter XII, p. 181.

prove, the matter. Whether we can account for the facts or not, it *is* a fact that we know many beings, and so we know them as different, else we wouldn't know them as many; it is a further fact that many beings are not known to be so "all-fired" different as to differ in the way that "is" differs from "is not." When, for example, we say that *x is* and *y is*, we do not mean that *x is* and *y is not*. No, we mean that *both* are, and that *x is not y*. Maybe one will succeed in explicitly extracting from that knowledge situation the realization that existential act does *not* expire in being *x*, else there would not be *y*; and yet *x*'s existential act *does* expire, so far forth as *x* is concerned, in being *x*, else it would not be *x* which exists—and maybe one will not succeed. If one does succeed in reaching that realization, one has separated *esse* from all its possessors.

The explicit knowledge-separation of existential act from all its possessors so as not to exclude any of them is not an easy insight, and indeed it is easier to get the insight than it is to maintain it. At any rate, if one does succeed in separating one's knowledge of *esse* from all of its quidditative factors so as to hold that *esse* steadily before one's eyes as not being involved or not not-involved in those quidditative factors, and so as to see eventually that when *esse is* involved in quiddity it is caused, one can talk like a metaphysician. If one does not succeed in that venture, one must talk only about quiddities in *esse*—the field of science, not about *esse* itself—the field of metaphysics. In the former case, one's discourse must assume the separation which the metaphysician practices—if one wishes to talk at all.

The Analogue and Analogy in Knowledge After the Demonstration

As we just saw, before the demonstration that there is a cause of the analogue and its analogy both in knowledge and in things, the analogue and its analogy stand in our knowledge as known existential act which anticipates the knowledge of all analogates or possessors of existential act. Such knowledge yields us this much: every being which exists or can exist is in *that* respect alike; yet not so

much alike as to cause our knowledge of one being to be identically
the knowledge of another being, otherwise we couldn't know two
beings, and we do. Thus, before the demonstration we know the
analogue and its analogy all right, even though we don't know why
existential act *must* be an analogue.

The knowledge of the cause of the analogue yields us the assurance which the anticipatory knowledge promised: there *is* a Being
which everything else is like, but Itself is not like them, because that
Being is not a possessor of existential act. Rather, It is existential act.

Consider, the demonstration of a cause is at one and the same time
a demonstration that the effect is like its cause.[5] For, the contradictory of this proposition: *every agent produces its like*, viz., *some
agents do not produce their like*, is an assertion that some effects
are not like their causes as well as that some causes are not like their
effects. In the area of causes of the generation of specific as well as
of accidental kinds of being, this amounts to saying that some generative causes as well as some generated effects are of no particular kind
whatsoever. Now, that is a contradiction in terms; for, a being of no
kind is no being. In the area of the cause of *esse*, the contradiction
is even more flagrant: a cause of *esse* is not *esse*. It remains, then, that
every cause produces its like.[6]

[5] That the demonstration of a cause is at one and the same time a demonstration that the effect is like its cause, see St. Thomas, *Sum. Theol.*, I, 4, 2,
Resp.; *De Pot.*, III, 4, ad 9; *Contra Gentiles*, I, 29; II, 16; III, 19; *Contra Gentiles*, II, 15: ". . . the order of causes necessarily corresponds to the order of
effects, since effects are commensurate with their causes. . . . Now, being is
common to everything that is. Above all causes, then, there must be a cause
whose proper action is to give being. But we have already shown in Book I
that God is the first cause. Everything that is must, therefore, be from God."
Contra Gentiles, III, 49: "It is possible to know a cause from its effect in several
ways. First, when the effect is taken as the means of knowing the existence
and character of the cause. This happens in the sciences which prove the
cause from the effect. Second, when the cause is seen in the effect itself,
inasmuch as the likeness of the cause is reflected in the effect. . . . Third, when
the very likeness of the cause in the effect is the form by which the cause is
known by its effect. . . . But by none of these ways is it possible to know from
its effect *what* the cause is, unless the effect be equal to the cause, and express
the whole power of the cause."
[6] Plato was not wholly wrong in his exemplarism. His mistake seems to
lie in his failure to locate formal causality within the framework of efficient
causality. Two apples are not related as cause to effect merely because they
are the same in kind, but the apple-effect has the apple-cause nonetheless.

The Univocal, the Universal, the Equivocal

The likeness of generated effects to their generative causes is an identical likeness in kind: the generator of a man is a man, and so also is the generated a man; and heat is heat, whether it be the heat of the heater or of the heated. Since an identical likeness in kind is described by one and the same word, the word which describes that likeness is named a univocal word, and the likeness itself may be called a quiddity or, if quiddity is viewed in relation to its many instances, a universal. Furthermore, the causes of univocal likeness, generative causes, that is, are named univocal causes. An equivocal word is one which happens to describe totally different situations, e.g., the "bark" of a dog and of a tree.

The Equivocal Cause

Sometimes a cause, though like its effect, is not like its effect in kind: a knowledge cause for instance, and some causes in nature.[7] Now, though we cannot say that medicine is in kind like the health which it causes, nor that God in kind is like the *esse* which He causes, nevertheless there is that about those causes which has what it takes to account for the kind of their effects. Belloc, in his attempt to explain Henry VIII's attraction to Ann Boleyn, remarked: "there was *that* about her." Quite. There is that about all causes which explains why their effects are such as they are, even when we don't know what the "that" is.[8]

"It is precisely by the title of an equivocal cause that God contains the effects which He creates. . . ."[9] This is why both the *esse*

Once an efficient cause has been demonstrated, one may thereafter utilize the exemplarism of a demonstrated cause as a principle of demonstration. On Plato's exemplarism, see *Phaedo*, 100b–c; *Timaeus*, 29a–32c, 53a; *Philebus*, 27a, 30d; *Laws*, X, 891b–892c.

[7] St. Thomas, *Contra Gentiles*, I, 29.

[8] See St. Thomas, *Contra Gentiles*, III, 49; *De Verit.*, II, 11, *Resp.*; E. Gilson, *Le Thomisme*, pp. 154 ff.

[9] See E. Gilson, *Le Thomisme*, p. 152.

of creatures as well as their kinds of *esse* are like God, because He is *esse*, though they are not. Creatures are *esse* only to the extent that their *esse* is a kind of being in *esse*.

And here we seem to be stumped: if creatures are like, but are not, God's *esse*, we must, it seems, either equivocate or univocate when speaking of God and creatures. We must indeed, unless the analogal is not quite equivocal. Such is the case: the analogal is not quite equivocal (*non omnino aequivoce . . .*)[10] when predicated of God and creatures. In other words, the "not quite equivocal" *is* the analogal. The "quite equivocal" simply *happens* to be the same word which describes totally different situations. The "not quite equivocal" or the separated *esse*, or its equivalents, we make designedly[11]—whether overtly as in metaphysics, or occultly as in knowledge which falls short of overt metaphysical knowledge—in order that we may understand our present as well as our eventual knowledge that things exist. Like the x in an equation which will represent an odd or even, a plus or minus number, even before we know which of the two the number is, we make the not-quite-equivocal in order to understand that it is something-which-exists which we *do* understand when we understand that something *does* exist. Separated *esse* is of course not an equational x, but it is the intellect's constant presence to *esse*, even before the intellect is fully present to *esse* in the judgment. To be able to know being, this is to be an intellect, and the actuation of that ability is twofold: a covert knowledge of being as being in *any* knowledge; an overt knowledge of being as being in metaphysical knowledge, which not only sees being as given but not identical with quiddities, but also sees it as caused.[12]

[10] See St. Thomas, *Contra Gentiles*, I, 33. See also *De Pot.*, VII, 7, *Resp.*; *Sum. Theol.*, I, 13, 5, *Resp.*; *De Verit.*, II, 11, *Resp.*; *Contra Gentiles*, I, 34; *In Boet. de Trin.*, VI, 3; J. Maritain, "Sur la doctrine de l'aséité divine," *Mediaeval Studies*, Vol. V (1943), pp. 39-50.

[11] This "design" is not the *finis operantis;* it is the *finis operis.*

[12] This point would demand a book-size development. See H. Schwartz, "Plato, Aristotle, St. Thomas and Univocity," *The New Scholasticism*, Vol. XXVII, n. 4 (October 1953), pp. 373-403; "Analogy in St. Thomas and Cajetan," *The New Scholasticism*, Vol. XXVIII, n. 2 (April 1954), pp. 127-144. Suffice it to say here that the relation of potency to act still obtains as between the intellect and its masked or overt knowledge of existential

The Components of Our Knowledge of Being

We now seem to have the pieces of our mental picture of being. First, each one of us has the covertly separated *esse* in all his knowledge. This knowledge of separated *esse* is knowledge of an analogue and, when we predicate *esse*, knowledge of the *esse*'s analogy. Second, when we overtly separate *esse* from its analogates, and eventually come to see by proof that there is a cause of *esse*, we have overt knowledge of being, viz., the knowledge that being is caused and uncaused.

Let us run through both points once more. First, if when we judge that, e.g., a man exists, we saw that to-be-an-existent is necessarily to be a man, we would never know any existent except a man. Against the fact, for we know many existents besides a man, and so we know *esse* is not identical with quiddity. On the other hand, if to know a man were *not* to know an existent, actual or possible, we would not even know a man. Against the fact, for we do know a man exists. So, quiddities are not *esse*, because quiddity is given as multiple, and *esse* of itself is neither multiple nor nonmultiple. We now have our knowledge of the analogue or separated *esse* and, when we predicate *esse*, our knowledge of analogy. Secondly, since the *esse* of quiddities is theirs (given), though not *from* them—for then quiddity would be unique whereas it is not unique (given), the *esse* of quiddities must come to them from an *esse* which is unique (proved). Thus and only thus is assured the unity of an existent or the undividedness of its quiddity from its *esse* in knowledge and in fact. Certainly, we cannot find that unity between a quiddity and its nonnecessary *esse*. We must, then, find that unity between a quiddity and its nonnecessary but given, because caused, *esse*. This amounts to saying that the source of unity is divine *esse*. We now have our demonstration that *esse* must be an analogue: the

---

act, but the potency in question here is the potency of the intellect itself. It is not a potency abstracted from matter as genus is abstracted from differences. Intellect is a power which is *capax entis*, and surely that potency is meaningless unless existential act is somehow present to it in and from its first knowledge act.

verb-predicate "exists" cannot be scientifically understood as multiple "exist's" except in relation to a unique "exist's" which causes the multiple "exist's." The "cannot be understood" means that the many and diverse relations of beings to their *esse* cannot be scientifically understood unless we know there is a unique *esse*, causative of all multiple *esse*'s.

Summary of the Solution

A philosopher is always trying to reduce plurality to unity so far forth as he can.[13] The reduction occurs in two areas: in the area of multiple acts of existing, and in the area of our knowledge of multiple acts of existing.

In the Area of Being

In the first area the reduction is accomplished thus: if the act of existing were identical with the many beings which we see do exist, it would follow that it is of the nature of those many things to exist. If such were the situation, it would not only follow that one nature is not another, as is the case; it would also follow that the nature of any one of many beings would be unique, because it would have absorbed *esse* into its own nature, and such is not the case. There are many different natures, and besides, even within one nature there are many individuals of that one nature. There is nothing unique about there being a man if there is another man; nor is there anything unique about there being Peter if he can be and also not-be. Peter certainly cannot be unique until he exists, and when he does exist, in order to be unique, he would have to possess the perquisite of being unable not to exist, just as he possesses the perquisite of being unable not to be Peter. Against the fact. In short, to exist is not the perquisite of any nature as nature. To exist is nonetheless the perquisite of any existent nature. Where, then, shall

[13] St. Thomas, *De Verit.*, V, 9, *Resp.*

we locate the source of that perquisite of any existent nature? Certainly not in nature. In a unique act of existing, then, whose "nature" is not nature but being.

In the Area of Our Knowledge of Being

Now change the ontological register of the above to the register of our *knowledge* of the above. Ask, how do many beings stand in our knowledge of the many? They stand in our knowledge of the many as recognized fulfillments of our, explicit or implicit, knowledge of separated *esse*. Those knowledge fulfillments of our expectant knowledge, which is the knowledge of separated *esse*, can be recognized from sense evidence or from proof. In either case, the knowledge fulfillments must have what it takes to answer our knowledge expectation: they must be known to be, actually or possibly, and so they are. If one cares to push on and ask, what the source is of our knowing that knowledge fulfillments fill the bill of our expectations, the answer is, that source is our knowledge that there is a cause of multiple being.

Knowledge of Analogals Versus Analogals Apart from Knowledge

The analogy of being thus seems to be a noetic version of causality. Causality explains why there are many beings. Analogy is knowledge that each being is different from each other being in the very spot in which each being is somewhat like each other one; and if, as was said, one wishes to know why analogical knowledge, which is given, must be analogical, the answer is: because we know there is a cause of many beings.[14] We see resemblances in being, and if we are to know why there are resemblances in being, we must first find out why there is any being around to be resemblant. That reason is this: beings are "around" because they are caused to be around.

[14] St. Thomas, *Sum. Theol.*, I, 13, 5, *Resp.*

Knowledge of Univocals

From the above it follows that knowledge of identities is never analogical knowledge. For example, the knowledge of many men is the knowledge of their identity in being the man-kind of being. This is not analogical but univocal knowledge. True, many men, known under the rubric of being many existents is analogical knowledge, because many men are not known as one man; knowing many "man's," however, adds up to knowing one "man."

Knowledge of Figures of Speech

Again, we often tag two operations with the same word or description, simply because it helps us to understand one or other of the operations better. For example, we say a man smiles and so do fields of grain—Vergil's *prata ridentia*. Here we are "hanging on" to the fields of grain a univocal predicate, and this analogical *use* we make of a univocal predicate is metaphorical analogy.[15] We do this in order, as was said, to help us understand better one or other of two operations. Thus, we understand better the sensation of the

---

[15] On metaphorical analogy, see St. Thomas, *Sum. Theol.*, I, 13, 6, *Resp.*: "All names applied metaphorically to God are applied to creatures primarily rather than to God, because when said of God they mean only similitudes to such creatures. For as *smiling* applied to a field means only that the field in the beauty of its flowering is like to the beauty of the human smile by proportionate likeness, so the name *lion* applied to God means only that God manifests strength in His works, as a lion in his. Thus it is clear that applied to God the signification of these names can be defined only from what is said of creatures." *Sum. Theol.*, I, 13, 9, *Resp.*: "A name is communicable in two ways, properly, and through likeness. It is properly communicable if its whole signification can be given to many; through likeness it is communicable according to some part of the signification of the name. For instance, this name *lion* is properly communicated to all beings of the same nature as *lion*; through likeness it is communicable to those who share in something of the lion's nature, as for instance courage, or strength, and such are called lions metaphorically."

See also R. Boyle, S.J., "The Nature of Metaphor," *The Modern Schoolman*, Vol. XXXI, n. 4 (May 1954), pp. 257–280; "The Nature of Metaphor: Further Considerations," *The Modern Schoolman*, Vol. XXXIV, n. 4 (May 1957), pp. 283–298.

blocked circulation in our foot when we say the foot has "fallen asleep," and it may also help us to understand better what that sensation is if we say it feels like gingerale. But if we wish to understand what falling asleep itself is, and maybe we never shall, we must either drop metaphors altogether or keep on piling them up. At bottom, figures of speech witness to our inability to understand the causes of some operation, and then we do the best we can by an analogical use of language, which is a sign of knowledge, which is a sign of things. We really don't know what makes a caterpillar crawl with a motion which looks like the crawling of a caterpillar truck. The cause of the truck's crawling we do know, because we put that cause there, but the cause of the caterpillar's crawling we don't, but it looks like a caterpillar-truck's crawling all the same. The surest sign of our inability to make some principles of nature's operations quite intelligible to ourselves is, as was said, our repeated use of figures of speech. On such occasions there's nothing else we can do.

Knowledge of Nonverbal Signs or the Analogy of Attribution

Again, at other times, we hang a univocal predicate on to a subject, as we do in figures of speech, and so we have a univocal predication, but the reason why we do so is not because we are using words or language analogically, but because we're using nonverbal signs analogically, natural signs that is. Thus, we say complexion is healthy and so is a man. But complexion is only a natural sign of health. It is not health itself. This naming of the natural signs of an attribute with the same name as the attribute itself is a univocal naming or predication and an analogy as between the natural sign (complexion) and the thing signified by that sign (health).[16] It is not the analogy of being.

[16] On the analogical use of natural signs, see St. Thomas, *In I Sent.*, d. 19, q. 5, a. 2, *ad* 1; d. 35, q. 1, a. 4, *Sol.*; *In IV Metaph.*, lect. 1, n. 537; *In XI Metaph.*, lect. 3, n. 2197; *De Pot.*, VII, 7, *Resp.*; *Contra Gentiles*, I, 32–34; II, 15; *De Princ. Nat.*, c. 6, nn. 365–367; *De Verit.*, I, 4, *Resp.*; II, 11, *Resp.*; *Sum. Theol.*,

The Analogy of Being, a Mean Between Univocity and Pure Equivocity

The analogy of being (*esse*) arises from our knowing many beings. Next, if we wish to assure ourselves why being must be analogous, we must know that being is caused to be, and upon that score every being is dissimilar and similar to every other being. Short of the knowledge that being is multiple and caused, our knowledge always involves some univocity. There is the univocity of the *universal*, e.g., of univocal words and descriptions used univocally: Peter and Paul are men. There is univocity in *words* used analogically: some music is cheerful, some sad, as persons are. There is univocity in *natural signs* used analogically: complexion is healthy and so is a person. But the multiplicity of being impedes univocity as well as perfect equivocity.

The Moments of Analogical Knowledge

There are two intellectual moments in analogical knowledge. First, the moment when we know, by the medium of our covert or overt knowledge of separated *esse* and by our knowledge of *esse* in predication that all beings are analogous. Second, when we know, by the demonstration of a unique *esse*, why beings must be analogous.[17] The first moment can be had without the second, but if it is, our

---

I, 13, 5, *Resp.;* 16, 6, *Resp.;* I–II, 20, 3, *ad* 3; *Sum. Theol.,* I, 13, 6, *Resp.*: "In names predicated of many in an analogical sense, all are predicated through a relation to some one thing; and this one thing must be placed in the definition of them all. And since *the essence expressed by the name is the definition,* as the Philosopher says, such a name must be applied primarily to that which is put in the definition of the other things, and secondarily to these others according as they approach more or less to the first. Thus, for instance, *healthy* applied to animals comes into the definition of *healthy* applied to medicine, which is called healthy as being the cause of health in the animal; and also into the definition of *healthy* which is applied to urine, which is called healthy in so far as it is the sign of the animal's health."
See Appendix D of this chapter.
[17] St. Thomas, *Sum. Theol.,* I, 13, 5, *Resp.*

analogical knowledge though valid is truncated. Truncated analogical knowledge is often the occasion of error. For example, if we don't know that multiple *esse* is caused by a unique *esse*, we might think that kinds of being, expressed in definitions, are analogous. Not so. We simply must define beings without involving ourselves in knowing that kinds of being are analogous, because they are not. But it is not possible to know the various "*esse*'s" of a kind as "*esse*'s" without involving ourselves in knowing that being is analogous and, in the upshot, caused.[18]

Summary

Caesar crossing-the-Rubicon, then, stands in our knowledge as a kind of being in *esse*, and since a kind of being in *esse* must be in *esse*, he stands there as necessary. Yet, since Caesar need not have existed at all nor therefore his crossing (one could also say since his crossing need not have existed at all nor therefore Caesar), the only way to explain the *esse* of an event which, once in *esse*, must be there, but which need not have been there at all, is to trace that *esse* to a giver of it. *Then* we have the source both of the event's contingency *and* necessity: of its contingency, because God need not have given the event's *esse;* of its necessity, because God gave it.

Subtending the above situation is our realization, overt or covert, that *esse* is not involved in quiddities *because* of quiddities. Such realization is the knowledge of an analogue, and when we predicate, of analogy. Such knowledge is had by all, even apart from a demonstration that being must be analogous. If one does so demonstrate, one sees that multiple beings, coming from God, imitate the *esse* of God. They are caused bits, so to say, of the being of God; like Him in their *esse* and so like Him in the kind which their *esse* is. They are not like each other when their kinds are different, but only like each other in the *esse* of their kinds, because their *esse* is like God's, the cause of their *esse*.

In sum, we first make a knowledge identity in *esse* between

Caesar's crossing and the existence of that event; and we make that
identity because a thing in *esse* is identical with itself; but, since the
event's "self" is not *esse*, we can understand that "self" only as coming from a cause which, in making the event to be, makes it to be
itself. Second, in the context of analogy, we see that all things are
dissimilar and similar in being beings, and we can't see any reason
why this is so unless we see that they are all like their cause, whereas
He isn't like them. How indeed *could* He be like them if He be only
esse, whereas they are kinds of being in *esse*?

Appendix to Chapter XII

APPENDIX (A). Aristotle on the analogy of being.

Aristotle, *Metaphysics*, XI (K), 3, 1060b 31–1061a 17: "Since the
science of the philosopher treats of being *qua* being universally and
not in respect of a part of it, and 'being' has many senses and is not
used in one only, it follows that if the word is used equivocally and
in virtue of nothing common to its various uses, being does not fall
under one science (for the meanings of an equivocal term do not
form one genus); but if the word is used in virtue of something
common, being will fall under one science. . . . Everything that is,
then, is said to 'be' in this same way; each thing that is is said to 'be'
because it is a modification of being *qua* being or a permanent or a
transient state or a movement of it, or something else of the sort.
And since everything that is may be referred to something single
and common, each of the contrarieties of being, whether the first
differences of being are plurality and unity, or likeness and unlikeness, or some other differences; let these be taken as already discussed."

APPENDIX (B). The analogy of cause to effect.

St. Thomas, *De Verit.*, II, 11, *Resp.*: "It is impossible to say that
something is predicated univocally of a creature and God because in
all univocal predication the nature signified by the name is common

to those of whom the univocal predication is made. Hence, from the point of view of the nature signified by the predicate, the subjects of the univocal predication are equal, even though from the point of view of its real existence one may take precedence over another. For example, all numbers are equal from the point of view of the nature of number, even though, by the nature of things, one number is naturally prior to another. No matter how much a creature imitates God, however, a point cannot be reached where something would belong to it for the same reason it belongs to God. For things which have the same formal characters but are in separate subjects are common to the same subjects in regard to substance or quiddity but distinct in regard to the act of being. But whatever is in God is His own act of being; and just as His essence is the same as His act of being, so is His knowledge the same as His act of being a knower. Hence, since the act of existence proper to one thing cannot be communicated to another, it is impossible that a creature ever attain to the possession of something in the same manner in which God has it, just as it is impossible for it to attain the same act of being as that which God has. The same is true of us. If *man* and *to exit as man* did not differ in Socrates, man could not be predicated univocally of him and Plato, whose acts of existing are distinct.

"Nevertheless, it cannot be said that whatever is predicated of God and creature is an equivocal predication; for, unless there were at least some real agreement between creatures and God, His essence would not be the likeness of creatures, and so He could not know them·by knowing His essence. Similarly, we would not be able to attain any knowledge of God from creatures, nor from among the names devised for creatures could we apply one to Him more than another; for in equivocal predication it makes no difference what name is used, since the word does not signify any real agreement.

"Consequently, it must be said that knowledge is predicated neither entirely univocally nor yet purely equivocally of God's knowledge and ours. Instead, it is predicated analogously, or, in other words, according to a proportion."

St. Thomas, *De Verit.*, XXIII, 7, *ad* 9: "Man is conformed to God since he is made to God's image and likeness. It is true that, because

man is infinitely distant from God, there cannot be a proportion
between him and God in the proper sense of proportion as found
among quantities, consisting of a certain measure of two quantities
compared to each other. Nevertheless, in the sense in which the
term proportion is transferred to signify any relationship of one
thing to another (as we say that there is a likeness of proportions in
this instance: the pilot is to his ship as the ruler to the common-
wealth), nothing prevents our saying that there is a proportion of
man to God, since man stands in a certain relationship to Him
inasmuch as he is made by God and subject to Him.

"Or the answer could be given that, although there cannot be
between the finite and the infinite a proportion properly so called,
yet there can be a proportionality or the likeness of two proportions.
We say that four is proportioned to two because it is the double;
but we say that four is proportionable to six because four is to two
as six is to three. In the same way, although the finite and the infinite
cannot be proportioned, they can be proportionable, because the
finite is equal to the finite just as the infinite is to the infinite. In
this way there is a likeness of the creature to God, because the creature stands to the things which are its own as God does to those
which belong to Him."

APPENDIX (C). Univocal, equivocal and analogous predication.

St. Thomas, *Contra Gentiles*, I, 34: "Names said of God and creatures are predicated neither univocally nor equivocally but analogically, that is, according to an order or reference to something one.

"This can take place in two ways. In one way, according as many
things have reference to something one. Thus, with reference to
one *health* we say that an animal is healthy as the subject of health,
medicine is healthy as its cause, food as its preserver, urine as its
sign.

"In another way, the analogy can obtain according as the order or
reference of two things is not to something else but to one of them.
Thus, *being* is said of substance and accident according as an accident has reference to a substance, and not according as substance and
accident are referred to a third thing.

"Now, the names said of God and things are not said analogically according to the first mode of analogy, since we should then have to posit something prior to God, but according to the second mode.

"In this second mode of analogical predication the order according to the name and according to reality is sometimes found to be the same and sometimes not. For the order of the name follows the order of knowledge, because it is the sign of an intelligible conception. When, therefore, that which is prior in reality is found likewise to be prior in knowledge, the same thing is found to be prior both according to the meaning of the name and according to the nature of the thing. Thus, substance is prior to accident both in nature, in so far as substance is the cause of accident, and in knowledge, in so far as substance is included in the definition of accident. Hence, being is said of substance by priority over accident both according to the nature of the thing and according to the meaning of the name. But when that which is prior in nature is subsequent in our knowledge, then there is not the same order in analogicals according to reality and according to the meaning of the name. Thus, the power to heal, which is found in all health-giving things, is by nature prior to the health that is in the animal, as a cause is prior to an effect; but because we know this healing power through an effect, we likewise name it from its effect. Hence it is that the health-giving is prior in reality, but animal is by priority called healthy according to the meaning of the name.

"Thus, therefore, because we come to a knowledge of God from other things, the reality in the names said of God and other things belongs by priority in God according to His mode of being, but the meaning of the name belongs to God by posteriority. And so He is said to be named from His effects."

APPENDIX (D). The analogical use of natural signs.

St. Thomas, *De Verit.*, II, 11, *Resp.:* "Since an agreement according to proportion can happen in two ways, two kinds of community can be noted in analogy. There is a certain agreement between things having a proportion to each other or some other relation to each other, like the proportion which the number two has to unity in as far as it is the double of unity. Again, the agreement is occasionally noted not between two things which have a proportion between them, but rather between two related proportions—for example, six has something in common with four because six is two times three, just as four is two times two. The first type of agreement is one of proportion; the second, of proportionality.

"We find something predicated analogously of two realities according to the first type of agreement when one of them has a relation to the other, as when being is predicated of substance and accident because of the relation which accident has to substance, or as when healthy is predicated of urine and animal because urine has some relation to the health of an animal. Sometimes, however, a thing is predicated analogously according to the second type of agreement, as when sight is predicated of bodily sight and the intellect because understanding is in the mind as sight is in the eye.

"In those terms predicated according to the first type of analogy, there must be some definite relation between the things having something in common analogously. Consequently, nothing can be predicated analogously of God and creature according to this type of analogy; for no creature has such a relation to God that it could determine the divine perfection. But in the other type of analogy, no definite relation is involved between the things which have something in common analogously, so there is no reason why some name cannot be predicated analogously of God and creature in this manner."

Suggested Reading

The Anticipative Knowledge of Existential Act:

Aristotle, *De Anima*, III, 8, 431b 21.
St. Thomas Aquinas, *De Verit.*, I, 1; II, 2; XVI, 1; *De Ente et Essentia*, Introduction and ch. I; *Sum. Theol.*, I, 5, 2; 14, 1; I–II, 94, 2; *Contra Gentiles*, II, 21.

The Analogy of Being:

Aristotle, *Metaphysics*, IV (Γ), 2; XI (K), 3.
St. Thomas Aquinas, *In IV Metaph.*, lect. 1, n. 535; *In V Metaph.*, lect. 8, n. 879; *In XI Metaph.*, lect. 3, n. 2197; *In I Sent.*, d. 19, q. 5, a. 2, *ad* 1; d. 22, q. 1, a. 1; d. 35, q. 1, a. 4, *sol.*; *De Pot.*, III, 4, *ad* 9; VII, 5-7; *De Verit.*, II, 1; II, 11; XXIII, 7, *ad* 9; *Contra Gentiles*, I, 32-34; II, 15; *Sum. Theol.*, I, 4, 3; 12, 1, *ad* 4; 13, 5; *De Princ. Nat.*, ch. 6, nn. 365-367; *In Boet. de Trin.*, I, 2; IV, 2; *De Malo*, II, 9, *ad* 16.
Cajetan, *In De Ente et Essentia*, c. II, q. 3; *De Nominum Analogia. De Conceptu Entis*, c. I, n. 6; c. II, nn. 19-20; c. III, n. 23.
John of St. Thomas, *Ars Logica*, Pars II, q. 13, a. 3.
Anderson, J., *The Bond of Being*, chs. I, VIII, XIII, XVII.
Arnou, R., S.J., *Metaphysica Generalis*, pp. 95-109.
Geiger, L.-B., O.P., *La participation dans la philosophie de s. Thomas d'Aquin*, pp. 77-84, 156-217, 238-258, 365-398.
Gilson, E., "Cajétan et l'existence," *Tijdschrift voor Philosophie*, Vol. XV (1953), pp. 267-287.
   Le Thomisme, pp. 150-160.
Lyttkens, H., *The Analogy between God and the World*, pp. 18-58, 164-175.
Maritain, J., *Distinguer pour unir, ou les degrés du savoir*, pp. 821-826.
Mascall, E., *Existence and Analogy*, ch. V.
Maurer, A., C.S.B., "St Thomas and the Analogy of Genus," *The New Scholasticism*, Vol. XXIX, n. 2 (April 1955), pp. 127-144.
Penido, M.T.-L., *Le rôle de l'analogie en théologie dogmatique*, pp. 11-78, 85-87, 96, 134 ff.
Phelan, G., *St. Thomas and Analogy*.

The Univocal, the Universal, the Equivocal:

St. Thomas Aquinas, *Contra Gentiles*, I, 29; I, 33-34; III, 49; *De Verit.*, II, 11; *De Pot.*, VII, 7; *Sum. Theol.*, I, 13, 5; *In Boet. de Trin.*, VI, 3.
Gilson, E., *Le Thomisme*, p. 152.
Maritain, J., "Sur la doctrine de l'aséité divine," *Mediaeval Studies*, Vol. V (1943), pp. 39-50.
Schwartz, H., "Plato, Aristotle, St. Thomas and Univocity," *The New Scholasticism*, Vol. XXVII, n. 4 (October 1953), pp. 373-403.
———, "Analogy in St. Thomas and Cajetan," *The New Scholasticism*, Vol. XXVIII, n. 2 (April 1954), pp. 127-144.

Metaphorical Analogy:

St. Thomas Aquinas, *Sum. Theol.*, I, 13, 6 and 9.
Boyle, R., S.J., "The Nature of Metaphor," *The Modern Schoolman*, Vol. XXXI, n. 4 (May 1954), pp. 257–280.
———, "The Nature of Metaphor: Further Considerations," *The Modern Schoolman*, Vol. XXXIV, n. 4 (May 1957), pp. 283–298.

Analogy of Attribution:

St. Thomas Aquinas, *In I Sent.*, d. 19, q. 5, a. 2, *ad* 1; d. 22, q. 1, a. 1; d. 35, q. 1, a. 4; *In IV Metaph.*, lect. 1, n. 537; *In XI Metaph.*, lect. 3, n. 2197; *De Princ. Nat.*, ch. 6, nn. 365–367; *In Boet. de Trin.*, I, 2; *De Pot.*, III, 4, *ad* 9; VII, 5–7; *De Verit.*, I, 4; II, 1; II, 11; XXIII, 7, *ad* 9; *Sum. Theol.*, I, 13, 5; 16, 6; I–II, 20, 3, *ad* 3; *Contra Gentiles*, I, 32–34; II, 15.

XIII · RECAPITULATION OF CHAPTERS X, XI, XII, AND THE VOCABULARY OF ANALOGY

The Problem

We have been trying to find a knowledge connection between pairs of known items which are not known as identical. The instances of that situation were the following, and they cover all types of knowledge. First, to know "John" is not to know "shaving," yet we know at times that John *is* shaving. Secondly, to know "anyone-like-John" is *not* to know that "anyone's" necessary predicates, either singly or in combination, as being identically "anyone-like-John"; yet we know that anyone-like-John *is* those necessary predicates. Thirdly, to know the definition of anyone-like-John, viz., a rational animal, is *not* to know that a rational animal exists, yet we know that a rational animal *does* exist. Then we telescoped all those three examples into this one: to know that an historical event was in existence is *not* to know something which must have been in existence, yet we know that once in existence a thing must *be* in existence. The problem is, in *what* are two unidentical knowledge items known to be the same, and *why?*

We took the telescoping example first, because in that example the problem is at its peak, in the citadel so to say. If the problem can be answered there, the answers to the three preceding problems are a matter of detail. So, to change the figure, we seized the problem at its throat and asked, why is our knowledge of an historical event or an event in *esse*, knowledge of an identity between an event in *esse* and the event itself, whereas there is no identity between the event and its own *esse?*

Seize well the data: an event in *esse* is known to be identical with itself. That proposition is self-evident from the self-identity of being. Next, the event is known to be accidentally related to its own *esse*. This is to say that the event is known to be unidentical with the *esse* by which it is itself or an event. That proposition is evident, because it is given that an event which need not have existed did or does exist. So much, then, is given: two knowledge items, Caesar's crossing and the existence of that event, unidentical in knowledge and in fact (before the event) are nevertheless known to be identical in the *esse* of the fact and in our knowledge of the fact when we know that Caesar did cross. The question is, why?

The Answer to the Problem

Obviously, the answer must be, because those two unidentical items *are* and are *known* to be identical in *esse*. But this answer doesn't account for the accidentality of the event's *esse*, either in fact or in our knowledge of the fact! That is right. It doesn't. And so we must explain the fact and our knowledge of it. The explanation is, as any explanation must be, through a cause, that is, a cause of accidental *esse*. Thus is assured the identity of an event in *esse* with itself, as well as our knowledge that this is so.

The Answer Evolved

Clearly, two unidentical knowledge items which turn up in the knowledge of any existent event cannot be known to be identical in *esse*, as they are, if the knowing of the *esse* of one event is the knowing of no more than the *esse* of that event, for this would reduce the knowing of existential act to the knowing of just one existential act. Against the fact. We know many existential acts. Concretely, if to know that *x is* is to know an "is" which is strictly identical with or private to *x*, we couldn't know that *y is*. And so when we know that *x is*, we know an "is" which is, covertly or overtly, a knowing of existential act. On the other hand, to know the "is" of *x*, as when we say that *x is,* is assuredly to know that it is *x* and none other which is. And so, when we know the existential act of any one being, as when we say *x* exists, we know, overtly or covertly, more than the existential act of just that one being, otherwise we would never be prepared to know the existential act of any other being, as when we say *y exists.* That "more" which we know is the relation which existential act bears to any being, a kind of "public" feature of existential act whereby anything at all which exists or can exist will be recognized, when it *is* recognized, as belonging to, or as an authentic citizen of, the republic of being.

If, now, we ask why existential act bears such a relation to any being, the answer would run as follows. The accidental *esse* of many beings cannot be located as in its source either in them or in our knowledge of them. Not in them, precisely because their *esse* is accidental to them, though *esse* is not an accident. Not in our knowledge of them, precisely because our knowledge is also an accident, a cognitive accident of the knower. Where, then, should we locate the source of those two accidental acts, the *esse* of things and the *esse* of our knowledge of things? In the *esse* of the cause, both of things and of our knowledge of things. It may be added once again that it is not necessary to know the cause of being and of our knowledge of being in order to know the relation which existential act bears to any being and to our knowledge of any being. Analogy, or the relation, is given, just as multiple beings are given, whether we can demonstrate its source or not. Nevertheless, once the cause of *esse* is demonstrated, we have the reason why the analogue or separated *esse* bears the relation it does to all beings, and also the reason why our knowledge of separated *esse* also bears the relation it does to the same cause. Just as the analogates have one source, so our knowledge of them has one source, God.

The Names of the Knowledge Situation

The names for what is known when we know being as being are separated *esse,* common being (*ens commune*), being in its universality or commonness (*ens in communi*), common *esse* (*esse commune*), an analogue, a transcendental, that which is, absolute being, being absolutely considered, etc.[1]

The analogy of being, then, seems to be a noetic version of causality, and because we cannot jam the cause of being under the head of separated *esse*, common being, etc., as we jam a member of a genus under a genus, we cannot call being as being a genus. We cannot do this because, whereas there are kinds of being, nonetheless being is not a kind. Being as being, or separated *esse*, or common being, and so on, are properly understood, then, only when they stand in our knowledge as separated *esse*, etc., *and* as being caused, both in fact and in our knowledge of the fact. Thus, the mystery of common *esse* can be somewhat understood, and scientifically understood at that, only when it is referred to a cause of common being, both in fact and in our knowledge of the fact. This understanding of common being and of its source leaves the mystery of common being mysterious, because such an understanding is not an understanding of the cause of common *esse* except to the extent that there *is* a cause of common esse. We don't understand God's *esse* as It is. We understand It only to the effect *that* It is. To paraphrase, God is in our knowledge only as in the truth of the proved proposition that He is. He is not in our knowledge as in the truth which *He* is. We don't see God when we see, overtly or covertly, being as being, nor do we see Him even when we prove His existence. Yet we see something like Him in all those insights, and we are assured by the demonstration of His existence that absolutely everything is like Him in the sense that He is everything (being) without being like anything (beings). He is the storm and the calm, peace and disquiet, justice and mercy, the lion and the lamb. Yet He is none of these things, for they are caused to be in existence, whereas He is existence. As St. Augustine says: "Behold the heavens and the earth; they shout that they are created. . . . Thou, therefore, Lord has made them, who are beautiful, because they are beautiful; who are good, because they are good; who are, because they are; yet they

---

[1] The nuances in this vocabulary will be explained in Chapter XX.

are not as beautiful, nor good, nor are they, as Thou their Creator, in comparison with whom they are neither beautiful, nor good, nor are they."[2]

The Vocabulary of Analogy

There is considerable fluidity in the vocabulary of analogy, a fluidity in fact which can cause a pretty mess. About all that can be done about it is to attempt to clear up the mess so far as the terms in this text are concerned.

The Analogy of Attribution

The analogical knowledge of the cause in the knowledge of its effect is called the *analogy of attribution*. The same name is also given to the analogical knowledge of a nature-sign and that which is signified by the nature-sign, e.g., complexion, a natural sign of health, is said to be healthy, and so is an organism, the thing signified by the predicate, healthy. Nothing much can be done about this except to note that the second analogy which bears the same name as the first is not an analogy of being. The second analogy is knowledge of a univocal natural sign (complexion) which is *used* analogically, i.e., as a natural sign of health. If, however, one runs the relation the other way about by saying that a healthy organism is

---

[2] St. Augustine, *Confessions*, XI, 4; PL 32, 811. See St. Thomas, *In I Sent.*, d. 22, q. 1, aa. 1 and 2; *De Pot.*, VII, 5, *Resp.*; *Sum. Theol.*, I, 13, 3 and 5; *Contra Gentiles*, I, 30: "With reference to the mode of signification there is in every name that we use an imperfection, which does not befit God, even though the thing signified in some eminent way does befit God. This is clear in the name *goodness* and *good*. For *goodness* has signification as something not subsisting, while *good* has signification as something concreted. And so with reference to the mode of signification no name is fittingly applied to God; this is done only with reference to that which the name has been imposed to signify. Such names, therefore, as Dionysius teaches, can be both affirmed and denied of God. They can be affirmed because of the meaning of the name; they can be denied because of the mode of signification."

the cause of a healthy complexion, then the analogy is an analogy of being.[3]

The Analogy of Proper Proportionality

Assume now as proven that what is accidentally related to its own *esse* and nevertheless is in *esse* is due to a cause of *esse*. Here we are confronted with a situation which has more in it than the wonder over a problem. The situation here, being no longer problematic, is astounding, stupendous. Any description of the situation must needs sound like "wild and whirling words," as will straightway appear.

Since the cause of *esse* is being, and we know this, that cause would be being even if it never caused anything; and we know this also. The knowledge that God is being, then, in its first moment, is knowledge of Him by the analogy of causal attribution: we know God in His effects, or as a cause of His effects. In its second moment, namely, in the knowledge that God is being even though He never caused anything, we have cut the *esse* of God loose from our *way of knowing* that *esse*, namely, as a cause of being, or as in the effects of a cause of being. There is then left in our knowledge only the knowledge of *esse* which is common to God and creatures. This knowledge is knowledge of a *properly proportionate analogue*. "Properly," because now each being, God included, is known as an existent without pretense. "Proportionate," because the analogue is different and somewhat the same in each of its instances. If we wish to name the relation of the properly proportionate analogue to all its analogates, that relation is named the *analogy of proper proportionality*.

We may again go into this a bit. Let us say, first, we know God is wise, because we know He causes wisdom. This is the analogy of causal attribution: knowledge of God through knowledge of some-

[3] See Chapter XII, pp. 181–183, 194. The following texts are pertinent to the analogy of attribution and the analogy of proper proportionality: *In I Sent.*, d. 19, q. 5, a. 2, *ad* 1; d. 22, q. 1, a. 1; *De Princ. Nat.*, c. 6, nn. 365–367; *In Boet. de Trin.*, I, 2; *De Pot.*, III, 4, *ad* 9; VII, 5–7; *De Verit.*, II, 1 and 11; XXIII, 7, *ad* 9; *Sum. Theol.*, I, 13, 5.

thing like Him, His effects. Ask now, is God wise because He causes wisdom? The answer must be, no. A cause of wisdom is not wise *because* He causes wisdom. That "because" clause is simply the reason why we *know* He is wise, not the reason why He *is* wise.[4] Just so, God doesn't exist or isn't a being *because* He causes beings, although if He had not caused beings, we would never know He is an existent, since we wouldn't be around to know anything. We are thus left with the knowledge that God is and is not the way we know Him. "God is the way we know Him," because He is a cause of being and we know that. "God is not the way we know Him," because He is, even though He had caused nothing, and we know that also. Let us say, then, that the proportionate analogue, which in the second moment of our knowledge of God is cut loose from the way we know Him, leaves us with a knowledge of Him which transcends all the ways we have of knowing Him. Those ways we have of knowing Him are innumerable. In none of those ways can we find Him. Yet we find Him nonetheless in the proportionate analogue which is like Him, although He isn't like any of the ways we know that proportionate analogue. And so, the proportionate analogue, cut loose from the attributive analogue, which latter started the whole business, reveals God for what He is, namely, being. We would never know Him as being unless we knew Him as a cause of being, but once we know Him as a cause of being we know Him by His most secret name, being—unless indeed He were to tell us more about Himself.[5]

At this point begin the "wild and whirling" words about God. How can one start talking about God Who transcends all our talk? How can one stop talking about Him Who nonetheless dwells in every thing we say about the covert *esse* of science, about the overt *esse* of metaphysics, about the proved *esse* of God? He is in all we *say* about those "*esse*'s," yet He is none of the ways we talk about

---

[4] St. Thomas, *De Pot.*, VII, 6, *Resp.*: "Non ergo sapiens dicitur Deus quoniam sapientiam causet, sed quia est sapiens, ideo sapientiam causat." See *Sum. Theol.*, I, 13, 2, *Resp.*: "It does not follow that God is good because He causes goodness; but rather, on the contrary, He causes goodness in things because He is good. As Augustine says, 'Because He is good, we are.'"

[5] See note 2 of this chapter. See also G. Smith, S.J., *Natural Theology*, pp. 174-175.

any thing, including the way we talk about Him. He is identically the perfections and the necessities of nature which science describes; He is also the perfections and the necessities which metaphysics and natural theology describe. Yet He is none of those perfections or necessities as having them; He is not even the necessities of those perfections. This amounts to saying that God doesn't exist because He is those perfections or because He is necessary. He is necessary and is all those perfections because He is.[6]

In sum, it is given, first, to our knowledge that things exist. Second, with that first "given" is also given to our knowledge that the "existing" of things is not identical with them, for then they would be a totalized, unique existent, and this is against the fact: things are multiple. Hence, third, the existence of things is now known to be caused by a cause of existing, whose existence is not caused. Fourth and last, the cause of being may now stand in our knowledge as cut loose from all the three ways which we have of knowing being, and He is revealed for what He is, being. What is common but different in all those analogates, multiple beings, causes of being, uncaused cause of being, is the *proportionate analogue*, being.

Metaphors and Similes

These have been sufficiently noticed.

Sometimes figures of speech are called *analogies of proportionality*, but not of proper proportionality. The reason is: one of the terms in figures of speech is only a word-sign of something we can't quite understand, a name for the appearance of things. For example, *noble* is a word-sign of a lion, and some men *are* noble. We don't quite know what it is about a lion which gives it the appearance of nobility, but he certainly has the appearance of a

[6] See St. Thomas, *De Pot.*, VII, 2, *ad* 1; *Sum. Theol.*, I, 13, 5; 3, 4, *ad* 2; 4, 2, *Resp.*: "God is being itself, of itself subsistent. Consequently, He must contain within Himself the whole perfection of being. . . . Since therefore God is subsisting being itself, nothing of the perfection of being can be wanting to Him. Now all the perfections of all things pertain to the perfection of being; for things are perfect precisely so far as they have being after some fashion."

noble man whose nobility is not an appearance, and which we do understand. A lion is not really or properly noble, but a lion looks noble, and so we say he is. Just so, a boxer dog looks like a judge, stern, just, incorruptible, whereas he is really a big, lovable fool of a dog, not like a judge at all except in appearance.[7]

Proportion and Proportionality

Many metaphysicians distinguish proportion from proportionality as if they were two sacraments, and then they invest their language and voices with a proportionate sacramentality, breathing heavily about the "formality of being." There is no real need for this distinction.

There is proportion where there is proportionality, and *vice versa*. Both are relations, expressed concretely or abstractly. However, there may be more or less proportion and proportionality. If so, there is a dividing line between *univocal* proportion and proportionality and *analogous* proportion and proportionality. There is *univocal* proportion when we use univocal word- or nature-signs analogically. This means that there is an analogy or likeness between knowledge of univocals and knowledge of analogals.

We may, as some do, name these univocal proportions of figures of speech *analogies of proportionality*, but not of proper proportionality; so too, we may name the analogous use we make of univocal nature-signs *analogies of attributions;* we may even name the identical mathematical proportions of, e.g., a half to its double, in size or numbers, *mathematical analogies*. However, all the analogies underlined in the last sentence fall short of the *analogy of attribution* which is the noetic version of causality, and so they also fall

[7] See Chapter XII, pp. 192-193. See also St. Thomas, *Sum. Theol.*, I, 13, 6, *Resp.*; 13, 9, *Resp.*: "A name is communicable in two ways, properly, and through likeness. It is properly communicable if its whole signification can be given to many; through likeness it is communicable according to some part of the signification of the name. For instance, this name *lion* is properly communicated to all beings of the same nature as *lion;* through likeness it is communicable to those who share in something of the lion's nature, as for instance, courage, or strength, and such are called lions metaphorically."

short of the knowledge-developed analogue of causal attribution, which is the knowledge of the properly proportionate analogue, *esse*. The analogy *between* the knowledge of univocals and the knowledge of true analogals does not make the knowledge of univocals knowledge of analogals. Just because our knowledge of nature is like our knowledge of nature in *esse* is no reason why our knowledge of nature is analogous knowledge. Our knowledge of nature is like, but is not, our knowledge of nature in *esse*. This last is always the knowledge of a true analogue of being.

The Analogies of Inequality

St. Thomas Aquinas had said that those predicates are analogal which are made one (*parificantur*) in intention but not in being,[8] e.g., "body" is made one in intention when it is predicated of celestial and terrestrial bodies, but "body" is not made one in being because celestial and terrestrial bodies are known to *be* different. The cosmology of this is erroneous, but not the metaphysics. St. Thomas is saying that "body" is "parified" from two *different orders* of potency, namely, the potency of celestial and the potency of terrestrial bodies. This of course, as was said, is not true. The potential knowledge of both celestial and terrestrial bodies is univocal knowledge, knowledge of the genus body or material substance.

Suppose, however, that *there really are two potential knowledges*, as there are *not* in St. Thomas' example. What then? St. Thomas' remark would stand fast in metaphysics, and with him we would

---

[8] *In I Sent.*, d. 19, q. 5, a. 2, *ad* 1: ". . . aliquid dicitur secundum analogiam . . . *secundum esse et non secundum intentionem:* et hoc contingit quando plura parificantur in intentione alicuius communis, sed illud commune non habet esse unius rationis in omnibus sicut omnia corpora parificantur in intentione corporeitatis. Unde Logicus, qui considerat intentiones tantum, dicit hoc nomen corpus de omnibus corporibus univoce praedicari; sed esse huius naturae non est eiusdem rationis in corporibus corruptibilibus et incorruptibilibus. Unde quantum ad metaphysicum et naturalem, qui considerant res secundum suum esse, nec hoc nomen corpus, nec aliquid aliud dicitur univoce de incorruptibilibus et incorruptibilibus."

See St. Thomas, *Sum. Theol.*, I, 4, 3, *Resp.*; *De Verit.*, II, 11, *Resp.*; *De Malo* II, 9, *ad* 16; *In Boet. de Trin.*, IV, 2, *Resp.*

have to say of two *such* potential knowledges that one of them is
the knowledge of a true genus, whereas the other is not. The other
such potential knowledge is the knowledge of a true analogue. The
issue then is this: are there two such potential knowledges?

There are. There is, first, the knowledge of the potency which is
drawn from matter.[9] This is the knowledge of material substances,
the proper subject of accidents, true genera. This knowledge develops into the knowledge of differences, of descriptions of species,
and sometimes even into definitions of species, pretty much as matter
itself develops through its successive actuations into the spiky, hard
and fast lines of essence in *esse*. Second, there is knowledge of
substance as that "to which it is owed to exist" (*id cui debetur
esse*).[10] This second potential knowledge will not issue or develop

[9] On the knowledge of genus, see St. Thomas, *In I Sent.*, d. 19, q. 5, a. 2,
ad 1; *In X Metaph.*, lect. 12, n. 2142; *In VII Phys.*, lect. 8, n. 8; *Sum. Theol.*, I, 66,
2, *ad* 2; 88, 2, *ad* 4; *In Boet. de Trin.*, VI, 3, *Resp.*; ed. Maurer, pp. 70–71: "Created immaterial substances, however, are indeed in a genus; but even though
considered logically they are in the same remote genus as these sensible substances, namely the genus of substance, considered naturally they do not belong
to the same genus, just as also heavenly and terrestrial bodies are not in the same
genus. For, as the *Metaphysics* says, the corruptible and the incorruptible are not
of one genus. It should be noticed that the logician considers concepts in themselves; and from this viewpoint nothing prevents the immaterial and the material, the incorruptible and the corruptible, from having something in common.
But the natural philosopher and the metaphysician treat of essences as existing
in reality; and therefore they say that there are diverse genera wherever they
find diverse modes of potency and act and consequently diverse modes of existing."

See *De Ente et Essentia*, c. II; Marietti, n. 13: ". . . the unity of the genus
comes from its very indetermination and indifference; not in such a way, it is
true, that the genus expresses a nature numerically identical in different species,
to which might be joined another thing—the difference—determining it as
form determines matter which is numerically one. On the contrary, the genus
expresses some form—although not in a determinate way this one or that one
—which the difference signifies determinately, and which is not other than that
which the genus signified indeterminately. That is why the Commentator
declares in the eleventh book of the *Metaphysics* that prime matter is said to
be one because of the removal of all forms, whereas genus is called one because of the commonness of the designated form. It is thus clear that, by adding
the difference and removing the indetermination which was the cause of the
unity of the genus, essentially diverse species remain."

See also A. Maurer, C.S.B., "St. Thomas and the Analogy of Genus," *op. cit.*,
pp. 127–144.

[10] See St. Thomas, *Sum. Theol.*, I, 3, 5, *ad* 1; *Contra Gentiles*, I, 25; *De Pot.*,
VII, 3, *ad* 4: "According to Avicenna, substance is not rightly defined as a self-

into a defining knowledge as the first does. If this second sort of
potential knowledge is to develop at all, its increment will simply
be to the effect that "that to which it is owed to exist," whatever
it may be, *exists*. It is of this knowledge of substance as *id cui debetur
esse* which St. Thomas seems to be thinking of when he calls it an
analogal which is made one (*parificatur*) in intention but not in
being.

"Made one"! By what? By the intellect itself in order that it may
understand, when evidence or proof supply the facts, the facts: material and immaterial substances (God and angels) do exist. "Made
one" means, then, made "univocal" or "equivocal" by design (*a
consilio*), not by the design of the operant, but by the design of the
nature of the intellect itself and of its operation. A sort of cocking
and aiming of its own gun so that when it does fire, the intellect
may hit its mark, i.e., so that it may know that those things exist
to which it is owed to exist. After all, when we know that substances
exist, we must have furnished ourselves, by a priority of cause and
nature, with the knowledge of what it is that exists, viz., that to
which it is *owed* to exist. This prior knowledge seems to be what
St. Thomas meant by the analogal, parified in intention but not in
being. *We* make the knowledge of "that to which it is owed to
exist," in order to understand existents. How, indeed, could we
understand that things exist unless we had already furnished ourselves with the knowledge of what to expect? Now, that expectant
knowledge (parified intention) is knowledge of that "to which it is
owed to exist"; it is knowledge *before* the proof or evidence that
something exists, of the prescription which any existent must fill.
Small wonder is it that our knowledge of existents fits the prescription of existents. An impossibility it is that we should know existents
without having known the prescription which our knowledge of

---

subsistent being; for *being* cannot be the genus of a thing according to the
Philosopher, because nothing can be added to being that has not a share of
being, and a difference should not be a part of the genus. If, however, substance
can be defined notwithstanding that it is the most universal of genera, its
definition will be *a thing whose quiddity is owed to have being not in a subject.*
Hence the definition of substance cannot be applied to God, Whose quiddity
is not distinct from His being."

existents demands. The prescription is the parified intention: substance as that to which it is owed to exist.

From a slightly different angle, to be beings is true of all beings,
God, angels, men. If we knew the definition of just one of those
beings, that definition would not be true of any other of those beings.
A clear case of equivocity. But how do we know that those three
beings which exist are *not* truly univocal or equivocal in our knowledge? We know this by designedly *making* them univocal or equivocal in our knowledge, by a factitious univocal or equivocal in other
words. When we do this, the designed univocity or equivocity is
not drawn either from our knowledge of the potency of substance
as the proper subject of accidents, or from our knowledge of two
totally different things which happen to have the same name. It is
drawn from our factitious knowledge (the parified intention) of
substance as the proper subject of "exists." This bit of intellectual
art seems to be one with the intellect itself; it is a knowledge that
if there were many beings they would all be and be known as beings
(here is the parified intention). Certainly, everyone who comes to
know there are many beings, knew all along that each one would
be a being, else how would he recognize them as beings?

The univocal or equivocal by design thus seems to be the preknowledge state of the true analogal, being as being, and the analogue
of causal attribution and, when that analogue of causal attribution
is developed into the properly proportionate analogue, the analogue
of proper proportion. That preknowledge state of the true analogal
is not prior as no-knowledge is prior to knowledge, but as knowledge of the parified intention is prior to knowledge of its evident
or proved instances. The parified intention is a "genus" of being
and of all the predicates of being, the genus St. Thomas means when
he speaks in the Five Ways of the maximum *in genere entis*, in the
genus of necessity, of mover, of cause, of knowledge, of perfections,
etc., the genus to which nothing is added as if the added bit were
lacking in the original, *esse commune*.[11]

[11] St. Thomas, *Sum. Theol.*, I, 3, 4, *ad* 1: ". . . (esse sine additione), sicut
animal commune est sine ratione, . . . nec . . . careat ratione . . . est esse
commune." But to *esse divinum*, nothing can be added. See also *Sum. Theol.*,
I, 13, 5, *Resp.* As to substance, see *Sum. Theol.*, I, 3, 5, *ad* 1: ". . . substantiae

Now, Cajetan[12] understands St. Thomas' remark about the parified intention of "body" to mean this: just as "body" is parified in intention, so every genus is parified as "body" is. Cajetan must, then, with a logic commensurate with his genius, go on to say that although any genus can be called an analogue in that sense, nevertheless it is an abuse of language to call a genus an analogue; and furthermore, these genera or *analogues of inequality*, as he calls them, are what St. Thomas meant by saying that "all animals are equally animals but are not equal animals."[13]

Cajetan seems to have missed the point here. The point St. Thomas is making is this: an intention which is *designedly made* univocal or equivocal is a true analogue. The example St. Thomas uses to illustrate this point is poor: "body" is not designedly made univocal or analogal; "body" *is* univocal because it is drawn from the knowledge of the potency of matter. But the knowledge of substance as that to which it is owed to exist (if it exists) *is* designedly made univocal and equivocal by the intellect in order that it may understand, when it does understand, that it is substances which exist, no matter what they may be. Hence, in saying that his *analogues of inequality* are not true analogues, Cajetan is right. In saying that it is an abuse of words to call them analogues, he is right again. But if one says that it is an abuse of words to call the parified intention of substance (*id cui debetur esse*), which is drawn from the potency of intellect itself, an analogue, one is denying precisely what St. Thomas had asserted: "those predicates *are* analogal which are made one in intention but not in being." St. Thomas' example of such analogals ("body" said of celestial and terrestrial bodies) is

---

nomen non significat solum quod est per se esse, quia hoc quod est esse, non potest per se esse genus . . . Sed (substantiae nomen etiam) significat essentiam cui competit sic esse, id est per se esse, quod tamen esse non est ipsa eius essentia." "Substance means not only . . . but also . . ." hits on the nose the parified notion of substance. For an analysis of this text, see E. Gilson, *The Christian Philosophy of St. Thomas Aquinas,* p. 30, p. 445, nn. 3-4; "Cajétan et l'existence," *op. cit.,* pp. 267-286.

[12] Cajetan, *De Nominum Analogia,* cc. I and III; *In De Ente et Essentia,* c. II, q. 3.

[13] St. Thomas, *De Malo,* II, 9, *ad* 16: "Dicendum quod omnia animalia sunt aequaliter animalia, non tamen sunt aequalia animalia, . . ."

indeed a poor one, but there *are* such analogals nonetheless: the analogals of substance (*cui debetur esse*), e.g., of necessity, of cause, etc. As to St. Thomas' remark that "all animals are equally but not equal animals," it is a "true and important" remark, but it is not to the point which Cajetan is trying to make. Cajetan, in making St. Thomas' parified intention, wrongly illustrated by St. Thomas' example of "body," an *analogue of inequality*, seems to have "unwittingly made univocity analogical," or if one prefers, he seems to have made the analogical univocal.[14]

In view of all this, it seems best simply to drop the whole business about *analogues of inequality* from the metaphysics and the vocabulary of analogy.

Suggested Reading

The Knowledge of Substance as Genus; and the Knowledge of Substance as "That to Which it is Owed to Exist":

St. Thomas Aquinas, *Contra Gentiles*, I, 33; *De Pot.*, VII, 7, *Resp.*; *Sum. Theol.*, I, 13, 5, *Resp.*; *De Verit.*, II, 11, *Resp.*; *In Boet. de Trin.*, VI, 3.
Gilson, E., *Le Thomisme*, p. 152.
Maritain, "Sur la doctrine de l'aséité divine," *Mediaeval Studies*, Vol. V (1943), pp. 39-50.

---

[14] See the two remarkable articles of H. Schwartz, "Analogy in St. Thomas and Cajetan," *op. cit.*, p. 143; "Plato, Aristotle, St. Thomas and Univocity," *op. cit.*, pp. 373-403. Dr. Schwartz' articles seem to be decisive on this point.

XIV · SOLUTION TO THE PROBLEM ABOUT OUR FIRST INTENTIONAL KNOWLEDGE OF BEING WITHIN THE CATEGORIES: KINDS OF BEING AND CHANGING BEING

The Object of Knowledge

We may now address ourselves to the third, second, and first instance[1] in which we connect two knowledge items which are not known as identical items. There may be method in this crablike madness of backing into the solution. . . . At any rate, the solution is in principle a single one, though it will have to be adjusted to each problem.

The essential point to seize in that single solution seems to be the following. If two men speak truly but differently about the same thing, the reason why they do simply cannot be the "thing" about which they are speaking. "Something else," i.e., some qualitative multiplicity in the thing itself, must be the reason for different and true statements about the same thing.[2] For example, if man number one says of an apple that it is green, and man number two says of the same apple that it is sour, and if we assume that they are both right, the reason why simply cannot be the apple as apple. The apple is the subject of their discourse, the subject matter one might say. Now, if it were because of the apple as apple that both men were talking and both were right, it would follow that each would be saying *the apple is an apple*. A true enough statement, but though twice repeated, it is still the same statement. "Something else," then,

---

[1] See Chapter X, pp. 161–165.
[2] W. O. Martin, *The Order and Integration of Knowledge*, Ann Arbor, University of Michigan Press, 1957, p. 7.

or a qualitative multiplicity in the apple, must be the reason for
those true but different statements: *the apple is green and the apple
is sour.*

That reason must be because the apple stands in man number one's
knowledge as *green*, in man number two's knowledge as *sour.* Thus,
an aspect of the brickbat reality of apple *plus the way that aspect
stands in each man's knowledge,* this is the reason why the different
statements about the apple are both true. We must name the aspect
of the brickbat reality plus the way it stands in knowledge. The
name of the situation is "an object of knowledge." Since the way
the apple stands in the knowledge of man number one, who sees the
apple as green, differs from the way the apple stands in the knowledge of man number two, who tastes the apple as sour, there are
different objects of knowledge.[8]

Where lies the difference? It lies, first, here: an object of knowledge is an aspect, a viewpoint, a knowledge perspective, the spot
where one sits in order to get the "hang" (*ratio*) of a thing. Thus,
if you are going to get the hang of the color of a thing, you must

---

[8] A more precise terminology may be helpful. An *object of knowledge* is
something which achieves a power of knowledge *in the way in which it
achieves that power.* For example, we *see* (the achievement of the power to
see) a colored thing *as colored* (the way in which a colored thing achieves
the power of sight). Thus, the "colored" is the object of the power to see, and
the "sounding" is the object of the power to hear, etc. If we wish to make an
abstract concept of the "colored" by saying "color," then we may distinguish
the colored (*proper object*) from its abstract trait, color (the *formal object*).
If we wish to speak of the colored thing in all its unknown residue of in-
telligiblity, we may call it a *material object.* There is no need to see a sacramental difference between proper and formal object. The proper object is
simply a concrete way (colored) of expressing the abstract trait (color).
  On the object of knowledge, see John of St. Thomas, *Cursus Philosophicus,
Ars Logica,* Pars II, q. 1, a. 3; Reiser, t. I, p. 260a 36—260b 18; Pars II, q. 21, a.
4; Reiser, t. I, pp. 674b 34—675a 3: "Ex his distingues alias divisiones obiecti,
ut in primarium et secundarium, formale et materiale. Id enim, quod per se vel
primo aut *formaliter* specificat seu est forma et ratio specificandi, dicitur per se
obiectum seu ratio obiecti; reliquum vero dicitur secundario seu per aliud et
materialiter obiectum. Et ipsa ratio specificandi secundum se sumpta solet etiam
dici *ratio sub qua* seu *obiectum quo.* Ut autem consideratur in aliqua re
afficiendo ipsam, dicitur res sic effecta *ratio quae,* obiectum vero materiale
obiectum quod. Exemplum facile est in pariete colorato et lucido respectu visus."
Cursus Philosophicus, De Anima, Pars IV, q. 2, a. 3; Reiser, t. III, p. 77a 23–38:
"Ex quo colligitur, quid sit obiectum formale, quid materiale, quid adaequatum.

see the color; if of its taste, you must taste it. But, second, within the aspect or viewpoint from which each man knows the apple there are many other subaspects which are nevertheless within that one overall aspect. Thus, the man who sees an apple as green will not only see the apple from one over-all viewpoint, viz., as colored; he will also and from precisely that same overall viewpoint see the apple as red if it is red. Red too is a color. The object of knowledge, then, is, first, one aspect or viewpoint from which a thing is known; to that one viewpoint, second, are referred all other subviewpoints of *that same one viewpoint*. The object of knowledge, as we saw, is not the apple as apple (the apple may be called the subject-matter of knowledge); nor is the object of knowledge, in the example, green or sour. "Green" and "sour" are instances or subobjects of an object of knowledge. The object is not "the green," because it is as colored that the apple hits the eye, and it would hit the eye as colored quite as well if its color were red. The object is not "the sour," and for the same reason: it is as having taste that the apple hits the taste buds, and it would still be as having taste that the apple hit the taste buds if the apple tasted sweet instead of sour. The object of knowledge, then, is one viewpoint of a thing to which one viewpoint all other viewpoints of the same kind are referred. Since there are many such "one viewpoints," there are many objects of knowledge.

We may also understand an object of knowledge in this way. We have many different ways or powers of knowing: the power to see, to touch, to understand, to reason, for example. Sometimes these powers are habituated, i.e., well- or ill-disposed to act, and then the habituated powers are called habits, good (intellectual virtues) or

---

Dicitur enim *obiectum adaequatum* illa ratio, quae terminat et complectitur, quidquid potest cadere sub attingentia alicuius potentiae, sive primario sive secundario, tam quoad rationem formalem, sub qua attingitur, quam quoad materiale, quod attingitur. *Obiectum formale* dicitur illa formalitas seu respectus, secundum quem fit proportio et coaptatio inter obiectum et potentiam. *Materiale* dicitur illud, quod tali habitudini seu formalitati substernitur et subiectum eius est"

See also J. Maritain, *An Introduction to Philosophy*, tr. E. I. Watkin, N.Y., Sheed & Ward, 1947, p. 106; *The Degrees of Knowledge*, pp. 58–59; Y. Simon, *Introduction à l'ontologie du connaître*, pp. 9–10.

bad (intellectual vices).[4] Sometimes these powers don't need any
habituation because they are usually well enough disposed to act
right from the start, e.g., the power to see, to hear, etc. In either
case, it is clear that the things known by a given power are known
under the rubric or the scope or perspective which is peculiar to
that power. This scope of power of knowledge is an object of knowledge. Should there be many powers, there are as many objects of
knowledge, and *vice versa:* as many as are the distinct objects of
knowledge, so many will be the powers of knowledge.[5] The object
of knowledge, therefore, is two-faced: the face which a thing presents to a certain way of knowing that thing is in the area of
"thingage"; the face of the kind of knowing of that kind of thing is
in the area of "thoughtage." The two areas *together* define an object
of knowledge.[6]

[4] See *The Material Logic of John of St. Thomas,* tr. Y. Simon, J. Glanville,
G. Hollenhorst, Chicago, University of Chicago Press, 1955, p. 611, n. 5, where
it is said that to use the English word "habit" for the Latin word *habitus* is
antipedagogical. It's not as bad as all that. "Habit" in English is an analogal,
just as *habitus* is in Latin. Besides, there is no sacramental value in the word
habitus which might efficaciously cause an understanding of its meaning. Both
English and Latin are difficult languages, even when one knows them, and any
language's difficulties are solved mainly *ex opere operantis.*
[5] On the distinction of powers and objects, see St. Thomas, *In Boet. de
Trin.,* V, 1, *Resp.; Sum. Theol.,* I, 1, 7, *Resp.;* 77, 3, *Resp.:* "A power as such
is directed to an act. Therefore we must derive the nature of a power from the
act to which it is directed; and consequently the nature of a power is diversified according as the nature of the act is diversified. Now the nature of an
act is diversified according to the various natures of the objects. . . . not any
variety of objects diversifies the powers of the soul, but a difference in that to
which the power of its very nature is directed. Thus the senses of their very
nature are directed to the passive quality which of itself is divided into color,
sound, and the like, and therefore there is one sensitive power with regard
to color, namely, sight, and another with regard to sound, namely, hearing.
But it is accidental to a passive quality, for instance, to something colored, to
be a musician or a grammarian, great or small, a man or a stone. Therefore
by reason of such differences the powers of the soul are not distinguished."
[6] Sometimes it is difficult or impossible to discern different objects, or powers,
of knowledge, but the broad distinctions are clear enough: sensory, e.g., and
intellectual objects, sight and touch, etc.

The Object of Metaphysical Knowledge

The face which things present to the metaphysician, as well as
the face of the kind of knowing of that face of things—the object
of metaphysical knowledge, that is, differs from the objects of all
other knowledges.[7]

Let us see what this means. Assume *John is shaving.* It is not because the knowledge which we have of *John* is identically the knowledge we have of *shaving* that we know John is shaving. If that were
so, two knowledge bits would be one knowledge bit. Against the
fact. Assume, next, that anyone-like-John, any man that is, is a
featherless biped, who can talk, cheat, cook his food, etc. The situation is the same: it is not because the knowledge we have of "any
man" is identically the knowledge we have of his necessary perinoetic
predicates that we know any man is his necessary predicates. If
that were so, two knowledge bits, e.g., "any man" and, e.g., *featherless biped,* would be one knowledge bit, as thus: *a featherless biped
is a featherless biped.* True, but that is not what we said in the
original proposition: we said "any man" is a *featherless biped,* not
a featherless biped is a featherless biped. Third, as for definitions and
the things defined, the situation is similar: dianoetic knowledge of

---

[7] On the object of metaphysical knowledge, see Chapter I, p. 1. See St.
Thomas, *In II Sent.,* d. 3, q. 3, a. 2; *In III Sent.,* d. 27, q. 2, a. 4, qa. 2; *In I Post.
Anal.,* lect. 20, n. 5; *In I Phys.,* lect. 1, n. 203; *In Metaph.,* Prooemium; *In I
Metaph.,* lect. 2, n. 47; *In IV Metaph.,* lect. 1, nn. 532, 534; lect. 5, n. 593; *In
VI Metaph.,* lect. 1, nn. 1163–1165; *In XI Metaph.,* lect. 3, n. 2194; lect. 4, n.
2210; lect. 7, nn. 2259, 2264; *In XII Metaph.,* lect. 2, n. 2427; *In Boet. de Trin.,*
V, 1, ad 6; V, 3, *Resp.;* V, 4, ad 6. See Appendix (A) of this chapter.
See also J. Maritain, *Distinguer pour unir, ou les degrés du savoir,* pp. 3–37;
Sept leçons sur l'être, et les premiers principes de la raison spéculative, pp.
5–21; *Court traité de l'existence et de l'existant,* pp. 23–78; *The Degrees of
Knowledge,* pp. 248–278; *A Preface to Metaphysics,* pp. 18–27; E. Gilson,
Being and Some Philosophers, pp. 154–215, 224–227; J. Owens, C.Ss.R., "The
Intelligibility of Being," *Gregorianum,* Vol. V, n. 36 (1955), pp. 169–193; "A
Note on the Approach to Thomistic Metaphysics," *The New Scholasticism,*
Vol. XXVIII, n. 4 (October 1954), pp. 454–476; *The Future of Metaphysics,*
Milwaukee, Marquette University Press, 1957, pp. 1–61; *The Doctrine of Being
in the Aristotelian Metaphysics,* pp. 147–180; Y. Simon, *Introduction à l'on-
tologie du connaître,* pp. 125–231; *Prévoir et savoir,* pp. 147–154; G. Smith, S.J.,
Natural Theology, pp. 9–17.

man (man is a rational animal) gives no assurance that a rational animal exists; it simply assures us that if a man exists, he exists as a rational animal. Yet, fourth, we know a rational animal exists or can exist. So, all those four propositions are true: (1) *John is shaving,* (2) *anyone like John or any man is a featherless biped, etc.,* (3) *man is a rational animal,* (4) *a rational animal exists or can exist.*

Since they are all true, but not because unidentical knowledge bits are identical, they must be true because there is an identity in knowledge, and in fact, of two knowledge bits in some knowledge and factual area which is outside the "bitty" area, so to say. Each pair of unidentical knowledge items is identical in the knowledge of the area which is their *esse* if not in the knowledge of the area which is the *kind* of *esse* which the *esse* occupies. We not only know what things are—the area of unidentical bits of knowledge; we also, sometimes, know that what-things-are *are*—the area where what-things-are is identical in *esse,* even though unidentical with the *esse* of those "what's." This area of *esse* is the aspect or knowledge object of the metaphysician, the way things hit *his* knowledge.

The Way in Which the Object of Metaphysical Knowledge Appears

How does the metaphysician ever land into that area? In this way. When any man, metaphysician or not, knows that *grass is green,* he not only knows what *grass* is, and what *green* is; he also knows that his knowing of the existing grass is the knowing of the existing green. In other words, the knowing of the proposition, *grass is green,* is a knowing that grass exists as green. So, too, in knowing the proposition *grass is not a stone* one knows that the existing grass is not the existing stone. The same goes for all true propositions and for anyone at all who knows them: the subject and predicate of any true proposition are two unidentical knowledge bits which are known as identical in *esse* (actual or possible), or as not identical in *esse.* Nevertheless—here is the spot where the object of metaphysical knowledge appears—though known as identical *in esse,* any two

knowledge bits of a true proposition are not known as identical
with their *esse*. Metaphysical knowledge appears here, not because
the metaphysician alone knows that not a single one of the many
beings which he knows as existing is identical with its *esse*. Everyone knows that in one way or another. Rather, metaphysical knowledge appears here because the metaphysician makes it his explicit
business to know that, and to keep on knowing that.

If we ask why the metaphysician is so sure that no one of the
many things he knows is identical with its *esse*, he will point to the
fact that from any one affirmative judgment there can and must
emerge two negative judgments. For example, from *grass is green*
(affirmative judgment) there emerges, first, a negation in any of
the three following ways: *one knowledge bit (grass) is not another
knowledge bit (green)*, or *green is not necessarily grass*, or *not all
green things are grass*. Second, from *grass is green* there also emerges,
whenever the occasion demands this emergence, this negation: *grass-
existing-as-green is not a stone*, whether the stone exists as green or
not. In both negations (to-be-green is not necessarily to-be-grass;
grass is not a stone) there is (1) a denial that two intelligible structures are alike: green-structure is not grass-structure, nor is green-
grass-structure stone-structure. Furthermore, in *grass is not a stone*
there is not only a denial that two intelligible structures are identical,
just as there is, implicitly, in *grass is green;* there is also (2) a denial
that one intelligible structure in *esse* is the other intelligible structure
in *esse: grass is not a stone*. Either one of these negative judgments
shows that *esse* is not identical with the intelligible structures involved.

Take the first denial, viz., *the grass structure is not necessarily the
green structure*. This is not a denial that *grass is green*. It is a denial
that *esse* is necessarily involved in being grass, for there are things,
and green things at that, which are not grass; nor is *esse* necessarily
involved·in being green, for there are things which are not green.
So for the second negation, *grass is not a stone*. Here, too, there is
no denial that *grass exists* and that a *stone exists*. There is a denial,
however, that *esse* is necessarily involved in being either grass or
stone: *esse* is not necessarily involved in being a stone, for there is

grass; *esse* is not necessarily involved in being grass, for there is stone. Thus, in any affirmative proposition there are two ready-to-make denials: (1) the denial of one intelligible structure to another; (2) the denial of one intelligible structure in *esse* to another intelligible structure in *esse*.[8]

Reflecting upon either one of those two negations, we see that *esse* is not necessarily involved in any given intelligible structure at all. At this point the metaphysician's object of knowledge appears. The *esse* which is involved in being both grass and green, as in *grass is green* (or in being *both* grass and stone, as in *grass is* and *stone is*) is not necessarily involved in being grass, or green, or stone, or anything else like them; for, if it were, only one structure would be in *esse*. Against the fact. Besides, one structure in *esse* would not differ from that same structure when it is not in *esse*. Against the fact. *Esse* has now moved from the wings, where it *was* involved in being grass and green and stone, or what have you, to the front center of the stage, where it is before the footlights, alone. It is the job of the metaphysician to move *esse* into that spot and to keep it there.

---

[8] See St. Thomas, *In II Periherm.*, lect. 2, n. 212 (2): "Circa primum duo oportet intelligere: primo quidem, quid est hoc quod dicit, est tertium adiacens praedicatur. Ad cuius evidentiam considerandum est quod hoc verbum est quandoque in enunciatione praedicatur secundum se; ut cum dicitur, *Socrates est:* per quod nihil aliud intendimus significare, quam quod Socrates sit in rerum natura. Quandoque vero non praedicatur per se, quasi principale praedicatum, sed quasi coniunctum principali praedicato ad connectendum ipsum subiecto; sicut cum dicitur, *Socrates est albus,* non est intentio loquentis ut asserat Socratem esse in rerum natura, sed ut attribuat ei albedinem mediante hoc verbo, *est;* et ideo in talibus, *est,* praedicatur ut adiacens principali praedicato. Et dicitur esse tertium, non quia sit tertium praedicatum, sed quia est tertia dictio posita in enunciatione, quae simul cum nomine praedicato facit unum praedicatum, ut sic enunciatio dividatur in duas partes et non in tres."

There is also a ready-to-make-denial in propositions of the "second adjacent," e.g., *New York is.* Here the denial is not of one essence structure in *esse* to *another* essence structure in *esse;* rather it is a denial of one essence structure not yet, or no longer, in *esse* to the same essence structure now in *esse* (*New York was not at one time*), or no longer in *esse* (*Troy is not*). The situation is basically the same as in the propositions in the text.

On the second and third adjacent, see also E. Gilson, *Being and Some Philosophers,* pp. 190–205.

The Two Objects of Knowledge: the Categorical, the Metaphysical

Let us now see how we may keep *esse* there. It is clear that we know *esse* in two dimensions: first, we sometimes know what the *esse* is—any old "what" will suffice; secondly, we sometimes know that *what* the *esse* is *is*. The first sort of knowledge is called conceptual, and the name of the content of that knowledge is essence. Thus, essence is the name of any "what," no matter which, whereas the *description* of any old "what" differs from the description of another "what." "Man" and "fish" are both essences, though the essence which each is differs. The second dimension of knowledge is called a judgment. In the first sort of knowledge no knowledge account is taken of *esse*, except the account of what the *esse* is: and we can know in a sense to be discussed later what things are without knowing whether or not they are. In the second sort of knowledge a knowledge account is taken of *esse*: we sometimes know that what-things-are are, or are not (grass *is* green, grass is *not* a stone).[9]

The wonderful feature of this double knowledge situation seems to lie here: one conceptual knowledge (grass) of any one thing (green grass) is *not* any *other* conceptual knowledge (green) either of that one thing (green grass) or of any other conceptual knowledge of any other thing (stone); and whereas the judgmental knowledge that a thing exists (*grass is green*) is *not* knowledge identity of two different knowledge bits or concepts (how could it be?), it is nevertheless a knowledge of the identity of two knowledge bits in

[9] On categorical and metaphysical knowledge, see Aristotle, *De Anima*, III, 6, 430a 26; 430b 26–30; St. Thomas, *In III de Anima*, lect. 11; *In I Sent.*, d. 38, q. 1, a. 3, *Sol.*; *Quodlibet.*, V, q. 5, a. 2; *In Boet. de Trin.*, V, 3, *Resp.*: "We must realize that, as the Philosopher says, the intellect has two operations, one called the 'understanding of indivisibles,' by which it knows *what* a thing is; and another by which it composes and divides, that is to say, by forming affirmative and negative enunciations. Now these two operations correspond to two principles in things. The first operation has regard to the nature itself of a thing, in virtue of which the known thing holds a certain rank among beings, whether it be a complete thing, as some whole, or an incomplete thing, as a part or an accident. The second operation has regard to a thing's act of existing [*esse*], which results from the union of the principles of a thing in composite substances, or, as in the case of simple substances, accompanies the thing's simple nature."

esse. See well those two "not's": any one essence is *not* another; any one essence's *esse* is *not* that essence, nor is it anything else's essence in *esse.* Those two *"not's,"* as well as the "not" which arises from the second adjacent ("the grass of the field, which is today, and tomorrow is cast into the oven") suffice to show that *esse* is not necessarily involved in any given intelligible structure whatsoever.

The Two Mental Operations Corresponding to the Categorical and to the Metaphysical Objects of Knowledge

What can possibly account for these two knowledge situations in which one essence is *not* known (or, known *not*) to be another, and in which one existent essence is *not* known (or, known *not*) to be identically its own *esse?* Only two distinct mental operations: one which considers one essence apart from considering another essence; another which considers, overtly or covertly, an *esse* apart from the essence which has that *esse.* "To consider apart" is to consider one knowledge bit as pulled away from another knowledge bit. Hence the name "abstraction," from *abstrahere,* to pull away from. There are, then, two sorts of abstraction: the abstraction of essence from *esse,* and the abstraction of *esse* from essence.[10] The difference between these two sorts of "abstraction" lies here. In the first sort of abstraction we distinguish mentally or conceptually that which is not always separate in *esse,* e.g., we distinguish *grass* from *green,* but grass is not separate in *esse* from green when grass *is* green. In the second sort of abstraction, which we shall call "separation" from now on, we separate in *esse* that which *is* separate in *esse,* e.g., *grass is not a stone.* Observe, however, that we cannot separate in *esse,* except according to the first kind of abstraction, that which is *not* separate in *esse.* We cannot say, e.g., grass is *not* green (when it is), though we do say that "green essence" is not "grass essence," for not all green things are grass. In sum, we cannot separate in our *judgments* the factors which are not separate but

[10] We have, following St. Thomas, been using the name "separation" for the second sort of "abstraction," and we shall continue to do so.

together in *esse:* we cannot say *grass is not green* when it is. We can and *do,* however, distinguish in our minds, according to the *first sort* of abstraction, the factors which are *not* separate in *esse,* e.g., grass essence is *not* green essence, although we do not separate in *esse* that which is not separate in *esse:* for grass *is* green.[11]

St. Thomas Aquinas and Plato on the Two Distinct Mental Operations

St. Thomas Aquinas thought that Plato confused these two sorts of "abstraction."[12] Because you can consider *man* apart from individual *men,* therefore Plato, as St. Thomas read him, thought that *man* must exist apart from individual *men.* If St. Thomas is right, Plato confused the knowledge of essence with the knowledge of

[11] On abstraction and separation, see St. Thomas, *In VI Metaph.,* lect. 4, n. 1236; *Sum.. Theol.,* I, 16, 2, *Resp.;* 85, 1, *ad* 1; *In Boet. de Trin.,* V, 3, *Resp.* See Appendix B of this chapter.
    See also M. D. Philippe, "Abstraction, addition, séparation," *Revue Thomiste,* Vol. XLVIII (1948), pp. 461–479; L.-B. Geiger, "Abstraction et séparation d'après s. Thomas," *Revue des sciences phil. et théol.,* Vol. XXXI (1947), pp. 3–40; *La participation dans la philosophie de s. Thomas d'Aquin,* pp. 315–341; C. Fabro, *La nozione Metafisica di Partecipazione secundo S. Tomaso d'Aquino,* Torino, Societa Editrice Internazionale, 1950, pp. 130–139; F. Blanche, O.P., "La théorie de la abstraction chez s. Thomas d'Aquin," *Mélanges Thomistes,* Paris, Vrin, 1934, pp. 237–251; J. Maritain, *Court traité de l'existence et de l'existant,* pp. 23–60; *The Degrees of Knowledge,* pp. 71–76, 265–268, 414–432; P. Hoenen, S.J., *La théorie du jugement d'après S. Thomas d'Aquin,* Romae, Univ. Gregorianae, 1946, pp. 5–9.
[12] See St. Thomas, *In de Div. Nom.,* c. V, lect. 1, n. 634; *De Ente et Essentia,* c. III; *In Boet. de Trin.,* V, 3, *Resp.; Sum. Theol.,* I, 85, 1, *ad* 2: "And because Plato failed to consider the twofold kind of abstraction, as above explained, he held that all those things which we have stated to be abstracted by the intellect, are abstract in reality."
    St. Thomas learned about Plato largely from Aristotle, not a bad witness. Aristotle gives the meat of Plato's doctrine from Plato's oral discourses rather than by way of quoting from his dialogues. Whether or not Aristotle, and consequently St. Thomas, correctly interpreted Plato must be decided from the texts. The main texts are these. Aristotle, *Nicomachean Ethics,* I, 4, 1095a 26–28; 6, 1096a 34–62; *Metaphysics,* I (A), 6, 987a 29–987b 14; 9, 990b 7; III (B), 2, 997b 8–13; XIII (M), 4, 1078b 32. Plato, *Republic,* VI, 18, 507b; 19, 508b–509a; *Parmenides,* 130b–e, 132d. For the Platonists, see Plotinus, *The Enneads,* VI, vii, 18, 21; ed. S. MacKenna, London, Faber and Faber, 1956; Proclus, *Elements of Theology,* Props. 8–10, 12; tr. E. R. Dodds, Oxford, Clarendon, 1933, pp. 9–13; Pseudo-Dionysius, *De Divinis Nominibus,* IV, 4, 10, 18; PG III, 697, 705, 716.

esse when he advanced the thesis that what can be *conceived* (*man*) apart from something else (*men*) must *exist* apart from that something else. This Platonic confusion seems to be against the facts. The fact is that whatever is known to exist together (e.g., *man* is known to exist together with *men*. There is no *man* apart from *a* man) can sometimes be known separately, according to the first kind of abstraction (for *man* is not *a* man). According to separation, however, whatever is known to exist separately (*man* and *stone*) cannot be known to exist together. And even when two different conceptual knowledge bits *are* known to exist together, as *grass* and *green* are known to exist together in *grass is green*, nevertheless these bits are not known to exist together in *esse* by a "togetherness" of those bits with an *esse* which is an identity of *esse* with either bit. Grass doesn't exist because *esse* is necessarily grass, nor does "green." Grass exists because of its *esse*, which is not grass, and so does "green"—for the same reason; and if that reason is because both have the same *esse*, but neither one is the *esse* which they both have, we might as well say so, and we do: *grass is green.*

Abstraction Within the Categories

It remains to work out the implications of the first sort of abstraction.[13] The separation of *esse* has been sufficiently noticed for the present.[14]

[13] Recall, an object of knowledge in a realist philosophy may be spoken of as a viewpoint of a thing, as St. Thomas constantly speaks of it; or it may be spoken of mainly as a viewpoint, as Cajetan and John of St. Thomas seem to speak of it. See Cajetan, *In De Ente et Essentia*, q. 1, n. 5; *De Nominum Analogia*, c. V, p. 50; John of St. Thomas, *Cursus Philosophicus, Ars Logica*, Pars II, q. 27, a. 1; ed. Reiser, t. I, pp. 818–830.
Maybe something of St. Thomas' doctrine is lost in speaking of an object of knowledge mainly in the second way, and maybe not. At any rate, Cajetan's and John of St. Thomas' *abstractio totalis* and *abstractio formalis* "are not equivalent to St. Thomas' *abstractio totius* and *abstractio formae*." "*Total* and *formal* qualify the act of abstraction [in his commentators]; *of a whole* and *of a form* designate the object of the abstraction [in St. Thomas]." See A. Maurer, C.S.B., *The Division and Methods of the Sciences*, Questions V and VI of St. Thomas' Commentary on the *De Trinitate* of Boethius, Toronto, The Pontifical Institute of Mediaeval Studies, 1953, p. xxiv, n. 29; p. xxv, n. 30.
[14] See Chapters X–XIII.

The Abstraction of a Whole ("Abstractio Totius")[15]

Abstraction is an act of leaving out of consideration whatever does not pertain to the "hang" (*ratio*) of a thing. Now, one never gets the hang or *ratio* of a thing, e.g., *rational animal*, by *explicitly* considering the individuals (these men) or their individuating traits (*this size* of this man), which are the instances of, or involved in the instances of, that *ratio*. Individuals clutter things up, that is, they make any *ratio* about them unscientific or nonnecessary. Individuals, then, and their individuating characteristics are not *explicitly* in the *ratio* of anything. Not that individuals and their individual traits are not in the *ratio* of anything. They are—but not explicitly. Implicitly, the knowledge of all individuals and of all their individual traits is already in the knowledge of their *ratio*. To illustrate, let something be known as *animal*. All that you will ever thereafter know about a thing according to that *ratio* will be found to have been a knowledge development of the knowledge of *animal*. This relation of the knowledge of a *ratio* to the further knowledge development of that *ratio* may be expressed as a relation of actual, implicit and therefore potential, knowledge to whatsoever further explicit, and therefore actual, knowledge may latterly actuate or develop the original actual, implicit knowledge: the relation of potency to act in the area of knowledge, in other words. Put it this way: the further knowledge development of the *ratio* of any "clunk" will be found to be knowledge of that *same* "clunk." One may also express the relation of the knowledge of a *ratio* of things to the further knowledge development of that same *ratio*—it makes no difference how far that knowledge development may go—in the following way. Knowledge of a *ratio* cuts off, leaves out of consideration, abstracts from, *explicit* knowledge of individuals and of their individual characteristics, but not from *implicit* knowledge of them. Knowledge of individuals and their individual traits was there

---

[15] St. Thomas discusses the abstraction of the whole in *Sum. Theol.*, I, 40, 3, *Resp.*; *In Boet. de Trin.*, V, 3, *Resp.* See Appendix C of this chapter.

implicitly all along, in the knowledge of their *ratio*. This abstraction from individuals so as not to leave them outside the knowledge of their *ratio* as if, when they *are* known, they are *not* known as instances of, or involved in the instances of, their *ratio*, this abstraction is called by St. Thomas "abstraction without precising" from individuals. It is the abstraction of a "whole." In this sense "Socrates is said to be a sort of essence [a whole]," because "essence" doesn't precise from Socrates, although essence abstracts from Socrates without precising from him.[16]

To abstract "without precising," then, is to abstract a whole which implies but does not express its parts. The parts of the whole are not expressly in the definition of the whole: no individual man, or his individual traits, is in any definition or description of man or of individuating traits. St. Thomas Aquinas named both the process of leaving out, i.e., of abstracting without precising from individuals, as well as the whole which is the resultant of that process, *abstractio totius*.[17]

The "Totum" of the "Abstractio Totius"

Sometimes *several* characteristics necessarily do pertain to the *ratio* of the same whole, and sometimes they do not. For example, to the *ratio* of the understanding of *living* pertains the characteristics which are body and soul (besouled matter); but *sentient* and *animal* need not be understood in the understanding of *living*, for plants

---

[16] St. Thomas, *De Ente et Essentia*, c. III; Marietti, n. 18: ". . . natura hominis absolute considerata abstrahit a quolibet esse, ita quod non fiat praecisio alicuius eorum. Et haec natura sic considerata est quae praedicatur de omnibus individuis." See *De Pot.*, V, 9, *ad* 16: "To abstract so as to precise from individuals is to reach a *ratio* which explicitly leaves out individuals and their individual traits. In this sense 'the essence of Socrates is not Socrates'"—*De Ente et Essentia*, c. II, n. 15. This latter abstraction is the abstraction of a "form," as we shall see, and the form so abstracted is a "precised form."

[17] Cajetan and John of St. Thomas thought that St. Thomas' *abstractio totius*, which they called *abstractio totalis*, is common to all sciences, "but properly defines none of them." See A. Maurer, C.S.B., *The Division and Methods of the Sciences*, pp. xxiv–xxv. Perhaps it is better to say that *abstractio totalis* is the only abstraction there is in the philosophy of nature, but it is not especially characteristic of the philosophy of nature.

live and they are neither *sentient* nor *animal*. Hence *sentient* and *animal* are left out of the understanding of *living:* it is not necessary to understand *them* in order to understand *living*. Thus, the *totum* (of the *abstractio totius*) is a whole, caused, first, by leaving out, but not precising from, individual traits, and by not considering the nonpertinent universal characteristics of that whole; it is caused, secondly, by taking into the understanding of that whole the universal and necessarily pertinent characteristics of that whole. Thus, in order to understand the "man" whole, you abstract but do not precise from the individuals (these men) and from their individual traits (these sizes of these men); and you leave out as well the universal traits which are not necessarily pertinent to the understanding of the "man" whole, e.g., six feet tall, white, flat-footed, etc.; but you take in *animal, rational, sentient,* etc. The *totum* which is the resultant of the *abstractio totius* is thus a *totum* not only because it abstracts without precising from individuals (though it does), not only because it leaves out the nonpertinent universal characteristics of the whole (though it does), but also because the *totum* itself may be made up of more than one universal and necessary[18] characteristic of the whole. Thus, the understanding of *man* not only abstracts without precising from the understanding of "this flesh"; but within the whole which is the understanding of *man* there is also the understanding of "flesh, bones," and so on.[19]

[18] Should a universal characteristic pertain to a whole, but not necessarily, except as a matter of fact, then we have an *accidental* relation of that characteristic to the whole: as, e.g., in *this man is fat,* or *man is fat*. Should a universal characteristic pertain to a whole and necessarily, but as derivative from, not as constitutive of that whole, then we have a property: *man is mirthful, cooks his food,* etc. A property is much easier to define than to discover.

[19] See St. Thomas, *In Boet. de Trin.,* V, 2, *Resp.:* ". . . the nature of man, which his definition signifies, and which is the object of science, is considered without *this* flesh and *these* bones, but not absolutely without flesh and bones. And since, as the *Metaphysics* says, individual things include determined matter in their nature while universals include common matter, we do not call this simply an abstraction of form from matter, but of the universal from the particular."

See also *De Ente et Essentia,* c. II; *Sum. Theol.,* I, 85, 1, *ad* 2: "Some have thought that the species of a natural thing is a form only, and that matter is not part of the species. If that were so, matter would not enter into the definition of natural things. Therefore we must disagree and say that matter is twofold, common and *signate,* or individual: common, such as flesh and

The Relation of the Understanding of the Whole to the Understanding of Matter

The understanding of a whole or of a *ratio* always involves simultaneously the understanding of that whole's appropriate but not of its inappropriate matter. The understanding of *some* matter, in other words, always tags along with, or is involved in, the understanding of the whole. We may see the point in this way: on the side of *things* we have composites of matter (prime and second matter) and form (substantial and accidental); on the side of our *knowledge* of those composites we have composite knowledge. The composite knowledge is made up of these components: the knowledge of the form of matter, and the knowledge of the matter of that form. The knowledge of *some* matter, in other words, always tags along with, or is in the understanding of formed matter; and that "some matter" is the appropriate matter of the form, not the form's inappropriate matter. One might put it thus: since the form of matter is always unintelligible without the understanding of some matter, form cannot be understood without understanding that "some" matter. In short, the form of matter cannot be understood without also some understanding of the matter of that form.[20] For example, *accidents* (forms of substance) cannot be abstracted from *substance*, nor can *quantity*. But *quantity* can be abstracted from the qualities of material substance. One dozen (form of divided units) can be understood without having to understand that it is a dozen eggs, good or bad, which are involved in the dozen; but one dozen cannot be understood without understanding one dozen uncharacterized but

bone; individual, such as this flesh and these bones. The intellect therefore abstracts the species of a natural thing from the individual sensible matter, but not from the common sensible matter. For example, it abstracts the species *of man* from *this flesh and these bones*, which do not belong to the species as such, but to the individual, and need not be considered in the species. But the species of man cannot be abstracted by the intellect from *flesh and bones*."

[20] The word "form" is thus ambiguous: it could mean the form of formed matter; or it could mean the form of the *understanding* of formed matter. It is this latter understanding of formed matter, which is a knowledge "form." The knowledge and abstraction of precised form will be explained later.

imagined divided units. So for continuous quantities: a line, a plane, a solid cannot be understood without understanding imagined lines, planes, solids.[21] Aristotle thought that the understanding of "form" (the *ratio* of informed matter) did not include the understanding of matter.[22] St. Thomas Aquinas thought that it did: the understanding at least of some matter, namely, the appropriate matter of that form,[23] and that is why St. Thomas saw that *esse* and all its properties can be known either with or without knowing matter. For, *esse* is *not* a form, though there are forms of *esse*.

The Abstraction of a Form ("Abstractio Formae")[24]

As we saw, *animal* is a whole or *ratio* which does not precise or leave out individuals and their individual traits, though it abstracts from them without precising. This means that the knowledge of animal neither explicitly includes nor excludes further knowledge bits about *animal* (*rational, of this size and weight*, etc.); the knowledge of *animal*, however, implicitly includes all those further knowledge bits.

[21] Should quantities be unimaginable or unpicturable, as in non-Euclidean mathematics, they are objects of second intentional knowledge. In Euclidean mathematics, the objects of knowledge are first intentional objects of knowledge. See J. Maritain, *Distinguer pour unir, ou les degrés du savoir*, pp. 107–110, 285, 325–326.

[22] Aristotle, *Metaphysics*, VII (Z), 7, 1032b 1–21; VII, 10, 1035a 17–22; VII, 11, 1037a 25–29. Aristotle thought that form was the ultimate act. St. Thomas did not.

[23] See St. Thomas, *In Boet. de Trin.*, V, 2, *Resp.*; V, 3, *Resp.*; *In III de Caelo et Mundo*, lect. 3, n. 4. To work this out a bit, the understanding of *act* leaves out the understanding of the inappropriate but not of the appropriate potency, but the understanding of *potency* does not leave out the understanding of *act*. Triangle leaves out the individual and the universal characteristics of *isosceles, scalene* and *right* angle triangles, but not *three joined lines*. *Accident* leaves out the *substance* to which it is actually related, but not its relation to *substance*. Man leaves out Peter, Paul, etc., but not *flesh, bones, animal, sentient*, etc. The *whole* leaves out a *part*, but not *vice versa*. In sum, *form* always leaves out the *matter* upon which the form doesn't depend for its *ratio* (the hang of the thing), e.g., *man* leaves out the matter of *this* and *that* man; but form does not leave out the matter upon which it depends for its *ratio*, e.g., *man* doesn't leave out *flesh, bones*, etc.

[24] On the abstraction of a form, see St. Thomas, *In Boet. de Trin.*, V, 3, *Resp.*; *Sum. Theol.*, I, 40, 3, *Resp.*; *De Ente et Essentia*, c. II; Marietti, nn. 14–15; c. III, n. 18. See Appendix D of this chapter.

Knowledge of Precised Form

We are now faced with the task of explaining the knowledge of *animality*. *Animality* is a "form" in the expression *abstractio formae*. The knowledge of that form is the knowledge of a characteristic which excludes, by precising from, individual traits. "Precised" form thus leaves out individual traits as a *totum* does not. Precised form excludes those traits; the *totum* neither includes nor excludes them explicitly.

In the *totum*, the individuals and their individual traits are indeed parts of the *totum*, and that is why the whole cannot leave them out or precise from them explicitly. Now, not explicitly to leave out is to include implicitly. Thus, the *totum* neither explicitly includes its parts nor does it explicitly exclude them; it includes them implicitly though, and excludes them as actual knowledge of a whole is also and only potential knowledge of the parts, which latter knowledge is the further knowledge development of the knowledge of the original whole.

On the other hand, the precised form in the *abstractio formae*, explicitly excludes—what? The precised form explicitly excludes individuating characteristics, precises from them, cuts them clean off. For example, *animality* precises from any individual or individuating trait, with the result that there is in the knowledge of *animality* no knowledge whatsoever, implicit or explicit, of any individual animal or its individuating traits. Knowledge of *animality* is knowledge of a *ratio* which we have divorced from any implicit or explicit reference to individualities. (The knowledge of *animal*, recall, is knowledge of a *ratio* which *has* an implicit reference to all the rest that may be known about *animal*.) There is, of course, in our knowledge of *animality* everything but knowledge of individualities. All the principles of *animality* are known in knowing it: substance is known, and accident, and matter, and form, etc., but not any individual instances of any composite, not even the *individuum vagum* (someone). The "vague individual," on the other hand, is implicitly known in the *ratio* which is his *totum*, but not in the *ratio* of the precised form, which precises from any individual, vague or not.

What then is this "form" which is the resultant of a precising abstraction? It is the knowledge of a whole which is *considered* as a part, though it may or may not be a part. To explain, there are parts which are considered as parts, because they are parts: the integral parts of a man, e.g., his arms, legs, and so on; then there are the parts which fall under the potency-act couplet, e.g., essence-*esse*, substance-accident, prime matter-substantial form. All these we consider as parts because they are. However, there are other "parts" which are parts only because we consider them as such, but they are not. The knowledge of *animality* is knowledge of a whole in which everything is known that pertains to *animality*, everything that is, except individuating traits. These we have explicitly excluded. Now, individuating traits are indeed parts of Socrates, say, but *animality* is not a part of Socrates as potency is, or as act is, or as arms, or as legs. *Animality* is only *viewed* as a part of Socrates. It follows that since no part is a whole, no part of a whole can be predicated of that whole. Thus, we cannot say a *man is his arm*, nor that the *composite of essence and esse is esse (or essence)*, nor that the *composite of substance and accident is accident (or substance)*, nor that the *composite of prime matter and substantial form is prime matter (or substantial form)*; nor can we say that a *man is animality*. In all these cases we can say the subject *has* the predicate, but not that the subject *is* the predicate. The reason is: a part is not the whole, not even that "part" (*animality*) which *is* a whole, because, though a whole, *animality* is considered by a precising abstraction as a part.

The Predication of a Whole (the Knowledge of Formed Matter) and of Precised Form

Language is basically a matter of predication about things, of saying something about them; but before anything is said about anything, there is a presupposed knowledge that the something about

which you are going to talk is a unit. Let us take John *que voila!*
Before you say anything about John, you know him in any old way,
for example, as a spot, smudge, a cough, a grunt, an odor . . . Now
here's the point: any or all of these knowledges about John presuppose that they are knowledges about *him.* Even if you recognize
a top and bottom to the smudge or spot which is John, even if there
is a difference between his cough and his grunt, even if there's a
variation in his scent, you are sure *before* you say anything about
him that both the top and bottom of the spot is his, John's, top and
bottom; that his cough is *his,* and so on.

Assume now that you say of John that *he is a man,* that you say
of George *que voila!* that *he too is a man,* that you say of *man* that
he is an animal, and *so is a horse,* that you say of John that *he is
white.* Here we have enough ways of predicating or talking about
John to make a point. The point is this: the unit, John, is given in
knowledge; and anything you say about that unit cannot possibly
fail to be knowledge of *that unit.* It cannot so fail if there is to be
knowledge of a being, for to be is to be a unit; not to be a unit is
not to be, and not to know a unit is not to know at all.

It remains to make explicit the relations of the predicates to their
subjects: the relation of species (man) to the individuals of the
species (John, George); the relation of genus (animal) to the species
of animal (man, horse); the relation of accident (white) to the subject of white (John).[25]

The relation of the predicates to the subjects must in all cases be
so explained as not to split the unity of the subject. Hence, in our
explanation we must first eliminate the possibility that precised
forms can be predicates. Precised forms cannot be predicates, precisely because they precise from individuals. We may say indeed
that *John has humanity, animality* (and *so has a horse animality*),
that *John has whiteness;* but in no case can we say that John *is* the
precised forms. The reason is: the precised forms are considered as
parts of their respective subjects, and, even though they may be
wholes (animality) or may not be (whiteness), they are not *con-*

[25] See St. Thomas, *De Ente et Essentia,* c. II; Marietti, n. 14; c. III, n. 16;
Sum. Theol., I, 85, 5, *ad* 3. See Appendix E of this chapter.

sidered as wholes. So we cannot predicate them of the subjects, because no part of a whole is the whole. If John's parts were, each, a whole, there wouldn't be any given unit, John, either in things or in our knowledge of units. Impossible, for not to be a unit is not to be, and the subject exists as a unit (given); moreover, not to know a unit is not to know.

However, second, a *ratio* in our knowledge, any knowledge, compounded of our knowledge of form *and* of our knowledge of form's appropriate matter, that *ratio* does not exclude explicitly any further knowledge development of that same *ratio;* on the contrary, it includes implicitly those further knowledge developments. Thus, any knowledge of the spot, the smudge, etc., which is that thing, John, is still knowledge of that thing, John: e.g., the knowledge of that thing, John, as being a *man* is still knowledge of *him;* the knowledge of George and John as being *men* is still knowledge of *them;* the knowledge of *man* and *horse,* known as being *animals,* is still knowledge of *them;* the knowledge of John, known as being *white,* is still knowledge of *him.* In all cases the predicates include the units (subjects). Not explicitly or expressly, of course. There is no explicit knowledge about John in the knowledge of *man,* but the knowledge of *man* doesn't exclude the knowledge of *John.* Our knowledge of *white, man, animal, rational* implicitly includes the knowledge of the subjects of those predicates, and if we must at times say so, we might as well say it, as indeed we do. This "saying" so is language or predication. There could be no true predication unless the predicate included its subject.

The Predication of Body

Some words are *clearly* signs of precised forms: *animality, whiteness,* etc.; some words could be signs either of precised forms, or of wholes implicitly inclusive of their subjects: *body, state, virtue, incendiarism, conflagration,* etc.

The only way to tell whether a word means a precised form or a whole is to work it out. The principle of the solution is as follows. Whereas in *things* form organizes matter into a unit of formed matter, and whereas in *thought* the thought-form organizes the "thought of" into a "thought of" unit, nevertheless the thought-form may organize the "thought of" differently. When, e.g., I think of *body* as having three dimensions and nothing else, no further specification, that is, then I am thinking of *body* as a part of all bodies; and that part is not a body, for no body has three dimensions and nothing else. So thought of, *body* is a precised form and is not a predicate any more than *animality* is a predicate. In this sense, John *has* a body, he *is* not a body. *However*, if I think of *body* as having three dimensions and further but as yet unspecified characteristics (*living, sentient,* etc.), then I am thinking of *body* as an implicitly determined whole even though that whole can be further determined explicitly, as, for example, by John's being a body. In this sense *John is a body.*[26]

The Relation of the Knowledge of the Whole to the Knowledge of the Precised Form

Is the "whole" in the "abstraction of a whole" the same as the "form" in the "abstraction of a form"? No. The whole (*animal*) is not a part, and although the part (*animality*) is a whole, it is nonetheless viewed as a part. In that whole which is viewed as a part (*animality*) there is lacking any knowledge reference, even implicit, to individual characteristics. However, minus those individual characteristics, the intelligible content of both the whole (*animal*) and the whole-viewed-as-a-part (*animality*) there is the same intelligible content. True, animality doesn't exist. Only animals exist. Nevertheless, all the intelligible content in *animal* is in *animality* minus, in the latter case, the implicit knowledge of individuals and of their individuating traits.[27]

[26] See St. Thomas, *De Ente et Essentia,* c. II; Marietti, nn. 9–10; *In I Sent.,* d. 19, q. 5, a. 2, *ad* 1; Cajetan, *In De Ente et Essentia,* c. III, nn. 42–44. See Appendix F of this chapter.

[27] Anyone of course can make make up words which seem to stand for precised forms: igneity, jugginess, or Shakespeare's *honorificabilitudinitatibus.* This is all good, clean fun, and it should be poked at decadent Scholastics. However, we are assuming here that *animality* is a sign of knowledge. It could be such a sign, and we speak only of the instances in which it is.

First and Second Intentional Wholes and Precised Forms

First and second intentions co-divide wholes and precised forms.
Recall that wholes are understandings of formed matter with implicit reference to individuals; and precised forms are understandings of those same wholes viewed as generic or specific or accidental
parts of an individual. These precised forms explicitly exclude individuals. Now, both understandings of wholes and precised forms
are in the *esse* of knowledge, namely, intentional *esse*.

The intentional *esse* by which both wholes and precised forms
exist in knowledge may function in two ways: first, so as to cause
knowledge to be knowledge of things; second, so as to cause knowledge to be knowledge of the knowledge of things. From the first
function of intentional *esse* the content or object of knowledge is
named a first intention; from the second, a second intention. First
intentional knowledge is knowledge of a whole or of a precised
form inasmuch as the wholes and precised forms are understood
according to their *ratio*, e.g., *as* animal (or *animality*), *as* living (or
life). Second intentional knowledge is knowledge of a whole or of
a precised form inasmuch as the whole and the precised form are
units which can exist in many individual things. The individuals *are*
the wholes (John is a *man*).[28]

The point needs some clarification. Take *animal*, a whole. View
animal as a unit understanding which explicitly leaves out the understanding of all the characteristics which are not pertinent to the
understanding of *animal*, e.g., *rational* and *individual* animals with
their *individual* traits. View *animal* also as an understanding which
explicitly includes the understanding of *sentient* and *living*. View
animal last as an understanding which implicitly includes the understanding of *rational* and of *individual* animals. Then that unit or
whole understanding of *animal* is such that it is an understanding of

---

[28] The precised form cannot exist in the individual as precised. Animality
does not exist. However, all the intelligible content of *animality* exists in each
animal. We can say that this animal and that *have* animality, just as we say this
and that animal *are* animals.

nothing but *animal*. That is, no understanding of any *other* kind of being would suffice for the understanding of *animal*. This understanding is a first intention. On the other hand, view the understanding of *animal* as the understanding of a unit which can exist in many individuals. In this latter sense any other unit, e.g., the *inanimate* or the *living*, would suffice just as well in order to understand the unit-which-can-exist-in-many individuals. This is a second intention. Synonyms of first intentions are: metaphysical universals, direct universals, metaphysical wholes. Synonyms of second intentions are: logical universals, reflex universals, logical wholes. The difference between the first and second intention, then, lies here: the first intention is an understanding of an intelligible content or structure; the second intention is the understanding of any old *ratio*, not according to its intelligible content, but according to the feature which any *ratio* whatsoever has of being universal or able to be in many. The fact that *animal* is the understanding of *besouled sentient matter* is the reason why it is called a first intention, etc. Any other *ratio* would *not* suffice for the understanding of *that ratio*. The fact that *animal* is also a unit understanding which abstracts, without precising, from individuals, and which leaves out nonpertinent but explicitly includes pertinent characteristics, and which implicitly includes everything else that an *animal* or, for that matter a *plant* may be—this is the reason why *animal* or *plant* is called a universal or a second intention. Any other such *ratio* does precisely the same thing. In short, no one *ratio* is another *ratio;* upon this score a *ratio* is a first intention. Each *ratio* is universal; upon this score it is a second intention.[29]

Let us say the same thing differently. In order to understand

[29] See Chapter X, pp. 153–158. See also Cajetan, *In De Ente et Essentia*, c. III, n. 40: ". . . we can speak of essences in a threefold way: first we can speak of them absolutely and without any relation to first or second intentions; secondly we can speak of them as they are expressed by terms of the first intentions; thirdly we can speak of them as they are expressed by terms of the second intention. For example, we can speak of human nature in itself, that is, inasmuch as it has predicates which are due it by reason of its essence; we can speak of it as it is expressed by the term *humanity*, or by the term *man*; and we can speak of it as it is expressed by the term species."

On direct and reflex concepts, see John of St. Thomas, *Cursus Philosophicus, Ars Logica*, Pars I, Summul., Lib. I, cap. iii; Reiser, t. I, p. 11a 5–15.

animal as *living* and *sentient* it is not necessary to understand that *ratio* (*living, sentient*) as universal or as not universal, as singular or as not singular. All you have to understand about *animal* in order to get the hang of it is this: animal is *besouled sentient matter,* and that understanding is neither universal nor not-universal, neither singular nor not-singular. This is the first intention, the direct, etc., universal. On the other hand, in order to understand *animal* or any thing else *as* universal you must understand it as a unit which can exist in many (*unum aptum esse in pluribus*); that is, you must understand it *as* universal. This is the second intention, the logical, etc., universal.

The Ambiguity in the Names Genus, Difference, etc.

There are *kinds* of universality in the logical universal: the universality of genus, of difference, of property, of accident. Hence, the logical universal does *not* exclude different universalities. Rather, it includes them as a potential understanding of them: the understanding of the *universality* of *animal* is a potential understanding of the understanding of the *universality* of *man* and *beast.* But the understanding of *animal* as besouled sentient matter neither explicitly excludes nor does it explicitly include the understanding of *man* and *beast.* However, the understanding of *animal* implicitly includes the understanding of *man* and *beast.* Nor does the understanding of *animal* as *animal* (besouled sentient matter) include explicitly the understanding of it as universal or not-universal, as singular or not-singular; however, the understanding of *animal* as besouled sentient matter implicitly includes the understanding of *animal* as singular and as universal.[30]

The word *genus* (and *difference,* etc.), then, as well as the word *animal* (*rational,* etc.) is ambiguous. *Genus* might mean a kind of universality, viz., generic universality; or it might mean the *ratio* which as a *ratio* neither has nor has not universality, neither has nor has not singularity. So too, *animal* might mean a kind of universality,

---

[30] See Chapter XIII, pp. 212–214.

viz., generic, or it might mean the *ratio*, viz., besouled sentient matter. About all we can do about the matter is to note the ambiguity and watch it.[31]

Appendix to Chapter XIV

APPENDIX (A). The object of metaphysical knowledge.

St. Thomas, *In Metaph.*, Prooemium: "From this it is clear that, although this demonstrative knowledge considers the three classes of objects spoken of [common principles, universal causes, separate substances], it does not have any one of them at all for its subject, but only being in common. For that is the subject of a knowledge of which we seek the causes and passions [properties]; but the causes themselves of a given genus are not the subject. For the knowledge of the causes of some genus is the end to which the consideration of a knowledge finally attains. Still, though the subject of this knowledge is being in common, the whole of it is said to be about those things which are separate from matter according to their act of existing and according to their intelligibility. For not only are those things which can never be in matter said to be separate from matter according to their *esse* and their intelligibility (such are God and intellectual substances), but also those things which are able to be without matter, such as being in common. But this could not be, if [the latter] depended on matter for their existence.

"According to these three classes of objects which have been mentioned, therefore, from which we weigh the perfection of this demonstrative knowledge, it comes to have three names. It is called divine knowledge, or *theology*, in so far as it considers the abovementioned substances. It is called *metaphysics* in so far as it considers being and those things which follow upon it; for these transphysical things are arrived at by the way of analysis, as the more

---

[31] Biological species are perinoetic understandings. We know that the perinoetic predicates of biological species are necessary, but the reason why escapes us. The species spoken of in the text are mainly species understood dianoetically.

common are arrived at after the less common. It is spoken of as *first philosophy*, in so far as it considers the first causes of things. Thus it is clear what the subject of this demonstrative knowledge is, in what way it is related to other knowledges, and by what name it is named."

St. Thomas, *In Boet. de Trin.*, V, 1, *ad* 6: "Although the subjects of the other sciences are parts of being, which is the subject of metaphysics, the other sciences are not necessarily parts of metaphysics. For each science treats of one part of being in a special way distinct from that in which metaphysics treats of being. So its subject is not a part of being according to that character by which being is the subject of metaphysics. But from the point of view of this character it is a special science distinct from the others."

St. Thomas, *In Boet. de Trin.*, V, 3, *Resp.*: "We conclude that in the operation of the intellect there is present a threefold distinction: one with respect to the operation of the intellect composing and dividing, which is properly called separation; and this belongs to divine science or metaphysics. There is another with respect to the operation by which the quiddities of things are formed, which is the abstraction of form from sensible matter; and this belongs to mathematics. And there is a third with respect to the same operation which is the abstraction of a universal from the particular; and this indeed belongs to physics and to all the sciences in general, because in every science we disregard the accidental and consider what is essential."

St. Thomas, *In Boet. de Trin.*, V, 4, *ad* 6: "The metaphysician deals with individual beings too, not with regard to their special natures in virtue of which they are special kinds of being, but in so far as they share the common character of being. And in this way matter and motion also fall under his consideration."

APPENDIX (B). Abstraction and separation.

St. Thomas, *In Boet. de Trin.*, V, 3, *Resp.*: "The first operation has regard to the nature itself of a thing, in virtue of which the known thing holds a certain rank among beings, whether it be a complete thing, as some whole, or an incomplete thing, as a part or an accident. The second operation has regard to a thing's act of existing (*esse*), which results from the union of the principles of a thing in composite substances, or, as in the case of simple substances, accompanies the thing's simple nature.

"Now, since the truth of the intellect results from its conformity with the thing, clearly in this second operation the intellect cannot truthfully abstract what is united in reality, because the abstraction would signify a separation with regard to the very existence of the thing. For example, if I abstract man from whiteness by saying, 'Man is not white,' I signify that there is a separation in reality. So if in reality man and whiteness are not separated, the intellect will be false. Through this operation, then, the intellect can truthfully abstract only those things which are separated in reality, as when we say, 'Man is not an ass.'

"Through the first operation, however, we can abstract things which are not separated in reality; not all, it is true, but some. For since everything is intelligible in so far as it is in act, as the *Metaphysics* says, we must understand the nature itself or the quiddity of a thing either inasmuch as it is a certain act (as happens in the case of forms themselves and simple substances); or by reason of that which is its act (as we know composite substances through their forms); or by reason of that which takes the place of act in it (as we know prime matter through its relationship to form, and vacuum through the absence of a body in place). And it is from this that each nature is given its definition. . . .

"Accordingly, in its various operations the intellect distinguishes one thing from another in different ways. In the operation by which it composes and divides, it distinguishes one thing from another by understanding that the one does not exist in the other. In the operation, however, by which it understands that a thing is, it distinguishes one from the other by knowing what one is without knowing anything of the other, either that it is united to it or separated from it. So this distinction is not properly called separation, but only the first. It is correctly called abstraction, but only when the things, one of which is known without the other, are one in reality. For if

we consider animal without considering stone, we do not say that
we abstract animal from stone."

APPENDIX (C). The abstraction of the whole.

St. Thomas, *In Boet. de Trin.*, V, 3, *Resp.*: "It follows that since,
properly speaking, we can only abstract things united in reality,
there are two sorts of abstraction corresponding to the two modes
of union mentioned above, namely, the union of part and whole,
and the union of form and matter. The first is that in which we
abstract form from matter, and the second is that in which we abstract a whole from its parts. . . .

"Furthermore, we cannot abstract a whole from just any parts
whatsoever. For there are some parts on which the nature of the
whole depends, that is, when to be such a whole is to be composed
of such parts. It is in this way that a syllable is related to letters and
a mixed body to the elements. Parts of this sort, which are necessary
for understanding the whole because they enter into its definition,
are called parts of the species and of the form. There are some parts,
however, which are accidental to the whole as such. The semicircle,
for instance, is related to the circle in this way, for it is accidental
to a circle that by division two of its parts or more are considered
equal or unequal. But it is not accidental to a triangle that three
lines are designated in it, for because of this a triangle is a triangle.
Similarly it is an essential characteristic of man that there be found
in him a rational soul and a body composed of the four elements.
So man cannot be understood without these parts and they must
be included in his definition; so they are parts of his species and
form. But finger, foot, and hand, and other parts of this kind are
outside the notion of man; and thus the essential nature of man does
not depend on them and man can be understood without them. For
whether or not he has feet, as long as he be granted as made up
of a rational soul and a body composed of the elements in the
proper mixture required by this sort of form, he will be a man.
And these parts are called parts of matter, which are not included
in the definition of the whole, but rather the converse is true. This

is how all determined parts are related to man; for instance, *this* soul, *this* body, *this* nail, *this* bone, etc. These indeed are parts of Socrates' and Plato's essence, but not of man precisely as man. And for this reason the intellect can abstract man from these parts. And this sort of abstraction is the abstraction of the universal from the particular.

"So there are two abstractions of the intellect: one which corresponds to the union of form and matter or accident and subject. This is the abstraction of form from sensible matter. The other corresponds to the union of whole and part; and to this corresponds the abstraction of the universal from the particular. This is the abstraction of a whole, in which we consider a nature according to its essential character, in independence of all parts which do not belong to the species but are accidental parts. But we do not find abstractions opposed to these, in which a part is abstracted from a whole or matter from form, because a part either cannot be abstracted from a whole by the intellect if it is one of the parts of matter in whose definition the whole is included; or it can indeed exist without the whole if it is one of the parts of the species; for instance, a line without a triangle, a letter without a syllable, or an element without a mixed body. . . .

"We conclude that in the operation of the intellect there is present a threefold distinction: one with respect to the operation of the intellect composing and dividing, which is properly called separation; and this belongs to divine science or metaphysics. There is another with respect to the operation by which the quiddities of things are formed, which is the abstraction of form from sensible matter; and this belongs to mathematics. And there is a third with respect to the same operation which is the abstraction of a universal from the particular; and this indeed belongs to physics and to all the sciences in general, because in every science we disregard the accidental and consider what is essential. And because certain persons, like the Pythagoreans and the Platonists, did not understand the difference between the last two and the first they fell into error, asserting that mathematicals and universals are separate from sensible things."

APPENDIX (D). The abstraction of a form.

St. Thomas, *De Ente et Essentia*, c. II; Marietti, nn. 14–15: "But if the nature of the species is signified in precision from designated matter, which is the principle of individuation, then it will have the role of a part. This is the way it is signified by the word *humanity*, for humanity expresses that by reason of which man is man. Now, it is not designated matter by which man is man; so it is not in any way included among the things by which man is man. Since the concept of humanity, then, includes only those things by which man is man, it manifestly excludes or omits from its signification designated matter. And because the part is not predicated of the whole, humanity is predicated neither of man nor of Socrates. Hence, Avicenna declares that the quiddity of a composite is not the composite itself whose quiddity it is, although the quiddity itself be the composite. Although humanity, for instance, is composite, it is not man; it must be received in something which is designated matter. . . .

"By humanity, therefore, we mean a certain form, called the form of the whole. It is not as something added to the essential parts, namely, form and matter, as the form of a house is added to its integral parts; rather, it is the form which is the whole, embracing both form and matter, excluding, however, those things which enable matter to be designated.

"The word *man* and the word *humanity*, then, clearly signify man's essence, but, as we have said, they do so in different ways. . . . The word *humanity*, . . . signifies man's essence as a part, because it signifies only what belongs to man as man, excluding all designation of matter. Therefore it is not predicated of individual men. And this is why we sometimes find the word *essence* predicated of a thing (for we say that Socrates is a certain essence), and sometimes denied (as when we say that Socrates' essence is not Scorates)."

St. Thomas, *De Ente et Essentia*, c. III, n. 18: "Yet, the nature itself, considered properly—that is to say, absolutely—demands none of these acts of existing. It is false to say that the nature of man as such exists in this individual man, because, if existing in this individual belonged to man as man, it would never exist outside this individual. Similarly, if it belonged to man as man not to exist in this individual, human nature would never exist in it. It is true to say, however, that it does not belong to man as man to exist in this or that individual, or in the intellect. Considered in itself, the nature of man thus clearly abstracts from every act of existing, but in such a way that none may be excluded from it. And it is the nature considered in this way that we predicate of all individual beings."

APPENDIX (E). The relation of predicates to their subjects.

St. Thomas, *De Ente et Essentia*, c. II, n. 14: ". . . the nature of the species is indeterminate with respect to the individual, as the nature of the genus is with respect to the species. As a consequence, just as the genus, predicated of the species, implies indistinctly in its signification everything which is determinately in the species, so too the species, predicated of the individual, must signify, although indistinctly, everything essentially in the individual. In this way the word *man* expresses the essence of the species, and so man is predicated of Socrates. . . . relative to the genus the species is designated by forms, while relative to the species the individual is designated by matter."

St. Thomas *De Ente et Essentia*, c. III, nn. 16, 20: ". . . the essence has the nature of a genus or species in so far as it is expressed after the manner of a whole, for instance, by the word *man* or *animal*, as containing implicitly and indistinctly everything that is in the individual. . . . We may predicate of Socrates everything which belongs to man as man. Yet, it belongs to the genus in virtue of its very nature to be predicated, since this is part of its definition. For predication is something accomplished by the intellect's act of combining and dividing, having for its foundation in reality the very unity of those things, one of which is said of the other."

St. Thomas, *Sum. Theol.*, I, 85, 5, *ad* 3: "In a material thing there is a twofold composition. First, there is the composition of form with matter. To this corresponds that composition of the intellect whereby the universal whole is predicated of its part: for the genus is derived from common matter, while the difference that completes the species is derived from the form, and the particular from individual matter. The second composition is of accident with subject; and to this composition corresponds that composition of the intellect whereby accident is predicated of subject, as when we say *the man is white*. Nevertheless, the composition of the intellect differs from the composition of things; for the components in the things are diverse, whereas the composition of the intellect is a sign of the identity of the components. For the above composition of the intellect was not such as to assert that *man is whiteness;* but the assertion, *the man is white*, means that *the man is something having whiteness*. It is the same with the composition of form and matter. For *animal* signifies that which has a sensitive nature; *rational*, that which has an intellectual nature; *man*, that which has both; and *Socrates* that which has all these things together with individual matter. And so, according to this kind of identity our intellect composes one thing with another by means of predication."

APPENDIX (F). The predication of body.

St. Thomas, *De Ente et Essentia*, c. II, nn. 9–10: "The word *body* has several meanings. Body in the genus substance means that which has such a nature that three dimensions can be designated in it. But the three designated dimensions themselves are a body according as body is in the genus quantity. . . . Similarly, over and above the perfection of having such a form that three dimensions can be designated in it, another perfection can be added, such as life, or something of the kind. The word *body*, therefore, can signify something having a form such that it admits the possibility of designating in it three dimensions, to the exclusion of any further perfection following upon that form. If anything else is added, it is outside the meaning of *body* in this sense of the word. In this sense body will be an integral and material part of animal, because soul then will not be included in the meaning of the word *body*, and it will be additional to body itself; so that, as parts, these two—soul and body—constitute the animal.

"We also can understand by the word *body* a thing having a form such that three dimensions can be designated in it, no matter what that form may be, whether some further perfection can come from it or not. In this sense body will be the genus *animal*, because there is nothing to be found in animal which is not implicitly contained in body. Soul is not a form different from that through which three dimensions could be designated in that thing. Consequently, when we said that a body is that which has a form such that in virtue of it three dimensions can be designated in the body, it was understood of whatever the form might be, whether animality, or stoneness, or any other form. Thus, the form of animal is implicitly contained in the form of body, inasmuch as body is its genus. Animal likewise bears the same relation to man. For, if *animal* were the name simply of a thing having a perfection such that it is capable of sensation and movement through an intrinsic principle, to the exclusion of another perfection, then any other additional perfection would be related to animal as a part, and not as implicitly contained in the notion of animal; so, animal would not be a genus. But it is a genus inasmuch as it signifies a thing from whose form sensation and movement can issue, no matter what that form may be, whether it be simply a sensitive soul or a soul that is both sensitive and rational."

Suggested Reading

The Object of Knowledge:

Cajetan, *In De Ente et Essentia*, Prooemium, q. 1, n. 5; *De Nominum Analogia*, c. V.

John of St. Thomas, *Ars Logica*, Pars II, q. 1, a. 3; q. 21, a. 4; q. 27, a. 1; *De Anima*, Pars IV, q. 2, a. 3.

Maritain, J., *An Introduction to Philosophy*, p. 106.

———, *The Degrees of Knowledge*, pp. 58–59.

Simon, Y., *Introduction à l'ontologie du connaître*, pp. 9–10.

The Object of Metaphysical Knowledge:

St. Thomas Aquinas, *In II Sent.*, d. 3, q. 3, a. 2; *In III Sent.*, d. 27, q. 2, a. 4, qa. 2; *In I Post. Anal.*, lect. 20, n. 5; *In I Phys.*, lect. 1, nn. 2–3; *In I Metaph.*, Prooemium; lect. 2, n. 47; *In IV Metaph.*, lect. 1, nn.

532, 534; lect. 5, n. 593; *In VI Metaph.*, lect. 1, nn. 1163-1165; *In XI Metaph.*, lect. 3, n. 2194; lect. 4, n. 2210; lect. 7, nn. 2259, 2264; *In XII Metaph.*, lect. 2, nn. 24-27; *In Boet. de Trin.*, V, 1, 3 and 4.

Gilson, E., *Being and Some Philosophers*, pp. 154-215.

Maritain, J., *Distinguer pour unir, ou les degrés du savoir*, pp. 3-37.

———, *Sept. leçons sur l'être, et les premiers principes de la raison spéculative*, pp. 5-21.

———, *Court traité de l'existence et de l'existant*, pp. 23-78.

———, *The Degrees of Knowledge*, pp. 248-278.

———, *A Preface to Metaphysics*, pp. 18-27.

Owens, J., C.Ss.R., "The Intelligibility of Being," *Gregorianum*, Vol. V, n. 36 (1955), pp. 169-193.

———, "A Note on the Approach to Thomistic Metaphysics," *The New Scholasticism*, Vol. XXVIII, n. 4 (October 1954), pp. 454-476.

———, *The Future of Metaphysics*, pp. 1-61.

———, *The Doctrine of Being in the Aristotelian Metaphysics*, pp. 147-180.

Simon, Y., *Prévoir et savoir*, pp. 147-154.

Smith, G., S.J., *Natural Theology*, pp. 9-17.

Categorical and Metaphysical Knowledge:

Aristotle, *De Anima*, III, 6.

St. Thomas Aquinas, *In III de Anima*, lect. 11; *In I Sent.*, d. 38, q. 1, a. 3, sol.; *Quodlibet.*, V, q. 5, a. 2; *In Boet. de Trin.*, V, 3, *Resp.*

Abstraction and Separation:

St. Thomas Aquinas, *In VI Metaph.*, lect. 4, n. 1236; *Sum. Theol.*, I, 16, 2; 85, 1, *ad* 1; *In Boet. de Trin.*, V, 3, *Resp.*

Blanche, F., O.P., "La théorie de la abstraction chez s. Thomas d'Aquin," *Mélanges Thomistes*, pp. 237-251.

Fabro, C., *La nozione Metafisica di Participazione secundo S. Tomaso d'Aquino*, pp. 130-139.

Geiger, L.-B., "Abstraction et séparation d'après s. Thomas," *Revue des sciences phil. et théol.*, Vol. XXXI (1947), pp. 3-40.

———, *La participation dans la philosophie de s. Thomas d'Aquin*, pp. 315-341.

Hoenen, P., S.J., *La théorie du jugement d'après S. Thomas d'Aquin*, pp. 5-9.

Maritain, J., *Court traité de l'existence et de l'existant*, pp. 23-60.

Maurer, A., C.S.B., *The Division and Methods of the Sciences*, Questions

V and VI of St. Thomas' Commentary on the *De Trinitate of Boethius*, p. xxiv, n. 29; p. xxv, n. 40.

Philippe, M.D., "Abstraction, addition, séparation," *Revue Thomiste*, Vol. XLVIII (1948), pp. 461–479.

Abstraction of the Whole:

St. Thomas Aquinas, *In Boet. de Trin.*, V, 2 and 3; *Sum. Theol.*, I, 40, 3, Resp.; *De Ente et Essentia*, ch. II; Marietti, n. 15; ch. III, nn. 18, 20; *De Pot.*, V, 9, ad 16; *Sum. Theol.*, I, 85, 1, ad 2.

Maurer, A., C.S.B., *The Division and Methods of the Sciences*, pp. xxiv–xxv.

Abstraction of the Form:

St. Thomas Aquinas, *In Boet. de Trin.*, V, 2 and 3; *In III de Caelo et Mundo*, lect. 3, n. 4; *Sum. Theol.*, I, 40, 3; 85, 5, ad 3; *De Ente et Essentia*, cc. II and III.

The Prediction of Body:

St. Thomas Aquinas, *De Ente et Essentia*, c. II; *In I Sent.*, d. 19, q. 5, a. 2, ad 1.

Cajetan, *In De Ente et Essentia*, c. III, nn. 42–44.

The Cause, Under God, of Our Knowledge of Separated "Esse"

The separated *esse*, as we saw, is not reached by an abstraction within the categories. We may now see more closely why it is not. A knowledge bit, a whole or a precised form, is always a *ratio* or intelligible structure which is made up of two components: the knowledge of an actuation of potency, and the knowledge of the appropriate actualized potency. Thus, just as the "thought of" is a unit of matter and form, or of potency and act; so, proportionately, the "thinking" of the "thought of" is an organization by thought of appropriate potency and its act.

Now, there is no appropriate potency drawn from matter or from the potency to exist, which can be a necessary part of the thinking of *esse*. The reason is this: *esse* could actuate formed matter (the *esse* of material bodies), or it could actuate only the potency to exist (as does the *esse* of angels), or it could be the actuation *of* nothing at all, but simply God, Act Itself.[1] In no case except the

---

[1] See St. Thomas, *De Ente et Essentia*, c. V; Marietti, nn. 30-33: ". . . we find in substances a threefold manner of having essence. There is a being, God, whose essence is His very act of existing. That explains why we find some philosophers asserting that God does not have a quiddity or essence, because His essence is not other than His act of existing. . . . In a second way, we find essence in created intellectual substances. Their act of existing is other than their essence, although their essence is immaterial. Their act of existing is thus not a separated, but a received, one; and it is therefore limited and restricted to the capacity of the receiving nature. Their nature or quiddity, however, is separated and unreceived in any matter. . . . We find essence in a third way in substances composed of matter and form. Their act of existing

last, so it would seem, *must* one know *esse*, because nothing short of God is known as a "must" existent; and in the case of God, the knowledge of His *esse* is had only by demonstration. Whence, then, comes the knowledge of separated *esse*, which is not necessarily involved in knowing creatures (material or spiritual), and which does not necessarily involve knowing that God exists until we demonstrate that He does? Be very sure you see that the question is not this: what is the ultimate cause of separated *esse* in itself and in our knowledge of it? The answer to that question has already been given: God causes the separated *esse* both of things and of our knowledge of separated *esse*.[2] The question is rather this: what is the cause, under God, of our knowledge of separated *esse*?

---

is received and limited because they have it from another; what is more, their nature or quiddity is received in designated matter. So, they are limited both from above and from below."

[2] God doesn't cause the separated *esse* to exist as separated either from things or from our knowledge of things, because there isn't any *esse* which is separate from things or our knowledge of them. Separated *esse* is a viewpoint (hence *only* in the mind) of any being as having an *esse* (physical or intentional) which does *not* come, as from a cause, from any quiddity either physical or in knowledge. Now, *esse* is caused by a cause of *esse*, and this means that any quiddity in *esse physico vel intentionali* is caused to be in *esse physico vel intentionali*. Thus, "meaning" (not meaningfulness nor the operation of "meaning," i.e., the signifying operation) *is* the "meant," and so since the "meant" is caused, so also is the "meaning" of the meant caused (for meaning *is* the meant).

The following texts are pertinent to the above point. St. Thomas, *De Pot.*, III, 5, *Resp.*: "Oportet enim, si aliquid unum communiter in pluribus invenitur, quod ab aliqua una causa in illis causetur; non enim potest esse quod illud commune utrique ex se ipso conveniat, cum utrumque, secundum quod ipsum est, ab altero distinguatur; et diversitas causarum diversos effectus producit. Cum ergo esse inveniatur omnibus rebus commune, quae secundum illud quod sunt, ad invicem distinctae sunt, oportet quod de necessitate eis non ex se ipsis, sed ab aliqua una causa esse attribuatur. Et ista videtur ratio *Platonis*, qui voluit, quod ante omnem multitudinem esset aliqua unitas non solum in numeris, sed etiam in rerum naturis."

De Pot., III, 6, *Resp.*: ". . . in quibuscumque diversis invenitur aliquid unum commune, oportet ea reducere in unam causam quantum ad illud commune, quia vel unum est causa alterius, vel amborum est aliqua causa communis. Non enim potest esse quod illud unum commune utrique conveniat secundum illud quod proprie utrumque eorum est, ut in praecedenti quaestione, art. praec. est habitum. Omnia autem contraria et diversa, quae sunt in mundo, inveniuntur communicare in aliquo uno, vel in natura speciei, vel in natura generis, vel saltem in ratione essendi: unde oportet quod omnium istorum sit unum principium, quod est omnibus causa essendi. Esse autem, in quantum huiusmodi,

The Cause of the Knowledge of Separated "Esse" Is "Esse" and the Intellect Itself

That cause is of course the *esse* of creatures. Above all, however, that cause is the human intellect itself which knows that no creature's *esse* is necessarily involved in that creature.[3] But here precisely is where the shoe pinches, namely, in the intellect itself. If the intellect knows separated *esse*, which is *not* necessarily involved in knowing natures, *because* of its knowing of natures in *esse*, in which the knowledge of *esse is* involved, how can that knowledge of separated *esse* fail to have tagging along with it the knowledge of the appropriate potency, material potency, or the potency to exist? And if the knowledge of separated *esse* does have tagging along with it the knowledge of an appropriate potency, how can that be the knowledge of separated *esse*, which does not necessarily involve potency at all?

The question may reveal the force of the original answer. If *esse* is known in terms of its quiddities, then knowing is a knowing of the categories, and this sort of knowing is abstractive. If, however, *esse* is known as the very actuation of the quiddities themselves, then in knowing *esse* we are knowing an act which overtops quiddities themselves, yet, when these quiddities are given, includes them withal. Thus, *ens est primum quod cadit in intellectu*, could

---

bonum est: quod patet ex hoc quod unumquodque esse appetit, in quo ratio boni consistit, scilicet quod sit appetibile; et sic patet quod supra quaslibet diversas causas oportet ponere aliquam causam unam, sicut etiam apud Naturales supra ista contraria agentia in natura ponitur unum agens primum scilicet caelum, quod est causa diversorum motuum in istis inferioribus. Sed quia in ipso caelo invenitur situs diversitas in quam sicut in causam reducitur inferiorum corporum contrarietas, ulterius oportet reducere in primum motorem, qui nec per se nec per accidens moveatur."

Quodlibet, VII, q. 1, a. 1, *ad* 1: ". . . esse per se subsistens est causa omnis esse in alio recepti." *Contra Gentiles*, II, 21: "Esse autem est causatum primum: quod ex ratione suae communitatis apparet. Causa igitur propria essendi est agens primum et universale, quod Deus est." See also *Sum. Theol.*, I, 3, 4; *ad* 2; 44, 2; *Contra Gentiles*, II, 16.

[3] See Chapter IV, pp. 62–65.

mean: the "being" which is intellect's first quidditative encounter with it,[4] and then "being" means the quiddity of material substances; or it could mean this: the "being" which is intellect's first existential encounter with it, and then "being" means the actuation of material quiddities, viz., their *esse* or the *ratio entis*.[5] In this latter sense the object of metaphysical knowledge is separated *esse*, overt or covert. The word "first" in either case does not mean a chronological "first." "First" means a causal first: in the order of essence, knowledge of quiddity is a causal first; in the order of *esse*, knowledge of the *ratio entis* is a causal first.

The Meaning of the Answer that Intellect Itself Causes the Knowledge of Separated "Esse"

What does this answer really mean? Apparently it means that the knowledge of *esse* always involves somehow the knowledge of essence, and *vice versa*. But the answer looks impossible! After all, we seem to know what-things-are without knowing that they are, and *vice versa*.

It is not so. We never know *what* the things are which exist without knowing in some sense *that* they exist. Nor do we ever

---

[4] See St. Thomas, *De Ente et Essentia*, Prooemium; Cajetan, *In De Ente et Essentia*, q. 1, n. 5: "It now remains to prove the first part of our conclusion from St. Thomas and Avicenna, who say that being is that which is first impressed upon our intellect. This conclusion is proved thus: the most imperfect concept of all is the first in origin; but the actual confused concept of being is the most imperfect of all concepts; therefore it is the first in origin. . . . the concept of being is something natural to the intellect, as is also the knowledge of a first principle: for upon the presence of being, it is immediately conceived by all. The concept of being must, therefore, be essentially prior to other concepts, just as it is universally true that a natural act is prior to to those which have their origin outside the necessity of nature. This does not hold, however, in the case of other concepts in themselves." See also John of St. Thomas, *Cursus Philosophicus, Ars Logica*, Pars II, q. 14, a. 1; Reiser, t. I, p. 500a 40–47: ". . . abstractio entis in communi ut analogum est confusissima, et licet actu includat omnia confuse, ideo potius non est abstractio formalis, quia non fit per segregationem imperfecti, sed per inclusionem omnium sub quadam confusione et caligine."

[5] See Chapter XI, p. 176; Chapter XII, p. 181.

know *that* things exist without knowing in some sense *what* they are.[6]

In order to clarify those last two propositions—they are really the same proposition—let us examine the instance of "absolute nature."

The Knowledge of Absolute Nature

Absolute nature is any *ratio*, e.g., animal (besouled sentient matter), which clearly does not have to exist physically in order to be known, and which just as clearly does not have to be known to exist physically in order to exist physically. Moreover, not only would *animal* be animal whether it existed physically or not, whether it were known or not to exist physically; *animal* would also seem to be animal whether it were known or not. That last clause contains its own qualification, "animal would also *seem*, etc." It would indeed so seem that *animal* is animal whether it be known or not.

It is not so. Absolute nature is indeed indifferent to being, physically, an animal, and it is also indifferent to be known to be, physically, an animal. This means that absolute nature does not exist except in knowledge, and *that* means that absolute nature has its *esse*, viz., a known *esse* which is the knowing that *animal* is animal, whether it exist or not, whether it be known or not known to exist, but *not* whether it be known or not known. Animal must be *known* to be animal if it be true that animal is animal. Apart from that *knowing*, namely, that animal is animal, there is no absolute nature.

Some further remarks[7] upon this knowledge of absolute nature may help us to understand the relation of absolute nature to its

---

[6] See St. Thomas, *De Ente et Essentia*, c. III; Marietti, n. 18: ". . . natura hominis absolute considerata abstrahit a quolibet esse, ita tamen quod non fiat praecisio alicuius eorum." See also *De Pot.*, V, 9, *ad* 16; *Sum. Theol.*, I, 44, 1, *ad* 1.

[7] See St. Thomas, *De Ente et Essentia*, c. III; *Quodlibet.*, VIII, q. 1, a. 1, *Resp.*

esse in knowledge. Ask, with St. Thomas Aquinas, is absolute nature one? No, for if it were one, it could not be predicated of Socrates and Plato, as it is. Is it many? No, for then it could not be predicated of Socrates, as it is. As absolute, nature has no *esse* in singulars. Nor as absolute, does it not have an *esse* in singulars. Thus absolute nature abstracts from any *esse*, physical or cognitive, but not so as to prescind from any *esse:* not so as to have prescinded from the physical *esse* of animals when they are known to exist; not so as to have prescinded from the cognitive *esse* of animal when *animal* is known as animal.[8]

Clearly, this cognitive *esse* of *animal*, when animal is known as animal, is the real issue. The issue is this: what must we mean when we say that animal, known as animal, must exist in knowledge? We must mean that absolute nature has a cognitive state of being, an intentional "self" so to say. Absolute nature peers at us clothed in the drapes of its intentional *esse*, not as though if it didn't peer at us through those drapes it would be behind them nevertheless, no more than physical *esse* peers at us through the curtain of physical beings as if there were a physical *esse* which is not physical beings. The absolute nature is a nature only in knowledge, just as physical natures are natures only in physical *esse*. So, absolute nature can be abstracted from any *esse*, physical or cognitive, but it cannot exist, either in nature or knowledge without its appropriate *esse*. Absolute nature, in other words, cannot prescind from any *esse*.[9]

The point can be made in another way. If absolute nature in the intellect could be abstracted from the intentional mode of existing which it has in the intellect (and absolute nature can be so abstracted), *and if abstractive knowledge is the only knowledge we have*, then absolute nature would have come loose with a mighty plop—from itself! Consider: unless absolute nature be in some existential state, it would not be at all; now, only *esse* assures an

[8] See St. Thomas, *De Ente et Essentia*, c. III; Marietti, nn. 16-18. See Appendix A of this chapter.

[9] See St. Thomas, *De Ente et Essentia*, c. III; Marietti, n. 18: "Sed verum est dicere quod homo inquantum est homo non habet quod sit in hoc singulari vel in illo aut in anima. Patet ergo quod natura hominis absolute considerata abstrahit a quolibet esse, ita tamen quod non fiat praecisio alicuius eorum. Et haec natura sic considerata est quae praedicatur de individuis omnibus."

existential state of absolute nature, in the instance, a knowledge
esse. Just so, if a physically existent nature could be abstracted
from its physical mode of existing (and physical nature can be so
abstracted), and *if abstractive knowledge is the only knowledge we
have*, then physical nature would have come loose with a mighty
plop—from itself! Consider: unless physical nature exists, it would
not be at all, nor would we know it to be at all; now, only *esse*
assures the existential state of physical natures, and only our
knowledge of such *esse* assures us that physical natures exist. Abstractive knowledge, however, is not the only knowledge we have.
We have, besides, the knowledge that things exist physically, and
also only in our knowledge. We cannot abstract any *esse*, physical
or intentional, from any nature, physical or absolute. Rather, we
abstract nature, physical or absolute, from any *esse*, physical or
intentional. Yet the knowledge of *esse* can be separated both from
the knowledge of physical and intentional beings, and this separation
of *esse* from all its modes includes all those modes.[10] This fact is
perhaps the best guarantee of the objectivity of knowledge, as we
shall straightway see.

"Separation" of *esse* from its modes, yet "inclusion" of all modes
within the separated *esse!* The thing looks impossible. The only
way to settle the issue of the possibility or impossibility of separating *esse* from all its modes of being so as to include all those
modes is to conduct an experiment, once more, in order to ascertain
whether this is or is not precisely what we do.

There are two modes of being: a physical and an intentional
mode.[11] Let us conduct the experiment, first, for the physical mode
of being. Since it is not *because* an existent is an animal that an
animal exists, else only an animal would be an existent (against the
fact), therefore physical *esse* is not by identity an animal. Here we
have separated physical *esse* from its physical mode of being, viz.,
the mode of being an animal. So much for the "separation" of *esse*
from physical animal *esse;* and note that the same result would
occur in any instance of physical nature in *esse*. Now for the
"inclusion" by *esse* of all its physical modes. If, in the separation

[10] See Chapter XI, p. 176; Chapter XII, p. 181.
[11] See Chapter X, pp. 153–158.

just practised, there were closed off all the modes of being other than the animal mode, those other modes of being would not be at all. Against the facts: plants, etc., exist. Make, second, a similar run for the separation of *animal's* intentional *esse* from the knowing-animal-mode which it has in knowledge. Since it is not *because* animal is *known* as animal that animal *is* animal, else only animal could be known (against the fact), therefore the knowing or the intentional *esse* is not by identity the knowing of animal. Here we have separated intentional *esse* from its intentional mode, viz., a knowing-animal-mode of knowledge, instead, e.g., of a knowing-plant-mode of knowledge. So much for the "separation" of intentional *esse* from the knowing-animal-mode of knowing; and note that here too the same result would occur in any instance of intentional beings in intentional *esse*. Now for the "inclusion" by intentional *esse* of all its intentional modes. If, in the separation just practised, we had closed off from intentional *esse* all the modes of knowing which are other than the knowing-animal-mode, then those other modes of being known could not be known at all. Against the fact: we know plants, etc. Thus, *esse*, physical or intentional, is separated from all its modes, physical or intentional, yet each separated *esse* respectively includes them withal.

"Esse" in Being and in Knowledge Redescribed

All this leaves us facing a situation which is at once a knowledge situation and a situation in being, which we may now redescribe simultaneously. The human intellect is so structured that in any judgment which it proffers, it knows, explicitly or implicitly, an *esse* which is not identically its *knowing* of the essence, or identically the *essence* of that *esse*. A marvelous resource of spirit, this: or better, a marvelous resource, this, which is a spirit: to be all set, prepared, readied to know what it means to exist in its very first encounter with existential act! For, the intellect in that first encounter with *esse* knows that its knowing that *x exists* is not a knowing of an "exists" which expires in being *x*. "More, more," a spirit ever cries. More of what? More of that *esse* which doesn't expire in being *x*, of course. But there isn't any more! This, a spirit cannot admit. The admission would kill it. True, a spirit can develop its quidditative knowledge of *x*, from the bottom to the top of any Porphyrian tree, but reflection will reveal to it that such additions to knowledge are knowable and known only because they are known to be, actually or possibly. Just as quiddities in *esse* exist only because of their *esse*, so quiddities in knowledge are there only because they are known to exist, intentionally or really. And so, although the quest for quiddities is a great and laudable venture, the spirit would die from refusing the food upon which it lives, if it refused to know the *esse* of those quiddities. For, if quiddities are not in *esse*, real or intentional, there aren't any quiddities at all.

Let us assist at the last gasp of an intellect's life which refuses quiddities in *esse*. Absolute nature or form, precised or a *totum*, exists only by an intentional *esse* whose content or intelligible structure is nonetheless not that intentional *esse*. The knowledge of separated *esse* also exists only by an intentional *esse* whose content is—what? It is the very marrow, the readied structure of intellect itself, a covert or overt knowing-separated-*esse*-structure, and this knowing is implicit in its every judgment. Deny that and you deny spirit, kill it, that is. A spirit simply must move on by a necessity of its nature to know more than the separated *esse* which is involved in quiddities but which transcends them. That "more" is, first, more quiddities in *esse*, and, next, the knowledge that God exists. Should the knowledge that God exists be not enough to satisfy spirit (God's existence is known as in the truth of the proposition *God exists;* and this truth is not the truth which He is), this would mean that a spirit cannot be satisfied without seeing God, although philosophy cannot tell us how a spirit is to see God. A spirit's knowledge of God is here and now a knowledge of something like God, viz., knowledge of separated *esse;* and, furthermore, it is knowledge that God exists as a cause of that separated *esse*, both in knowledge and in things.[12]

[12] See St. Thomas, *De Pot.*, III, 5, *ad* 1: ". . . licet causa prima, quae Deus est, non intret essentiam rerum creatarum; tamen esse, quod rebus creatis inest, non potest intelligi nisi ut deductum ab esse divino; sicut nec proprius effectus potest intelligi nisi ut deductus a causa propria."

Here is where the shoe pinches. Just as we might like to be God instead of being like Him, so we might like here and now to know God instead of knowing something like Him. Both situations show up in our knowledge of sensibles: just as we might prefer sensibles, including ourselves, to be in themselves, so we might like to know them in themselves. The trouble is they are *not* in themselves, nor can they be known in themselves as *esse* if their *esse* is accidental, and if in order to explain that accidental *esse* of theirs, and so have science about it, we must know that they are caused.

Christianity's Version of Metaphysics Versus Hellenism's Version

All the issues raised from Chapter X to the present one inclusive boil down to a single one. That single issue seems to be this: how does Christian philosophy understand metaphysics, and how does Greek philosophy understand it? And that single issue boils down to this point: what is the place of sensibles in the science of metaphysics?

The Sensibles and Metaphysics

To see unity in multiplicity is to see a cause of multiplicity. This is to possess a science.[13]

So far as can be ascertained no one ever successfully denied that consequents (multiplicity) lie in their antecedents (cause), that is, no one ever successfully denied that there exists scientific knowledge. There are, however, different interpretations of science, especially of the science of metaphysics. These different interpretations arise, naturally, from the different ways the data are interpreted and, consequently, from the way the causes of those data are interpreted. The two different versions are the Christian and the Greek. Let us, first, propose the Christian version.

[13] St. Thomas, *In Boet. de Trin.*, VI, 1, *ad tertiam quaest.*; *Sum. Theol.*, I, 79, 8; *De Verit.*, X, 8, *ad* 10; XV, 1; *In II Metaph.*, lect. 1, n. 278.

The Christian Version of the Place of Sensibles in Metaphysics

The first move the Christian version makes is to describe multiplicity, the data, the situation of the many. The many are passive potentials, related to their respective actuations.

The Passive Sensible Potentials

A passive potential is anything which exists in such wise that whatever it can be is consistent with nonbeing.[14] Let us run through the cases. First, what is possible in being man, e.g., a man *can* be white, is consistent with a man's *not* being white. Again, what is possible in being a living being, e.g., a living thing *can* die, is consistent with the fact that a living thing is *not* dead. In both cases the data (the many, consequents, multiplicity) stand in the following situation: the many exist, and in that existential situation of theirs, whatever they, the existents, can be is in *them* nonbeing; but *they* are not nonbeing. *They* are beings, existents, existing in such wise that whatever they *are* in the order of existence is consistent with their *not* being whatever they *can* be.

The insight is not the easiest in the world. We must have several go's at it. It is as *not* being white, but nonetheless as *being* a man, that a man *can* be white. It is as *not* being dead, but nonetheless as *being* alive, that a living thing *can* die. To be a white man is impossible unless there *be* a man. To be organically alive is impossible unless there *be* the dead. To put it again, it is not because passive potentials do *not* exist that they are ordered to their actuations. It

[14] St. Thomas, *Sum. Theol.*, I, 9, 2, *Resp.*: ". . . in every creature there is a potentiality to change: either as regards substantial being as in the case of corruptible things; or as regards being in place only, as in the case of the celestial bodies; or as regards the order to their end, and the application of their powers to diverse objects, as is the case with the angels; and universally all creatures generally are mutable by the power of the Creator, in Whose power is their being and nonbeing. Hence, since God is mutable in none of these ways, it belongs to Him alone to be altogether immutable."

is rather because they *do* exist, but not so as to be affected by the surplus of whatever they can be, it is upon *that* score that they are passive potentials. It is as an *existent* that a man is not but can be white. It is as an *existent* that a living thing is not but can be dead. Were passive potentials not in an already existential situation, they would not be at all, and so they would not be ordered or related to anything at all. The bare cupboard cannot be filled, even though there are things to fill it with, unless there is a cupboard.

Aristotle saw the point about passive potentials. None better: ἔτι τῶν πρός τι ἡ ὕλη,[15] he says, and his description still holds. St. Thomas Aquinas also saw the point: *cum esse in potentia nihil aliud sit quam ordinari in actum.*[16] The operative word in St. Thomas' text seems to be *esse:* to *be* in potency is nothing else but to be ordered to act. St. Thomas further notes that "potency is a principle, not because it is the very relation which the word principle means, but because it is that which *is* the principle".[17] In other words, potency as a principle is an existent which is not that which it can be. Potency does not exist. The potential exists, but it does not exist as being in the actuation to which it is related as to that which the potential is not but can be; nevertheless the potential exists with its own acuation. In sum, to be in potency or to be a passive potential, is to exist, but not with the perfection to which the potential is related as to its possible actuation.

The Greek Version of Passive Potentials in "Esse"

There was something, however, which the Greeks did not see: they did not see the relation of the passive sensible potential in *esse* to its *esse*. That Plato did not see this is intensely clear. For Plato the sensibles were not veritable existents.[18] And Aristotle! Surely

---

[15] Aristotle, *Physics*, II, 2, 194b 9; St. Thomas, *Q.D. de Anima*, a. 12, *Resp.*
[16] St. Thomas, *De Malo*, I, 2, *Resp.*
[17] St. Thomas, *De Pot.*, I, 1, *ad* 3: ". . . potentia dicitur principium non quia sit ipsa relatio quam significat nomen principii sed quia est id quod est principium."
[18] See Plato, *Theaetetus*, 156; *Republic*, VII, 423-524. For Plato's reason for denying that sensibles were true existents, see Aristotle, *Metaphysics*, I (A), 6,

the man who opposed Plato all his life on this point was convinced
that sensibles exist! Surely the man who thought that sensibles simply
cannot be nonbeing had a place in his metaphysics for sensible existents![19] He did indeed, but the place sensibles occupied in Aristotle's
metaphysics is a place from which they cannot be dislodged.
Sensibles for Aristotle could not not-be.[20]

St. Thomas Aquinas' Version of the Place Occupied by Sensibles and Nonsensibles in Metaphysics

Whatever Aristotle may have thought, St. Thomas Aquinas most
certainly meant that sensibles as well as nonsensibles are in themselves nonbeing,[21] and this without the slightest surrender to
Platonism. The point is essential, it seems, to the validation of metaphysics as a science.

In order to see that it is, let us recur to the notion of the passive
potential. The passive potential is that which exists in such wise that
it is not whatever it can be, although the passive potential does exist.
We must now run the crucial case. Any sensible or nonsensible existent in Christian metaphysics can quite well not exist at all, and

---

987b 4–10: "Plato . . . held that the problem applied not to sensible things but
to entities of another kind—for this reason, that the common definition could
not be a definition of any sensible thing, as they were always changing. Things
of this other sort, then, he called Ideas, and sensible things, he said, were all
named after these, and in virtue of a relation to these; for the many existed by
participation in the Ideas that have the same name as they." St. Thomas
follows Aristotle's interpretation of Plato in *Sum. Theol.*, I, 84, 1, *Resp.*

[19] See L. Eslick, "What Is the Starting-Point of Metaphysics?" *The Modern
Schoolman*, Vol. XXXIV, n. 4 (May 1957), p. 254.

[20] For Aristotle's position on sensible being, see J. Owens, C.Ss.R., *The
Doctrine of Being in the Aristotelian Metaphysics*, pp. 293-296.

[21] See St. Thomas, *Sum. Theol.*, I, 2, 3, *Resp.*: ". . . that which does not exist
begins to exist only through something already existing." *In I Sent.*, d. 8, q. 1,
a. 2, *sol.*: "God is the being of everything, not the essential, but the causal
being." *Sum. Theol.*, I, 44, 1, *ad* 1: "Though relation to its cause is not part of
the definition of a thing caused, still it follows as a result of what belongs
to its nature. For, from the fact that a thing is being by participation, it
follows that it is caused. Hence such a being cannot be without being caused
. . . But, since to be caused does not enter into the nature of being taken
absolutely, that is why there exists a being that is uncaused."

so that which is possible in regard to an existent, viz., its complete nonbeing, must be consistent with the fact that it does exist. At this point we must ask, on what grounds could this be true? Upon the score that *in* the existent there is the possibility of nonexistence? Impossible. Here Aristotle seems to be dead right, and Plato dead wrong. It is unthinkable that a sensible, which exists but can also not exist, be able not to exist as though its existential act were affected by a coefficient of nonbeing when nonbeing means precisely not to exist at all. So to exist, viz., so as by not existing, is complete nonsense. True, a sensible's existential act *as* sensible can be affected with a coefficient of relative nonbeing. For, the nonbeing of a sensible *as* sensible is a nonbeing of this or that accidental or substantial way of being; it is not a nonbeing without qualification. Complete or unqualified nonbeing simply cannot reside in a being, though a qualified being, or if you will, a qualified nonbeing, can exist in a sensible. Yet in Christian philosophy, every sensible or nonsensible being which exists can also not exist at all. Where, then, are we to locate the sensible's and nonsensible's possibility of not being at all? St. Thomas Aquinas answers: ". . . in its Creator, in Whose power lies both its being and nonbeing."[22] It would seem, then, that sensibles and nonsensibles in themselves are nonbeing.

To resume the matter, all passive potentials are (1) in *some* existential situation, and (2) are ordered to *another* existential situation in either of two ways: (a) as to actuations which are as yet inexistent, be those actuations accidental or substantial; (b) as to actuations which are existent either in the cause of those actuations, or which are existent as effects of those causes.

The Sensibles and Their Existential Act

The crucial case is the sensible's actuation which is existential act (*esse*). The crux is here: how can one say that a nonexistent sensible being can exist, whereas there is no *esse* in it by which it can exist, and *esse* there must be, somehow, somewhere, if the nonexistent

---

[22] St. Thomas, *Sum. Theol.*, I, 9, 2, *Resp.*

sensible can be? Or run the question this way: how can one say that an existent sensible being can not be at all, whereas there is no foothold in the existent sensible for its nonbeing? One cannot answer either question unless the being (*esse*) of the existent sensible, as well as its nonbeing, lies in the power of God. Is this to destroy the *esse* of the sensible? On the contrary, this, it seems, is to establish the *esse* of the sensible. It is not in or of themselves that passive potentials exist. If they did, we should have an unexplained sensible world, a world without a cause. Sensibles themselves exist indeed, and this must be stated without any *arrière pensée* whatsoever, but they do not exist in or of themselves. In or of themselves they are nothing except either in the *esse* of their divine cause, or in the *esse* which is their own but is not *from* them. In their divine cause, it may be added, they are not like pins in a pin cushion. In God, they are the power of God, that is, they are God. Outside of God they themselves exist, but they do not exist in or of themselves. *Non nostri sumus* each creature proclaims, and this proclamation of theirs is equivalent to each creature's proclamation that it is caused.

Metaphysics as a Science

Having located the being and nonbeing of sensibles in the power of God, we have a science.

At this stage the point needs only elaboration. Sticks and stones are surely beings, and so is a straight stick and a hard stone. We have no difficulty about saying these things, because there is no difficulty in there being these things. However, if we ask, how can a stick be straight, or a stone be hard? and if we desiderate an answer which is above ($\mu\epsilon\tau\acute{a}$) the testing level of feeling and measuring the stick and stone, above the level of physics and mathematics, that is; if, in other words, we wish to answer the question in terms of metaphysics, then we must see that our question is precisely the one put by any Platonist. It is this: how can one distinct object of thought (stick) be another distinct object of thought (straight)? The question is not about the identity of a subject (stick) with a predicate (straight), not about the fact that this stick is straight. The question is rather about the nature of that identity, or if you will, about the meaning of the copula "is." Now, it is impossible to see how one can answer the question if a stick is allowed an *esse* in the stick's own right, or if "straight" is allowed an *esse* in "straight's" own right. For, if you allow that a stick is *esse* in its own right, you thereby confine a stick to being a stick, and by the same token you eliminate the possibility that a stick may be straight. Similarly for "straight": if "the straight" is nothing but straight, there could not be, e.g., a straight arm instead of a straight stick; for that matter, nothing could be straight except "straight." Nonsense. No, it is only when two distinct objects of thought *are* one in an area other than their area as objects that you can say that they are one another. And one cannot say *that*, as when we say that *a stick is straight*, unless each distinct object of thought shares but is not by identity the nature of being. The *esse* of a stick lies in being a stick, and the *esse* of a straight stick lies also in being a stick. Further, precisely because neither stick nor straight are, of or in themselves, *esse*, yet both are in the same *esse*, therefore the *esse* of both is caused. To see this, namely, to see the effect in the cause, is to possess a science, and since we are here seeing in God, its cause, the shared *esse* of God, we are within the science of metaphysics.[23]

There should be no illusion that the point made here is clear, or that it can be made very clear. One reason why the point cannot be made clear is because it cannot be made in physical or mathematical terms. Another, and the main reason, is this: the predicate, "is caused to be," said of any sensible's being, is no clearer than the predicate "is," said of God, and for exactly the same reason. Both propositions are conclusions of *quia* demonstrations. We do not know what the predicate "is" said of God means when that predicate is viewed as in God. We know what that predicate means only in so far as it is involved in the truth of the proposition *God is*. Just so, we do not know what the predicate "is caused" means in so far as that predicate is in sensibles, but only in so far as that predicate is in the truth of the proposition, *the sensible is caused*

[23] See St. Thomas, *De Pot.*, III, 5, *Resp.* and *ad* 1 and 2.

to be.[24] There is indeed a difference between the two propositions, *God is* and *a sensible is caused to be*. For a sensible to be caused to be is for a sensible to exist, and we can quite well know what it means for a sensible *as* sensible to exist: it means that a sensible is hot, cold, a man, fish, six feet tall, thin, etc. On the other hand, we do not know what God is. Thus, we neither know what God's "is" may mean except in the sense that "is" is true of Him; nor do we know what the sensible's predicate, viz., a caused "is," may mean except in so far as that caused "is" is true of the sensible, and of course, in so far as that sensible's caused "is" is describable in sensuous terms. These sensuous terms, however, are not the sensible's "is" at all. These considerations show that the science about sensibles is, because more familiar, easier to possess than the science about their *esse*. Perhaps also it shows one source of our perennial difficulties about metaphysics: we should dearly love to know what "is" means, and we cannot, except in terms of nature; but the sensible's "is" is not a nature predicate at all.

We may see the same point in another way. We all love to make necessary propositions. Indeed this is one of our deepest loves, the love of knowledge at knowledge's peak. These necessary propositions are in one way or another in the area of science. Now, the only absolutely necessary proposition we can make about sensibles in terms of their *esse* is that *if they are they must be*, and *when they are they are caused to be*, and the propositions derivative therefrom. Should we make a necessary proposition about sensibles in terms of their nature, which is involved in their *esse*, or in terms of their *esse* as involved in their nature, we are not talking about the sensible's *esse as esse*. In order to talk about the sensible's *esse* as existential act, we must first see that its *esse* is accidental to it in the sense that "accidental" means nonnecessary. Next, we must see that this nonnecessary *esse* of sensibles, which is the source of their necessity and their contingency, would be an impossible accident if sensibles had either perforce to be, or if, once in *esse*, they did not have perforce to be. The only way, it seems, to understand the sensible's *esse* as at

[24] See St. Thomas, *Sum. Theol.*, I, 2, 3, *Resp.; De Ente et Essentia*, c. IV; *Contra Gentiles*, I, 22.

once necessary and contingent is to understand it as being caused by that which is only *esse*. The "only-*esse*-cause," being alone *esse*, is a free cause.[25] Thus the sensible has no "must be" or "must be caused" predicate about it at all. It has only the "caused to be" predicate, and that predicate is proved by the acknowledgment that since the sensible exists and since its existence is accidental to it, therefore it is caused to be.

One may submit that rational animals do not like this situation one bit. They would much prefer, as the history of philosophy shows, to reduce the accidental *esse* of sensibles to some nature predicate, and make that nature predicate accidental, as in modern existentialism;[26] or else they would much prefer to make the nature predicate absolutely necessary, something in itself, as in some variety of Platonism.[27] Doubtless the reason for this is because we should like to have a God Whom we can handle. We cannot handle the God of Abraham, Isaac, and Jacob. We might as well get used to our similar philosophical inability to handle the One Who Is. If faith seeks intellect, which, if faith found, would no longer be intellect but the beatific vision, then intellect must seek faith, which, if intellect found, would no longer be faith but a kind of syllogizing of ourselves into heaven.[28] There is, it seems, an intellectual prostration before *esse*, just as there is a faith prostration before God the Father, and nobody likes to prostrate himself before anything.

The only doubt which might be left as to the status of sensibles and nonsensibles in the area of *esse* would be over the status of absolute nature. Perhaps one might feel that one should adore absolute nature! After all, absolute nature is other than sensible and nonsensible existents and other also than our knowledge of them; and if God in any version of Him is "other" than His creation, maybe absolute nature is God or at least a reasonable facsimile of Him.[29] In answer, once more, one might say that not even absolute

[25] See Chapter XI, pp. 177–178.
[26] See Chapter XI, pp. 171–172.
[27] See Chapter XI, pp. 171–172.
[28] B. Lonergan, S.J., *Insight*, N.Y., Philosophical Library, 1957, pp. xxix, 743–744.
[29] See, for example, Avicenna, *Metaph.*, V, 1, fol. 86v; *Log.*, I, fol. 2r; III, fol. 12r; in *Opera*, Venetiis, 1508.

nature is without its *esse*, namely, intentional *esse*, and that *esse* too is caused by God and, under Him, by the intellects which He causes.

Summary

Abstraction is a mental operation by which a certain essence feature of a being, real or intentional, can be distinguished from the *esse* of that essence feature, although that essence feature is always in *esse*, real or intentional.

Separation is a mental operation by which the *esse* of a being, real or intentional, can be known as distinct from, yet inclusive of, that being's essence feature, real or intentional.

In things, separated *esse* is an actuation which is not identically the essence which it actuates. In knowledge, separated *esse* is— knowledge of that act. Both separated *esse*'s, in things, and in our knowledge, are caused by God.

Under God there is no cause in *nature* of the separated *esse* of things. Under God the cause of the *knowledge* of separated *esse* is beings of course, but above all the cause is the human intellect.

As to the history of the problem which issues into the doctrinal difference between the meaning of those two propositions: *sensibles exist in or of themselves,* and *sensibles themselves exist;* the doctrine that the first proposition is not true, whereas the second one is true may indeed seem to be only a doctrinally verbal difference. If one cares to read the difference between the two propositions as being only verbal, one surely may. There is no point in being finicky about verbal differences. Apart, nevertheless, from what seems to be only a verbal difference between the two propositions, there is a vast and real difference between Christian and Greek philosophy, and one way of locating that difference is to see the way in which each philosophy understands the relation of a passive potential to its *esse*.

St. Thomas Aquinas did not like to hear people go around saying that essence "has of itself a potency to *esse*." He thought that there *is* no essence unless it be in *esse*. He suggests that we say rather, "essence does not of itself have *esse*."[30] Clearly, for him, essence is *always* in *esse:* either its own, which comes from God; or if not in its own *esse* and not yet caused, then it is in the *esse* of its cause; or, if essence is in intentional *esse*, then that intentional *esse* is also created by as much as God creates the operations of a created intellect.

Appendix to Chapter XV

APPENDIX (A). Absolute nature.

St. Thomas, *De Ente et Essentia*, c. III; Marietti, nn. 16–18: ". . . essence has the nature of a genus or species in so far as it is expressed after the manner of a whole, for instance, by the word *man* or *animal*, as containing implicitly and indistinctly everything that is in the individual.

"If nature or essence is understood in this sense, we can consider it in two ways. First, we can consider it according to its proper meaning, which is to consider it absolutely. In this sense, nothing is true of it except what belongs to it as such; whatever else is attributed to it, the attribution is false. For example, to man as man belong rational, animal and whatever else his definition includes, whereas white or black, or anything of this sort, which is not included in the concept of humanity, does not belong to man as man. If someone should ask, then, whether the nature so considered can be called *one* or *many*, neither should be granted, because both are outside the concept of humanity and both can be added to it. If plurality were included in the concept of humanity, it could never be one, although it is one inasmuch as it is present in Socrates. Similarly, if unity were contained in its concept, then Socrates' and Plato's nature would be one and the same, and it could not be multiplied in many individuals.

"Nature or essence is considered in a second way with reference to the act of existing it has in this or that individual. When the nature is so considered, something is attributed to it accidentally

[30] St. Thomas, *In VIII Phys.*, lect. 21, n. 5; *Contra Gentiles*, II, 53.

by reason of the thing in which it exists; for instance, we say that man is white because Socrates is white, although whiteness does not pertain to man as man.

"This nature has a twofold act of existing, one in individual things, the other in the mind; and according to both modes of existing, accidents accompany the nature. In individual beings, moreover, it has numerous acts of existing corresponding to the diversity of individuals. Yet the nature itself, considered properly—that is to say, absolutely—demands none of these acts of existing. It is false to say that the nature of man as such exists in this individual man, because, if existing in this individual belonged to man as man, it would never exist outside this individual. Similarly, if it belonged to man as man not to exist in this individual, human nature would never exist in it. It is true to say, however, that it does not belong to man as man to exist in this or that individual, or in the intellect. Considered in itself, the nature of man thus clearly abstracts from every act of existing, but in such a way that none may be excluded from it. And it is the nature considered in this way that we predicate of all individual beings."

Suggested Reading

The Knowledge of Separated "Esse":

St. Thomas Aquinas, *De Ente et Essentia*, Prooemium; cc. III, V; *De Pot.*, III, 5, and 6; V, 9, *ad* 16; *Sum. Theol.*, I, 44, 1, *ad* 1.
Cajetan, *In De Ente et Essentia*, Prooemium, q. 1, n. 5.
John of St. Thomas, *Ars Logica*, Pars II, q. 14, a. 1.

The Knowledge of Absolute Nature:

St. Thomas Aquinas, *De Ente et Essentia*, c. III; *Quodlibet.*, VIII, q. 1 a. 1, *Resp.*

The Sensibles and Metaphysics:

Plato, *Theaetetus*, 156; *Republic*, VII, 523-524.
Aristotle, *Physics*, II, 2; *Metaphysics*, I (A), 6.

St. Thomas Aquinas, *Sum. Theol.*, I, 2, 3; 9, 2; 44, 1, *ad* 1; *Q.D. de Anima*, a. 12, *Resp.*; *De Malo*, I, 2, *Resp.*; *In I Sent.*, d. 8, q. 1, a. 2, *sol.*; *De Pot.*, III, 5; *De Ente et Essentia*, c. IV; *Contra Gentiles*, I, 22; II, 53; *In VIII Phys.*, lect. 21, n. 5.

Eslick, L., "What Is the Starting-Point of Metaphysics?" *The Modern Schoolman*, Vol. XXIV, n. 4 (May 1957), pp. 247–263.

Owens, J., C.Ss.R., *The Doctrine of Being in the Aristotelian Metaphysics*, pp. 293–296.

The Operations of the Created Intellect Which Are Relations of Reason Only. Preliminary Remark

Metaphysics is a reduction of the many beings to the causality of Being in both the order of being and of knowledge. This reduction is a demonstration, in the orders of being and of knowledge that Being causes the many; in other words, a demonstration that the many are causally *related* to Being.[1] Implied in the demonstration is a theory of relations, which must now be made explicit. Not that the theory of relations adds anything new to the demonstration. The theory of relations is nothing but a fresh viewpoint of what we have already seen, an attempt to clarify further the mysterious interdependence of creatures upon one another and their far more mysterious dependence upon God.

Relations in Being[2]

Relation is a way of existing so as by being referred to some other existent. For example, "to be a taller than" is a way of existing o

---

[1] See Chapter XV, pp. 268–272.

[2] On relations in being, see Aristotle, *Metaphysics*, V (Δ), 15, 1020b 26–1021l 11; St. Thomas, *Sum. Theol.*, I, 13, 7, Resp.; 28, 1–2; *In I Sent.*, d. 26, q. 2, a 1; d. 26, q. 2, a. 2, *ad* 4; *In IV Metaph.*, lect. 17, nn. 1004–1005; *Quodlibet.*, I, q 2, a. 1; *De Pot.*, VII, 11, Resp.; VIII, 1, Resp.; *De Verit.*, I, 5, *ad* 16; IV, ! Resp.; *Contra Gentiles*, II, 12; IV, 14. See Appendix A of this chapter.

A study of relation may be found in C. Kossel, S.J., "The *Esse* and *Ratio* o Relation," *The Modern Schoolman*, Vol. XXIV (1946), pp. 28–36; "St. Thoma Theory of the Causes of Relation," *The Modern Schoolman*, Vol. XV (1948) pp. 151–172.

"a taller than" so as by existing *in reference to* "a smaller than." This way of existing which a "taller than" has *in* the man who is "taller than" (*esse in*) so as by being referred to (*esse ad*) some other being, e.g., to "a smaller than," is a relation, a category of being.[3]

Categories of course explain nothing. They are simply descriptions of the various modes of being.[4] The explanation of the categories, as are all explanations, is an explanation through causes.

The Subject as a Cause of a Relation

The first and most obvious cause of a relation is in the related thing itself, e.g., in John, who is taller than George.[5] Let us analyze this related thing.

The whole existential feature of a relation in being, the place where a relation resides, so to say, is in the subject (*esse in*) of the relation, John. From this point of view a relation is an accident, like any of the other eight categorial accidents of being.[6] This existential feature of a relation, the *esse* of an accident in other words, provides a base or starting point for a reference (*esse ad*)

---

[3] Aristotle, *Categories,* ch. 7, 6a 36–38: "Those things are called relative, which, being either said to be *of* something else or *related to* something else, are explained by reference to that other thing." St. Thomas, *In I Sent.,* d. 20, q. 1, a. 1: ". . . relation is something according to the *esse* which it has in its subject, but according to its intelligibility it is not a 'something,' but only a being referred to another." *De Pot.,* VII, 8, *Resp.:* ". . . relation differs from quantity and quality in that quantity and quality are accidents residing in the subject, whereas relation, as Boethius says, signifies something not as adhering to a subject but as passing from it to something else. . . ." See also *Sum. Theol.,* III, 2, 7, *ad* 2.

[4] Aristotle, *Categories,* ch. 5, 1b 25–2a 4.

[5] Aristotle, *Categories,* ch. 7, 8a 35–8b 14; St. Thomas, *De Pot.,* II, 5, *Resp.:* "Quod [relatio] sit vero aliquid secundum rem, habet ex illa parte qua inest, vel ut idem secundum rem, ut in divinis, vel ut habens causam in subiecto, sicut in creaturis."

[6] On the *esse* of accidents, see St. Thomas, *Sum. Theol.,* III, 77, 1, *ad* 2: ". . . an accident is defined as an essence which is apt to exist in a substance as in a subject." See also *De Princ. Nat.,* c. 1, nn. 338–339; *De Ente et Essentia,* c. VI; *In VII Metaph.,* lect. 1, n. 1256; *Quodlibet.,* IX, q. 2, a. 2; *Sum. Theol.,* I, 45, 4. An analysis of the *esse* of accidents may be found in J. Albertson, S.J., "The *Esse* of Accidents According to St. Thomas," *The Modern Schoolman,* Vol. XXX, n. 4 (May 1953), pp. 265–278.

to some other being whenever there is another being to which the first may actually refer. Add that other being, George, and then what could be related, viz., John, who is of a given size, *is* related (*esse ad*) to George without any change in John. In default of another being or a correlative, the "accidented" subject provides only a virtual relation, that is, the possibility of being related. And note here this curious situation: the size of John could be taller than George's, or less than George's if George grew taller than John; or equal to George's if George grew to John's height, and this without the slightest change in John's size. Clearly, then, a relation is explained in part by something *in* John, viz., by the accident of his size which is *not* actually related to George until George is around; and indeed, as was just said, John's size could be differently related to George's, even when George is around, without the slightest change in John's size.[7]

A relation in being, then, compounds with a subject as being *in* a subject, as size is an accident *in* a man, and from this point of view there is nothing particularly significant about a relation, nothing which differentiates it from the other eight categorial accidents, no actual relation at all (*esse ad*), that is. However, John's size as *referred* to George's so as by being greater, equal to, or less than George's, *that* accident does *not* compound with John. Rather, as referred to George's, John's size "stretches" toward George's, and this "stretch" is precisely an *esse ad*, a new category of accident, a relation.[8] A relation is thus a sort of "in-between" being, in between an accidented subject and its correlative, a sort of metaphysical antenna by which John's size "feels" George's (this "feeling" is the *esse ad*), and by which even *before* John's size "feels" George's it is all set (*esse in*) to do the "feeling" without the slightest change in John's size even when it "feels" differently, that is, even when John's size is differently related to George's. Less figuratively, actually related subjects communicate in, give or take, perfections of other beings, because before they give or take there is in them a

---

[7] Aristotle, *Categories*, ch. 7, 7a 22–7b 34.

[8] On relation as an accident, see St. Thomas, *Sum. Theol.*, I, 28, 2, *Resp.*; *De Pot.*, VII, 8, *Resp.*; VII, 9, *ad* 7; VIII, 2, *Resp.* See Appendix B of this chapter.

demand, a want, a need, an uneasiness (in psychic agents), a tendency which is fulfilled by other beings.[9] This fulfillment is a relation (*esse ad*); the one fulfilled by the relation is the subject of it; the existential status (*esse in*) of the relation (*esse ad*) is either identical with the subject, as in God, or has a cause in the subject, as with creatures.[10] Thus, before an *esse ad* exists by reason of the fact that a term or correlative of the *esse in* exists, there is only the *esse in*, an accidented subject, the starting point, the base or foundation of a relation. When a correlative exists, then the *esse in* reveals itself for what it was all the time, viz., as a "stretching" accident, a tendency of an accidented subject to its term, not just as an accident in a subject, as "fat" is an accident in a man. The "stretching accident" has two phases: first, the tendency of the accidented subject to stretch to other beings; second, its actual stretching (*esse ad*) to other beings. The second phase comes into existence when there is another being around towards which the tendency to stretch may actually stretch.

The Extrinsic Cause of a Relation

Hamelin says that if one were without the illusions of a rudimentary metaphysics which mistakes the abstract for the concrete, one would view each being as a solid block isolated and definitively distinct from any other solid block.[11] Yes and no. Yes, in the sense that each being has its *own* act of existing, each being is surely a solid block, definitively isolated from each other being. Nonetheless, within each solid being there are potential elements, and although those potential elements are always actuated up to a point, nevertheless precisely because they are never actuated to the point of being the "nature of being," those actuated potentials still have a residue of vacuity which *they* cannot fill up, but other beings can.

---

[9] There is but cold comfort in the relations of sizes. Nevertheless the size of the prehistoric monsters apparently kept them from "making it." Related qualities on the other hand are great enrichments.

[10] St. Thomas, *De Pot.*, II, 5, *Resp.*

[11] O. Hamelin, *Essai sur les éléments principaux de la répresentation*, 2 éd., Paris, Alcan, 1925, p. 365.

In this sense, no, beings are *not* solid, isolated blocks. Rudimentary or sophisticated, a metaphysics which does *not* mistake the abstract for the concrete sees relations in concrete things. In any one being there is inscribed a demand for other beings. To fill up or to be filled up by other beings, this is a demand written in the very heart of limited beings, not so much because they are limited as because they are beings, and beings always press on towards the fulfilling of themselves, because being is fulfillment, and partial fulfillments are not yet *ful*fillments. And so, the analysis of any one being brings the insight that other beings are written in any one being as in a passive or active potential which those other beings can fill or be filled with.

Now, if this give and take among beings is only among themselves, intramural so to say; if beings merely link hands and dance together in an unbreakable fairy ring, it is impossible that any member of the ring should get from, or give anything *new* to, any other. They would be fooling away their time by getting or giving what was there in the ring all the while. No doubt there is a real give and take within limited beings, but notice: the give and take is of being, and being, though *in* the ring, is not *from* the ring. The *esse* within the ring is from its cause, God. Instead of a closed ring, then, we have a double spiral, from God as from an efficient cause, and to God as to a final cause.

Not to let the figure get out of hand—the second cause of a relation is the accidented subject itself, or another second cause of the accidented subject; the First cause of a relation is the cause of any accidented subject. The First cause of the accidented subject causes that subject to exist as demanding fulfillment in *esse* by or in other beings, and as being fulfilled by or in other beings; and since *esse* is from the First cause, beings are interrelated as well as related to God. For, since the *esse* of a creature is from God, and since that same *esse* is ever more fully expanded by giving to or taking from other beings, which are also from God, it is God Who is the ultimate efficient and final source of a relation.[12] The fairy ring, then, if not broken, is at least open to the reception of its *esse* from God and to

---

[12] On creation as a relation, see *De Pot.*, III, 3, *Resp.*; VII, 9, *Resp.*; *Sum. Theol.*, I, 45, 3, *Resp.* and *ad* 1. See Appendix C of this chapter.

the fulfillment of its *esse* by or in other beings, which are also from the same source.

In sum, like the three musketeers, who always turn out to be four, any one being shows two faces: (1) its own; (2) the face of being related to others. This being-related-to-others face exists as an accident exists, in the subject; however, this accident in a subject is not like the categorial accidents which compound with the subject and seal it off from others; rather, this sort of accident, of being related, is that *to* which the *esse in* tends and *in* which the *esse ad* terminates.[13] To be related to others, then, is a mode of *esse*, rich with its own capital precisely because its own capital grows from and causes to grow, the capital of others. To be related to others, this, for a created being, is also to exist. And since existence is from God, so also are relations of *esse* from Him.[14]

The basic difficulty about understanding relation, then, is this: what *is* that size of John's which is greater or less than or equal to George's? The question, note, does not mean that we wish to know what John's size is as being, say, six feet tall. No, we wish to know what there is about size, any size, which makes it greater or less than or equal to, any other size. To put the question in another way, if any size is an absolute, then how can anything else (an *esse ad*) be added to the absolute? And if size is *not* an absolute but also a relation (*esse ad*), then what is that relation when the subject of it has no term, no other size, that is, for the first size to be related to; and indeed what is size, which can be differently related to other sizes without change in itself? Certainly, the facts seem to be as described: *any* size is an absolute, and any *other* size is a term of that absolute's relation to that other size; furthermore, any size is differently referrable to any other whether there is or is not any other size.[15] To recur to our example, if John's height is six feet and George's is five feet, John's height is related to George's by

[13] St. Thomas, *Sum. Theol.*, I, 28, 2, *Resp.*: ". . . relations are found as such to be *assistant*, and not intrinsically affixed, for they signify as it were, a respect which affects the thing related, inasmuch as it tends from that thing to something else. . . ." See also *De Pot.*, VII, 8, *Resp.;* VIII, 9, *ad* 7; VIII, 2, *Resp.*

[14] St. Thomas, *De Pot.*, VII, 9, *Resp.; De Pot.*, III, 3, *Resp.; Sum. Theol.*, I, 45, 3, *Resp.* and *ad* 1.

[15] St. Thomas, *In V Phys.*, lect. 3, n. 3; *De Pot.*, VII, 8, *Resp.;* VII, 9, *Resp.* and *ad* 7; VIII, 2, *Resp. ad fin.*

being one foot taller than George's, and this relation would persis
even if George were four feet tall and John five. What is more
something would persist or survive in John's height even if there
were no George to be related to, and even if John's height were
differently related to George's. Apparently, then, there is something
in a "one foot taller" which survives even when the relations of the
"one foot taller" change to, e.g., one foot shorter, and indeed even
when there is no "shorter than, taller than, or equal to" at all. The
question is what *is* this surviving factor?

It is an explanation of the relative, John's size. In other words
actual sizes do not survive in the explanation of them; only the explanation of them survives. This is to say that the category of
relation is not explained by describing it. It is explained by its causes

The Explanation of the Relative in Being

We wish to know why a given quantity, a size or a number, is
differently related to other quantities without change in the given
one, and indeed why any given quantity is referrable even to inexistent quantities. Let us run through the states of the explanation.
To be "a taller than," is to be quantified. To be quantified is to be
the size of a material substance. To be a material substance is also.
besides being a subject of accidents, to be under the quasi genus of
"that to which it is owed to exist." To be "that to which it is owed
to exist" is, when a substance whether material or immaterial does
exist, to exist. To exist is to be caused to exist in every case where
there is no peremptory or contractual claim of that "to which
it is owed to exist" (even if it does exist) upon its own existential
act. Such is the situation of every existent short of God. Finally,
to be caused to exist is to be related to a cause of being, and so to
be related, namely, as to a cause of its being, is for the related thing
to exist. Here at last is disclosed the identity of "being related" with
the existent so related. Here one sees that the relation of a caused
being to its cause is the very *esse* of the being so related. Here one
sees that to be an existent is to be related to a cause of being, that is,

to be an existent is to be an absolute which is its relation to its cause; and because that absolute is merely one of many such absolutes, each is related to God and to others through its *esse*. Obviously, the subject (the existent) of the relation (of creation) stands in our knowledge as prior to the relation, just as substance stands in our knowledge as prior in *esse* to its accident; but *this* accident (creation) *in* a creature *is* a creature.[16] This, of course, involves the relation of our knowledge to being, but before the knowledge relation can be settled, the relations themselves must be settled, and the settlement lies in there being a First cause of beings and their relations.

The same explanation holds for all relations, even relations of quality, e.g., a "whiter than" or a "more intelligent than," etc.

We may see this more clearly as follows. Assume as true these propositions: *x is, x was*. Now clearly, if *x is* and *x was* are statements of facts, those facts do not get their situs in being from the one who makes those statements, nor from the time or place in which he makes them, nor from the statements themselves, nor even from the meaning of those statements. The utterer, his utterance, the time and place of his utterance, even the meaning of his utterance, none of these has anything to do with the situs in being of the uttered. If facts begin to be, continue, at least for a while, and sometimes cease to be—but do not cease to have been—this is not because the nature of being is to begin, to continue, and to cease to be. Rather, this is because *they*, the facts, which are *not* the nature of being, *they* begin, continue, and cease to be. The nature of being is to exist, pretty much as it is the nature of the liver to secrete bile. The nature of being is *not* to begin and cease to be. Put it this way: the nature of being does not shove its way into itself; if facts come and go, this is because *they* come and go, not because the nature of being comes and goes; and *they* come and go because they are *not* the nature of being. The situation is of course unintelligible if

---

[16] St. Thomas, *Sum. Theol.*, I, 45, 3, *ad* 2: ". . . passive creation is in the creature, and is a creature." *Sum. Theol.*, I, 45, 3, *ad* 3: "The creature is the term of creation as signifying a change; but it is the subject of creation taken as a real relation, and is prior to it in being, as the subject is to the accident."

there be no "nature of being," no cause of facts, no being whose nature it is to exist and not, as with the past and present facts, whose nature it is to be past or present *if* they exist.[17]

The drift of these remarks is not to demonstrate a cause of being. It is rather to help us realize that existential acts, signalized here by past and present facts, are not intrusions into being, not *their* entry into being. It is rather the entry of existential act into them, from a cause of them of course, and this entry of *esse* into them is not so much an entry of *esse into* something as it is the "something" itself. The entry *is* the facts. Facts are quite at home in *esse*. Indeed they have no other home. And if we are forced to say that the past and present are intrusions of *esse* into modes of *esse*, we are also forced to recall that those modes of being have no existential status whatsoever until they were or are in *esse*. Once in *esse*, facts are not intruders. They are invited guests, quite at home where they have been invited, especially so since that home of theirs is nothing less than they themselves, the facts. As St. Augustine remarked, "what is so much yours as you, and what is so little yours as you if it belongs to another—that 'you'?"[18] In sum, past and present facts do not depend for their factual status upon themselves but upon a cause of them; if so, they do not depend for the factual status upon our knowledge of them.

Relations of Knowledge to Being

It is the other way about. Our knowledge of them depends upon them, and in the most astounding way, short of divine grace, possible. Knowledge is surely a physical mode of being, a physical accident of the soul. But so to describe knowledge as if there were nothing more to it than to be a physical qualification of the knower as fatness is a physical qualification of a fat man is to miss the specificity, the location of the mystery of knowledge. Besides qualifying the knower as a physical accident of his soul, knowledge

[17] See Chapter XI, pp. 170–179.
[18] St. Augustine, *Tract.* XXIX super *Joan.*, PL 35, 1629: "Quid enim tam tuum quam tu? et quid tam non tuum quam tu, si alicujus est quod es?"

is above all a qualification of the knower in terms of the known.[19]
It is here that the mystery of knowledge lies. One may locate that
mystery thus: let a man see red and later see green. These two
operations, these two seeings are indistinguishable as physical accidents. Nevertheless, they are distinguishable as a-seeing-red-opera-
tion is not a-seeing-green-operation. The difference, in other words,
between the two operations is a difference as between the knowns,
red and green. Just so, to say that *x* is or was—those two "sayings"
are operations qualified by the past and present *x*'s. So to be qualified, namely, by something which is not the knower, nor his knowledge act, but which is the known, this is knowledge: an awareness
of something other than the knower and his knowledge.

There are other ways to see the same point. Assume as true these
two propositions: *x is white and a body*. The two assertions are
cognitive accidents of any asserter of them. Yet what is asserted by
the two propositions, though accidental to the *x* in *x is white*, is *not*
accidental to *x* in *x is a body*. X could exist without being white,
but if *x is a body* is true, *x* could not exist unless it were a body.
Thus the "is" of the assertion or the act of judging is always accidental to the judger, but the "is" of the judged is sometimes accidental to the judged as in *x is white*, and sometimes not, as in *x is
a body*.[20]

The question now is this: is the "is" of the judged which is accidental to *x* in *x is white*, and not accidental to *x* as in *x is a body*,
is that "is" accidental to the judged in the same way as the assertion
of that "is" is always accidental to the judger? In other words, is
the "is" of the judgment a category like the "is" of the judged, like
whiteness, for example, which is an accident? No, not even though
the judging that *x is white*, or for that matter, the judging of anything, e.g., that *x is a body*, is always accidental to the judger. To
see this one has only to recall that any true saying is not just a

---

[19] On knowledge as a qualification of the knower in terms of the known,
see Chapter X, pp. 149–153.

[20] St. Thomas, *De Verit.*, III, 3, *Resp.*: "We find, moreover, in certain forms,
a double relation: one relation to that which is informed by these forms, and
this is the kind of relation that knowledge has to the knower; another to
that which is outside, and this is the kind of relation that knowledge has to
what is known."

saying. It is a saying of something which is *not* the saying of it: it is being. Now surely the accidental being of "being white" is not the accidental being of the sayer's "saying" that something is white. However accidental either status may be, being white is certainly not the saying that a being is white. You can say that *x is white* until you are blue in the face, but your sayso, even when true, is not *x*'s being white.[21]

There is another way of grasping the point. Assume as true this proposition: *x can be or cannot be.* If the *can be* and *cannot be* predicates are accidental to the *x* in the same way that the *assertion* of them is accidental to the asserter, then the assertion of either predicate is a true or false assertion solely and simply upon the score that the predicates are asserted. This means that the *can be* and *cannot be* predicates can be true of *x* conjunctively, because both predicates can surely be *asserted* conjunctively of *x*. And yet it is impossible that *can be* and *cannot be* be conjunctively true of *x*, even though they can be conjunctively *asserted* of *x*. X can be or not be, not because one *says* either or both predicates, but because it is the *x* which can be or not be. If one insists that the assertion *is* the asserted, to insist that *x*'s *can be* is the assertion of it, and so for *x*'s *cannot be*, there is no point in pursuing the matter with one whose intellectual life has thus become vegetal.[22]

A last and similar version of the same point. Assume as true that *x is or is not.* Here too if the *is* and *is not* predicates are accidental to the *x* in the same way that the assertion of them is accidental to their asserter, then *x* is because one *says* so, and *x* is not, also because one *says* so. Here at last is fully revealed a situation that was present in all the examples. Whereas one can state either predicate or both, only one of them is true of the *x*, and maybe it is not the one stated! If the one stated is true, then that one is more than the assertion of it. That "more than" means this: the existence of the asserted, a factor which is outside the genus of knowledge.[23] And if

---

[21] See Chapter XV, pp. 260–263.

[22] Aristotle, *Metaphysics,* IV (Γ), 4, 1006a 15; St. Thomas, *Sum. Theol.,* I–II, 51, 1.

[23] St. Thomas, *De Verit.,* III, 3, *Resp.:* ". . . knowledge is about those things whose natures are such that they cannot be produced by the knowledge of the knower, as is true for example, when we think about natural things."

a stated contradictory is not true, then the unstated one stands as a witness, ready, able and willing to accuse the thinker of not knowing the fact. In sum, any true judgment is true not only because it is in the mind, but mainly because the mind's judgment is in being, knocking around in being so to say. When the mind knows that it is *x* which is white and a body, etc., knowledge is bumping its way into, hitting its nose against being. View knowledge merely as an assertion, and knowledge bumps into nothing but knowledge, into nothing but an assertion. View knowledge as more than an assertion, and the mind runs smack into the asserted, into being. Two colliding trucks feel no shock, but the drivers do, and it is the latter collision which is the collision of knowledge with being.

To ask, then, how one "goes from knowledge to the known" is to presuppose that one does so go. The presupposition is false, not because it contradicts any known fact or principle, but because it is given in knowledge that *it is x* which is white and a body, etc. And so, knowledge is not the only given in knowledge. Being is also given in knowledge. Descartes will always be there to remind us that the thinker (Descartes' *cogitatum*) is given with his thinking.[24] Unfortunately, Descartes did not realize that the *cogitata* which are *not* the thinker (Descartes' *cogitatum* was *only* the thinker) are no more and no less being, though in a less privileged way, no more and no less given in knowledge, than is the thinker himself. Not realizing this, Descartes tried to prove that there are beings which are other than the thinker, with no resounding success, as everyone knows. Neither for Descartes' thinker nor for the *cogitata* which are not thinkers is any proof that they exist possible or necessary. Descartes' *cogitata* or nonthinkers, though he did not realize this, are quite as authentically beings as his thinker is.

Knowledge, then, is an entry of a knower into being. It is not an entry of being into knowledge. We have our heads in the clouds

---

[24] Descartes, *Principia Philosophiae*, Pars I, princ. X; ed. Adam-Tannery, Vol. III, p. 8; *Discours de le méthode;* ed. Adam-Tannery, Vol. VII, pp. 86-89, 165-167, 201-202, 292, 301-307.

Descartes shows that the thinker is given with his thinking in *Meditations*, II; ed. Haldane and Ross, Vol. I, pp. 151-152. See Appendix D of this chapter.

Descartes' proof for beings other than the thinker, i.e., God and the sensible world, may be found in *Meditations*, IV; ed. Haldane and Ross, Vol. I, pp. 171-172; *Meditations*, VI, p. 19. See Appendix E of this chapter.

when we know them. The clouds are not in our heads. We are aware of *them*, they are not aware of us. Being does not invade knowledge. Knowledge invades being. To say that knowledge invades being, this is to say that being is first: first, as waiting to be invaded by our knowledge; secondly, as prior even in knowledge to the knowledge of being and to the knower. Knowledge speaks to me of something which is not-me even when it speaks to me of me.

This foray, then, of knowledge into being causes knowledge to come back burdened simultaneously with two items. Knowledge brings back the booty that *it is x* which is white and a body, etc., etc. Besides that loot (the knowing of being), knowledge also brings back this item: knowledge knows that it *knows* being. But the latter knowledge, simultaneous and co-essential with the first, is not the only spoils which knowledge has reaped. To know you know being is the main *title* to your *spoils*, but it is not the only spoils. To know being is also the first spoils. Thus again, to know being is not so much being's venture into knowledge as it is knowledge's venture into being by way of knowing being. One may see it this way: say *x is;* say next *I know x is.* The second statement adds nothing to the first, although it does proffer the title which assures us that *x is* is knowledge about being. That title was there in the first statement, though not explicitly proffered there. This title of *knowing* you know being is a "relation of reason."

Relations of Reason

The relations of reason are first intentional relations, or second, or the "relations of reason only." First intentional relations have been sufficiently noted:[25] they are relations of our knowledge of *animal*, say, to our knowledge of the species of animal, e.g., to our knowledge of *fox, man*, etc.; and again, the relations of our knowledge of the species of animal, *fox, man*, etc., to our knowledge of *individual existent* animals. In other words, the first intentional knowledge relation is a relation of explicitly known wholes in *esse* to those

[25] See Chapter X, pp. 153-165.

wholes' implicitly known parts. Second intentional relations are the relations of, e.g., our knowledge of generic universality to specific universality; and again, the relation of our knowledge of the necessary to our knowledge of the nonnecessary or accidental; and again, the relation of our knowledge of the constitutive necessary to our knowledge of the nonconstitutive but derivative necessary or property. Generic, differential, specific, accidental, proprietal universalities, all these second intentional knowledges (there are others) of the relation of predicates to their subjects are *discovered* in our knowledge pretty much as fish are discovered in water; only, these fish are not in physical *esse* at all. They are only in intentional *esse*. (First intentional knowledge relations, however, involve a content which is both in intentional and physical *esse*.) The "discovered" second intentional relations can be examined and reexamined because they *stay* discovered, with enormous profit to the sciences of logic, formal and material, and also to the profit of the metaphysics of intentions, first and second. The relations of "reason only" are something else again. They do not stay discovered as logical relations do. They are in consequence of having discovered being, and if you wish to find them, you must have known being; if you wish to find them a second and a third, etc., time, you must have known being a second and a third, etc., time. We must see this better.

The Relations of Reason Only

The relations of reason only can be discovered indeed, but only as one discovers one's footprint—after having made it. This latter discovery is, of course, a perfectly idle occupation compared with the job of having reached one's destination which is to have known being. Nevertheless, the relations of reason only will tell one where he had been headed all along, because they are but the tracks left by one's knowledge of being, structures one has made whenever one has known being. These structures are not one's knowledge of being, but they reveal what one's knowledge of being is. Hence it is no small advantage to know what "the relations of reason only" are if only because they help to lay bare what it means to know being.

The "Relations of Reason Only" Enumerated[26]

We shall now list the "relations of reason only." Occasionally we understand some "two's" as beings, whereas only one of them, or neither, is a being. For example, we understand a present and a future event, or a past and present event, or two future events. Past events are no longer beings, and future events are not yet beings. Yet we understand the past and the future as beings. In further illustration of "the relations of reason only," of any unit we understand that it is not other than itself: to be not other than oneself is not a being, whereas to be oneself is; and yet we understand a "self" as being not other than itself all the same. And again, we understand that a known is not affected by or related to our knowledge of it: known or not the North Pole is not affected by or related to our knowledge of it. Here too we are understanding as related to knowledge something which is not so related, a being (the related to knowledge) which is not a being (not related to knowledge). Lastly, as we have seen, we understand a unit of quantity as being a relatedness, even when there is no other unit of quantity to which the first is related: a relatedness which is not related to anything, a being which is not a being.[27]

The Subject as Cause of the Relations of Reason Only

Common to all the listed relations of reason only is this feature: each is a result of having known being.

For example, to know that a unit is not other than itself, this

[26] St. Thomas discusses the "relations of reason only" in *Sum. Theol.*, I, 13, 7, *Resp.*; *De Pot.*, VII, 11, *Resp.*; *De Verit.*, I, 5, *ad* 16; *Sum. Theol.*, I, 28, 1, *ad* 4. See Appendix F of this chapter.

[27] St. Thomas, *De Pot.*, VII, 11, *Resp.*

is not to know being; rather this is to have known being, viz., a unit. Again, to know the past or future, or when we say *this was* or *this will be,* this is to have known a *this is;* for, *was* and *will be* simply repeat *is.* So, *this is* is past or future only in knowledge. In itself the "this" in the proposition *this is* is being, and the knowledge that *this is* is knowledge of being. Of course our knowledge of the future is knowledge of a pattern, a law, a description of what the future will be if it is. It is not fixed knowledge about *one* of two contradictories. Yet the description of the future will hold, just as the description of extinct species holds, because in both cases it is the incorruptible formula of a corruptible existent. Besides, although we don't know which of these two alternatives is true: "there will be, or there will not be, a sea-fight here tomorrow,"[28] nevertheless we do know that one of them *must* eventuate. Now, to say that one of two contradictories must occur, this is to say that we know that the one which will occur is already fixed in knowledge; and to say *that* is to say that we know, however obscurely, God. Again, to say of *x* that it "is known," this is to have known *x;* the "is known" predicate is no skin off or on *x*'s nose. *We* relate knowns to our knowledge only because our knowledge is related to knowns, and that relation which *we* make is in consequence of our having known being; it is not our knowledge of being. The known is a term of a knowledge relation, but there is no relation of the known to knowledge, no relation in reverse. That factitious relation in reverse is a relation of reason only, a consequent of having known being.

The feature common to all relations of reason, including the "relations of reason only" is explained in part by the subject of those relations. Let us run through the stages of the explanation by simply adding "to know" to the explanation already given of the relative in being.[29] To know a "taller than" is to know the quantified. To know the quantified is to know the size of a material substance. To know a material substance is also, besides knowing being as a subject of accidents, to know the quasi genus which is "that to which it is owed to exist." To know "that to which it is owed to exist" is,

---

[28] Aristotle, *On Interpretation,* ch. 9, 19a 30–33.
[29] See p. 282 of this chapter.

when we know that a substance, material or immaterial, *does* exist, to know an existent. To know an existent which has no contractual or peremptory claims upon its own existential act (even if it does exist) is to know that an existent is caused. To know that an existent is caused is to know its cause. To know there is a cause of existents is to know God. Here at last is revealed a relation of the intellect to being and to its cause, which relation *is* the intellect.[30]

The point is not so much that we make assertions as that in any assertion we make there are involved unasserted absolute elements.[31] Say, for example, *John is here, now*. In order to be intelligible that statement involves these unasserted, absolute statements: *a man can be here, now,* and *no man can be the place where he is or the time at which he is there, a man can be or not be, a man is or is not*, etc. Or, say *a genus is*. If that statement is true, then this one is true: *a species is*, for a genus cannot exist except as a species. If *a species exists* is true, then this statement is true: *individuals of a species exist,* for species cannot exist except as in individuals. If *individuals exist* is true, then this is true: *quantified individuals exist,* for men cannot exist except as quantified. If quantified individuals exist, then this is true: *they are related or relatable to other quantified individuals,* for the quantified cannot exist except as so related or relatable. If quantified individuals exist as so related or relatable, then the following is true: *no bearer of nonnecessary or accidental esse or of esse's relations can exist except as necessarily related to its cause,* for the accidental has no root except in the absolute. Here at last is revealed an expectancy, which is the intellect, which was present in all the instances, an expectancy of a power to know, which is always partially fulfilled because that power has always seen *esse*, but never fully fulfilled because it has not yet seen God.[32]

It is not so much, as was suggested, that we assert the statements which follow the first one, not so much that we state, *sotto voce,* all the propositions following the first one. We don't go around asserting God. It is rather that the assertion of all the statements

---

[30] See St. Thomas, *Sum. Theol.,* I, 13, 7, *Resp.;* 28, 1, *ad* 4; *De Pot.,* VII, 11, *Resp.; De Verit.,* I, 5, *ad* 16.

[31] See J. Maréchal, S.J., *Le point de départ de la métaphysique,* Vol. V, pp. 379, 389.

[32] See Chapter XI, p. 176; Chapter XII, p. 181.

following the first one is ahead or in front of the assertion of the first. In other words, the knowledge of the absolute, God, is the end of the intellect's thrust, of its tendency, of its drift. Any assertion has written within it the expectancy of making more assertions up to and including the final one, God exists. And even after that final assertion, the expectancy is still expectant of knowing what God is. God is thus moulding, shaping, directing all knowledge unto Himself. The mould is the intellect itself, or to change the figure, in the thrust of the intellect itself is written the image of God. That image cannot be effaced. It may be troubled and distorted indeed, but only as an image reflected in a clear but rippling pool is wiggly. And yet that thrust to knowing being, which hits creatures so readily and well, comes to know so much about creatures that we like to stare at them instead of seeing God. The vast amount we know about creatures hides from us the little we know about God.

In any assertion, then, there are unasserted knowledges; in any knowledge there is unemployed knowledge.[33] To know the simple fact that a writer is becoming boring is also to know a feature whose only limit is nonbeing, for surely a writer can be nonboring without ceasing to be. If he ceased to be, he would be neither boring nor nonboring; he wouldn't be at all, and so he wouldn't be known at all. Now, to know that there is no limitation in the knowledge of being except the nonlimit of nonbeing, this is to have known being. It is not to know being. To know being has, then, as its consequences this: to have known a feature which is either absolute or involves knowing the absolute. Or put it this way, to know that all being is knowable is to have known being. The first statement (to know that all being is knowable) is a relation of reason only, a relation which would not be in our heads, so to say, unless our heads had been occupied in knowing being. Just as physical beings, then, have a built-in physical thrust (*esse in*) to other beings so as by completing or being completed by other beings (*esse ad*), so the soul has a built-in intentional thrust (*esse in*) towards knowing other beings (*esse ad*) up to and including the knowing of God.[34]

This thrust is a relation of the intellect to the absolute even in

[33] J. Maréchal, S.J., *op. cit., loc. cit.*
[34] See Chapter XII, p. 181.

the intellect's knowledge of the contingent. The actuation of that thrust is the knowing, implicitly or explicitly, of the absolute in the knowing of the contingent. No one ever denied or can deny that thrust and its actuation, because even in knowing the contingent (Socrates is running) there is also the knowledge of the absolute (if Socrates is running, run he must).[35] The thrust is there all right, in any bit of knowledge. The difficulty is about the interpretation of that thrust or incipient relation.

You might say, for example, that knowledge of the absolute is *not* illusory, whereas the knowledge of the contingent *is*. Plato thought so.[36] He reasoned thus: because the outstanding characteristic of being is its self-identity, and because no sensible being is completely self-identical, therefore ideas are being because *they* at least are self-identical. No one ever felt easy about Plato's solution, not even Plato. Or, you might say with Plotinus that the outstanding characteristic of being is its unity, and so unity is above being; or, if you wish, the peak instance of being a being is to be the One.[37] This solution satisfies still less, for how can being be one before it exists? With Aristotle you might say that neither the knowledge of the absolute nor the knowledge of the contingent is illusory.[38] You would then have on your hands two knowledge itsems which for the life of him Aristotle can't get together, though like the honest

[35] St. Thomas, *Sum. Theol.*, I, 86, 3, *Resp.*

[36] Plato, *Republic*, V, 476a-d; VI, 510e; *Parmenides*, 129a-135d; *Sophist*, 240b-246a; *Philebus*, 15a ff.; *Phaedo*, 78d; "'But now let us return to those things we have been dealing with in the previous discussion. The very essence of being which we have accounted for by means of questions and answers, is it always in the same manner and in the same way, or is it now this way now that way? Equality itself, beauty itself, each and every itself, which being is, are they liable at times to some degree of change? Or does each one of these things, whose form is single, remain always itself in itself, being changeless in every way and in every respect?' 'They must remain always the same, Socrates,' replied Cebes."

[37] Plotinus, *The Enneads*, V, 3, 15: "The One is the ultimate principle of being: The nonone is preserved by the One, and it is owing to the One that it is what it is; so long as a certain thing, which is made up of many parts, is not yet become one, we cannot yet say of it: *it is*. And, if we can say of each and every thing what it is, it is owing to its unity as well as to its identity." *Enneads*, V, 3, 17: "It is manifest that the maker of both reality and substance is itself no reality, but is beyond both reality and substance."

[38] See Aristotle, *Metaphysics*, I (A), 9, 990b 1-991b 20; IX (Θ), 6, 1048a 31-1048b 4; XIII (M), 5, 1079b 12-1080a 10.

man he is he hangs on to both bits. Aristotle reasoned thus: before
the event one of two contradictories *must* occur; after the event
the one which occurs is the one which must *have* occurred, and
you can't say that![39] An honest man, as was said. He is hanging on
grimly to two data, refusing to surrender either, but unable to get
them together. There are other less penetrating suggestions. Kant
thought that there was an absolute, but it is unknowable.[40] A pietistic
hope. Christian Wolff thought that essence (a possible being) can
be known without knowing *esse*, and since *esse* too can be known,
therefore the knowing of *esse* is complementary to knowing
essence.[41] This solution makes the intelligible intelligible (whoever
denied this!) without indicating the source of intelligibility, viz.,
an essence in *esse*, or an essence which is *esse*—being in short. Far
from being a complement of essence, *esse* for a realist is comple-
mented by essence. Still lower on the scale is Cassirer's explanation
to the effect that the knowledge of the absolute is an illusion we
can't get along without.[42] William James thinks that we should wash

[39] See Aristotle, *On Interpretation*, ch. 9, 19a 30–35. See also Chapter XI,
pp. 174–179.
[40] Kant, *Prolegomena to Any Future Metaphysics*, Pt. I, Remark II; ed.
P. Carus, Chicago, The Open Court Publishing Co., 1926, pp. 42–43: "All our
intuition however takes place by means of the senses only; the understanding
intuits nothing, but only reflects. And as we have just shown that the senses
never and in no manner enable us to know things in themselves, but only
their appearances, which are mere representations of the sensibility, we conclude that 'all bodies, together with the space in which they are, must be
considered nothing but mere representations in us, and exist nowhere but in
our thoughts.' You will say: Is not this manifest Idealism?
"Idealism consists in the assertion, that there are none but thinking beings,
all other things, which we think are perceived in intuition, being nothing but
representations in the thinking beings, to which no object external to them
corresponds in fact. Whereas I say, that things as objects of our senses existing
outside us are given, but we know nothing of what they may be in themselves,
knowing only their appearances, i.e., the representations which they cause in
us by affecting our senses."
[41] C. Wolff, *Philosophia prima, sive Ontologia, methodo scientifica pertractata, qua omnis cognitionis humanae principia continentur*, Pars I, Sec.
II, cap. 3; ed. Francofurti et Lipsiae, 1736, n. 134, p. 115: "Ens dicitur quod
existere potest, consequenter cui existentia non repugnat." N. 135, p. 116:
"Quod possibile est, ens est." N. 174, p. 143: "Hinc existentiam definio per com-
plementum possibilitatis."
[42] For Cassirer's position, see E. Cassirer, *An Essay on Man. An Introduction
to a Philosophy of Human Culture*, N.Y., Doubleday, Inc., 1956, p. 286; *The*

our hands of the job of trying to hitch a knowledge of the contingent on to a knowledge of the absolute: "to a painted nail you
can hitch only a painted chain."[43] Semanticists think that words are
signs of thinking,[44] and they have become so bemused with the
marvels of the signs of thinking that they have forgotten that thinking itself is a sign of the things which are thought about.

A realist thinks that the outstanding characteristic of being, both
in itself and in our knowledge of it, is being: the fact that being

Philosophy of Symbolic Forms, Vol. I; tr. R. Manheim, New Haven, Yale
University Press, 1953, pp. 87-93: "We find indeed that, beside and above the
world of perception, all these spheres produce freely their own *world of
symbols* which is the true vehicle of their immanent development—a world
whose inner quality is still wholly sensory, but which already discloses a
formed sensibility, that is to say, a sensibility governed by the spirit. Here we
no longer have to do with a sensible world that is simply given and present,
but with a system of diverse sensory factors which are produced by some form
of free creation.

"The process of language formation shows for example how the chaos of
immediate impressions takes on order and clarity for us only when we 'name'
it and so permeate it with the function of linguistic thought and expression.
In this new world of linguistic signs the world of impressions itself acquires an
entirely new 'permanence,' because it acquires a new intellectual articulation.
. . . In the immanent development of the mind the acquisition of the *sign*
really constitutes a first and necessary step towards knowledge of the objective nature of the thing. . . . Through the sign that is associated with the
content, the content itself acquires a new permanence. . . . what language
designates and expresses is neither exclusively subjective nor exclusively objective; it effects a new mediation, a particular *reciprocal relation* between
the two factors. . . . language arises where the two ends are joined, so creating
a new synthesis of 'I' and 'world.'"
[43] W. James, *The Meaning of Truth*, N.Y., Longmans, Green, 1927, p. 109:
"Should we not say here that to be experienced as continuous is to be really
continuous, in a world where experience and reality come to the same thing?
In a picture gallery a painted hook will serve to hang a painted chain by,
a painted cable will hold a painted ship. In a world where both the terms and
their distinctions are affairs of experience, conjunctions that are experienced
must be at least as real as anything else. They will be 'absolutely' real conjunctions, if we have no transphenomenal absolute ready, to derealize the
whole experienced world by, at a stroke."
[44] See, for example, H. Reichenbach, *Elements of Symbolic Logic*, N.Y.,
Macmillan, 1947, p. 6: "It appears advisable, however, to restrict the predicates
meaning and *truth* to linguistic signs, or symbols, since a complete interpretation of these terms can be given only with a system of rules constituting a
language."
See also R. Carnap, *The Logical Syntax of Language*, London, Routledge
& Kegan Paul, 1949, p. 279: ". . . Philosophical questions are logical questions. . . . The supposed peculiarly philosophical point of view from which the

exists and that it is known to exist.[45] If so, knowledge of *that* characteristic is more than the *meaning* of that characteristic; the meaning of that characteristic *is* that characteristic, viz., being. This seems to be, then, the basic description of a realist's knowledge: meaning *is* the thing meant. This fundamental description of knowledge is open to two distortions.

Distorted Idealistic Explanation of Knowledge

That description can be distorted by confusing the operation of knowing with the known. Surely the mind's operation is the mind's alone, and so we incline to think that if there is such a thing as knowledge, it must be knowledge of the mind's operation, not knowledge of the known. A clear case of confusing the word "meaning" as meaning the *signified* with the word "meaning" as meaning the operation of signifying.[46] As realists, we must be quite clear that the meaning of the signified *is* the signified; the meaning of the signified is *not* the signifying operation. Idealists think that "meaning" is the signifying operation.

Distorted Pseudo-realistic Explanation of Knowledge

Nevertheless, the mind *does* know its signifying operation as well as what is signified by that operation. This fact is the occasion for a second, this time a pseudo-realist's, distortion of the statement that the meaning of the signified *is* the signified. Because the mind

---

objects of science are to be investigated proves to be illusory, just as, previously, the supposed peculiarly philosophical realm of objects proper to metaphysics disappeared under analysis. Apart from the questions of the individual sciences, only the questions of the logical analysis of science, of its sentences, terms, concepts, theories, etc., are left as genuine scientific questions. We shall call this complex of questions the *logic of science. . . . the logic of science takes the place of the inextricable tangle of problems which is known as philosophy.*"

[45] For the realist position of the knowledge of being, see Chapter X, pp. 149–153.

[46] B. Russell, *Problems of Philosophy*, N.Y., Holt, 1912, p. 65. Russell is at his best here.

knows that it knows being, viz., something other than itself and its operation, therefore (this is the pseudo-realist's distortion) the knowing of *knowing* is not the knowing of being. To see this distortion better, ask, of what are we conscious when we are conscious? Answer: we are conscious of something other than ourselves. If so, what about our consciousness of our knowing, the while we are conscious that our knowing is also consciousness of something other than our knowing? Surely (here comes the pseudo-realist's distortion) the consciousness of our knowing is *not* the consciousness of being, for to know is not to exist. Knowers exist even when they do not know. In reply to this distortion one might say that the consciousness of ourselves as knowing, the while it is also consciousness of something other than the consciousness of our knowing, is precisely the deliverance over to the knowledge of being, our own being as knowing, and other beings as well. Look at the facts. The knower is not his knowing; yet knowing is both the knowing of things and of *knowing* that we know things. These facts can be explained only thus: both "knowings" are two phases of one operation in which both "things" are given to knowledge as well as that "thing" which is the knowing of being. In both cases being is given to knowledge, the being of things, and the being of the knowing of things. In that latter "knowing" we find that phase of knowledge which indicates its unlimited range.

The Realistic Explanation of Knowledge

We may break this down. The operation of knowing (*intelligere*) is a nonnecessary accident of the power to know (*intellectus*). It is employed knowledge. It comes and goes. The power to know (*intellectus*) is a necessary or proprietal accident of the soul (*anima*). It does not come and go. It stays with us. As accidents of the soul, all we can say about the operation and its power is that they inhere in their proper subjects: the operation in the intellect, the intellect in the soul. And yet, because the intellect knows both the intelligibles as well as its own operation, it knows itself as an unlimited power in its limited operations. The operation of knowing (*intelligere*) as being *what* is known by the power to know (*intellectus*), that operation is precisely "knowing." Knowing what? Knowing of both intelligibles and of the unemployed knowledge of more intelligibles including the absolutely intelligible. The reason is as follows. The operation of knowing (*intelligere*), taken as meaning *what* it is that is understood (*ut quod intelligitur*) by the power to know (*intellectus*), and taken, as well, as meaning the operation itself *by which* (*ut quo intelligitur*) the act of knowing itself (*intelligere*) is understood, *that* operation *is* the intellect in actuation. Whence, "knowing" (*intelligere*) *is* what is understood by the intellect, and "knowing" is also that by which (*intelligere*) the intellect understands.[47] Look now at the "knowing" or operation. It is (1) specified by "the other," viz., something which is *not* the intellect or the intellect's knowing; (2) it is an assertion or denial that the known exists, or doesn't, *on its own*, an assertion that the known has a way of being which is *different* from its way-of-being-asserted, or denied. If this is so, it makes little difference whether one says "I know being" or "I know my *knowing* of being." Both statements amount to the same thing. To know being is also to know one's *knowing* of being, for *knowing* is knowing of being.

We may see the point also from this angle. To exist is an actuation of an existent, but to know (*intelligere*) is *not* an actuation of the thing known. Rather, to know is an actuation of a knower. Now, the *power* to know (*intellectus*) is a personal endowment of the knower, a necessary accident residing in the soul as in its proper subject. But the actuation of the power to know or the act of knowing doesn't reside in the intellect, nor, therefore, in the soul, as in *its* proper subject. It's the other way about: it is in the act of knowing that the power to know (*intellectus*), when in an operation (*actus intelligendi*)—it is in its operation that the intellect resides as in its proper subject. Thus, in the intellect as in an actuated power we find both that *by which* we know and *that which* we know.[48]

---

[47] St. Thomas, *De Verit.*, X, 8, *ad* 12 and 13.

[48] St. Thomas, *De Verit.*, X, 8, *ad* 13: ". . . intellectiva potentia est forma ipsius animae quantum ad actum essendi, eo quod habet esse in anima, sicut proprietas in subiecto; sed quantum ad actum intelligendi nihil prohibet esse e

Whatever, then, be the explanation of the genesis of knowledge, an explanation which must leave to the instrumentality of knowledge all its rights, in the upshot every phase of that instrumentality must leave untouched the unity of this instrument (the intellect and its operation) and its object, being. It is not upon the score of its instrumentality that knowledge loses its relation to being. Rather, because *this* instrument, which is the intellect in operation, is related to being in all its genetic phases, therefore in each of those genetic phases there is found—being. Take a crucial phase, the *species*, e.g., by which we know. It is not because the species is that *by* which we know that it is different from that *which* we know. The *species* by which we know is *not* different from that which we know.[49] Why not? Because the *species* is nothing but the prolongation into intentional *esse* of what anything in physical *esse is*. To assert that such is the case, this is to know.

Summary

A relation as a category of being inheres in (*esse in*) a subject just as any accident does. On that score there is nothing which sets off the category of a relation from the other eight categorial accidents, nothing particularly significant about it at all. As a distinct and significant category of being a relation is a reference to another being. That reference is significant only as a reference, though its existential status is *in* the subject. Just as an "action" has no special significance as being *in* the agent but only as being *from* the agent, yet action must be *in* the agent all the same; so a relation has no especial status as being *in* the related but only as being *to* another being, though a relation is *in* the related all the same.[50]

---

converso (scil., quod ut actus intelligendi, intellectus est quo et actus intelligendi est quod)." See *De Verit.*, X, 8, *ad* 12: ". . . quo intelligitur et quod intelligitur, non hoc modo se habent ad invicem sicut quo est et quod est. Esse enim est actus entis; sed intelligere non est actus eius quod intelligitur, sed intelligentis; unde quo intelligitur comparatur ad intelligentem sicut quod est et quo est."

[49] St. Thomas, *De Verit.*, X, 8, *ad* 12.
[50] St. Thomas, *De Pot.*, VIII, 2, *Resp.*

The reason or explanation for the above is this: the subject of a relation is caused to be, and so, the subject's relations are caused to be; for, to be is also to be related.

Now, the relation of a being to its cause is not *significant* as something inhering *in* a being but only as related to its cause, though that relation is *in* the related all the same. In fact, that relation of creation in a creature *is* the creature.

The situation is the same for the created intellect. The relation of the intellect to the things known by the intellect, that relation *is* the intellect.

Last, the relations of reason only are not even *in* the intellect.[51] They are simply the occupational results of having known being, and those occupational results will reveal what the occupation was all along.

These occupational results are the transcendentals: (1) a being (2) of reason only, which is (3) a relation of (4) that which perfects to that which is perfected.

Appendix to Chapter XVI

APPENDIX (A). Relations in being.

St. Thomas, *Sum. Theol.*, I, 13, 7, *Resp.*: ". . . things themselves have a mutual order and relation. Nevertheless it is necessary to know that, since a relation needs two extremes, there are three conditions that make a relation to be real or logical. Sometimes from both extremes it is an idea only as when a mutual order or relation can be between things only in the apprehension of reason; as when we say that *the same is the same as itself*. For the reason, by apprehending one thing twice, regards it as two; and thus it apprehends a certain relation of a thing to itself. And the same applies to relations between *being* and *nonbeing* formed by reason, inasmuch as it apprehends nonbeing as an extreme. The same is true of those rela-

---

[51] St. Thomas, *De Pot.*, VIII, 2, *Resp. ad fin.*: ". . . quando [relatio] vero est secundum rationem tantum, tunc non est inhaerens."

tions that follow upon an act of reason, as genus and species, and the like.

"Now there are other relations which are realities as regards both extremes, as when a relation exists between two things according to some reality that belongs to both. This is clear of all relations consequent upon quantity, as great and small, double and half, and the like; for there is quantity in both extremes. The same applies to relations consequent upon action and passion, as motive power and the movable thing, father and son, and the like.

"Again, sometimes a relation in one extreme may be a reality, while in the other extreme it is only an idea. This happens whenever two extremes are not of one order, as sense and science refer, respectively, to sensible things and to knowable things; which, inasmuch as they are realities existing in nature, are outside the order of sensible and intelligible existence. Therefore, in science and in sense a real relation exists, because they are ordered either to the knowledge or to the sensible perception of things; whereas the things looked at in themselves are outside this order. Hence in them there is no relation to science and sense, but only an idea, inasmuch as the intellect apprehends them as terms of the relations of science and sense. Hence, the Philosopher says that they are called relative, not because they are related to other things, but because others are related to them. Likewise, *on the right* is not applied to a column, unless it stands on the right side of animal; which relation is not really in the column, but in the animal.

"Since, therefore, God is outside the whole order of creation, and all creatures are ordered to Him, and not conversely, it is manifest that creatures are really related to God Himself; whereas in God there is no real relation to creatures, but a relation only in idea, inasmuch as creatures are related to Him. Thus there is nothing to prevent such names, which import relation to the creature, from being predicated of God temporally, not by reason of any change in Him, but by reason of the change in the creature; as a column is on the right of an animal, without change in itself, but because the animal has moved."

APPENDIX (B). Relation as an accident.

St. Thomas, *Sum. Theol.*, I, 28, 2, *Resp.*: ". . . in each of the nine genera of accidents there are two points for remark. One is the nature belonging to each one of them considered as an accident, and this is, in the case of all of them, that their being is to inhere in a subject; for the being of an accident is to inhere. The other point of remark is the proper nature of each one of these genera. In the genera, apart from that of *relation*, as in quantity and quality, even the true notion of the genus itself is derived from a relation to a subject; for quantity is called the measure of substance, and quality is the disposition of substance. The true notion of relation is not taken from its respect to that in which it is, but from its respect to something outside. So, even in creatures, relations are found as such to be *assistant*, and not intrinsically affixed; for they signify, as it were, a respect which affects the thing related, inasmuch as it tends from that thing to something else; whereas, if relation is considered as an accident, it inheres in a subject, and has an accidental being in it."

St. Thomas, *De Pot.*, VII, 9, *ad* 7: "The very relation that is nothing but the order between one creature and another may be considered as an accident, or as a relation. Considered as an accident it is something adhering to a subject; but not considered as a relation or order, for then it is mere towardness, something passing as it were from one thing to another and assisting that which is related. Accordingly a relation is something inherent, but not because it is a relation: thus action as action is considered as issuing from the agent; but, as an accident, is considered as inherent to the active subject. Wherefore nothing prevents such an accident from ceasing to exist without any change in its subject, because it is not essentially complete through its existence in its subject but through transition into something else: and if this be removed, the essence of this accident is removed as regards the action, but remains as regards its cause: even so, if the matter be removed, the heating is removed, although the cause of heating remain."

APPENDIX (C). Creation as a relation.

St. Thomas, *De Pot.*, VII, 9, *Resp.*: ". . . relation to God is something real in the creature. . . . Now if relation had no objective
reality, it would not be placed among the predicaments. Moreover
the perfection and goodness that are in things outside the mind are
ascribed not only to something absolute and inherent to things but
also to the order between one thing and another; thus the good of
an army consists in the mutual ordering of its parts, to which good
the Philosopher compares the good of the universe. Consequently
there must be order in things themselves, and this order is a kind
of relation. Wherefore there must be relations in things themselves,
whereby one is ordered to another. Now one thing is ordered to
another either as to quantity or as to active or passive power; for
on these two counts alone can we find in a thing something whereby
we compare it with another. For a thing is measured not only by its
intrinsic quantity but also in reference to an extrinsic quantity. And
again by its active power one thing acts on another, and by its
passive power is acted on by another: while by its substance and
quality a thing is ordered to itself alone and not to another, except
accidentally, namely, inasmuch as a quality, substantial form or
matter is a kind of active or passive power, and inasmuch as one may
ascribe to them a certain kind of quantity. Thus, one thing produces the same in substance; and one thing produces its like in
quality; and number or multitude causes dissimilarity and diversity
in the same things; and dissimilarity in that one thing is considered
as being more or less so and so than another,—thus one thing is said
to be whiter than another. Hence the Philosopher in giving the
species of relations, says that some are based on quantity and some
on action and passion. Accordingly, things that are ordered to something must be really related to it, and this relation must be some
real thing in them. Now all creatures are ordered to God both as
to their beginning and as to their end, since the order of the parts
of the universe to one another results from the order of the whole
universe to God; just as the mutual order of the parts of an army
is on account of the order of the whole army to its commander.

Therefore creatures are really related to God, and this relation is something real in the creature."

St. Thomas, *De Pot.*, III, 3, *Resp.:* ". . . creation does not denote an approach to being, nor a change effected by the Creator, but merely a beginning of existence, and a relation to the Creator from whom the creature receives its being. Consequently creation is really nothing but a relation of the creature to the Creator together with a beginning of existence."

St. Thomas, *Sum. Theol.*, I, 45, 3, *Resp.:* "Creation posits something in the created thing only according to relation; for what is created is not made by motion or by change. For what is made by motion or by change is made from something preexisting. This happens, to be sure, in the particular productions of some beings, but it cannot happen in the production of all being by the universal cause of all beings, which is God. Hence, when God creates, He produces things without motion. Now when motion is removed from action and passion, only relation remains, . . . Hence creation in the creature is only a certain relation to the Creator as to the principle of its being; even as in passion, which supposes motion, is implied a relation to the principle of motion."

St. Thomas, *Sum. Theol.*, I, 45, 3, *ad* 1: "Creation signified actively means the divine action, which is God's essence with a relation to the creature. But in God relation to the creature is not a real relation, but only a relation of reason; whereas the relation of the creature to God is a real relation, . . ."

APPENDIX (D). Descartes shows that the thinker is given with his thinking.

Descartes, *Meditations*, II; ed. Haldane and Ross, Vol. I, pp. 151–152: "What of thinking? I find here that thought is an attribute which belongs to me; it alone cannot be separated from me. I am, I exist, that is certain. But how often? Just when I think; for it might possibly be the case if I ceased entirely to think, that I should likewise cease altogether to exist. I do not now admit anything which is not necessarily true: to speak accurately I am not more than a thing which thinks, that is to say a mind or a soul, or an understanding, or a reason, which are terms whose significance was formerly unknown to me. I am, however, a real thing and really exist; but what thing? I have answered: a thing which thinks."

APPENDIX (E). Descartes' proof for God and the sensible world.

Descartes, *Meditations*, IV; ed. Haldane and Ross, Vol. I, pp. 171-172: "And when I consider that I doubt, that is to say, that I am an incomplete and dependent being, the idea of a being that is complete and independent, that is of God, presents itself to my mind with so much distinctness and clearness—and from the fact alone that this idea is found in me, or that I who possess this idea exist, I conclude so certainly that God exists, and that my existence depends entirely on Him in every moment of my life—that I do not think that the human mind is capable of knowing anything with more evidence and certitude. And it seems to me that I now have before me a road which will lead us from the contemplation of the true God (in whom all the treasures of science and wisdom are contained) to the knowledge of the other objects of the universe."

Descartes, *Meditations*, VI, p. 191: "There is certainly further in me a certain passive faculty of perception, that is, of receiving and recognizing the ideas of sensible things, but this would be useless to me [and I could in no way avail myself of it], if there were not either in me or in some other thing another active faculty capable of forming and producing these ideas. But this active faculty cannot exist in me [inasmuch as I am a thing that thinks] seeing that it does not presuppose thought, and also that those ideas are often produced in me without my contributing in any way to the same, and often even against my will; it is thus necessarily the case that the faculty resides in some substance different from me in which all the reality which is objectively in the ideas that are produced by this faculty is formally or eminently contained, as I remarked before. And this substance is either a body, that is a corporeal nature in which there is contained formally [and really] all that which is objectively [and by representation] in those ideas, or it is God Himself, or some other creature more noble than the body in which that same is contained eminently. But, since God is no deceiver, it is very manifest that He does not communicate to me these ideas immediately and by Himself, nor yet by the intervention of some creature in which their reality is not formally, but only eminently, contained. For since He has given me no faculty to recognize that this is the case, but, on the other hand, a very great inclination to believe [that they are sent to me or] that they are conveyed to me by corporeal objects, I do not see how He could be defended from the accusation of deceit if these ideas were produced by causes other than corporeal objects. Hence we must allow that corporeal things exist. However, they are perhaps not exactly what we perceived by the senses, since this comprehension by the senses is in many instances very obscure and confused; but we must at least admit that all things which, speaking generally, are comprehended in the object of pure mathematics, are truly to be recognized as external objects."

APPENDIX (F). The relations of reason only.

St. Thomas, *De Pot.*, VII, 11, *Resp.:* ". . . just as a real relation consists in order between thing and thing, so a logical relation is the order of thought to thought; and this may occur in two ways. First, when the order is discovered by the mind and attributed to that which is expressed in a relative term. Such are the relations attributed by the mind to the things understood as such, for instance, the relations of genus and species: for the mind discovers these relations by observing the order between that which is in the mind and that which is outside the mind; or again the order between one idea and another. Secondly, when these relations arise from the mode of understanding, namely, when the mind understands one thing in its relation to another, although that relation is not discovered by the intellect but follows by a kind of necessity its mode of understanding. Such relations are attributed by the intellect not to that which is in the intellect but to that which has objective reality. This happens inasmuch as certain things not mutually re-

lated are understood in relation to one another, although the mind
does not understand them to be related, for in that case it would
be in error. Now in order that two things be related they must
each have existence, be distinct from each other (for nothing bears
a relation to itself), and be referable to the other. Now the mind
sometimes conceives two things as having existence, whereas one
or neither of them is a being; just as when it considers two futures,
or one present and one future, and considers one in relation to
the other by placing one before the other. Wherefore, such relations are purely logical since they arise from the mode of understanding. And sometimes the mind considers one thing as though
it were two, and considers them in the light of a certain relationship; as when a thing is said to be identical with itself, and such a
relation is purely logical. Sometimes the mind considers two things
as referable to each other, whereas there is no relation between them;
in fact one of them is itself essentially a relation; as when a relation
is said to be accidental to its subject. Wherefore, such a logical
relation has merely a logical relationship to anything else. Again
the mind sometimes considers something in relation to another inasmuch as it is the term of the relationship of another thing to it, and
yet itself is not related to the other; as when it considers something
knowable as terminating the relationship of knowledge to it; and
thus it imputes to the thing knowable a certain relation to knowledge, and such a relation is purely logical. In like manner our mind
attributes to God certain relative terms, inasmuch as it considers
God as the term of the creature's relation to him; wherefore such
relations are purely logical."

St. Thomas, *Sum. Theol.*, I, 28, 1, *ad* 4: "Relations which result
in the things understood from the operation of the intellect alone
are logical relations only, inasmuch as reason observes them as existing between two understood things. Those relations, however, which
follow the operation of the intellect, and which exist between the
word intellectually proceeding and the source whence it proceeds,
are not logical relations only, but real relations, inasmuch as the
intellect itself or reason is a real thing and really related to that

which proceeds from it intelligibly; as a corporeal thing is related to that which proceeds from it corporeally."

St. Thomas, *De Verit.*, I, 5, *ad* 16: "All genera as such, with the exception of relation, posit something in reality. For example, quantity by its very nature posits something. But relation alone, because of what it is, does not posit anything in reality, for what it predicates is not *something* but *to something*. Hence there are certain relations which posit nothing in reality, but only in reason. This occurs in four ways, as can be seen in the writings of the Philosopher and Avicenna.

"First, there occurs a relation merely in reason when a thing is referred to itself; for example, when we say that a thing is identical with itself. If this relation posited something in reality in addition to the thing which is declared to be identical with itself, we should have an infinite process in relations; for the very relation by which something is said to be identical with itself would also be identical with itself through an added relation, and so on to infinity. Second, a relation existing only in reason occurs when the relation itself is referred to something. For example, one cannot say that paternity is referred to its subject by some intermediate relation; for that mediate relation would need another intermediate relation, and so on to infinity. Consequently, the relation signified when paternity is compared to its subject is not real but only rational. Third, a relation existing in reason alone occurs when one of the related things depends on the other and not conversely. For example, knowledge depends on the thing known but not the other way about. Hence, the relation of knowledge to a thing known is something real, but the relation of the thing known to knowledge is merely rational. Fourth, a rational relation occurs when a being is compared with a nonbeing. For example, we say that we are prior to those who are to come after us. If this were a real relation, it would follow (if future generations were infinite) that there could be an infinite number of relations in the same thing."

Suggested Reading

Relation in Being:

Aristotle, *Metaphysics*, V (Δ), 15; *Categories*, ch. 7.
St. Thomas Aquinas, *In I Sent.*, d. 20, q. 1, a. 1; d. 26, q. 2, a. 1 and 2;
In V Metaph., lect. 17, nn. 1004-1005; *In V Phys.*, lect. 3, n. 3;
Quodlibet., I, q. 2, a. 1; *Sum. Theol.*, I, 13, 7; 28, 1-2; 45, 3; *Contra
Gentiles*, II, 12; IV, 14; *De Pot.*, II, 5; III, 3; VII, 8; VII, 9 *ad* 7;
VII, 11,; VIII, 1 and 2; *De Verit.*, I, 5, *ad* 16; III, 3; IV, 5.
Kossel, C., S.J., "The *Esse* and *Ratio* of Relation," *The Modern School-
man*, Vol. XXIV (1946), pp. 28-36; "St. Thomas' Theory of the
Causes of Relation," *The Modern Schoolman*, Vol. XXV (1948),
pp. 151-172.

Relations of Reason Only:

St. Thomas Aquinas, *Sum. Theol.*, I, 13, 7; 28, 1, *ad* 4; *De Pot.*, VII, 11;
De Verit., I, 5, *ad* 16.
Maréchal, J., S.J., *Le point de départ de la métaphysique*, Vol. V, pp.
379, 389.

This chapter will review and enlarge the preceding one.

The Nature of Assertion

Any assertion has two components: the *something* asserted; the *assertion* of that something.[1] The first component specifies an assertion. The second component is actual knowledge, an awareness that the something asserted exists in a way different from its way-of-being-asserted. Assertion is knowledge. The asserted is not.

The Cause of an Assertion

Back of every assertion (*actus intelligendi, intelligere*) lies the power to assert (*intellectus*). The power to assert or the intellect, viewed as a property or necessary physical accident of the soul, has no especial place in the explanation of knowledge. It is simply a sort of form of the soul.[2] Viewed in its actual operation, however, the intellect is tremendously significant as a factor in the explanation of knowledge. For, the intellect actuated by the accident of its assertion is the intellect actuating its assertion.[3]

[1] See St. Thomas, *De Verit.*, III, 1, *ad* 1–3; III, 3, *Resp.*
[2] St. Thomas, *De Verit.*, X, 8, *obj.* 13: ". . . quasi quaedam forma essentiae eius [scil., animae]."
[3] St. Thomas, *De Verit.*, X, 8, *ad* 13: ". . . intellectiva potentia est forma ipsius animae quantum ad actum essendi, eo quod habet esse in anima, sicut proprietas in subiecto; sed quantum ad actum intelligendi nihil prohibet esse e converso [scil., quod intellectus habet esse in suo actu intelligendi sicut in subiecto]."

Why is that significant? Because, unless the actuated intellect were the intellect actuating its own assertion, an assertion would have to find its explanation in some theory of illumination . . .[4] Now, any theory of illumination tends to destroy either the notion of nature or the supernaturality of grace . . . In order, then, to preserve the notion of nature, a given,[5] as well as to allow for the fact that we know being, also a given, the following points must be admitted. First, in that genetic phase of knowledge in which the knower contributes only his passivity, the thing known stamps the knower as the signet stamps the wax.[6] However, Aristotle's example

[4] On illumination, see St. Augustine, *De Lib. Arb.*, II, 12, 34; PL 32, 1259–1260: ". . . there exists an immutable truth, containing within itself all these things that are immutably true, which you cannot call yours or mine or any man's, but which is rather present and offers itself in common in ways that are wonderful as a private and public light, to all those who behold immutable truths. Now who will say that whatever is present in common to all who reason and understand is part of the individual nature of any one of them? . . . if this truth were equal to our minds it too would be mutable. For our minds sometimes see more and sometimes less, and by this they show that they are mutable. On the other hand, this truth, abiding in itself, neither progresses when we see more, nor loses ground when we see less; rather, remaining whole and uncorrupted, to those who turn to it it gives joy by its light, and those who are turned away it punishes with blindness. . . . Therefore, if truth is neither inferior to our minds, nor equal to them, it must be superior and more excellent."
See also *De Lib. Arb.*, II, 14, 38; PL 32, 1261–1262; *De Vera Relig.*, XXXI, 58; PL 34, 148; XXXIX, 73; PL 34, 154; *Soliloq.*, I, 6, 12; PL 32, 875; *De Civ. Dei*, XI, 25; PL 41, 338; *De Trin.*, IX, 7, 12; PL 42, 967; XII, 15, 24; PL 42, 1011; *In Joan. Evang.*, XXXV, 8, 3; PL 35, 658.
St. Thomas' criticism of Augustinian illumination may be found in *De Spir. Creat.*, a. 10; *De Verit.*, X, 6; XIX, 1; *Sum. Theol.*, I, 84, 1; *Q.D. de Anima*, a. 15.
For an excellent analysis of Augustinian illumination, see E. Gilson, *Introduction a l'étude de saint Augustin*, 2 éd., *Études de philosophie médiévale*, XI, Paris, Vrin, 1929, pp. 21–23; 103–125.
[5] See Aristotle, *Physics*, II, 1, 192b 8–34; 193a 1–8; *Metaphysics*, V (Δ), 4, 1015a 13–19.
[6] Aristotle, *De Anima*, II, 12, 424a 16–21: "By a *sense* is meant what has the power of receiving into itself the sensible forms of things without the matter. This must be conceived of as taking place in the way in which a piece of wax takes on the impress of a signet-ring without the iron or gold; . . ." See St. Thomas, *In II de Anima*, lect. 24, n. 551.
This knowledge stamping and the knowledge stamp are both in the order of efficient, *intentional*, causality. Both the stamping and the stamp are *from* the agent (the known) and *in* the patient (the knower) *intentionally*. The signet-wax situation is one which is in physical *esse*, but it illustrates very well a similar sort of transaction in intentional *esse*.

illustrates only partially, but very well, the total situation. His point is this: just as the stamp *in* the wax no longer has the matter of the stamper, viz., gold, but only the matter which is wax, so the known *in* the knower no longer has the matter which it had in the known, but only the matter of the knower. Clearly, this describes only part of the situation. The wax does not react. It simply lies around exemplarizing the seal with which it has been stamped. Knowers do not just lie around exemplarizing the stamps which have pressed into them intentionally. Knowers react. They hit back. This hitting back, second, is an operation which is the knower's very own. It is *his* assertion, and precisely because every assertion is specified or is *something* asserted, therefore the peak of knowledge which is an assertion that the asserted exists in a way which is different from its-way-of-being-asserted, this peak of knowledge is reached by the knower alone.[7] In other words, no factor except the knower alone is up to the job of creating his own knowledge. True, the knower is subject-cause or patient of the specification or stamp which has been pressed into him intentionally. That specification is a penny-in-the-slot affair of which the patient is quite unaware, and which as a patient he cannot help. You can't help hearing, for example, B flat if B flat is sounded. The knower even causes, as an agent, the meaning of the assertion which he will make.[8] But the specification of the assertion itself, which is the knower's operation alone, that specification comes into being only by way of being asserted by the knower, as when one says, "it *is* B flat."

---

[7] The knower of course understands *through* his soul; his soul understands through the intellect; his intellect, *through* its acts; the acts are understood through their objects: *Sum. Theol.*, I, 75, 2, ad 2. The niceties of these distinctions should not obscure the main issue: who does the knowing?

[8] This is the famous thesis of the possible and agent intellect: the same intellect is passive as receiving the stamp, active as reissuing that stamp within its causal mechanism by which assertions become meaningful even before they are asserted; but above all, the intellect and the intellect alone is active in its assertions: *Sum. Theol.*, I, 54, 4, *Resp.*; 79, 3–4; *Contra Gentiles*, II, 75–78; *De Spir. Creat.*, aa. 9 and 10; *Q.D. de Anima*, aa. 3–5.

Human Knowledge Is of Being, but Being Is not Human Knowledge

A while back it was said that knowledge bumps its nose into being, but that being does not bump its way into knowledge.[9] The statement may now be qualified. Being makes its way into knowledge (1) by way of *intentionally* specifying the knower as subject-cause of his knowing, quite as the signet *physically* specifies the wax as a physical subject-cause of the stamp which the signet has impressed upon the wax. Being even makes its way into knowledge (2) by way of supplying a recognizable and recognized meaning of itself. But view knowledge as a personal reaction of the knower, as a knower's hitting back, as an assertion that what is meant exists— and not simply as the *meaning* of an assertion, then knowledge runs smack into being. It is not in order to be specified by the known, although the knower *is* specified by the known, that the knower makes assertions. Rather, it is in order to make assertions that the knower is specified by the known. It is not in order to become "the other" that we assert "the other." It is in order to assert "the other" that we become "the other." Intentional causality pervades all causes except prime matter: the power of the instrument, e.g., is the power of "the other," viz., the principal cause; and the good of the means is the good of "the other," viz., the end; and the motion of the moved is the "moving" of the "other," viz., the efficient cause.[10] None of these intentional causalities does justice to knowledge. The statement that "thar's gold in them teeth" is highly intentional from the viewpoint of meaning. But it is not until one has taken a good look that one can assert that "there *is* gold in those teeth." And so, it is in order to assert that the asserted exists, this is the basic reason why we assert. Assertion of being is the goal of all knowledge. Let a man say, for example, that *x is red*, or that *x is*. The asserter isn't the red or the *x* which he asserts to be. Indeed, the knower's assertions are not even those genetic phases of knowledge in which he *is*, inten-

[9] See Chapter XVI, pp. 287–288.
[10] See Chapter II, pp. 17–19; Chapter VIII, pp. 115, 120–121.

tionally, red and being. Assertions are to the effect that the asserted exists, not to the effect that the asserted is its assertion, or that assertions exist, or that assertions are meaningful. Assertions are to the effect that the asserted exists, that there *is* red, or there *is* being.[11]

The Relation of the Asserted Contingent to the Absolute

As was said,[12] any assertions about a contingent being, e.g., Socrates is running, involves assertion about absolutes, e.g., if Socrates runs, run he must. This must be so if the assertion about a contingent is to make sense. For how can a man be running, unless while running he must run? The relation of the assertion of the contingent to the assertion of the absolute is this: the assertion of absolutes is the end, goal, objective, towards which the assertion of the contingent is always headed.

"End" in philosophy does not mean a stopping point, a place where you are told to get off, not even the place where you do get off. End rather means something which an agent causes to exist in himself or in a patient.[13] For example, the end of medical art is the health of the patient. This end of medical art is not something which a doctor causes to be his end. Rather, he causes that which *is* the end of his art, namely, the health of the patient, to exist in the patient. Just so, the assertion of absolutes is the end which the asserter of contingents does not cause to be his end. Rather, he causes those assertions of absolutes to exist in himself if and when he thinks things over and sees that he cannot reasonably assert contingents unless he also assert absolutes. There is this difference, however, between the ends of transitive action and the ends of immanent action.[14] After healing one patient the doctor will say "next." And if there is another patient, he will have to be the "next" one. After knowing a contingent and an absolute involved in the contingent,

[11] See Chapter XVI, p. 286; Chapter X, pp. 149–153.
[12] See Chapter XVI, pp. 292–294.
[13] See Chapter VIII, pp. 112–117.
[14] See Chapter VIII, pp. 109–111.

however, there is no "next" absolute which was not involved in the very first one; and that very first one, in the knowing of a contingent. Not even the knowing that God exists? No, not even the knowing that God exists. To put the question positively, is even God known in knowing a contingent? Yes. (Indeed, even in the beatific vision there is progress in knowing the same God. God's knowledge of Himself has no progress.) The reason for the involution of absolutes within the contingents is this: the end of human knowledge, which is knowledge of absolutes and the demonstration of God's existence and, later, the beatific vision, the end of knowledge cannot be so fully given to a creature that he has it on tap so to say, as his personal capital which he owes to nothing and nobody, as a capital which is not *always* coming to him from "the other." Even in possession of his end a creature also owes the *continuance* of that possession to "the other" or end. And the reason for *that* is this: a creature does not cause itself to be. To be a knowing creature is to aspire to something not-me as to me; to aspire to the knowledge of God as to a perpetual donation of that knowledge, as to something which is given indeed but never in fee simple. Ever to aspire to more and more assertions of something not myself as to something which is I, this is another way of saying I am not God. But I would mighty like to be God, because I would mighty like to be myself. Yet I am never fully a self, because I am never God. To be a knowing creature is to be an intense desire to be like God in the knowledge of Him, but that desire's fulfillment is always short of the fulfillment which is divine knowledge.

More simply, the assertion of absolutes is given. The question is, how *can* it be given if we always start with the assertion of contingents? The suggested answer is this: the assertion of absolutes is already within the assertion of contingents, as an end is already written within an agent, as a "tended toward" is already within the "tending towards."[15] Now, since nature and its tendencies, two components which make but one composite or nature—since nature and its tendencies are both from God, therefore God is the first efficient and final cause of any assertion. If, in other words, an assertion is

[15] See Chapter III, pp. 44–46; Chapter XVI, pp. 292–294.

not the asserted, and if nevertheless the *meaning* of an assertion ("meaning" here is *not* the signifying operation, nor the meaningfulness of an assertion) *is the thing meant* by the assertion; if, last, the thing meant by the assertion involves absolutes up to and including God; it follows that any assertion is an implicit assertion of God.[16]

The Transcendental Relation

It is this relation of the intellect, through its assertion of contingent beings, to its implied assertion of absolute being, it is this relation which is known as "a transcendental."[17] Of course all creatures are related to God as to the source of their physical *esse*. One may, if one wishes, call *that* relation also a transcendental one. But the relation we speak of here is a knowledge relation, an implicit *knowledge* of a First Cause in the explicit *knowledge* of any given being. The relation of a physical effect to its cause would persist even if there were no knowers. The relation of a knowledge effect to its cause would not.

In further illustration of that knowledge situation, assume (1) that I know Peter, (2) that I see Peter as a speck upon the horizon. Ask, in the number (2) situation, do I know Peter? Yes and no. No, I don't know that the speck is Peter. Yes, I know something which Peter is, viz., the speck. Now substitute for "speck" the word "being," and ask, in knowing a being do I know God? Yes and no. No, I don't know that a being is God, or positively, I know that a being is *not* God. Yes, I know something which God is, viz., a being.[18]

[16] St. Thomas, *De Verit.*, XXII, 2, *ad* 1: ". . . omnia cognoscentia cognoscunt implicite Deum in quolibet cognito."

[17] See Chapter XVI, pp. 292–294.

[18] St. Thomas, *Sum. Theol.*, I, 2, 1, *ad* 1: "To know that God exists in a general and confused way is implanted in us by nature, inasmuch as God is man's beatitude. For man naturally desires happiness, and what is naturally desired by man is naturally known by him. This, however, is not to know absolutely that God exists; just as to know that someone is approaching is not the same as to know that Peter is approaching, even though it is Peter who is approaching; for there are many who imagine that man's perfect good, which is happiness, consists in riches, and others in pleasures, and others in something else."

Compare now the number (2) situation when Peter heaves into sight with the number (2) situation when God heaves into sight. When Peter gets close, I see him. And when God heaves into sight by demonstration? I do *not* see Him, I only prove Him. This situation is at once the misery and the greatness of a knowing creature. We are miserable because we have to prove God, and we are still miserable after proving Him, because we have only proved Him.

God is thus an unknown known, an unexplained explanation, an absolute without which the relative cannot be pronounced to be, or better, an absolute which is impliedly pronounced whenever anything is pronounced to be. Every philosopher who is not a sophist has always recognized this; and even the sophist, who denies all absolutes, is but living an illusion without admitting it. Nonsophists do not deny the absolute in knowledge. Many of them only deny that the absolute exists, or, if it does, they deny that we can know that it does. Nothing much can be done about those nonsophists until they admit that knowledge is of being. Once that is admitted, then something can be done. For, it may be pointed out that to know that a being exists is like sticking your finger into a tar barrel of absolutes. The tar is all over you, though you thought only to stick your finger into it. Still, a man who is covered with tar can keep on swearing that he is not—but only if there *is* no tar.[19]

The relation of knowledge to *a* being, and the relation of the knowledge of *a* being to the knowledge of being as being, and the relation of the knowledge of being as being to knowing that God exists is a transcendental relation. Obviously the relation of an effect in *esse* to the cause of *esse* is also a transcendental one. But we are not talking about that latter relation at present. The latter relation would persist even if there were no knower. The noetic relation would not.

[19] On the presence of God to the soul, see C.J. O'Neil, "St. Thomas and the Nature of Man," *Proceedings of the American Catholic Philosophical Association*, Vol. XXV (1951), pp. 47–66.

Knowledge Media

Yet the similarity of the two relations, of created knowledge and of created being to God, may suffice to bare the root of the matter. Both created knowledge and created being come into existence from the creative cause. Both "creations," in creatures, are creatures.[20] Neither is related to its first cause as the effect which is *fieri* is related to its cause. Water, for example, which is becoming hot, is related to the cause of its becoming hot only while it is becoming hot. After the "becoming" is over, the heat of the water persists without any further influx of the heater's heating. The created *esse* of creatures, however, persists only because of the *continued* creation of God. So, as *fieri* is related to its cause, created *esse* is related to God.[21] *Fieri* demands a cause the while there is *fieri*. So does a

[20] St. Thomas, *Sum. Theol.*, I, 45, 3, *Resp.*: "Creation posits something in the created thing only according to relation; for what is created is not made by motion or by change. For what is made by motion or by change is made from something preexisting. This happens, to be sure, in the particular productions of some beings, but it cannot happen in the production of all being by the universal cause of all beings, which is God. Hence, when God creates, He produces things without motion. Now when motion is removed from action and passion, only relation remains, as was said above. Hence creation in the creature is only a certain relation to the Creator as to the principle of its being; even as in passion, which supposes motion, is implied a relation to the principle of motion."

[21] St. Thomas, *De Pot.*, V, 1, *Resp.*: ". . . things are preserved in existence by God, and they would instantly be reduced to nothing were God to abandon them. . . . the form of the thing generated depends naturally on the generator in so far as it is educed from the potentiality of matter, but not as to its absolute existence. And, therefore, when the act of the generator ceases, the eduction of the form from potentiality into actual being, that is the *becoming* of the thing generated, ceases, whereas the form itself whereby the thing generated has its existence, does not cease. Hence it is that the existence of the thing generated, but not its becoming, remains after the action of the generator has ceased. On the other hand, forms that do not exist in matter, such as intellectual substances, or that exist in matter in no way indisposed to the form, as the heavenly bodies wherein there are no contrary dispositions, must proceed from a principle that is an incorporeal agent that acts not by movement, nor do they depend on something for their *becoming* without depending on it also for their *being*. Wherefore just as when the action of their efficient cause which acts by movement ceases, at that very instant the becoming of the thing generated ceases, even so when the action of an incorporeal agent ceases, the very existence of things created by it ceases. Now this incorporeal agent by whom all things, both corporeal and incorporeal are created, is God, . . ."

creature's *esse*, the while there *is* a creature's *esse*. Consider, next, that a creature's *esse* is permanent (a creature's *esse* doesn't come and go as its accidents do) and that it is none of its modes. It is this *persistent* relation of the *esse* of a creature to its creator both in the order of its physical *esse* as well as in the order of the creature's *knowledge* of physical *esse*, it is this persistent relation ("persistent" because "esse" does not cease to be; only its modes flicker) that is distinctive of the transcendental relation. A father generates a son. The son stays generated even when the father dies. Not so with the relation of creature to creator. The creature and its knowledge, both are in *esse;* and in order to stay in *esse* they need the *constant* influx of the creative cause. Thus, the power which creatures need in order to persist in their physical *esse* and in their knowledge of physical *esse* is not a power which would knock down anything which kept them from so existing and so knowing, a power which, so to say, prevents them from not-existing and not-knowing as if, apart from that *removens prohibens* power which knocks over whatever gets in their way, they would do all right on their own. No, the power which keeps creatures in physical or cognitive *esse*, is a power which—keeps them there, just as it put them there, namely, as *staying* put. Now, the relation of creatures to *such* a power is precisely the transcendental relation. If we look upon that relation of created *esse* to its creative cause as a *physical* situation, that situation is simply the relation of an effect in *esse* to the cause of its *esse*—without any intermediary. If we look upon the relation of our *knowledge* of being to the creative cause of our knowledge, that relation is a relation of an effect to its creative cause—*with* intermediary, viz., the medium which is the knowledge of *esse*. That knowledge of *esse* is the knowledge of *a* being in *esse*, in which is involved the knowledge of being as being, in which is involved, impliedly, or by demonstration, the knowledge of God. "Intermediary" in the second instance, then, does *not* mean something which we know as God but which isn't God, nor does it mean something which we know as not-God but which is God.[22] "Inter-

---

[22] Ontologists think that God is known just as anything else is, or that anything not-God is known as He is known. In other words, God is a creature

mediary," then, in the expression "with intermediary," means a knowledge medium.

Kinds of Knowledge Media

A knowledge medium is threefold. First, a knowledge medium could be a universal "thing," e.g., the universal nature of *man* or *triangle*. To know these universal "things" is to know imperfectly the singular things: *this* man, *this* triangle. Individuals are far richer in their individuality than in the formula (the universal "thing") of their individuality. Nonetheless, without knowing their formulae we can never know what individuals are, and not to know *that* is not to know at all, not at least with any scientific knowledge. Individuals must be tagged if we are ever to sort them out. These tags, these media, these universal "things" are objects of first intentional knowledge.[23] Second, a knowledge medium could be, not a universal thing, but the universality of a thing, e.g., the universality of the nature of *man* or *triangle*. This second medium of knowledge is an object of second intentional knowledge.[24]

From the viewpoint of the thing known, the first medium is a poorer way of knowing singulars. You won't know much about *a* man from knowing him as *man*. Not that knowing *a* man as *man* is not first rate knowledge. It is. Nevertheless, the comprehension or content of the knowledge of *man* is far poorer than its extension or its relation to singulars. The knowledge of the universal thing which

---

or a creature is God. Yet if the ontologists' assertions were understood of the medium which is the knowledge of *esse*, they would not be far wrong.

The ontologist position on the knowledge of God may be seen in the following. Descartes, *Méditations*, V; ed. Adam-Tannery, Vol. IX, p. 52; Malebranche, *Dialogue on Metaphysics and on Religion*, II, 4–5; tr. M. Ginsberg, N.Y., Macmillan, 1923, pp. 89–90; Leibniz, *Monadology*, nn. 44, 45; tr. R. Latta, London, Oxford University Press, 1925, p. 242; Spinoza, *Ethics*, I, 1 and 6; IV, Preface; ed. R.H.M. Elwes, N.Y., Tudor, 1936, pp. 39, 190; *Kant Selections*; ed. T. M. Greene, N.Y., Scribner's, 1929, pp. 360, 373–374. See also E. Gilson, *God and Philosophy*, pp. 74–108.

[23] See Chapter X, pp. 153–158.
[24] See L. M. Régis, O.P., *Epistemology*, tr. I. C. Byrne, N.Y., Macmillan, 1959, pp. 289 ff. See also Chapter X, pp. 153–158.

is *man* catches all individuals in one and the same net: each man is
what any other man is, viz., a man; but so to catch all men in one
net is to acknowledge that the net lets much else, besides the characteristic which is *man*, slip through its meshes.

From the viewpoint of the *universality* of *man*, the second
medium, that is, it is far better to know *a* man as *man*. The reason
is this: what slips through the net of the first medium is nonetheless
caught by the net of the second medium. How caught? So as by
being characteristics which, when known, will be known to be
characteristics of *man*. When, for example, we know *man* as being
six feet tall, in this room, studying metaphysics, unshaved, and chewing gum, we are not astonished. Why should we be? Those further
known qualifications of *man* are simply knowledge developments of
our knowledge of *man*, *actual* knowledges of what was already
known *potentially* in knowing *man*.[25]

The Third Knowledge Medium Which Is Knowledge of Being

Now compare the above relation, of our knowledge of universals
to our knowledge of singulars, to the relation of our knowledge of
being to our knowledge of beings. This last relation is a third knowledge medium.

Our knowledge of singulars limits the universal, pinpoints it, con-
fines the universal to being *this* man. Our knowledge of beings, however, does not quite pinpoint our knowledge of being. *This* man,
indeed, cannot be any other man. But whether you view being as
something which has *esse* or as the *esse* which something has, in
neither case does our experience attest that there is only one *habens*

[25] St. Thomas, *Sum. Theol.*, I, 55, 3, *ad* 2: "To know anything universally can
be taken in two senses. In one way, on the part of the thing known, namely,
that only the universal nature of the thing is known. To know a thing thus is
something less perfect; for he would have an imperfect knowledge of a man
who only knew him to be an animal. In another way, on the part of the
medium of such universal knowledge. In this way it is more perfect to know
a thing in the universal; for the intellect, which by one universal medium can
know singulars properly, is more perfect than one which cannot."

esse (as there *is* only one "this man"), or only one *esse* (as there *is* only one nature of man). Put it this way: our knowledge of *this* being does not exhaust our knowledge of being, for if it did, we would never know any other being; our knowledge of *this man*, on the other hand, will never be knowledge of any other man. In sum, whether you view being as any old subject of *esse*, or as the *esse* of any old subject, the knowledge of being is not limited by the subject in which it resides as universals *are* limited by the subjects in which *they* reside; nor is the knowledge of the *esse* of a subject of *esse* limited at all, because the only "limit" of *esse* is nonbeing, and that is no limit at all. Knowledge of being is knowledge of an actuated by an act or knowledge of an act which is the source of anything that deserves the name of being.[26]

The universality of being, then, is not the universality of a universal "thing," known as something potential, something undetermined; nor is it the universality of a medium like the universality of *man*. It is the universality of a medium in which all beings are known in so far as they are. It is not the universality of a medium in which things are known in so far as they are this, that, or the other *kind* of being, nor in so far as they are this, that, or the other *being* of a kind. The universality of this medium is the universality of a transcendental. This medium is like a dim light in which everything is

[26] St. Thomas, *De Pot.*, VII, 2, *ad* 9: "*Being*, as we understand it here, signifies the highest perfection of all: and the proof is that act is always more perfect than potentiality. Now no signate form is understood to be in act unless it be supposed to have *being*. Thus we may take human nature or fiery nature as existing potentially in matter, or as existing in the power of an agent, or even as in the mind: but when it has being it becomes actually existent. Wherefore it is clear that *being* as we understand it here is the actuality of all acts, and therefore the perfection of all perfections. Nor may we think that being, in this sense, can have anything added to it that is more formal and determines it as act determines potentiality: because *being* in this latter sense is essentially distinct from that to which it is added and whereby it is determined. But nothing that is outside the range of being can be added to *being*: for nothing is outside the range of being except *nonbeing*, which can be neither form nor matter. Hence *being* is not determined by something else as potentiality by act but rather as act by potentiality: since in defining a form we include its proper matter instead of the difference: thus we define a soul as the act of an organic physical body. Accordingly this *being* is distinct from that *being* inasmuch as it is the *being* of this or that nature. For this reason Dionysius says that though things having life excel those that merely have being, yet being excels life, since living things have not only life but also being."

seen darkly.[27] Let but the dawn of first principles appear, or let demonstration or evidence appear, and the shadows become substance.

The matter had better receive a technical and scientific expression. Being is "that to which nothing is added." "That to which nothing is added" can be understood in two senses. First, an addition to "that to which nothing is added" is not made, because it cannot be made, e.g., the addition of *rational* is not made to *irrational animal*, because it cannot be made. There cannot be an *irrational-rational animal*. Secondly, an addition is not made to "that to which no addition is made" because the "added to" neither excludes nor includes the addition, e.g., *animal* neither includes nor excludes *rational*. The first "that to which nothing is added" is the *esse* of God; the second is the common *esse* of which we have been speaking.[28] It is in this third medium of the knowledge of the subject of *esse* (*ens*), or of the *esse* of a subject, that the human intellect comes to know everything it knows. This sort of knowledge is of the widest extension and, unlike the comprehension of universals, of the fullest *implicit* comprehension.

The Mystery of the Knowledge of Being

In this fullest implicit comprehension of the knowledge medium of being we must finally locate the mystery of knowledge. The mystery is not so much that in that knowledge medium is present an implied knowledge of absolutely everything, though that is true.

[27] See A. C. Pegis, "In Umbra Intelligentiae," *The New Scholasticism*, Vol. XIV, n. 2 (April 1940), pp. 146–180.

[28] St. Thomas, *Sum. Theol.*, I, 3, 4, ad 1: "A thing-that-has-nothing-added-to-it can be understood in two ways. Either its essence precludes any addition (thus, for example, it is of the essence of an irrational animal to be without reason), or we may understand a thing to have nothing added to it, inasmuch as its essence does not require that anything should be added to it (thus the genus animal is without reason, because it is not of the essence of animal in general to have reason; but neither is it of the essence of animal to lack reason). And so the divine being has nothing added to it in the first sense; whereas being-in-general has nothing added to it in the second sense."

That St. Thomas uses nature predicates here to illustrate his point should not disturb us. What else can he use?

The mystery lies in the *way* everything is present in that medium. Everything is present as being the end of the operation of a knower. View knowledge merely as a signifying operation, or view it merely as meaningful, in neither case are we seeing common *esse*. A signifying operation is the signifier's alone, and the meaning of meaningful enunciations leaves us unassured that such meaning has any root beyond itself. But view our knowledge of being as having a term, viz., being; view that term as given impliedly in its starting point, *then* knowledge is not just of the being of the knower or of his knowing; *then* knowledge of being is a term which includes, always implicitly and sometimes explicitly, the knower, his knowledge, *and* the known. The known is being. And so it is not just the sensuous experience or the intellectual assertion of being which is delivered over to us when we experience or assert being; it is being which is delivered over to our experience or assertion of being. The experience, or assertion, of being is *ours*, nobody else's. Yet there is something in the knowledge of being which is not we nor is it our knowledge of being. That something is being, not just the being of the one who sees it, not even just his seeing of being. It is the "seen," inviscerated within, but transcending the knowledge of it. To put it slightly differently: our knowledge of being is—ours; our own physical being is also—ours. But the being in knowledge is not ours in the sense that *we* make it; nor is our physical *esse* ours in the sense that *we* made that either. Both the being which is we, and the being which is in our knowledge are perpetual donations: given forever and all given. "Given forever" means that, since there is no foothold for nonbeing in being, everything is made to last. Things change, thank God; but change is not the fully truthful witness of being. If it were, a changing being would eventually turn into nothing; but being, thank God, will never change into nothing. Certainly, like one fingering a tabletop for something which is not there, a changing being might as well give up pawing over accidental actuation after accidental actuation, none of which completely fulfills it. No, once given, being is given for good. "All given" means that in any given being there is inscribed a demand for the rest, including God; and that the rest are given. To exist, then, is, for a being whose existence is caused, to be dripping with the causality of God which forever keeps a being from being—nothing. To know being is to be dripping with that same causality which forever keeps knowers from—knowing nothing. Both relations, of created beings and created knowledge to the creator of beings and of their knowledge, are transcendental relations, relations of an effect in *esse* to the cause of *esse*. The relation of a *knowledge* effect in *esse* to a *knowledge* cause of that effect, that knowledge effect cannot be given except as a *knowledge of that cause;* and the knowledge of that cause cannot be given (except in the beatific vision) unless it be given in the penumbrous knowledge of common *esse* and in the proved knowledge that *God exists.* Everyone knows God in his penumbrous knowledge of common *esse.* No man understands discourse about God as a blind man understands discourse about colors. To be a knowing creature is to know God. All of us know God, even those who do not or cannot name Him. To know God, even when we cannot name Him, this is the minimal situation of a knowing creature. Just as we are created to last, so our knowledge is created to last—in both cases with a perpetuity and a density of being which transcend all beings' modes, but that perpetuity and that density, because they are modes of *esse* and *esse* is not a mode, are borrowed from, or better, are caused by, an *esse* which is modeless.

Summary

The transcendental relation of a creature to God both in the dimension of a creature's *esse* and in the dimension of the creature's knowledge of *esse* is a one way relation and a relation which is constitutive of a creature and of its knowledge. There is no relation in reverse, except the factitious relation we make, not in order to understand ourselves, our knowledge, or God, but rather because we *have* understood ourselves, our knowledge, and God. One might say that we have understood that triad when we have seen that our physical *esse* and the cognitive *esse* of our assertions are both accidental or nonnecessary: the physical, accidental to the subject which exists; the assertion, accidental to the asserter. For, if we understand both *esse's* as accidental, we nonetheless understand that neither *esse* is an accident. Why? Because neither *esse* qualifies its subject as accidents do. Both *esse's* qualify their subjects in terms of "the other": physical *esse* in terms of the other upon which physical *esse* comes, viz., God; intentional *esse* in terms of "the other" which is known, viz., being and God. The "qualification" in both cases is creaturely *esse* and creaturely knowledge. This amounts to saying that we have understood the triad when we have understood that God exists, or, if you prefer, that we have understood that God exists when we have understood that two members of the triad are not, but have, their *esse*.

In any case, the *esse ad* of a predicamental relation is *explained* only by explaining the *esse ad* of a transcendental, and that latter explanation is this: God causes the being of creatures, which is inter-related intramurally because it is related extramurally, so to say, namely, to God. This extramural relation is of something given (physical *esse* and the knowledge of *a* being in physical *esse* and the knowledge of being as being and, within that knowledge of being as being, the penumbrous knowledge of God) to its giver. Only, the "given" here is not given to something. The given here *is* the something, and the giver is not any one of His gifts; He is not even like His gifts. His gifts are like Him. We are like God; He is not like us. Also, we know there is a God, because we know there is an "is." Within that "is" God dwells, not as a contingent part of a contingent "is," nor even as an absolute which is involved in a contingent "is" as is the absolute which is Socrates' "must-be-running" predicate involved in his "running" predicate; but as the absolute to which the contingent "is" points, as an absolute which the contingent "is" is *not*, but which explains the contingent "is."

To put the matter technically: the relation of physical and cognitive *esse* to God is the relation of a potential to an actuation. True, each foundation or potential (each creature) is *in* actuation and is in relation to the actuation which it is not but has. For example, prime matter is *in* the actuation of its form, which it is not but has;

formed matter is in the actuation of its accidents which it is not, but
has; and accidentally formed matter is in the actuation of the *esse*,
which it is not but has. But the *esse* of each creature is the reason
why each one of the enumerated potentials has its act; and the *esse*
of a creature cannot be explained except as related to a cause of
esse. The same goes for the cognitive *esse:* knowledge is knowledge
of *being*, and the knowledge of being cannot be explained except
as knowledge, at least in terms of knowing common *esse*, of the
being which God is. In short, at whatever level you take the composite which a creature is, you cannot in the upshot explain the
interrelation of the components of that composite except as related
to an incomposite *esse*. In that last relation we see the transcendentals,
see, that is, that creatures *are* their transcendental relations.

Suggested Reading

The Meaning of Assertion:

Aristotle, *De Anima*, II, 12.
St. Thomas Aquinas, *In II de Anima*, lect. 24, n. 551; *De Verit.*, III, 1 and
    3; VIII, 8, *ad* 13; *Sum. Theol.*, I, 2, 1, *ad* 1; 54, 4; 75, 2, *ad* 2; 79, 3-4;
    Contra Gentiles, II, 75-78; *De Spir. Creat.*, aa. 9 and 10; *Q.D. de
    Anima*, aa. 3-5.

The Transcendental Relation:

St. Thomas Aquinas, *Sum. Theol.*, I, 2, 1, *ad* 1; 3, 4, *ad* 1; 45, 3; *De Pot.*,
    V, 1; VII, 2, *ad* 9.
O'Neil, C., "St. Thomas and the Nature of Man," *Proceedings of the
    American Catholic Philosophical Association*, Vol. XXV (1951), pp.
    47-66.
Pegis, A. C., "In Umbra Intelligentiae," *The New Scholasticism*, Vol.
    XIV, n. 2 (April 1940), pp. 146-180.

XVIII · THE MEANING OF THE
TRANSCENDENTALS. UNITY

We are now ready to understand the meaning of the transcendentals.

Summary of Chapters XVI, XVII

Up to now we have been engaged in seeing what a transcendental relation is. It is a pointing of a nature to God—like the pointing of a boomerang which heads back to its thrower from the very moment it left his hand. The figure fails. The boomerang here, a creature, is so pointed, because its pointing *is* the boomerang, and the boomerang *is* its pointing. Not so with the authentic boomerang. Its pointing is *not* the boomerang, nor is the boomerang its pointing. Creatures, however, *are* their pointing, and their pointing *is* a creature. The accidental relation of a boomerang to the accident of its directed motion is indeed ultimately *explained* by the transcendental relation. The explanation is this: whereas the directed motion of the boomerang lies partly in the instrument itself and partly in its thrower, the accidental relation of a creature to its *esse* is explained by a cause of that *esse*. Now, the relation of a being to its *esse* is not an accident, and the relation of a being in *esse* to its cause is not an accident either. The reason is: *esse* is not an accident. The *esse* of a creature is a creature, and that *esse* is caused, and so the relation of a creature to its *esse* and to the cause of its *esse* is caused.[1] We might put it this way: a transcendental relation is not

[1] See Chapter XVI, pp. 280–283.

so much explained as it is an explanation of the predicamental relation—like God, Whom a transcendental relation involves: God explains the rest, but *He* is not explained. Or this way: a creature is a
glance backwards to its efficient cause, and a glance forward to its
final cause, and this complex involves both the creature and that to
which it glances in either direction, namely, God. This figure too
fails, because those glances *are* the creature. Or this way: a creature
is not properly an existent, nor is it known as such if it is or is
known as one of Hamelin's "solid blocks."[2] A creature, in order
properly to be and to be understood, i.e., in order to be understood
as transcendentally related to God, a creature is *any* creature viewed
as coming from or headed to the cause of its *esse*. For surely, only
that is a being which either is, or is and comes from, and is headed
to, being. And just as surely, only that is knowledge of *esse* (given)
which involves us in knowing, by penumbrous, or demonstrated, or
beatifying knowledge—God.

This, then, is *one*, and the basic, meaning of the transcendental
relation: it is a creature, which involves not only its own *esse* but
also, as its explanation, the *esse* of its cause; and this, both in the
area of physical and of cognitive *esse*. Of course that meaning would
not mean a blessed thing if a cause of *esse* is not proved. Without
the demonstration of a cause of *esse*, that meaning would be only
meaningful.

Modes of "Esse"

There are *other* meanings of that fundamental relation. We may
get at those other meanings as follows. A creature in *esse* is in a
mode of *esse*, e.g., the *man* mode, or the *fish* mode of *esse*. Moreover, the mode of *esse* is not the *esse* which is in those modes, and
this is so not merely because one mode of *esse* is not another (a man
is not a fish), though that is true. It is true mainly because the mode
of *esse* is *in esse*. There lies the basic reason why a man is not a fish.

---

[2] O. Hamelin, *Essai sur les éléments principaux de la réprésentation*, p. 365.
See Chapter XVI, p. 284.

That basic reason, to repeat, is this: a *man* being is not a *fish* being, because there *is* a *man*-being, and there *is* a *fish*-being, not just because *man* and *fish* are different modes of being, though they are. Put it thus: if the *man* mode differed from *fish* mode *only* because the modes differ, then to say that *a man is not a fish* would be to say that a man and a fish differ because one exists and the other doesn't; now that is impossible for a man and a fish are *still* different beings by hypothesis. Yet to say that a man and a fish are different beings only because their modes differ, this is to say that a man is, whereas a fish is not. A difference indeed, but against the facts: both a man and a fish exist. It is not upon the score that they exist that two beings differ, nor is it solely because two different beings are in two different modes of being either. It is because each being's mode is in *esse* that beings differ in their modes. For, once more, if each mode were not in *esse*, the modes of beings would differ indeed but not as beings. They would differ *only* as modes, and then how on earth are we to explain the difference of two beings which are in the same mode, two men for instance? We could not. Two men would not differ at all, would not be two beings at all. Against the fact. Modes of *esse*, then, differ not just because the *man* mode is not the *fish* mode, though that is true; they differ because its mode is not the only or the main feature of a being. Its *esse* is the main feature of a being, and its *esse*, by being in a mode of *esse*, causes that mode to be the mode of a different *being* and not just a different *mode* of being, even when the modes of being are the same. Two beings, whether of the same mode or not, are different beings.[3]

The above shows what it *means* to say that essence and *esse* are distinct. The proof that essence and *esse* are distinct is the demon-

[3] St. Thomas, *De Pot.*, VII, 2, *ad* 9: "This *being* is distinct from that *being* inasmuch as it is the *being* of this or that nature." *De Verit.*, II, 11, *Resp.*: "If *man* and *to exist as man* did not differ in Socrates, man could not be predicated univocally of him and Plato, whose acts of existing are distinct." *In I Sent.*, d. 35, q. 1, a. 4, *sol.*: "The nature of humanity is not in two men according to the same act of existing; and thus whenever the form signified by the name is existence itself, it cannot be attributed univocally since being (*ens*) also is not predicated univocally." *Sum. Theol.*, I, 3, 5, *Resp.*: ". . . the being of a man and of a horse is not the same; nor is the being of this man and that man."

stration of an *esse* which is not in any mode, for if there be *that* *esse*, it follows that *esse* is not a mode of *esse* even when *esse* is in a mode.

The "Esse" of the Modes

If a transcendental relation is the cognitive or physical *esse* of any-creature-as-referred-to-God (through its reference to its own *esse* and through the reference of that *esse* to God), and if that basic relation can be differently described, it follows that those different descriptions are descriptions of the *same* relation.

See this by the following contrast. The relation of the *man* mode of *esse* to the *esse* in that *man* mode is totally different from the relation of the *fish* mode of *esse* to the *esse* in that *fish* mode. A man is not a fish. (And, as we saw, even if two modes of *esse* are identical, as for example in two men, nevertheless two men are totally different beings. George is not John.) Now contrast that situation with this: the predicate, "exist," said of George and John, is not totally different in meaning or in being, nor is it totally the same in meaning or in being. That predicate which is neither totally the same nor totally different when said of any existent is the separated *esse*, an *esse* which implies all its modes and, as well, the modeless *esse* of God.[4] Such is the *esse* of the modes, namely, an *esse* separated from its modes.

Why the Separated "Esse" can be Differently Described

It follows that anything else which can be said of that separated *esse* will have to be said of it because those further descriptions will be different descriptions of *esse*, not descriptions of some factor which is not *esse*. In other words, the predicates, if any, which can be hitched to separated *esse* are not descriptions of *other* tran-

[4] See Chapter XVI, pp. 283–284.

scendental relations; they are rather other facets of the same relation, other epiphanies of being. Now, there *are* other predicates or descriptions of separated *esse*, e.g., *esse* is one, good, true, beautiful, etc. The point is this: it is because it is *esse* which is one, good, etc., that we can so describe *esse*; it is not because to-be-one, etc., is *esse* that we can so describe *esse*. You may indeed say that a man's "is" causes him to exist and to exist as a man. This will make him different from a fish and from another man as well. But you cannot say that it is a man's unity which makes him to be or to be a man; it's the other way about, namely, it is a man's *esse* which makes him, at one stroke, to be, to be a man, and to be a unit. So for the *other* descriptions of separated *esse*.[5]

Variant Descriptions of Separated "Esse." Unity

To be a unit is "to be in one piece."[6] One piece of being? No, for a piece is a fraction, and such a fraction, say a ½ being, would mean that a being half is and, by the same token, half isn't. This is more than faintly ridiculous. It is absurd. He who does not understand a unit does not understand.[7] Just so, that which is not a unit, isn't at all.

No doubt some beings can be fractioned and some cannot. Divide the divisible being and you have as many units as there are divisions plus one. For example, divide a man and you have two beings, each of which is in one piece because it is a being. Whether or not one

---

[5] St. Thomas, *Sum. Theol.*, I, 4, 1, *ad* 3: "Being is the most perfect of all things, for it is compared to all things as that which is act; for nothing has actuality except so far as it is. Hence being is the actuality of all things, even of forms themselves. Therefore it is not compared to other things as the receiver is to the received, but rather as the received to the receiver."

[6] G. Klubertanz, S.J., *Introduction to the Philosophy of Being*, N.Y., Appleton-Century-Crofts, 1955, pp. 193–194.

[7] Among those who do not know the meaning of a unit, Aristotle refers especially to Protagoras and says, "such thinkers are saying nothing, then, while they appear to be saying something remarkable": *Metaphysics*, X (I), 1, 1052a 15–1053b 8. See St. Thomas, *In X Metaph.*, lect. 2, n. 1946: ". . . ab eo non possit aliquid auferri sensibile vel addi quod lateat. Et tunc putant se cognoscere quantitatem rei certitudinaliter, quando cognoscunt per huiusmodi mensuram minimam."

of the pieces is still a man depends upon where you make the division. Cut off his arm and he can survive. Cut off his head and he can't. At any rate, after one division there will be two pieces or units, and each piece is still in one piece. Some beings cannot be divided, e.g., the soul, an angel, God. Any being, therefore, has to be in one piece. Yet it is not because it is in one piece that a unit is a being; rather, it is because it is a being that any being is in one piece. A being is a unit *because* it is a being. It is not a being *because* it is a unit. Oneness is indeed convertible with being, and *vice versa*, but that is because being is convertible with being.[8]

From the negative point of view a unit is *not* divided, but that negation is a "relation of reason only," consequent upon our understanding that any being is in one piece.[9] So too if there are two

[8] See Aristotle, *Metaphysics*, X (I), 2, 1054a 13-19: "In a sense unity means the same as being which is clear from the facts that its meanings correspond to the categories one to one, and it is not comprised within any category (e.g., it is comprised neither in 'what a thing is' nor in quality, but is related to them just as being is); that in 'one man' nothing more is predicated than in 'man' (just as being is nothing apart from substance or quality or quantity); and that to be one is just to be a particular thing."
See also St. Thomas, *In III Metaph.*, lect. 12, n. 501; *In IV Metaph.*, lect. 2, n. 549; *De Pot.*, IX, 7, *Resp.*; *Sum. Theol.*, I, 30, 3, *Resp.*; *Quodlibet.*, VI, q. 2, a. 1, *Resp.*; X, q. 1, a. 1, *Resp.*; *Q.D. de Anima*, a. 1, ad 2; *In III Sent.*, d. 18, q. 1, a. 1, *ad* 3: "The unity of a being is consequent upon its act of existence. . . . The subject cannot be one if its act of existence is not one." *Sum. Theol.*, I, 76, 3, *Resp.*: ". . . nothing is absolutely one except by one form, by which a thing has being; because a thing has both being and unity from the same source, . . ." *Contra Gentiles*, II, 40: "There is a cause of the distinction that obtains between all things whose existence is caused and which, therefore, are distinct from one another. For each and every thing is made a being according as it is made one, undivided in itself and distinct from others."
[9] See Aristotle, *Metaphysics*, X (I), 1, 1052b 15-20: ". . . 'to be one' means to be indivisible, being essentially a 'this' and capable of being isolated either in place, or in form or thought; or perhaps 'to be whole and indivisible' ". . . ; *Metaphysics*, X (I), 1, 1053b 4-8: ". . . unity in the strictest sense, if we define it according to the meaning of the word, is a measure, and most properly of quantity, and secondly of quality. And some things will be one if they are indivisible in quantity, and others if they are indivisible in quality; and so that which is one is indivisible, either absolutely or *qua* one."
See also St. Thomas, *Sum. Theol.*, I, 6, 3, *ad* 1; 11, 4, *Resp.*; 30, 3, *Resp.*; *Sum. Theol.*, I, 11, 1, *Resp.*: "One does not add any reality to *being*, but is only the negation of division; for *one* means undivided *being*. This is the very reason why *one* is convertible with *being*." *In III Metaph.*, lect. 12, n. 501: "One . . . is used in two senses. In one way, inasmuch as it is convertible with being, and thus everything is one by its essence . . . and 'one' does not add anything to

beings, one is not the other, but that negation also leaves untouched the basic situation that a being is a unit even if there were no other being. So, to say that one being is not another one, this is consequent upon having first seen that each being is a unit. The positive characteristic of a unit is that it is in one piece. The negative aspects, namely, the indivision of any unit and its division from other units if any, follow upon the understanding of the positive aspect.

The Units of Quantity

Some beings, not all, are big or small, i.e., have sizes.[10] These are called *quanta*. (A) *Quanta* may be discrete. A discrete *quantum* is divided from other *quanta* and undivided in itself, e.g., *this* man is not divided in himself but is divided from *that* man. (B) *Quanta* may be *divided*. A divided *quantum* is one which is at least in two pieces (but not two pieces of being).[11]

(A) A discrete *quantum* may be described in many ways. (1) Its name may be a number, e.g., man number 1, man number 2, etc. (2) If you view it according to the *shape* it has in your mind, its

---

being except only the notion of 'being undivided.' In the second way, 'one' is used inasmuch as it signifies the notion of the first measure, either simply or in some genus."

On relations of reason only, see Chapter XVI, pp. 288-290. See also St. Thomas, *De Verit.*, I, 1, *Resp.*; *In IV Metaph.*, lect. 2, n. 560: "'One' which is convertible with being designates being itself, adding the notion of indivision, which, since it is a negation or a privation, does not posit any nature added to being. And thus 'one' in no way differs from being in reality, but only in intelligibility. For, negation and privation are not beings in the real order, but beings of reason." *De Pot.*, IX, 7, *Resp.*: "The unity that is convertible with being adds nothing to being except the negation of division, not that it signifies indivision only, but substance with indivision, for *one* is the same as individual being."

[10] See Plato, *Parmenides*, 144b: "Being is distributed over the whole multitude of things, and nothing that is, however small or however great, is devoid of it . . . and it is divided into the greatest and into the smallest, and into being of all sizes, and is broken up more than all things; the divisions of it have no limit." See also Aristotle, *Physics*, I, 4, 187b 14-17: ". . . if the parts of a whole may be of any size in the direction either of greatness or smallness (by 'parts' I mean components into which a whole can be divided and which are actually present in it), it is necessary that the whole being itself may be of any size."

[11] See Aristotle, *Categories*, ch. 6, 4b 20-5a 5. See Appendix A of this chapter.

name will be a line, or a plane, or a solid (lines, planes and solids
may also be numbered); (3) view it according to the shape it has in
itself, and its name will be the name of an approximate shape, e.g.,
a cylindroid. (4) Besides the names in (A) (1), (2), (3), you may
also give a discrete *quantum* the name "being" and, therefore, the
name "one."

(B) *Quanta* which are divided may also be variously described:
(1) View each piece as undivided in itself, and its name could be
any in (A) (1), (2), (3), (4). (2) View each piece as a part of
a whole, and the name of that piece would be a fraction, e.g.,
½ of 1. You may fraction wholes mentally as well as physically.
Further, you may, if you view each of the pieces of a divided or
fractioned *quantum* as undivided in itself, you may name those pieces
with any name in (A) (1), (2), (3), (4).

Quanta, therefore, are kinds of units, namely, units of sizes. Sizes
are sizes of unsplit or split *quanta*. The unsplit *quanta* provide
answers to the questions, how much is each? or how many of them
are there? The question, how much? may be answered by saying,
for example, as much as is the distance between A and B, or as
much as is within this plane or this solid. The question, how many?
may be answered by whole numbers or fractions. Split *quanta* provide the answers to the question, how many? by giving their whole
or fraction numbers; or, if you view each piece as unsplit, by giving
them the names of unsplit *quanta*.

At any rate, both the split (divided) and unsplit (discrete) *quanta*
can be named beings and therefore "ones."[12] Thus the name "one"

---

[12] See St. Thomas, *De Pot.*, III, 16, *ad* 3: "It must be observed that unity
is twofold. There is a unity that is convertible with being: it adds nothing
to being save that it excludes division, and it excludes multitude—in so far as
multitude results from division—not extrinsic multitude that is composed of
unities as parts, but intrinsic multitude that is opposed to unity; since when
we say that a thing is one we do not deny the existence of others extrinsic
thereto with which it constitutes a multitude, but we deny its division into
many. The other kind of unity is the principle of number, and to the idea
of being it adds that of measure; it is this kind of unity that multitude excludes,
since number results from the division of continuity. Yet multitude does not
entirely exclude unity, since when a whole is divided the parts still remain
undivided; but it does exclude unity of the whole. . . ." *De Pot.*, IX, 7, *Resp.*:
". . . *one* which is convertible with *being* posits *being* but adds nothing except
the negation of division. And the *number* corresponding to it adds this to the

as meaning being-in-one-piece (but not a piece of being) cuts across and includes all beings, *quanta* or not. One might say that there are many ways of being-in-one-piece, but being-in-one-piece is not a way of being. Being-in-one-piece *is* a being. To put it in another way, there are degrees of unity. In the descending order there is the unity of God, Whose unity is His *esse* because *He* is *esse*. Then there is the unity of any being which has just one *esse*, but is not identically that *esse* (a *per se* unit). Then there is the unity of natural aggregates, e.g., a heap of stones, each stone having its own *esse;* or the unity of artificial aggregates, each member having its own *esse*, e.g., a mosaic, a watch, an army, etc. (accidental units).[18] (It is very difficult to say at times which things have just one *esse*. Living things, clearly, do. But the nonliving? We cannot always decide what, in the inanimate world, is the *per se* unit. Yet we know what a *per se* unit is, and we know there *are per se* units in the inanimate world, because there must be if there are inanimate beings.) In all cases, being-in-one-piece, which is an epiphany of being, is the source of all unities including the unity of number. Number is not the cause of unity. Being is.

You may view the transcendental "one" as a relation of a being in physical *esse* to the cause of its *esse*, and then each being's unity is to be in one piece, because it is from and to God Whose being-in-one-piece is just *esse*. Surely anything which is *esse*, is from *esse*, or is to *esse*, must be *esse*, and if *esse* must be in one piece, then anything which is *esse*, is from *esse*, or is to *esse*, must be in one piece as well. You may also view the transcendental "one" as a relation of our knowledge of that "one" to our knowledge of the One

---

things described as *many*, that each of them is *one*, and that each of them is not the other, wherein lies the notion of distinction. Accordingly then, while *one* adds to *being* one negation inasmuch as a thing is undivided in itself, *plurality* adds two negations, inasmuch as a certain thing is undivided in itself, and distinct from another, i.e., one of them is not the other." *De Verit.*, I, 1, *Resp.*: "Just as a being is said to be *one* in so far as it is without division in itself, so it is said to be *something* in so far as it is divided from others."

[18] On the unity of God, see St. Thomas, *Sum. Theol.*, I, 11, 1–4; *De Pot.*, IX, 7, *Resp.*

On *per se* and accidental unity, see Aristotle, *Metaphysics*, V (Δ), 6, 1015b 16–1016a 17; 1016b 18–31; 13, 1020a 6–33. See Appendix B of this chapter. See also St. Thomas, *In I Sent.*, d. 24, q. 1, a. 1, *sol.; In V Metaph.*, lects. 7 and 8.

Which is God, and then our knowledge of the transcendental one
is knowledge, penumbrous, demonstrated, or beatifying—of the
One Which is God.[14]

The Realistic and Idealistic Views of Unity

Both realists and idealists share the conviction that any being
must be in one piece. And indeed they must unless their minds are
to blow apart along with the being with which their minds are
occupied.

The realist explains the feature of being-in-one-piece in this way.
He sees first that *esse* is accidental or non-necessary to any experienced being, e.g., to George, who can be or not-be. Next he sees
that the meaningfulness of the assertion of the accidentality of
esse is not merely meaningful, but is also true of the physical *esse*
of any experienced being. He sees this the moment he has demonstrated the existence of an *esse* which is not of the nature or kind
of *a* being, but is the "nature of being" itself, namely, a being
whose "nature" it is to be, and not, as with an experienced being,
whose nature it is to be of the sort it is. For, if it be proved that
there is a being whose *esse is* its nature, then it is demonstrated that
esse is not a mode or kind of *esse* even when *esse is* in a mode or
kind. Lastly, he sees unity in this way. Give that feature of a being
which falls upon the side of its kind, give it the name "essence"; or
name that feature of a being which is the proper subject of *esse*,
name it "substance"; or name that feature of a being which gets
its name from *esse* "*ens*"; or name any being "a thing."[15] Now

[14] St. Thomas, *In IV Metaph.*, lect. 2, n. 561; *In V Metaph.*, lect. 15, n. 978;
In X Metaph., lect. 2, n. 1952; lect. 3, n. 1976; *Quodlibet.*, X, q. 1, a. 1; *De Unit.
Int.*, ch. 3; ed. Keeler, nn. 68–69; ch. 5, n. 101.
[15] See St. Thomas, *Contra Gentiles*, I, 25: "The nature of substance, therefore, must be understood as follows. A *substance* is a thing to which it belongs
to be not in a subject. The name *thing* takes its origin from the *quiddity*, just
as the name *being* comes from *to be*. In this way the definition of substance
is understood as that which has a quiddity to which it belongs to be not in
another."
In IV Metaph., lect. 2, n. 553: "Sciendum est enim quod hoc nomen Homo,
imponitur a quidditate, sive a natura hominis; et hoc nomen Res imponitur

comes the discernment of unity: it is *not* because there belongs to essence, or to substance, or to *ens*, or to a thing, an *esse* which is other than essence's *esse*, or other than the substance's *esse*, or other than the *ens' esse*, or other than the thing's *esse* that each is called a being. Rather, essence, substance, *ens*, thing are called, respectively, beings because of an *esse* which each respectively *is*. Essence is a being by an *esse* which the *essence* is. Substance is a being by an *esse* which the *substance* is. *Ens* is a being by an *esse* which the *ens* is. The insight is, then, simply this: all you see in a being is all that is there. The to-be of an essence *is* an essence; the to-be of a substance *is* a substance; the to-be of an *ens is* an *ens;* the to-be of a thing (*res*) *is* a thing. It is quite pointless, therefore, to ask if essence, substance, *ens*, *res* are beings by some *esse* feature which *they* are not. And to see the pointlessness of such questions is to see the unity of being. It is *not* pointless, however, to ask whether any essence, or substance, etc., is a being because it is *esse* itself, or because there *is* an *esse* itself which causes those essences, substances, etc., to be. To see that there *is* an *esse* which causes the rest to be, this is to see the cause of *esse* and, at the same moment, of unity.[16]

An idealist too has a profound respect for unity. He too sees that any being must be in one piece, and he sees that "one piece" as an identity of any being with itself. In this and basic feature of unity both idealist and realist are at one. The point at which idealism and realism begin to diverge seems to lie here. Since any experienced being changes and is generated, and since such beings are *not* absolutely self-identical, the question, what is "really" (ὄντως) a being (ὄν)?[17] becomes pertinent. The answer to that question divides the two positions. For Plato, an idea is a being because an idea at least stays self-identical even if the changing and generated being

a quidditate tantum; hoc vero nomen Ens, imponitur ab actu essendi: et hoc nomen Unum, ab ordine vel indivisione. Est enim unum in se indivisum. Idem autem est quod habet essentiam et quidditatem per illam essentiam, et quod est in se indivisum. Unde ista tria, res, ens, unum, significant omnino idem, sed secundum diversas rationes."

[16] St. Thomas, *De Verit.*, XXI, 1, *Resp.;* 4, *Resp.;* 5, *Resp.* and *ad* 8. This whole question XXI had better be read over time after time.

[17] See Plato, *Republic*, V, 476a–d; VI, 510e; *Parmenides*, 129a–135d; *Sophist*, 240b–246a; *Philebus*, 15a ff.; *Phaedo*, 78d.

does not. Upon this Platonic conviction, as upon a base, can be
erected various prolongations, all of which must locate unity in a
unit which is *not* changing and generated. The examination of
each of these variant prolongations of the basic Platonic conviction
would yield only this much: no matter what is finally stated to be
a unit, and therefore a being, it will *not* be a changing and a generated being. Now, a realist *starts* with the conviction, borne in upon
him by evidence, that the changing and generated beings *do* exist,
and so they are beings, and so they are units. And if these units are
not absolutely self-identical, this must be so, not because they are
not beings, but rather because unity and self-identity vary precisely
in the measure that being varies. The absolutely self-identical is only
God. The rest have a measure of self-identity in the measure that
they have being. The realist in short thinks that it is amusing to
start talking about given beings, and therefore about given units,
and then to wind up talking about something which is not a being
nor therefore a unit.[18]

Appendix to Chapter XVIII

APPENDIX (A). Divided and discrete *quanta*.

Aristotle, *Categories*, ch. 6, 4b 20–5a 5: "Quantity is either discrete or continuous. Moreover, some quantities are such that each
part of the whole has a relative position to the other parts: others
have within them no such relation of part to part. Instances of
discrete quantities are number and speech; of continuous, lines,
surfaces, solids, and, besides these, time and place. In the case of the
parts of a number, there is no common boundary at which they
join. For example: two fives make ten, but the two fives have no
common boundary, but are separate; the parts three and seven also
do not join at any boundary. Nor, to generalize, would it ever be

[18] St. Thomas, *Sum. Theol.*, I, 84, 1, *Resp.*: "... derisibile videtur ut, dum rerum
quae nobis manifestae sunt notitiam quaerimus, alia entia in medium afferamus,
quae non possunt esse eorum substantiae, cum ab eis differant secundum esse;
..." The context of St. Thomas' remark is slightly different, but he is smiling
at the same joke in a different guise.

possible in the case of number that there should be a common boundary among the parts; they are always separate. Number, therefore, is a discrete quantity. . . . A line, on the other hand, is a continuous quantity, for it is possible to find a common boundary at which its parts join. In the case of the line, this common boundary is the point; in the case of the plane, it is the line: for the parts of the plane have also a common boundary. Similarly, you can find a common boundary in the case of the parts of a solid, namely, either a line or a plane."

APPENDIX (B). *Per se* and accidental unity.

Aristotle, *Metaphysics*, V (Δ), 13, 1020a 6–33: " 'Quantum' means that which is divisible into two or more constituent parts of which each is by nature a 'one' and a 'this.' A quantum is a plurality if it is numerable, a magnitude if it is measurable. 'Plurality' means that which is divisible potentially into noncontinuous parts, 'magnitude' that which is divisible into continuous parts; of magnitude, that which is continuous in one dimension is length, in two breadth, in three depth. Of these, limited plurality is number, limited length is a line, breadth a surface, depth a solid. Again, some things are called quanta in virtue of their own nature, others incidentally; e.g., the line is a quantum by its own nature, the musical is one incidentally. Of the things that are quanta by their own nature some are so as substances, e.g., the line is a quantum (for 'a certain kind of quantum' is present in the definition which states what it is), and others are modifications and states of this kind of substance, e.g., much and little, long and short, broad and narrow, deep and shallow, heavy and light, and all other such attributes. And also great and small, and greater and smaller, both in themselves and when taken relatively to each other, are by their own nature attributes of what is quantitative; but these names are transferred to other things also. Of things that are quanta incidentally, some are so called in the sense in which it was said that the musical and the white were quanta, viz., because that to which musicalness and whiteness belong is a quantum, and some are quanta in the way in which movement

and time are so; for these also are called quanta of a sort and continuous because the things of which these are attributes are divisible.
I mean not that which is moved, but the space through which it
is moved; for because that is a quantum movement also is a quantum,
and because this is a quantum time is one."

Suggested Reading

The Modes of "Esse":

St. Thomas Aquinas, *De Pot.*, VII, 2, *ad* 9; *De Verit.*, II, 11; *In I Sent.*,
   d. 35, q. 1, a. 4, *Resp.*; *Sum. Theol.*, I, 3, 5; 4, 1, *ad* 3.

Unity:

Aristotle, *Metaphysics*, V (Δ), 6; X (I), 1 and 2; *Categories*, ch. 6.
St. Thomas Aquinas, *In III Metaph.*, lect. 12, n. 501; *In IV Metaph.*, lect.
   2, nn. 549, 560; *In V Metaph.*, lects. 7 and 8; *In X Metaph.*, lect. 2,
   n. 1946; *In I Sent.*, d. 24, q. 1, a. 1; *In III Sent.*, d. 18, q. 1, a. 1, *ad* 3;
   De Pot., III, 16, *ad* 3; IX, 7; *Contra Gentiles*, II, 40; *Sum. Theol.*, I,
   6, 3, *ad* 1; 11, 4; 30, 3; 76, 3; *Quodlibet.*, VI, q. 2, a. 1; X, q. 1, a. 1;
   De Verit., I, 1; XXI, 1, 4 and 5.
Klubertanz, G., S.J., *Introduction to the Philosophy of Being*, N.Y.,
   Appleton-Century-Crofts, 1955, pp. 193-195.

XIX · THE MEANING OF THE TRANSCENDENTALS. TRUTH. GOODNESS. BEAUTY

The True *Is a Transcendental*

To see that any being is true because it is a being, this is to discern another epiphany of being. Here, too, as with the transcendental "one," "being" and "true" are convertible terms, but this is so because "to be true" is "to be," not the other way about, not at least by a priority of perfection or nature.[1] Any being has to be kicking around first before anything can be said of it.

The True *Is Primarily a Predicate of Knowledge*

The "true" is above all a predicate of knowledge, as when we say that the knowledge that x exists, when in effect x does exist, is true

[1] On the true as a transcendental, see St. Thomas, *De Verit.*, I, 1, *ad* 4 and 6; I, 4, *Resp.*; XXI, 1, *Resp.*; *Sum. Theol.*, I, 16, 3, *ad* 1; *De Verit.*, I, 1, *Resp.*: ". . . the truth or the true has been defined in three ways. First of all, it is defined according to that which precedes truth and is the basis of truth. This is why Augustine writes, 'the true is that which is'; and Avicenna, 'the truth of each thing is a property of the act of being which has been established for it.' Still others say, 'the true is the undividedness of the act of existence from that which it is.' Truth is also defined in another way—according to that in which its intelligible determination is formally completed. Thus Isaac writes, 'truth is the conformity of thing and intellect'; and Anselm, 'truth is a rectitude perceptible only by the mind.' This rectitude, of course, is said to be based on some conformity. The Philosopher says that in defining truth we say that truth is had when one affirms that 'to be which is, and that not to be which is not.' The third way of defining truth is according to the effect following upon it. Thus Hilary says that the true is that which manifests and proclaims existence. And Augustine says, 'truth is that by which that which is, is shown'; and also, 'truth is that according to which we judge about inferior things.' "
See Appendix A of this chapter.

knowledge.[2] The question is, what is that truth of true knowledge? Is it perhaps the identity of knowledge with material being (Parmenides)? Or with ideas (Plato)? Or with reasoning (Hegel)? Or with essence (Kant, Wolff)?[3] Though all these identifications and many others have been suggested, and though each has some sound basis in it, let us say bluntly that truth is none of these identities, and leave it to the history of philosophy to evaluate the near misses. True knowledge is an identity of thinking with being.

The True *Is Primarily a Predicate of Knowledge Because It Is Primarily a Predicate of Being*

To say that true knowledge is an identity of thinking with being seems fantastic. Surely "to think" is not "to be," surely "thinking" cannot be the "thought of." And yet that seemingly fantastic statement must somehow be true if "to be true" is "to be," and indeed that statement is true because "to be true" *is* "to be."

[2] See St. Thomas, *In I Sent.*, d. 19, q. 5, a. 1: "Truth has a foundation in the thing, but its intelligibility is completed by the action of the intellect—when, that is, the thing is apprehended in the way it is. Therefore, the Philosopher says that the true and the false are in the mind, but good and evil are in things. Now, in the thing there are its essence and its *esse*; truth is founded rather on the *esse* of the thing than on the essence. As the name 'being' is given to something from the act of existing, so in the operation of the intellect which takes the *esse* of the thing as it is (by becoming like to it), the relation of equality is completed, and the intelligibility of truth consists in this relation. Therefore, I assert that the very *esse* of the thing (as it is in the knowledge of the intellect) is the cause of truth."
See *Sum. Theol.*, I, 16, 2, *Resp.*; *De Verit.*, I, 1, *Resp.* See Appendix B of this chapter. See also G. B. Phelan, "Verum Sequitur Esse Rerum," *Mediaeval Studies*, Vol. I (1939), pp. 11–22.
[3] See Parmenides, *On Truth*, in M. C. Nahm, *Selections from Early Greek Philosophy*, pp. 113–117; Plato, *Phaedo*, 65a–66e, 76a–77c, 101c–d; *Phaedrus*, 247c; *Republic*, IX, 585a–d; *Philebus*, 15a ff.; *Sophist*, 254b–257e; *Parmenides*, 132a–d; Hegel, *The History of Philosophy*, in *Hegel's Lectures on the History of Philosophy*, tr. E. Haldane, Vol. I, pp. 19–20; *The Philosophy of History*, in *The Philosophy of Hegel*, tr. C. Friedrich, N.Y., Modern Library, 1954, pp. 4–11; Kant, *Critique of Pure Reason*, Bk. II, ch. 1, in *Kant Selections*, ed. T. M. Greene, pp. 100–106; *Prolegomena to any Future Metaphysics*, tr. P. Lucas, pp. 9–10; Wolff, *Philosophia prima, sive Ontologia, methodo scientifica pertractata, qua omnis cognitionis humanae principia continentur*, Pars I, Sec. II, cap. 3; ed. Francofurti et Lipsiae, 1736, nn. 115, 134, 174.

The Truth Which Is God

Let us go straight to the privileged case where the truth is undoubtedly being. When God thinks of Himself, He, the "thought of," is identically the same as His "thinking" of Himself.[4] In this privileged instance, the "thought of" God gets this characteristic of "being thought of" not precisely from His "thinking" (in our "thinking," the "thought of" *does* get its characteristic of "being thought of" only from our "thinking"); rather, the "thought of" here gets its characteristic of "being thought of" precisely from the "thought of" and from nothing else. This means that God's "thinking" of Himself is precisely the "thought of." Here the "thought of" is "thinking" *because* "thinking" *is* the "thought of," namely, God. In the last analysis, then, the predicate, "true," gets its full meaning only when said of God's self-knowledge, and that full meaning is this: *this* true knowledge is completely identical with God's being. In sum, that which, *because* it exists, is also "thought of," *that* "thought of" is also thought. Here, then, "thinking" is unquestionably being.[5]

The Truth Which Is Our Thinking About Creatures, and the Truth Which Is Creatures

Short of the capital instance where thinking is past question being, we have our own knowledge. Our thinking is surely a product only

[4] See St. Thomas, *Sum. Theol.*, I, 16, 5, *Resp.*: ". . . truth is found in the intellect according as it apprehends a thing as it is; and in things according as they have being conformable to an intellect. This is to the greatest degree found in God. For His being is not only conformed to His intellect, but it is the very act of His intellect; and His act of understanding is the measure and cause of every other being and of every other intellect; and He Himself is His own being and act of understanding. Whence it follows not only that truth is in Him, but that He is the highest and first truth itself." See also *De Verit.*, I, 7, *Resp.*

[5] The Aristotelian basis for this is in *Metaphysics*, XII (Λ), 9, 1074b 15–1075a 11. See St. Thomas, *Contra Gentiles*, IV, 11: "Since in God, therefore,

of the thinker. Our thinking is *only* thought. The "thought of"
is *not* a work of thought, though the "thought of" gets its feature
of "being thought of" from thought alone.[6] Where else?

Grant, then, that our thinking invests the "thought of" with a
state of intentionality, of ideality, a state which the "thought of"
does not of itself have; for instance, the North Pole is the North
Pole whether thought of (discovered) or not. To state that much
is to see a problem, which is this: if the thinker alone produces the
ideality of the "thought of," the state, namely, of "being thought
of," how can his thinking (which is *not* the thought of) nevertheless express a state of affairs which holds fast in being, that is, a
state of affairs which holds fast even though it were *not* thought of
by us? That our thinking purports to express such a state of affairs
is given. We certainly don't say that our thinking is the "thought
of." We do say that thinking is *about* the "thought of," and that
means not that our thinking is primarily about our thinking; rather,
it means that our thinking expresses a state of natural being, not

---

being and understanding are identical, the intention understood in Him is His
very intellect. And because understanding in Him is the thing understood (for
by understanding Himself He understands all other things), . . . it follows that
in God, because He understands Himself, the intellect, the thing understood,
and the intention understood are all identical."

Obviously, none of the statement in this text is more than meaningful until
God's existence is demonstrated.

[6] See St. Thomas, *Sum. Theol.*, I, 16, 6, *Resp.*; *De Verit.*, I, 8, *Resp.*: ". .
among created things truth is found both in things and in the intellect. In
the intellect it is found according to the conformity which the intellect has
with the things whose notions it has. In things it is found according as they
imitate the divine intellect, which is their measure—as art is the measure of all
products of art—and also in another way, according as they can by their
very nature bring about a true apprehension of themselves in the human
intellect, which, as is said in the *Metaphysics*, is measured by things. By its
form a thing existing outside the soul imitates the art of the divine intellect;
and, by the same form, it is such that it can bring about a true apprehension
in the human intellect. Through this form, moreover, each and every thing has
its act of existing. Consequently, the truth of existing things includes their
entity in its intelligible character, adding to this a relation of conformity to
the human or divine intellect. . . . the truth found in created things can include
nothing more than the entity of a thing and conformity of the thing to intellect or conformity of intellect to things or to the privations of things. All
this is entirely from God, because both the very form of a thing, through
which it is conformed, is from God, and the truth itself in so far as it is the
good of the intellect, . . ."

just a state of thinking.[7] To ask how this can be so is to see a problem, as was said. To go on to say, after seeing the problem, that because our thinking is a product of the thinker alone, therefore the thinker attains only to his own product, viz., his thinking, this is to walk away from the problem at the very moment it is seen.

Not to walk away from the problem—if our thinking is *not* the "thought of," if nevertheless our thinking is about the "thought of" up to and including the point where thinking explicitly acknowledges that the "thought of" exists in a way which is not the way it exists when it is thought of (this acknowledgement is always implicit in every true statement we make), the only explanation of such a given situation must be as follows. The "thought of" is identically the same in its precognitive intentional *esse* (*species impressa*), in its cognitive or meaningful intentional *esse* (*species expressa* and in enunciations), and above all in that act of thinking, the judgment, which asserts that the "thought of" has a way of existing (*esse naturae*) which differs from its way of being thought of (*esse intentionale*). All these modes of *esse*, the *esse* of nature, the *esse* of intentionality, and, within that *esse* of intentionality, the intentionality of impressed and expressed species, of enunciations and of judgments, all those modes of *esse* are simply different existential modalities of the same thing, namely, the "thought of."[8]

And so, in our thinking, which we assume can be true, the "thought of" prolongs itself into another way of being, namely, the way of "being thought of." In all the genetic phases of that new way of being, and especially in the way of being which the "thought of" has when it is asserted to be "other" than that way of being which the "thought of" has when it is "being thought of," in all those ways of being, *man*, for example, stays the same *man*, whether unconsciously received *into* thought, or consciously conceived *by* thought, or asserted to be other than thought. The peak of the stages of "truth" is of course the last stage of it, namely, the assertion that there *is* a man.[9]

---

[7] See Aristotle, *Metaphysics*, IX (Θ), 10, 1051b 7–9: "It is not because we think truly that you are pale, that you *are* pale, but because you are pale we who say this have the truth."

[8] See Chapter X.

[9] See Aristotle, *De Anima*, III, 5, 430a 10–430b 30. St. Thomas, *In III de Anima*, lect. 10; Pirotta, n. 728; *De Verit.*, I, aa. 1 and 12; I, 6; *In IV Metaph.*,

The Location of the Transcendental True

If, then, you view God's thinking of Himself in relation to the "thought of" which is God, *that* thinking is not a transcendental. That thinking is God. Here we have the capital instance where thinking is past question being.[10] If you view the relation of creatures to God's thought of *them*, that relation is the very being of those creatures.[11] All that creatures are, from tip to toe, is all that God thinks of them, no more and no less. This relation is *their* transcendental truth-relation to God, the truth of *their* being. The point is: that truth *is* their being, the truth of *their* being. If you view the relation which *our* thinking of things has *to them*, that thinking is not their natural being. Nonetheless, that thinking has as its term the assertion of their natural being. Now, since our thinking, which at its peak is an assertion that natural beings exist, since our thinking makes no sense unless those natural beings *do* exist; since, further, the assertion that the asserted exists makes no sense unless the asserted is asserted to be either *esse* alone, or a being in *esse* which is from and to *esse*, therefore our thinking is transcendentally related to *esse*. In sum, our thinking is true because the being which terminates our thinking (and is *esse* itself, or is in *esse* which is from and to God), that being which terminates our thinking is true being. The truth of the knowledge situation is pretty much like the truth of beings: beings are true because their being, which is from God's knowledge, is true; our thinking is true because it is true thinking of those true beings. The difference between the truth of natural beings and the truth of our assertion of them is a difference as between the truth of thought and the truth of being, but the truth of thought makes no sense unless, in the upshot,

---

lect. 6, n. 605; *In XI Metaph.*, lect. 5, n. 2211; *Contra Gentiles*, II, 83; IV, 11; *Sum. Theol.*, I, 5, 2; 55, 1; 79, 7; I–II, 4, 2; II–II, 8, 1. See also J. Maritain, *Distinguer pour unir, ou les degrés du savoir*, ch. 3 and Annexe I; *Réflexions sur l'intelligence et sur sa vie propre*, ch. 2.

[10] See p. 345 of this chapter.

[11] See St. Thomas, *De Verit.*, I, 4, *Resp.*: "Truth predicated of things because of their relation to the divine intellect is inseparably attendant on them, for they cannot exist except by reason of the divine intellect which keeps bringing them into being."

our knowledge be related to knowing the Being which is the cause of being.[12]

Put it this way. When one asserts with truth that *x* is fat, the statement makes no sense unless *x is* fat. Now, that makes no sense unless to-be is either identically to-be-fat (against the fact, for there are thin men), or because "ising fat" is caused to be and, in the upshot, by a cause of being. So, in my knowledge that *x* is fat, there is involved a knowledge of *a* being, a knowledge of common being, and a proved, or a beatifying knowledge of a cause of common being.[13] Shortly, the truth of knowledge makes no sense except in relation to the truth of natural being; the truth of natural being makes no sense except in relation to the truth from which natural being issues.[14]

The Relation of Being to Our Knowledge Is a Relation of Reason Only

There are as many ways of being true as there are ways of being. Of all those ways of being we can say that they are relatable to our knowledge even when they are not actually related, that is, even when they are not actually known, because if they were known

[12] See pp. 345–347 of this chapter.

[13] See Chapter XVII, pp. 324–326.

[14] Falsity lies only in knowledge, never in being. See Aristotle, *Metaphysics*, VI (E), 4, 1027b 25: ". . . falsity and truth are not in things—it is not as if the good were true, and the bad were in itself false—but in thought; . . ." St. Thomas, *Sum. Theol.*, I, 17, 1, *Resp.*: "Now, in things, neither truth nor falsity exists, except in relation to the intellect." *De Verit.*, I, 10, *Resp.*: ". . . counterfeit gold is still true brass."

Knowledge is false when there is an irruption of the voluntary into our thinking. At the minimum, we make false statements because we *wish* to have something to say when we should keep our big mouth shut or simply say that we do not know. This is a disordered love of truth, a love so natural that we would rather speak than be silent. At the maximum, we make false statements because we wish for the great advantages which error sometimes brings us. For example, ask one who says he is losing his faith, "who is she"? Usually you will startle him into, "how did *you* know"? Try it some time.

On truth and falsity, see also Aristotle, *Metaphysics*, IV (Γ), 4, 1006a 1–1006b 35; V (Δ), 29, 1024b 19–21; IX (Θ), 10, 1051b 1–1052a 4; *On Sophistical Refutations*, ch. 1, 164a 23–164b 25; St. Thomas, *Sum. Theol.*, I, 17, 4, *Resp.* and ad 2; *In IV Metaph.*, lect. 22; *In VI Metaph.*, lect. 4; *In IX Metaph.*, lect. 11.

they would be known as beings. However, we say that being is relatable to our knowledge only in consequence of having seen that our knowledge is related to being. The relation of our knowledge to being is a real relation; the reverse relation is a relation of reason only. We have made the reverse relation only when and because we have seen that we know being. The reverse relation is thus a by-product of a real relation.

The picture then is this. The relation of creatures to the knowledge which God has of them is an accidental relation, but that relation is not an accident, because creatures are not accidents. That accidental relation *is* a creature. The relation of our knowledge to being is also an accidental relation, but that relation is not an accident either, except in relation to the knower. In relation to the known, namely, to being, that relation is the very being of knowledge. Knowledge is an accident of the knower indeed, but the relation of knowledge to being is not an accident of knowledge. It is the very stuff, the very being of knowledge. Lastly, the relation of God's knowledge to creatures, and the relation of creatures to our knowledge are both relations of reason only.[15]

Goodness. Its Meaning

As the "one" and the "true," so also the "good" is convertible with being.[16] Any being is good because it exists. It is not primarily because it is good that any being exists.[17]

---

[15] See Chapter XVI, pp. 288–290.

[16] See St. Thomas, *Sum. Theol.*, I, 5, 1, *Resp.*: "Goodness and being are really the same, and differ only in idea; which is clear from the following argument. The essence of goodness consists in this, that it is in some way desirable. Hence the Philosopher says: *Goodness is what all desire.* Now it is clear that a thing is desirable only in so far as it is perfect, for all desire their own perfection. But everything is perfect so far as it is actual. Therefore it is clear that a thing is perfect so far as it is being; for being is the actuality of every thing, as is clear from the foregoing. Hence it is clear that goodness and being are the same really. But goodness expresses the aspect of desirableness, which being does not express."
See Appendix C of this chapter. See also *Sum. Theol.*, I, 5, 3, *Resp.*; 16, 3, *Resp.*; 16, 4, *Resp.*; 54, 2, *Resp.*; 59, 2, *ad* 3; I–II, 29, 5, *Resp.*; 94, 2, *Resp.*; *Contra Gentiles*, II, 41; III, 7; *De Pot.*, IX, 7, *ad* 6; *De Malo*, II, 5, *ad* 1 and 2; *De Verit.*, I, 1, *Resp.*; XXI, 1, *Resp.*

[17] See St. Thomas, *De Verit.*, XXI, 2, *Resp.*: "Existence itself, therefore, has the essential note of goodness. Just as it is impossible, then, for anything to be

We may see the point in this way. First, dismiss from the expression, "a would-be being," any connotation of pretentiousness. Next, retain in that expression only the meaning of the optative mood. For example, dismiss from the meaning of "a would-be philosopher" any meaning but this one: a hard working, intelligent student of philosophy. When such "a would-be philosopher" becomes a philosopher, he is a philosopher without pretense, because he was one with intent. It is the same with any given being. At any point of its duration any being is the same in intent as it will be in fact when it has arrived at some future point in its duration; any being is now by intent what it will be later in fact.[18] This "would-be" status of a being is "being" as "good," another epiphany of "is," because a "would-be" is nothing if not an "is." The reason is this: whatever an "is" would be, and (when an "is" achieves a "would-be") whatever a "would-be" is—this is not a being which is pretending to be. This is a being which is.

The Validation That the Good Is Being

That this must be so may be seen thus: a changing being stays the same being. In terms of "would-be" and "is"—unless the "would-be" anticipates an "is," and unless the "is" be the anticipated "would-be," the "would-be" status of any being would be the status of another being, totally other, that is. This is impossible if there be a changing being. After all, as was said, "is" repeats "would-be" and "would-be" is but an anticipating "is." This being so, if what any being "would be" is its good, the "good" is "being."[19]

---

a being which does not have existence, so too it is necessary that every being be good by the very fact of its having existence, even though in many beings many other aspects of goodness are added over and above the act of existing by which they subsist. Since, moreover, good includes the note of being, as is clear from what has been said, it is impossible for anything to be good which is not a being. Thus we are left with the conclusion that good and being are interchangeable." See also *Sum. Theol.*, I, 5, 1, *ad* 1; 5, 2, *Resp.*

[18] On the chance event, see G. Smith, S.J., *Natural Theology*, pp. 148–152, 251–252. On violence, see St. Thomas, *De Verit.*, XXII, 1, *Resp.*; *Sum. Theol.*, I, 82, 1, *Resp.* →

[19] On evil, see G. Smith, S.J., *Natural Theology*, pp. 252–259.

One might put the matter this way. Any given being works hard at its job of being. This hard work at its job is another epiphany of being, the epiphany which is the "good." Hard work of this sort means tendency to, pursuit and, barring chance and violence, possession of one's own being. The hard work phase lies in tendency and pursuit, and that work is sometimes crowned by possession. The first two phases aim at, and the third secures, what a being would be. Now, to tend toward, to pursue, and to possess one's own being so as by possessing what one would be, all this is good, and all this is good because all this is being.[20] There is no such thing as an effortless, or better, an inert *esse,* *and* to see that *esse* is not inert is to see that facet of being which is the good.

Description of the Good

The good, then, may be described by its sign, namely, by the seeking for it. As Aristotle says, the good is "that which each thing for its part seeks."[21] Note well that Aristotle is not saying that the good is good because it is desired. He is saying that because it is good it is desired. Nor is he saying that what any one being seeks is good for any other being. As usual, he is saying exactly what he means: the good is the goal of *any* tendency. Aristotle also describes the good as that on account of which there is operation.[22] Whether the good be described as the sought for, or as the reason for that seeking, namely, because the sought for is good for the seeker, in either case the good is being. Certainly, neither the sought for nor the reason for seeking it can be nothing.

----

[20] St. Thomas, *De Verit.,* XXI, 2, *Resp.:* ". . . tendere in finem, et in fine quodammodo quiescere; . . . Haec autem duo inveniuntur competere ipsi esse." See *Sum. Theol.,* I, 5, 6, *Resp.*

[21] Aristotle, *Nicomachean Ethics,* I, 1, 1094a 2: ". . . the good has rightly been declared to be that at which all things aim."

[22] Aristotle, *Physics,* II, 3, 194b 32–38; II, 8, 199a 20–33; *Metaphysics,* V (Δ), 2, 1013a 32–35.

The Good Which Is a Creature

As we saw, any creature's *esse* comes to it from a cause. Furthermore and for the reason just stated, any creature's *esse* is so set up
that, although a creature actually exists, it is not actually all that
it will be: any creature is actuated but not ever completely actuated
as a nature. Here, then, is the point: a nature's completer actuation
cannot come to it from that nature's own resources, because if it
could, a creature would not change, as it does. Hence, the completion
of a creature's actuation must be fed into it.[23] The relation of the
incompletely actuated to its completer actuation is the relation of
act (incomplete) to act (completer). This relation is what is meant
by fittingness (*convenientia*).[24] Fittingness or the suitability of a
completion is not a "value" added to incomplete act as though that
"value" were not the value of incomplete act, as though that value
were not the value of being, in other words. No, this completion or
good is the very being of that which is completed by it. This rules
out the good conceived as something which looks good but isn't, because it rules out the denial that the good is being. Again, this rules
out something which *is* good, conceived as something valuable
which is not the value of being. In short, the completion or good of
a being *is* fitting to a being, because its completion *is* its being.

[23] St. Thomas, *Contra Gentiles*, III, 20; Aristotle, *Physics*, III, 1, 201a 28. See
Appendix D of this chapter.
[24] St. Thomas, *De Verit.*, XXII, 1, *Resp.*: ". . . omnia bonum appetunt, non
solum habentia cognitionem, sed quae sunt cognitionis expertia. Ad cuius
evidentiam sciendum est, quod quidam antiqui philosphi posuerunt, effectus
advenientes in natura, ex necessitate praecedentium causarum provenire; non ita
quod causae naturales essent hoc modo dispositae propter convenientiam talium
effectuum: quod Philosophus in II *Physic.* ex hoc improbat quod secundum
hoc, huiusmodi convenientiae et utilitates si non essent aliquo modo intentae,
casu provenirent, et sic non acciderent in maiori parte, sed in minori, sicut
et cetera quae casu accidere dicimus; unde necesse est dicere, quod omnes res
naturales sunt ordinatae et dispositae ad suos effectus convenientes. . . . omnia
naturalia, in ea quae eis conveniunt, sunt inclinata, habentia in seipsis aliquod
inclinationis principium, ratione cuius eorum inclinatio naturalis est, ita ut
quodammodo ipsa vadant, et non solum ducantur in fines debitos."

Psychic and Apsychic Creatures

There are as many ways in which its completion or its good is fed into a being as there are ways of being.[25] In all these ways the common feature is this: creatures exist as needing and getting completion.[26] They don't just lie around and get what is good for them by lying around. Rather, they get what is good for them by lying around disgruntled. This is perfectly clear when psychic agents are in question. They are always uneasy, always stirring about, always seeking satisfaction. And as for apsychic agents, although we don't know what the apsychic equivalent of uneasiness is in them, we do know that without some equivalent they would not thrive and indeed would not even be. A plant without water, sun, earth, etc., would not last long, indeed, without ever having had water, sun, etc., a plant would not be a plant at all. So, both psychic agent and apsychic have what they "would be" fed into them. When this good of theirs is fed into psychic agents, one might say they are "gruntled." Thus, the feature which is common to the disgruntled-"gruntled" couplet and the apsychic need-apsychic fulfillment couplet is this: the relation of incomplete act to completer act.

And precisely because this relation is common to both psychic and apsychic agents, it is not necessary for a being to *know* its needs in order to have them, nor is it necessary for a being to *know* its completion in order to be completed by other beings. All that is required in order to see that the good is being is to see that a creature has needs which are fulfilled by other beings. For, if other beings fill the needs of any being, and if that fulfillment is the good of any being, it follows that the good is any being.

One might say that any being desires itself if we enlarge the notion of desire so as to include the desires of nature, e.g., the tendency of bodies to fall, of trees to grow, etc. For, this desire of being oneself entails the desire of the not-self as needed for the continuance and enrichment of the self. Beings do not wrap their

[25] On the kinds of desirous *esse*, see Chapter IX.
[26] See note 23 above.

arms around themselves, hugging their small capital, flourishing within the small limits of their own hides. No, they must hug other beings to themselves, feed upon other beings, assimilate other beings into their own being. *Then* they flourish in themselves and the point is that they flourish *only* then. Nor is self love the horrid thing sin has made it. Properly conducted, self love is the love of the "other," which is one's *own* good. It is only in finding one's own good (self love) in the other-than-self (another self) that one's own good is authentically one's own. Thus, even in Eros can be found the outlines of Agape.

The Good Which Is God

God's good is God.[27] We may see the meaning of this in various ways. No good is fed into God's being, because no being can be fed into infinite being. Just as it is God's nature to exist, so it is His nature to be good. See this by contrast with a creature's nature. A creature's nature is not to exist. Rather, it is to exist as *a* nature, e.g., as a man. This means that no nature is all that being can be. Being can be much else besides a man nature, e.g., being can be a fish nature. Moreover, even a man or any nature for that matter is always being continuously fulfilled or completed. A creature is forever restless. This indicates that a nature as nature either has no complete rest, or else it is having fed into it a good which is above nature.[28] Certainly, there's no rest in contemplating one's own navel. If then we think of the good as the completion of being, then the good which is God is not the completion of His being. Rather, the good which is God is, since His being is complete, complete good.

Again, if we think of the good as "that which each thing for its part desires," some adjustment is needed in order to think properly

[27] St. Thomas, *Contra Gentiles*, I, 38: "To be in act is for each being its good. But God is not only a being in act; He is His very act of being, as we have shown. God is, therefore, *goodness itself*, and not only good." See *Contra Gentiles*, III, 20; *Sum. Theol.*, I, 6, 1, *Resp.* and *ad* 1; 6, 2, *Resp.*

[28] St. Augustine, *Confessions*, I, 1; PL 32, 661: "Fecisti nos ad te Domine, et irrequietum est cor nostrum donec quiescat in te."

of the good which is God. Desire, the pursuance of the desired and,
barring chance, violence, and the refusal of the desired, the possession of the desired—these three are but three phases of one love.
The first two phases, desire and pursuit, indicate that the beloved
is absent though loved.[29] The third phase, namely, the possession or
the presence of the beloved, this is the phase of love which is common to God's self-love and ours. The differentiating feature of the
two loves is this: God's self-love is the willed identity of Himself
with His being *because* He is, by physical identity with it, the
beloved.[30] In other words, the willed identity of Himself with His
being is precisely that identity. A creature's love is never a physical
identity of the lover with the beloved, because a creature is never
identically its *esse*, and it is into that *esse* that the creature's good
is fed. True, there are degrees of physical possession of the beloved
by creatures, but never a physical possession which is physical
identity. One being cannot be, physically, another being. Short of
physical identity, one being can possess another by having something effected in it by another, e.g., the heat of the heater is fed into
the heated. Then there is the delightful possession of the beloved
by the lover when they are physically together. What a joy to be
with those we love! The expression, "to be at home," will evoke
the proper meaning of possession here. Then there is sexual presence
of the beloved to the lover, an example whose familiarity makes this
sort of possession quite clear. Then there is the possession of the
known by knowledge. At this point the degree of possession
begins to grow. To be in a spot from which our minds are absent,
this is absentmindedness, or "mindedness" elsewhere. To have others
in our minds is to be present to them in a way which transcends any
physical proximity. And yet we may have others in our minds without having them on our minds. To have others on our minds, this is
to love them.[31] All these are examples of the way their good is fed

[29] St. Thomas, *De Caritate*, a. 2, *ad* 6: ". . . de ratione caritatis seu amoris est,
quod coniungat secundum affectum; . . . Sed coniungere secundum rem,
non est de ratione caritatis, et ideo potest esse et habiti et non habiti."
[30] St. Thomas, *De Verit.*, XXII, 1, *ad* 11: "Fini ergo ultimo non competit
tendere in finem, sed seipso fine fruitur."
[31] St. Augustine, *Confessions*, XIII, 9; PL 32, 849: ". . . pondus meum amor
meus, eo feror quocumque feror."

into creatures. Into God, however, no good can be fed, because His good is only God, and God is infinite. This leads us to examine the matter from another angle.

If we view love as self-love, and this is true of all love provided we keep in mind that self-love is always the love of the not-self-as-another self, then God's self-love has no possibility in it of being improperly conducted. There is no competition in God between His self-love which could refuse the good which "completes" Him and the good which He is, because there *is* no good which completes Him. In our love there can be such competition, and if our love does refuse the good which completes it, this is indeed a self-love, but one which refuses the very condition of being oneself, namely, the good of self which is fed into the self by other beings. The name of such self-love is selfishness. Not an authentic example of love. But if the self-love which is God can have nothing fed into it, how then can we say that He loves creatures, that His love is altruistic or other regarding? Well, we *cannot* say that creatures are God's good, and so we cannot say that He loves them and mean thereby that creatures are His good. He doesn't love creatures as if they contributed to His good, as if, should He not love them, *He* would be missing something. He does not love creatures for His own sake, as a man loves food for his own sake. Rather, He wishes creatures to be for His own sake. God wills creatures to be ordered to Himself, the end; but He does not will creatures because of that end.[32] That this is much more than a nuance may be seen in this, slightly fantastic, way. God does not create in order to have a rooting section to whose "rah, rah, God," He might listen to with complacence, and which if mute would leave Him without the satisfaction of hearing them root for Him. Rather, if we may keep the figure, God creates a rooting section whose rooting for Him is *their* good, not His. If the rooting section didn't root, He would miss nothing, but rooters would. They would miss their very *raison d'être*, which is to root for God. This leads to the relation of the good which is creatures to the good which is God.

[32] St. Thomas, *Sum. Theol.*, I, 19, 5, *Resp. ad fin.*: "Vult ergo hoc esse propter hoc, sed non propter hoc vult hoc."

The Relation of Created to Uncreated Good

Since the good completes a being, and since a being's completion
is still a being, and since a creature's being is from God, therefore a
creature's good, which is simply a creature's completer being, is
also from God. Thus the relation of created to uncreated good is the
same as the relation of created to uncreated *esse*. Only, here the
relation of created to uncreated *esse* is now seen to be also a relation of created to uncreated good. And so, just as created being
is a relation to uncreated being, so created good is a relation to
uncreated good. This, in the order of efficient causality.

In the order of final causality, since each creature desires, pursues,
and possesses, in a degree, its own *esse*, and since its *esse* is like uncreated *esse*, each creature is a likeness to God. This is to say that
each creature implicitly desires or is headed to God.[33] The transcendental relation of created to uncreated good is thus the old
transcendental relation of *esse* to its efficient and final cause; but
here the related *esse* is now viewed as what it really was all the
time, namely, as good.

There is no relation in reverse. This is to say that no creature's
good, not even God, completes a being until a being *is* or is *being*
completed. Before a being is or is being completed, we do indeed
view that able-to-complete-good as good, but we do this only in
consequence of a real relation of a being to its good. And that real
relation is not real until the actuation of incomplete by completer
act is a veritable actuation of incomplete act. Before the good is
being, i.e., before the good actuates a being, the good is only able
to actuate a being. This is to say that before actuating a being, the
good is not being; but we think of it then as if it were a being, because the good is and (when we are involved) we have understood
the good to be, in its actuating status, viz., the status of being.

[33] St. Thomas, *De Verit.*, XXI, 5, *Resp.* See *De Verit.*, XXII, 2, *ad* 2: ". . .
ipsum esse est similitudo divinae bonitatis; unde in quantum aliqua desiderant
esse, desiderant Dei similitudinem et Deum implicite." See also *Contra Gentiles*,
III, 20–21.

The able-to-actuate status of the good is a relation of reason only, involved in our understanding of the good's actuating status.[34]

The relation of a being to its good, then, is a transcendental relation, both in the order of the physical completion of a being's physical good and in the order of the knowledge completion of a knower's knowledge good. The relation of the being of God to His good *is* God, not a transcendental relation at all. The relation of a being's good, including the good which is God, to a being is not a real relation at all. It is a relation of reason only, a relation which we have posited only because we have understood the real or actuating transcendental relation of a being to its good. Such an understanding is to the effect that a being's "is" and "would-be" come to it as from its efficient and final cause, which is God.

The Meaning of the Beautiful

Sometimes we know things in an unusual way. For example, we have been hearing sounds all our lives, and one day we hear a certain combination of them, Beethoven's *Fifth*, say, and that hearing is extraordinarily delightful. Or we have been seeing things all our lives, and one day we see something, the curve of a hand or the flash of an eye, for example, and that seeing is extraordinarily delightful. Perhaps such experiences can also be gustatory, olfactory, or tactual. At any rate, these latter experiences are not as noteworthy as the auditory or visual ones.[35]

[34] St. Thomas, *De Verit.*, XXI, 6, *Resp.*: ". . . the essence of good implies a relation, not because the name *good* itself signifies only a relation, but because it signifies something which has a relation along with the relation itself. The relation implied in the word *good* is the status of that which perfects. This follows from the fact that a thing is capable of perfecting not only according to its own specific character but also according to the act of being which it has in reality."

[35] St. Thomas, *Sum. Theol.*, I-II, 27, 1, *ad* 3: "The beautiful is the same as the good, and they differ only in intelligibility. For, since the good is that which all things seek, the notion of good is that which quiets the desire; while the notion of the beautiful is that which quiets the desire by being seen or known. Consequently those senses chiefly regard the beautiful which are the most cognitive, viz., sight and hearing, as ministering to reason; for we speak of beautiful sights and beautiful sounds. But in reference to the other objects

If we ask what is unusual about such experiences, we cannot say
that it is just because they are knowledge acts. Knowledge acts are
indeed unusual as contrasted with the operations of nature. Yet
only some knowledge acts are delightful. The question is, why is
this so?

The explanation seems to lie here. Some knowns are integral
wholes, with properly proportioned parts and bathed, so to say, in
their own light.[36] The knowledge of such knowns causes an intense
knowledge delight. This knowledge delight is the sign that we are
knowing something beautiful. The beautiful, then, is a kind of good,
the good of cognition. One component of that good is the pleasure
of such cognition. Yet the beautiful thing is not the pleasure it
causes in the knowing of it. Rather, the beautiful thing is that which
causes the knowing of it to be a delightful knowing. Here we have
a special proportion or relation between the power to know and
some, not all, knowns. Some knowns are not integral, or not har-
moniously integrated, or not clear. Some are.[37] When there is defect

---

of the other senses, we do not use the expression *beautiful;* for we do not
speak of beautiful tastes and beautiful odors. Thus it is evident that beauty
adds to goodness a relation to the cognitive faculty; so that *good* means that
which simply pleases the appetite, while the *beautiful* is something pleasant
to apprehend."

[36] St. Thomas, *Sum. Theol.,* I, 39, 8, *Resp.:* "For beauty includes three conditions: *integrity* or *perfection,* since those things which are impaired are by
that very fact ugly; due *proportion* or *harmony;* and lastly, *brightness,* or
clarity, whence things are called beautiful which have a bright color." *Sum.
Theol.,* II–II, 145, 2, *Resp.:* ". . . beauty or comeliness results from the con-
currence of clarity and proportion. For, he states that God is said to be beautiful as being *the cause of the harmony and clarity of the universe.* Hence the
beauty of the body consists in a man having his bodily limbs well proportioned,
together with a certain clarity of color. Similarly, spiritual beauty consists in
a man's conduct or actions being well proportioned according to the spiritual
clarity of reason."

[37] St. Thomas, *Sum. Theol.,* I, 5, 4, *ad* 1: "Beauty and goodness in a thing
are identical fundamentally, for they are based upon the same thing, namely,
the form; and this is why goodness is praised as beauty. But they differ
logically, for goodness properly relates to appetite (goodness being what all
things desire), and therefore it has the aspect of an end (the appetite being
a kind of movement towards a thing). On the other hand, beauty relates to a
cognitive power, for those things are said to be beautiful which please when
seen. Hence beauty consists in due proportion, for the senses delight in things
duly proportioned, as in what is like them—because the sense too is by

on either side of the relation, between the power to know and
the known, then we don't know something beautiful. The beautiful,
then, may be described as a being, the very perception of which
pleases.[38] The pleasing perception is a sign of the beautiful. The
signalized is the beautiful.[39]

The beautiful thing as well as the knowledge of it need not be
very important. Blue smoke, curling from a cottage on a hill at
evening, this is not an important item in the hierarchy of knowns.
No matter. It is a beautiful sight, and as a sight it leaves little to be
desired. So too some "lines, the birth of some chance morning or
evening at an Ionian festival, or among the Sabine hills, have lasted
for generation after generation, for thousands of years, with a
power over the mind, and a charm, which the current literature . . .
with all its obvious advantages, is utterly unable to rival."[40] Indeed,
so splendid are some truths[41] that a man might well be tempted to
make the pursuit of them a vocation instead of an avocation.[42] A
complete vocation is to the moral good.[43] The beautiful should not
be pursued except in subordination to the moral good.

---

assimilation, and likeness relates to form, beauty properly belongs to the nature
of a formal cause."
    See *Sum. Theol.*, I–II, 27, 1, *ad* 3; *In D. de Div. Nom.*, c. IV, lect. 5;
Marietti, n. 356.
    [38] St. Thomas, *Sum. Theol.*, I, 5, 4, *ad* 1; 39, 8, *Resp.*; I–II, 27, 1, *ad* 3; II–II,
145, 2 and *ad* 1; 180, 2, *ad* 3; *De Verit.*, XXII, 1, *ad* 12; *In D. de Div. Nom.*,
c. IV, lect. 5.
    [39] The sign of the good is the seeking for it. The sign of the beautiful is the
pleasure of knowing it; and as the good is the completion of being, so the
beautiful is an aureole of a knowledge act: the good is related to being as
beauty is to knowledge. Any being is completed by its good; only knowers
see the beautiful.
    [40] J. H. Newman, *A Grammar of Assent*, N.Y., Doubleday, 1955, p. 79.
    [41] See St. Augustine, *De Vera Relig.*, XXIX, 52; PL 34, 145; XXX, 55; PL
34, 146. On the *splendor veri, splendor ordinis,* and *splendor formae,* see J.
Maritain, *Art and Scholasticism,* tr. J. F. Scanlan, N.Y., Scribner's, 1946, p. 20.
    [42] See J. Maritain, *Art and Scholasticism,* pp. 19–30; *Creative Intuition in
Art and Poetry,* N.Y., Meridian, 1957, pp. 122–128; *Neuf leçons sur les notions
premières de la philosophie morale,* pp. 63–66; E. Gilson, *Painting and Reality,*
The Mellon Lectures, N.Y., The Bollingen Foundation, 1957, pp. 3–45, 187–206.
    [43] See J. Maritain, *Art and Scholasticism,* pp. 58–67; *Neuf leçons sur les
notions premières de la philosophie morale,* pp. 61–77.

Beauty as a Transcendental

As we saw, the effect of a beautiful thing is the delightful knowledge it causes. That delight is, for us, mainly sensuous. Our knowledge is either mainly sensuous or mainly intellectual. It is never one exclusive of the other. To a knower without any sensorium, any being would be beautiful. To us it is not. When a being is beautiful, and when a knower is perceptive enough to know it, then occurs the breath-taking experience of the splendor of truth, the beautiful. By contrast, the good can be attained without knowledge as, for example, in the inorganic and the plant world; but not the beautiful, not even by purely animal knowledge. The beautiful is signalized by the pleasure of *knowing* the good.

Since the cause of knowledge is being as true, and since the cause of pleasure is being as good, the cause of knowing the beautiful must be a combination of two transcendentals, namely, the good and the true. The beautiful is the good of knowledge, the pleasant sensuous-intellectual knowledge of some good dwelling in matter.

Since, further, the transcendentals or any combination of them pervade all the categories, the beautiful can be in a category just as being can, but it is not a category.

The remarks already made about the transcendental relations are pertinent here.[44] Those remarks, in sum, amount to this: a transcendental is any being, viewed as related to its efficient and final cause, and that relation is the being so related; the knowledge and love of being is that same relation, viewed as constitutive of knowledge and love, just as any being's relation to its final and efficient cause is constitutive of its physical *esse*. A being's knowledge and love is constitutive of its intentional *esse*, whereas the relation of a being's physical *esse* to its cause is constitutive of its physical *esse*. Beings with intentional *esse*, whether that *esse* be the *esse* of knowledge or love, are much more than their lumpish physical selves; they are the beings who know and love, up to and including, implicitly at least, their status of being God-lovers and God-

---

[44] See Chapter XVII, pp. 317-318; Chapter XVIII, pp. 329-330.

knowers. In the matter of beauty, the beings who know beauty are, implicitly at least, enjoying the beauty of God.

Appendix to Chapter XIX

APPENDIX (A). The true as a transcendental.

St. Thomas, *De Verit.*, I, 1, *ad* 4: "The true is a state of being even though it does not add any reality to being or express any special mode of existence. It is rather something that is generally found in every being, although it is not expressed by the word *being*."

St. Thomas, *De Verit.*, I, 1, *ad* 6: "There is a conceptual difference between the true and being since there is something in the notion of the true that is not in the concept of the existing—not in such a way, however, that there is something in the concept of being which is not in the concept of the true. They do not differ essentially nor are they distinguished from one another by opposing difference."

St. Thomas, *Sum. Theol.*, I, 16, 3, *ad* 1: ". . . the true that is in things is substantially convertible with being, while the true that is in the intellect is convertible with being, as that which manifests is convertible with the manifested; for this belongs to the nature of truth, . . . It may, however, be said that being also is in things and in the intellect, as is the true; even though truth is primarily in the intellect, while being is primarily in things. This is so because truth and being differ in idea."

St. Thomas, *De Verit.*, I, 4, *Resp.*: "Truth predicated of things because of their relation to the divine intellect is inseparably attendant on them, for they cannot exist except by reason of the divine intellect which keeps bringing them into being. Again, truth is primarily in a thing because of its relation to the divine intellect, not to the human intellect, because it is related to the divine intellect as to its cause, but to the human intellect as to its effect in the sense that the latter receives its knowledge from things. For this reason, a thing is said to be true principally because of its order to the

truth of the divine intellect rather than because of its relation to the
truth of the human intellect."

APPENDIX (B). The "true" is a predicate of knowledge.

St. Thomas, *Sum. Theol.*, I, 16, 2, *Resp.:* ". . . since everything
is true according as it has the form proper to its nature, the intellect, in so far as it is knowing, must be true according as it has
the likeness of the thing known, which is its form as a knowing
power. For this reason truth is defined by the conformity of intellect
and thing; and hence to know this conformity is to know truth. . . .
truth resides in the intellect composing and dividing; and not in the
sense, nor in the intellect knowing *what a thing is.*"

St. Thomas, *De Verit.*, I, 1, *Resp.:* "*True* expresses the correspond-
ence of being to the knowing power, for all knowing is produced
by an assimilation of the knower to the thing known, so that
assimilation is said to be the cause of knowledge. . . . the first
reference of being to the intellect, therefore, consists in its agreement with the intellect. This agreement is called 'the conformity of
thing and intellect.' In this conformity is fulfilled the formal
constituent of the true, and this is what *the true* adds to being,
namely, the conformity or equation of thing and intellect. . . . the
knowledge of a thing is a consequence of this conformity, therefore, it is an effect of truth, even though the fact that the thing is a
being is prior to its truth."

APPENDIX (C). The good is convertible with being.

St. Thomas, *De Verit.*, XXI, 1, *Resp.:* "Good must, accordingly,
either add nothing to being or add something merely in concept.
For if it added something real, being would have to be narrowed
down by the character of good to a special genus. But since being
is what is first conceived by the intellect, as Avicenna says, every
other noun must either be a synonym of being or add something at
least conceptually. The former cannot be said of good, since it is
not nonsense to call a being good. Thus good, by the fact of its not
limiting being, must add to it something merely conceptual. What

is merely conceptual, however, can be of only two kinds: negation and a certain kind of relation. Every absolute positing signifies
something existing in reality. Thus to being, the first intellectual
conception, *one* adds what is merely conceptual—a negation; for it
means undivided being. But *true* and *good*, being predicated positively, cannot add anything except a relation which is merely conceptual. A relation is merely conceptual, according to the Philosopher, when by it something is said to be related which is not
dependent upon that to which it is referred, but vice versa; for a
relation is a sort of dependence. . . . The true and the good must
therefore add to the concept of being, a relationship of that which
perfects. . . . A being is perfective of another not only according
to its specific character but also according to the existence which
it has in reality. In this fashion the good is perfective; for the good
is in things, as the Philosopher says. Inasmuch as one being by
reason of its act of existing is such as to perfect and complete another, it stands to that other as an end. And hence it is that all who
rightly define *good* put in its notion something about its status as
an end. The Philosopher accordingly says that they excellently
defined good who said that it is 'that which all things desire.' First
of all and principally, therefore, a being capable of perfecting another after the manner of an end is called good; but secondarily
something is called good which leads to an end (as the useful is
said to be good), or which naturally follows upon an end (as not
only that which has health is called healthy, but also anything which
causes, preserves, or signifies health)."

APPENDIX (D). The completion of a creature's actuation.

St. Thomas, *Contra Gentiles*, III, 20: ". . . though God has His
own perfect and complete goodness, in accord with His simple existing being, creatures do not attain the perfection of their goodness
through their being alone, but through many things. Hence, although any one of them is good in so far as it exists, it cannot be
called good, without qualification, if it lacks any other things
required for its goodness. Thus, a man who is destitute of virtue

and host to vices is indeed called good, relatively speaking; that
is, to the extent that he is a being, and a man. However, in the
absolute sense, he is not good, but evil. So, it is not the same thing
for any creature to be and to be good without qualification, although
each of them is good in so far as it exists. In God, however, to be
and to be good are simply the same thing. So, if each thing tends toward a likeness of divine goodness as its end, and if each thing becomes like the divine goodness in respect of all the things that belong
to its proper goodness, the goodness of the thing consists not only
in its mere being, but in all the things needed for its perfection, as we
have shown. It is obvious, then, that things are ordered to God as
an end, not merely according to their substantial act of being, but
also according to those items which are added as pertinent to perfection, and even according to the proper operation which also
belongs to the thing's perfection."

Suggested Reading

Truth:

St. Thomas Aquinas, *In I Sent.*, d. 19, q. 5, a. 1; *De Verit.*, I, 1; I, 4; I, 7;
    I, 8; XXI, 1; *Sum. Theol.*, I, 16, 2; I, 16, 3; I, 16, 5; I, 16, 6.
Phelan, G. B., "Verum Sequitur Esse Rerum," *Mediaeval Studies*, Vol.
    I (1939), pp. 11–22.

Truth and Falsity:

Aristotle, *Metaphysics*, IV (Γ), 4; V (Δ), 29; VI (E), 4; IX (Θ), 10;
    On Sophistical Refutations, ch. 1.
St. Thomas Aquinas, *In IV Metaph.*, lect. 22; *In VI Metaph.*, lect. 4;
    In IX Metaph., lect. 11; *Sum. Theol.*, I, 17, 1 and 4; *De Verit.*, I, 10.

Goodness:

St. Thomas Aquinas, *Sum. Theol.*, I, 5, 1–3; 6, 1–2; 16, 3, *Resp.*; 16, 4,
    Resp.; 54, 2, *Resp.*; 59, 2, *ad* 3; I–II, 29, 5, *Resp.*; 94, 2, *Resp.*; *De
    Verit.*, I, 1, *Resp.*; XXI, 1–2; XXI, 6; XXII, 1; *Contra Gentiles*, I, 38;
    II, 41; III, 7; III, 20–21; *De Pot.*, IX, 7, *ad* 6; *De Malo*, II, 5, *ad* 1 and
    ad 2.

Salmon, E., *The Good in Existential Metaphysics.*
———, "Metaphysics and Unity," *Progress in Philosophy*, ed. J. McWilliams, S.J., Milwaukee, The Bruce Publishing Co., 1955, pp. 47–60.

Goodness and Evil:

St. Thomas Aquinas, *Sum. Theol.*, I, 48, 1–2; 49, 1–3; *Contra Gentiles*, III, 7; III, 11; *De Malo*, I, 1–2.
Smith, G., S.J., *Natural Theology*, pp. 252–259.

Beauty:

St. Thomas Aquinas, *Sum. Theol.*, I, 5, 4, *ad* 1; 39, 8, *Resp.;* I–II, 27, 1, *ad* 3; II–II, 145, 2, *Resp.;* 80, 2, *ad* 3; *In D. de Div. Nom.*, c. IV, lect. 5; *De Verit.*, XXII, 1, *ad* 12.
Gilson, E., *Painting and Reality*, pp. 3–45, 187–206.
Maritain, J., *Art and Scholasticism*, pp. 19–30.
———, *Creative Intuition in Art and Poetry*, pp. 122–128.
———, *Neuf leçons sur les notions premières de la philosophie morale*, pp. 61–77.

Preliminary Remarks

The only profit in a vocabulary of metaphysics is to let us know exactly what we are talking about, and if that is not clear by now, it is too late to remedy matters. It may be useful, however, to restate briefly in one chapter what it is that we have been talking about all along.

Before any attempt is made to state the meaning of the symbols or words descriptive of *Metaphysics*, it is well to remark that any investigation into the meaning of words is bound to be futile unless the decisive factor of meaning be the thing meant. If inquiry into meanings stopped with meanings alone, we should be confronted with many meanings and be utterly unable to say whether any meaning, or which one of them, meant anything at all. Say, for example, that a man is a biped, of the order of Mammalian primates, who uses fire, speech, etc. All this is very well. Yet if there *is* no man, or biped, etc., none of the meanings of those words means anything except meaning itself and signifying operations. This is a dead end. Question any meaning you please, but do not question *that* meaning which means the thing meant—when there *is* that thing. To rest satisfied with semantic inquiries is like chewing a bath towel. Worse, it is like eating oneself up. The invitation to do just that, which is implied in "it's all a matter of words," should not impress us with its promise of nourishment.[1]

And even when one allows that it is the thing meant which is

---

[1] See A. J. Ayer, *Language, Truth, and Logic*, London, Gollancz, 1949, pp. 45, 58–71, 124, 153. See also Chapter XVI, pp. 297–298.

chiefly to decide the validity of meaning, there is still the task of taking many a good look at the symbolized. Say, for example, that a man is a biped. Then what about a Long John Silver, who had only one leg? Does two-footed mean *"having* two feet?" If not, then *what?* Moreover, what words are you going to use to describe the "two-footed" which has only one foot?

Maybe you will have to coin words. Very good. It's risky business, but if you keep pointing to the symbolized whenever you use a new word, you may succeed.

Many other difficulties attend the task of fixing meanings. They can't all be overcome in one go, not even when the symbolized is as well explored as are the *metaphysicalia.*

The Situation Which the Vocabulary Describes

To say that there are beings, alive and kicking, or inanimate and changing, is true enough. The question metaphysics poses is this, how *can* there be such beings? And if we say, why ask such a question? we have failed to see that generated and corrupted beings don't have to be, precisely because they are generated and corrupted; and, more generally, we have failed to see that there is nothing in any experienced being which assures its existence. So, the question is valid.

This question does not arise at all at the level of science. A scientist may indeed raise the question. His science does not. And even when a scientist does raise the question, there is no answer to it to be found in, or needed by, his science. The question arises only when we wonder why beings which need not be, nevertheless are.[2]

One might try to answer the question thus. Beings which need not be but are come from other beings. Fair enough. Yet all that this answer says is this: beings are from other beings. Whoever doubted it? Beings are surely not nothings, nor can they come from nothings. So, beings which need not be come to be from other beings. Good. Is this answer sufficient?

[2] Leibniz, *Monadology,* 36–38, 43–45, 54–55; ed. Latta, pp. 237–238, 241–242, 247–248; *On the Ultimate Origination of Things,* ed. Latta, pp. 337–340.

It is not. The reason is this: the answer explains one unexplained being by another unexplained being. This is like entering a road marked "dead end." It's not so much that you cannot enter such a road. You may, and your journey might be indefinitely long. It is rather that a dead end will lead you nowhere—like taking off in a rocket missile of limitless range. *If* you keep on going, you can't by hypothesis get back. Now, an explanation must lead us back to the beings which are to be explained.[3] The proferred explanation keeps leading away, and away, and away. . . .

Or you might try to answer the question by denying that there are beings which need not be, or, positively, by saying that all beings must be, every single one of them. This won't do either, because it is against the facts. The facts are that some beings come into existence by generation, and go out by corruption. And indeed, if every single being had to be, and if each one came from another, then there are these alternatives: either a being causes itself (impossible), or else there is an indefinite series of them, each unexplained by its predecessor (for the predecessor came from another), or, lastly, all beings came from a cause of them.

The explanation offered in this book why beings which need not but do exist is the last alternative: they all come from a cause of them which, because it causes them to exist, is the nature of being "if I may put it that way."[4] What is this "nature of being" which St. Thomas, with such soft politeness, asks to put in that way? It is a Being whose nature it is to exist, not a being whose nature it is to exist as caused (creatures), nor even to exist as causing (God). God's causing is the reason why we know He exists, not the reason why He exists. His causing of other beings is—those other beings. They are new. Neither He nor His causing is new. He would be even if He caused nothing; but then we wouldn't know He existed, not being around to know anything. The "nature of Being," then, is simply to be, and One Who is that nature, simply is. And if one insists that, since God causes beings, therefore it is His nature to

---

[3] E. L. Mascall, *Existence and Analogy*, p. 47.
[4] St. Thomas Aquinas, *Sum. Theol.*, I, 45, 5, *ad* 1: ". . . quodcumque ens creatum participat, ut ita dixerim, naturam essendi; . . ."

cause as well as to be, one has simply missed the point that a cause of being who *had* to cause beings would not be a cause of being; in other words, one has missed the point that a causing God is not a limitation of God. A causing God is rather a limitation of the caused. The reason is this: if God's causing limits Him, then His causing would be caused in Him, just as the causing of creatures is caused in and along with creatures. This would leave a proved cause of being on our hands who is not a cause of being, for His causing of being would then be caused in Him—by another cause, and so on indefinitely. This leaves us exactly where we started, namely, there is a cause of being which does not cause being. In short, a causing God is one whose causing is so identical with Him that His being stays identically the same whether there be creatures or not. This surely is an inexplicable mystery. But we may not lose that mystery by losing the intelligibility of caused being, as Plato did. Plato located given diversity in the intelligibility of the One. This is to lose *both* the unity and the intelligibility of being. Certainly, a being is a unit, but it is a unit because it exists. If you say that it exists because it is a unit, it is impossible to say that a unit first of all exists,[5] and so it is impossible to say that there *is* a unit. And when we do locate unity in the cause of being, God, what precisely do we know of Him? Only this: He exists. We can't possibly know what a cause of being is whose causing, when viewed as identical with God, is not at all creatures, and, when viewed as creatures, is not at all God. No wonder St. Thomas is soft-spoken about such a mystery. If one may put it that way, there is quite an agnosticism here about what God is, but not about His existence.

The Vocabulary of Metaphysics. Being

The vocabulary of metaphysics is the meaningful words necessary to describe the above situation.

Start with these words, all synonyms, *an existent, a being (ens)*.

[5] A. C. Pegis, "The Dilemma of Being and Unity," *Essays in Thomism*, pp. 157, 176-178, 183.

An existent is that which exists, anything, that is, which you kick, or which kicks you, around. Second, see in any one of those existent beings these two features: first, the "that which" (*ens*) feature; second, its feature of "existing" (*esse*): for example, in an existing *x* you may discern the *x* feature (that which) and its "existing." See, third, that there is no "existing" feature in a being (in the *x* or "that which" feature) unless that "existing" feature be the feature of the "that which"; in other words, see that there is no "existing" *x* unless the "existing" be the *x*'s existing. Nor is there any "that which" feature of a being unless it be related to an "existing" feature. So for any existent. See, fourth, that the relation between the "that which" and its "existing" is not reciprocal. Thus, whereas there is no "existing" without "that which," there may well be a "that which" without its own "existing," e.g., your future child.

It is the fourth point which can cause metaphysics to blow up in one's face. For, if any being be something which exists, and if nonetheless a being which does *not* exist (your future child) is still a being, what becomes of point (3) above? It seems, if we allow point (3), that in allowing *also* that there are beings which do not exist, we have lost the "existing" feature of any being (point 1). So indeed we have, but *only if* we have admitted that a possible being is possible apart from its cause which can make the possible being to exist. This we cannot admit. A possible being's possibility (*posse*), just as an existing being's "existing," lies in "existing." Whose "existing"? Its own? No, for then the possible being would be. It would not be merely possible. Locate, then, the possible being's possible "existing" in the "existing" of its cause, able to make the possible to exist. It is there, in the actuality of the *esse* of its cause, that we find the possible "existing" of the possible which we thought to have lost.[6] In sum, you cannot understand a possible existent except in terms of an actually existing cause able to make the possible to be. Of course you may understand a possible existent in terms of "what it is" without understanding its cause, but those terms do not assure us that a possible can be. If they did, you

---

[6] St. Thomas Aquinas, *Sum. Theol.*, I, 44, 1, *ad* 1; *De Pot.*, III, 1, *ad* 17; III, 5, *ad* 2; *De Verit.*, IV, 6, *Resp.* and *ad* 3.

would be thinking of "possibles" as "queuing up in some nonexistent realm, jockeying for position and each putting in a claim to their 'is' in virtue of their *existuritio*."[7] Without a cause, a possible being is strictly nothing. Say, then, that an existent or a being (*ens*) is that which is or can be, and understand that "can be" of a possible existent as a cause's *esse* which can make the possible to be. Say, last, that such an existent, actual or possible, has two features about it: the "that which" feature, and the "existing" feature, either its own "existing" feature (when it exists), or the "existing" feature of its cause (when it doesn't but can exist).

Substance. Essence

We now need two words to describe the "that which" feature of an existent or a being. First, we need a word to describe the "that which" no matter what it may be. A man and a cockatoo, for example, are certainly "that which's," yet they are different "that which's." Second, we need a word to describe the kind situation of any "that which," a word, that is, which names the *man* situation of a man, or the *cockatoo* situation of a cockatoo. Both words will of course name the same "that which," but differently. The first word will name the "that which" no matter what kind it may be; the second will name the kind of the "that which."

The first word is *substance*. Substance is the name of the subject of the act of existing, no matter what kind it may be, no matter even if it be of no kind (God).[8] Some alternative descriptions of substance are these. (a) Substance is that to which it is owed to exist. The operative words are "owed to." See it this way: there are certainly many features in a being to which it is not "owed" that *they* exist as it is owed to the subject of existing that *it* exist. For example, it is not fitting, proper, "owed" to a smile that *it* exist as it *is*

---

[7] E. L. Mascall, *Existence and Analogy*, p. 48.

[8] In the instance of God, it is not good to say that there is no "that which" that exists, no subject of the act of existing. We should rather say that the "that which" of God *is* an act of existing. See St. Thomas, *In I Sent.*, d. 8, q. 1, a. 1, *Sol.*; *Sum. Theol.*, I, 3, 4, *Resp.*

owed to the smiler that *he* exist. A smile exists only as a qualification of a man. To *him* it is owed to exist, not to his smile. There is
no smile of the Cheshire cat without the cat.[9] (b) Substance may
also be described as a subject of predicates which is never a predicate. If that subject be viewed as an individual, it is called *first*
substance. If it be viewed as what is essential to, but is not, an individual, it is called *second* substance. For example *George, a man*,
is first substance; *man, body, living*, etc., are second substances.[10]
(c) Substance may also be described as a subject of accidents, if
any. If none, as with God, substance is used analogically as said of
God and creatures. Both God and a creature are subjects of the act
of existing.[11]

The second word we need is *essence*. Essence is the name of the
basic kind which the substance is, e.g., the name of the *man* kind
of substance, etc., is essence. Since an accident is also the name of
a kind, you may also name accident essence, but then you mean by
"essence" an accidental, nonbasic, qualification of the substantial
kind which the substance is. For example, *fat* is a kind of *man*, but
there would not be any "fat" unless there were *something* fat. The
name which describes that "something" in terms of what it is
basically or necessarily is essence; and the name of the further
qualifications of that basic essence is accidents, accidental qualities,
or, if you will, accidental essences. Essence, then, is the name of
that by which a being is what it is, either basically (necessarily)
or accidentally.

[9] St. Thomas Aquinas, *Sum. Theol.*, I, 28, 2, *Resp.*: ". . . accidentis enim esse
est inesse." See *In I Sent.*, d. 8, q. 4, a. 3, *Sol.*; *In V Metaph.*, lect. 9; *In VII
Metaph.*, lect. 1, n. 1253; *In XII Metaph.*, lect. 1, n. 2419; *Contra Gentiles*, IV,
14; *De Ente et Essentia*, c. VI.
[10] St. Thomas Aquinas, *De Pot.*, IX, 2, *ad* 6: "The division of substance into
'first' and 'second' is not a division into genus and species, since 'second' substance covers nothing that is not covered by 'first' substance; but it is a
division of a genus according to different modes of existence. Thus 'second'
substance denotes the generic nature in itself absolutely, while 'first' substance
signifies that nature as individually subsistent; wherefore the division is analogous rather than specific."
For the relation of second to first substances, see Chapter IV, pp. 65–67.
Man as second substance may certainly be defined, but the descriptions are
not really predicates.
[11] See note 8 above.

Corollaries

(1) A *definition* is a *statement*, verbal or mental, of the basic kind which a substance is. *Quiddity* is the mental expression, your thinking, of that basic kind which a substance is. Since definition and quiddity differ only as a statement differs from the meaning of a statement, and since meaning differs from the meant (essence) only as intentional differs from natural *esse*, the three words, definition, quiddity, essence, are practically interchangeable.[12] Also, since there is accidental quiddity or an accident of substance to reckon with, the description of accidental quiddity, that description's meaning and the thing meant by the description are practically interchangeable. And note that accidental quiddity always implies substance: *fat*, for example, always implies *something* fat, unless indeed you view *fat* abstractly, namely as fatness. Then accidental quiddity prescinds from individuals.[13]

(2) If substance be viewed as the subject of accidents and it may be, we are viewing a function of substance which the word *substance* (from *sub-stare*, to stand under) is nicely calculated to express. However, the philosophical, if not the etymological, meaning of "substance" is far more basic. The philosophical meaning of substance is not wholly that substance underlies accidents, though it sometimes does. The philosophical meaning of substance is this: the proper subject of the act of "existing." The negative aspect of substance, viewed as "that to which it is owed to exist," may bring the matter to a clearer focus: there is not any *other* substance to which it is owed to exist *in* any substance to which it is owed to

---

[12] St. Thomas Aquinas, *In V Metaph.*, lect. 10, nn. 902–903; *De Ente et Essentia*, cc. I and VI; *Sum. Theol.*, I, 29, 2, Resp.; *De Verit.*, I, 1, Resp.; *De Pot.*, IX, 1, Resp.

[13] Fatness is conceived *per modum substantiae*, i.e., it is not conceived as an accident at all. See St. Thomas, *In VII Metaph.*, lect. 4, n. 1353: "In recto quidem, quando accidens significatur ut accidens in concretione ad subiectum: ut cum dico, Simus est nasus concavus. Tunc enim nasus ponitur in definitione simi quasi genus, ad designandum quod accidentia non habent subsistentiam, nisi ex subiecto. Quando vero accidens significatur per modum substantiae in abstracto, tunc subiectum ponitur in definitione eius in obliquo, ut differentia; sicut dicitur, simitas est concavitas nasi."

exist. This basic viewpoint of substance is nicely expressed, both etymologically and philosophically, by renaming a substance a *subsistent*. "Subsistent" is from *sub-sistere* (to come to a stop at). And you must indeed "come to a stop at" a proper subject of "existing," because there isn't any proper subject of existing except it be one subject. Men are not made up of little men, nor houses of little houses.[14] A *subsistent*, then, is a substance viewed as *one* thing which exists. It is too bad that this basic meaning of substance skidded past Hume's mind.[15] Substance, then, is that which (an actual or possible being) an *esse* achieves or can achieve, but the *esse* doesn't achieve as accidents do, namely, as qualifying substance. *Esse* achieves so as by, in making substance to exist, making substance to be substance. (If its own *esse* does *not* achieve a substance, then we are confronted with a possible substance, which is not possible apart from the *esse* of a cause, able to cause it.)

(3) If you view a *substance* as a source of operation, its name is *nature* (from *nascor*, I am born). Certainly, any being is active, dynamic. Now, before (this is a metaphysical "before," not necessarily a temporal one; a stage of operation, the "falling" of the held rock before you release it, i.e., its *tendency* to fall), before there is operation, the agent will operate according to a pattern. This complex which is a being fixed, by tendency thereto, upon operating *before* it operates, plus the kind which that being is (which assures the kind which its operation will be), this complex is called a nature. Aristotle suggests that if you pronounce the words φύσις, or φύεσθαι, with a long, long stress, you will get a sort of phonetic equivalent of what he means by φύσις (nature).[16] Maybe, if you know Greek. If you don't, you might express his meaning thus: a nature is a being whose operation, before that operation exists, resides in it as a perpetual, anticipatory, and specified grunt which is about to issue into an operation which is appropriate to that grunt. At any rate,

[14] See Aristotle, *Physics*, III, 7, 207b 5; *Metaphysics*, VII (Z), 16, 1040b 5-10; X (I), 2, 1053b 13; St. Thomas Aquinas, *Sum. Theol.*, I, 11, 2, ad 2.

[15] Hume, *A Treatise of Human Nature*, Bk. I, Part I, sec. VI; Bk. I, Part IV, sec. V; ed. Selby-Bigge, pp. 16, 233-234.

[16] Aristotle, *Physics*, II, 1, 192b 8-22; *Metaphysics*, V (Δ), 4, 1015a 13-19. See W. D. Ross, *Aristotle's Physics, A Revised Text with Introduction and Commentary*, pp. 501-502.

nature, from the Latin *natura*, is not at all a poor word to express the situation. *Natura* means that which is "about to give birth" to an operation which will be according to the kind the operant is.

(4) Since essence is the name for what a substance is, and since that "what" must comprise all that a substance is and not just one of substance's components, and since both substance and essence have components, we must take another look at the components of substance and essence.

(A) As we said, the components of substance are the "that which" feature, no matter what it may be, and that "existing" feature of the "that which." The relation between the two may again be expressed thus: there is no "existing" feature unless it be the "that which's" existing feature. Conversely, there is no "that which" feature unless it be "existing," i.e., unless the "that which" be in *esse*, its own or in its cause's *esse*. Or one might express the relation thus: since every being is itself, it is through (*per*) or by way of being itself (*se*) that there is an "existing" of *that self*. Shorten the sentence to this: a substance is a being *per se;* or to this, a substance is a being of itself.[17] By contrast, some features of a being do not exist so as by being through (*per*) or of themselves (*se*). Rather, they exist as qualifications of a being which is a being *per se*. For example, the "fat" is not a being *per se*. It is a being through being the "fat" of "something" fat. That "something" is a being by way of being of itself, not by way of being fat.

By still further contrast, God is a being (substance) not through or by way of being Himself; rather, He is Himself through or by way of being Being. He is *per se* being, not a being *per se*. And so God is not a substance as creatures are. Yet the analogical community of substance between God and creature substance remains somewhat the same: both are authentic, unit, beings.[18]

[17] St. Thomas Aquinas, *De Pot.*, VII, 3, *ad* 4; *Sum. Theol.*, I, 3, 5, *ad* 1: "The name *substance* signifies not only what is being of itself—for being cannot of itself be a genus, as has been shown; but it also signifies an essence to which it belongs to be in this way—namely, of itself, which being, however, is not its essence."

[18] St. Thomas Aquinas, *Sum. Theol.*, I, 3, 5, *ad* 1: "What has to be said [in answer to this: a substance is a being which subsists of itself. But this is especially true of God. Therefore God is in the genus of substance] is this: the

Matter and Form

(B) Matter and form are names of the components of material essences. It is absolutely essential to see right at the start that those components are not beings. They are components of a material being, and it is the composite, not its components, which is a being. So we shall straightway clarify the point by an example which will cover all cases though it is not all the cases. The finger, e.g., of a curved finger is *nothing* apart from its curve. For, if the finger of the curved-finger complex were a being apart from its curve, the finger would exist because it is a finger, and it would also not exist, because it is not curved. There can't be a curved finger unless it be curved. Make the same run for the curve: if the curve existed apart from the curved, it would be, because it is a curve, and it could also not be, because there is nothing curved. There can't be a curve unless it be the curve of something curved. Much nonsense which is spoken and written about matter and form would be avoided if only it were grapsed from the start that neither feature is a being.

Matter and form enable us in part to explain, first, how there can be many kinds of body being.[19] Every kind of body being must be composed of determinable-but-always-determined-stuff, because all.body-being is of some kind of stuff. This stuff is matter, called prime or first matter in order to distinguish it from second matter,[20] which we shall see in a moment. And every kind of body being is

---

name *substance* means not only that which is being of itself [God] . . . but also an essence to which it belongs to be in this way, namely, of itself, [a creature] which being (*esse*), nonetheless, is not its very essence. Thus it is clear that God is not in the genus of substance."

The contrast here may be grasped by accenting the operative words. God is of Himself *being*; a creature is *of itself* a being, and lest one think that this is a matter of tweedle-dum and tweedle-dee, one must recall that in order to be oneself one must first of all *be*; God *is* that, namely, being; creatures are not being; *their* being lies only in being themselves, whereas God's self lies only in being.

[19] That there *are* kinds of body being is shown in Chapter III, pp. 37–41, 44–46, 53–54.

[20] See Chapter III, pp. 51–53.

determined by an always-determining-feature which is the reason why the determinable stuff is always determined to be of some kind. This always determining feature of determinable-but-always-determined kind of stuff, is called substantial form.[21]

Second, matter and form also enable us to explain how determined stuff or kinds of body being can be further qualified. For example, a man, a composite of prime matter and substantial form, can be drunk or sober without prejudice to the kind of being he is, viz., a *man* kind of being. As a *man* kind of being, the kind is named second or formed matter; as a drunk or sober kind of man, the qualifications are named accidental forms. Matter and form, then, are components of any unit *kind* of being; these components are named prime matter and substantial form. A unit which is a kind of being which has accidents is also compounded of matter and form; here matter is called second matter, and form, accidental form or simply accident.[22]

At this point it is well to remark that our knowledge of matter and form is always a knowledge of the two together. There is no knowing of matter without the knowing of form, nor is there any knowing of form without the knowing of its appropriate matter. The relation of the knowing of matter to the knowing of form is like the relation of matter to form thus:

$$\frac{\text{organizable thought}}{\text{organized thought}} :: \frac{\text{organizable matter}}{\text{organized matter}}$$

(5) Let us push on. Absolutely every feature in a being which falls on the side of essence or quiddity, even the "that which" feature, no matter what its essence may be, and the components of material essence as well, namely, matter and form, all these features are strictly *nothing* apart from one act of existing which causes the

[21] See Chapter III, pp. 51–52.

[22] No component of any unit is a unit. The composite is the unit. Yet there are integral components of a unit which, like matter and form, are *not* units, but which, unlike matter and form, are *not* related as the determinable-to-its-determining-component. A man's leg, arms, etc., are components of a man, who is the unit, but arms, legs, etc., are not determinable-determined composites like the composites of matter and form.

On accidental form, see Chapter III, pp. 51–52.

total composite to exist.[23] So, although material essences, or substances, be they material or not (angels), are composites in one
way or another, what is basic is not that they be *composites*. What
is basic is this: those composites do not jell, do not stiffen into being
spiky, resistent, existent beings except by their composition with
one act of existing. It is, therefore, the composition of a subject of
existing with its act of existing, or if you please, the composition
of essence with its *esse*,[24] which is prior to any composite of matter
and form, prior even to just form (angel). It is upon that basic composition of essence with *esse* that the other compositions are grafted.
And that basic composition is *not* like the composition of H_2O.
Essence or a subject of existing arises from *esse*. There simply *isn't*
any essence or subject of existing *before esse*, as there are hydrogen
and oxygen before *they* are compounded. Positively, there *is* essence or a subject of existing only by reason of the *esse* of that
essence or subject of existing. It is not enough to say that essence,
substance, *ens* connote *esse*. You must say that *esse* is the very actuation by which essence, substance, *ens* are—essence, substance, *ens*.
And this is so, not so much because *ens* gets its name from *esse*,
though it does,[25] and with the result that any being (*ens*) is named
a being because it has *esse;* this is so rather because even those features
of a being (substance and, within material substance, matter and
form, and the forms which are angels) which do *not* get their names

[23] St. Thomas Aquinas, *Contra Gentiles*, I, 54; *Sum. Theol.*, I, 4, 1, *ad* 3;
8, 1, *Resp. ad fin.*; *De Verit.*, XXI, 5. In *De Sub. Sep.*, c. VIII; Marietti, n. 89,
we have one of the best texts on the point: "Si igitur per hoc quod dico: 'non-
ens,' removeatur solum esse in actu, ipsa forma secundum se considerata, est
non ens, sed esse participans. Si autem 'non-ens' removeat non solum ipsum esse
in actu, sed etiam actum seu formam, . . . sic materia est non ens; forma vero
subsistens [angel] non est non ens, sed est actus, quae est forma participativa
ultimi actus, qui est esse."

[24] One may say that a material essence is the same thing as a material subject
of existing (substance) if one speaks of the essence of *that subject*. Thus, the
essence of *a* man is identically a *man* essence. But the accidental essence of a
subject is not identical with that subject. The accidental essence, *green*,
for example, is not identically the subject which is green. Only in God are
essence and subject of *esse* totally identical, because His essence is being.

[25] St. Thomas Aquinas, *In IV Metaph.*, lect. 2, n. 558: "Esse enim rei quamvis
sit aliud ab eius essentia, non tamen est intelligendum quod sit aliquod super-
additum ad modum accidentis, sed quasi constituitur per principia essentiae.
Et ideo hoc nomen Ens quod imponitur ab ipso esse, significat idem cum
nomine quod imponitur ab ipsa essentia."

from *esse* nevertheless do get all their existential sap from *esse;* it is for this reason that any being is—a being. Thus, the distinction between essence and existence is not as between two existents, nor even as between two abstract concepts of one existent; it is a distinction, as *within* a concrete being (*ens*), between a primary feature (*esse*) in it and another, less primary, feature, which latter feature gets all its existential juice from *esse*. To put the matter in another way: it is totally wrong to think of a being as made up of substance of which we predicate accidents, and of the accidents which we predicate of substance; it is wrong also to think of being as made up of substance and its *esse* as if each feature were a being. Rather, beings are unit existents, and all their components short of *esse* (substance-accidents and, within material substance, matter-form, and of course that component of an angel which is just his form) exist only in virtue of one and the same act of existing, namely, the *esse* of a being (*ens*).[26] In sum, each "self" is a composite in one way or another; and each "self" is *itself* compounded with an *esse* which is other than that self.

Variant Expressions of Being as Being (Ens in Quantum Ens)[27]

All the variant expressions or descriptions of being as being have one common feature, which is this: a thing-which-has-nothing-added-to-it.

From that one common feature we must first exclude the divine being. For, a thing-which-has-nothing-added-to-it can be understood as *precluding* an addition, e.g., an irrational animal precludes the addition of *rational:* an irrational animal cannot be rational. Similarly, the divine being cannot have *anything* added to it: God cannot be anything but the *esse* of God. The comparison fails in that "anything": an irrational animal precludes the addition of *rational;* God's

---

[26] St. Thomas Aquinas, *In V Metaph.*, lect. 9, n. 894; *In VII Metaph.*, lect. 1, n. 1245; *In XII Metaph.*, lect. 1, n. 2419.

[27] These expressions are: common being (*ens commune*); being in common or in general (*ens in communi*); being (*ens*); the common act of existing (*esse commune*).

being precludes *any* addition. So, none of the above expressions describes the *esse divinum;* God is not common being, being in general, etc.

Nonetheless, secondly, a thing-which-has-nothing-added-to-it can be understood as neither *requiring* an addition, as, for example, *animal* does not require the addition of *reason:* there are animals which are without reason; nor as lacking an addition, as, for example, *animal* does not lack *reason:* there are animals which have reason.[28] This second thing-which-has-nothing-added-to-it is variously described by calling it common being, being in general, being, the act of existing, being as being. All those expressions are descriptions of created being to the exclusion of the divine being (*ens*) which is the divine act of existing (*esse*).

Why the variations in those descriptions of created being? Because each created being has two features to it: (1) the feature of being *a subject* of the act of existing; (2) the feature which is the subject's *act of existing.* It makes little difference really which of the above expressions you use in order to describe a created being, because any one of those descriptions involves *both* features.

Let us see this more closely. The role of the subject of *esse* is to assure that it be the *subject* of that *esse* which exists; the role of *esse* is to assure that that subject *exist.* Neither role can be played solo. There is no subject of *esse* without *esse*, nor is there any *esse* (of a subject) without that subject: "existing" does not exist; only subjects of existing do.

Common being (*ens commune*), then, means any subject of *esse*, and so does being in common (*ens in communi*), and so does *ens.* The common act of existing (*esse commune*) means any act of existing of any subject thereof, and so does *esse.* Being as being (*ens in quantum ens*) is simply a reduplicative emphasis which hits hard the topic or subject with which metaphysics is concerned, namely, that which exists.[29] For, being (*ens*) is nothing but that

---

[28] St. Thomas Aquinas, *Sum. Theol.*, I, 3, 4, *ad* 1.
[29] St. Thomas Aquinas, *In I Periherm.*, lect. 5; Marietti, n. 71 (20): ". . . *ens* [in communi quod est objectum metaphysicae] nihil est aliud quam *quod est.* Et sic videtur et *rem* significare, per hoc quod dico *quod* et *esse*, per hoc quod dico *est.*"

which exists, and so being apparently means *both* a thing, when you
describe it as "that which," *and esse* when you speak of the "exists"
of the "that which." It may be added that the expression "that
which is" does not mainly mean *esse;* mainly the expression means
"a thing which has *esse.*"[30] But *ens* also means *esse* all the same.

Etymological considerations of metaphysical terms might further
clarify their meaning, and they might not. Perhaps we had better
leave the matter at that—after one last remark.

(6) The relation of common *esse* or *ens* to the divine *esse* may
be restated thus. First, common *esse* is not divine *esse.* Second, the
common *esse* is related to the divine as an effect to its cause. To say
that is to state precisely at what point God touches creatures. It is
here: since common *esse* or *ens* is always a potential (the subject of
esse) in *esse,* always a concrete actualization of any being by its *esse,*
God causes any being (*ens*) of which *esse* is the actualization.

Obviously our knowledge of common *esse* or *ens* is only—knowledge, but that knowledge is related to something which is *not*
knowledge, namely, to physical *esse* or *ens.* Now, that something-
not-knowledge, if we view it as the act of existing which is God
(and this we must do when we have proved that God exists), that
something is *not* common *esse,* nor do we know what It is; we know
only that It is. If we view that something as physical *being* or *esse,*
then it is the term of a relation. The related is the intellect, which
is constituted by being so related.[31] The point here is not so much
that the knowledge that God exists is the very end and capstone of
metaphysics, as that the subject or topic of metaphysics, namely,
common being, lays hold of the intellect, seizes it, molds it as something which demands an explanation. And even when the explanation, which is the proof that there is a cause of common *esse,* is
given, the intellect is still restless until it may know what the divine
being is. Our knowledge of common *esse* is pretty much like our-

---

[30] St. Thomas Aquinas, *In I Periherm.,* lect. 5, n. 71 (20): "Et si quidem haec
dictio *ens* significaret *esse* principaliter, sicut significat *rem* quae habet esse,
procul dubio significaret aliquid esse. Sed ipsam compositionem, quae im-
portatur in hoc quod dico *est,* non principaliter significat, sed consignificat
eam in quantum significat *rem* habentem esse."

[31] St. Thomas Aquinas, *Sum. Theol.,* I, 3, 4, *ad* 2.

selves, pretty thin stuff when compared to God's *esse* and the knowledge of the blessed. And yet, thin as both are, nevertheless they
are the image of God. Certainly, an image may well rejoice over
being an image and, at any rate, any other reason for rejoicing is
too thin to rely upon.

GENERAL BIBLIOGRAPHY

Primary Sources

Patrologia Graeca (J. P. Migne, *Patrologiae Cursus Completus*, Series I, Paris, 1857–66, with later reprints), 162 vols.

Patrologia Latina (J. P. Migne, *Patrologiae Cursus Completus*, Series II, Paris, 1844–64, with later reprints), 221 vols.

Aristotle, *Aristoteles Graece ex recensione Immanuelis Bekkeri*, ed. Academia Regia Borussica (Berlin: Reimer, 1831), 5 vols.

The *Works of Aristotle*, tr. W. D. Ross and others (Oxford: Clarendon, 1928–31), 11 vols.

The *Basic Works of Aristotle*, ed. R. McKeon (New York: Random House, 1941).

Aristotle's Metaphysics, a Revised Text with Introduction and Commentary, ed. W. D. Ross (Oxford: Clarendon, 1924).

Aristotle's Physics, a Revised Text with Introduction and Commentary, ed. W. D. Ross (Oxford: Clarendon, 1936).

Augustine, St., *Opera Omnia*, PL 32–47.

The *Works of Aurelius Augustine*, tr. M. Dods (Edinburgh: T. & T. Clark, 1871–76), 15 vols.

Avicenna, *Opera in lucem redacta ac nuper quantum ars niti potuit per canonicos emendata* (Venetiis, 1508).

Metaphysices compendium ex arabo latinum reddidit et adnotationibus adornavit Nematallah Carame (Romae: Pont. Institutum Orientalium Studiorum, 1926).

Berkeley, G., *A Treatise Concerning the Principles of Human Knowledge*, in *Berkeley's Complete Works*, ed. A. Fraser (Oxford: Clarendon, 1901), vol. I.

Boethius, *Opera Omnia*, PL 63–64.

Cajetan, Scripta philosophica: *De nominum analogia. De conceptu entis*, ed. P. N. Zammit, O.P. (Romae: Institutum "Angelicum," 1934).

In De Ente et Essentia, ed. P. M.-H. Laurent (Taurini: Marietti, 1934).

In Sum. Theol., in *S. Thomae Aquinatis Opera Omnia*, iussu Leonis XIII edita (Romae, 1882–1948), vols. IV-XII.

Scripta philosophica: *Commentaria in De Anima Aristotelis*, ed. P. I. Coquelle, O.P. (Romae: Institutum "Angelicum," 1938), 2 vols.

Descartes, R., *Oeuvres de Descartes*, ed. C. Adam and P. Tannery (Paris: Cerf, 1897–1910), 12 vols.

The Philosophical Works of Descartes, ed. E. Haldane and G. Ross (Cambridge: The Cambridge University Press, 1911–12), 2 vols.

Hegel, G., *The History of Philosophy*, in *Hegel's Lectures on the History of Philosophy* (London: Routledge and Kegan Paul, 1955), Vol. I.

Hume, D., *A Treatise of Human Nature*, ed. L. Selby-Bigge (Oxford: Clarendon, 1928).

John of St. Thomas, *Cursus Philosophicus*, ed. Reiser (Turin: Marietti, 1930), 3 vols.

Cursus Theologicus, ed. Solesmes (Paris: Desclée, 1931), 4 vols.

The Material Logic of John of St. Thomas, tr. Y. Simon, J. Glanville, G. Hollenhorst (Chicago: University of Chicago Press, 1955).

Outlines of Formal Logic. John of St. Thomas' "Textus Summularum," *Ars Logica*, tr. F. C. Wade, S.J. (Milwaukee: Marquette University Press, 1955).

Kant, I., *Kant's Schriften* (Berlin: Reimer, 1905), Vol. II.

Kant Selections, ed. T. M. Greene (New York: Scribner's, 1929).

Critique of Pure Reason, in *Kant Selections*, ed. T. M. Greene (New York: Scribner's, 1929).

Prolegomena to any Future Metaphysics, tr. P. Lucas (Manchester: Manchester University Press, 1953).

Prolegomena to any Future Metaphysics, ed. P. Carus (Chicago: Open Court, 1926).

Leibniz, G., *Discours de métaphysique*, ed. H. Lestienne (Paris: Vrin, 1929).

The Monadology and Other Philosophical Writings, tr. R. Latta (New York: Oxford University Press, 1925).

Liber de Causis, ed. H. Steele, in *Opera hactenus inedita Rogeri Baconi*, fasc. XII (Oxford: Clarendon, 1935).

Locke, J., *An Essay Concerning Human Understanding*, ed. A. Pringle-Pattison (Oxford: Clarendon, 1924).

Malebranche, N., *Dialogue on Metaphysics and on Religion*, tr. M. Ginsberg (New York: Macmillan, 1923).

Parmenides, *On Truth*, in M. C. Nahm, *Selections from Early Greek Philosophy* (New York: Crofts, 1941).

Plato, *Platonis Opera*, ed. J. Burnet (Oxford: Clarendon, 1905–13), 5 vols. in 6.

The Dialogues of Plato, tr. B. Jowett (New York: Random House, 1937), 2 vols.

The Dialogues of Plato, tr. B. Jowett (Oxford: Clarendon, 1871), 5 vols.

Plotinus, *Enneads*, ed. and tr. in French by E. Bréhier (Paris: Société d'Edition "Les Belles Lettres," 1924–38), 6 vols.

The Enneads, ed. S. MacKenna (London: Faber and Faber, 1956), 5 vols.

Proclus, *Elements of Theology*, tr. and ed. E. R. Dodds (Oxford: Clarendon, 1933).

Pseudo-Dionysius, *De Divinis Nominibus*, PG 3.

Scotus, J. D., *B. Joannis Duns Scoti . . . Commentaria Oxoniensia ad IV Libros Sententiarum*, ed. M. F. Garcia (Quaracchi: Ex Typographia Collegii S. Bonaventurae, 1912–14), Vols. I and II.

Spinoza, B., *Ethics*, ed. R. H. M. Elwes (New York: Tudor, 1936).

Ethic., tr. W. White and A. Stirling (Edinburgh: Oxford University Press, 1927).

Suarez, F., S.J., *Disputationes Metaphysicae*, in *Opera Omnia* (Paris: Vivès, 1856–77), Vol. XXVI.

Thomas Aquinas, St., *S. Thomae Aquinatis Opera Omnia*, iussu Leonis XIII edita (Romae, 1882–1948), 16 vols.

S. Thomae de Aquino Ordinis Praedicatorum Summa Theologiae, cura et studio Instituti Studiorum Medievalium Ottaviensis ad textum S. Pii V iussu confectum recognita (Ottawa: Impensis Studii Generalis O. Pr.), Vols. I–IV.

S. Thomas Aquinatis Opuscula Omnia necnon Opera Minora, ed. J. Perrier, *Opuscula Philosophica* (Paris: Lethielleux, 1949), Vol. I.

Opuscula Philosophica (Turin: Marietti, 1954).

Scriptum super Libros Sententiarum Magistri Petri Lombardi, ed. P. Mandonnet and F. Moos (Paris: Lethielleux, 1929–47), 4 vols.

In Metaphysicam Aristotelis Commentaria, ed. M. R. Cathala and R. M. Spiazzi (Turin: Marietti, 1950).

In Aristotelis Librum de Anima Commentarium, ed. A. M. Pirotta (Turin: Marietti, 1925).

Quaestiones Quodlibetales (Turin: Marietti, 1927).

Quaestiones Disputatae (Turin: Marietti, 1949), 2 vols.

De Ente et Essentia, ed. L. Baur (Münster: Aschendorff, 1933).

Le "De Ente et Essentia" de S. Thomas d'Aquin, Bibliothèque Thomiste, VIII (Kain: Le Saulchoir, 1926).

De Unitate Intellectus contra Averroistas, ed. L. W. Keeler, S.J. (Romae: Univ. Gregorianae, 1936).

Sancti Thomae de Aquino Expositio Super Librum Boethii De Trinitate, ed. B. Decker (Leiden: Brill, 1955).

In librum Boetii de Trinitate, Quaestiones Quinta et Sexta, ed. P. Wyser (Fribourg, 1948).

Basic Writings of St. Thomas Aquinas, ed. A. C. Pegis (New York: Random House, 1945), 2 vols.

On the Truth of the Catholic Faith (New York: Doubleday, 1955–56), 4 books.

Truth (Chicago: Regnery, 1952–54), 3 vols.

On the Principles of Nature, tr. R. Henle, S.J., and V. Bourke (St. Louis: St. Louis University Press, 1947).

The Compendium of Theology, tr. C. Vollert, S.J. (St. Louis: St. Louis University Press, 1947).

On Being and Essence, tr. C. Riedl (Toronto: St. Michael's College, 1932).

On Being and Essence, tr. A. Maurer, C.S.B. (Toronto: The Pontifical Institute of Mediaeval Studies, 1949).

The Division and Methods of the Sciences, tr. A. Maurer, C.S.B. (Toronto: The Pontifical Institute of Mediaeval Studies, 1953).

William of Ockham, *Guilhelmi de Ockam anglici super quatuor libros sententiarum subtilissimae quaestiones earumdemque decisiones* (Lugduni, 1495).

Wolff, C., *Philosophia prima, sive Ontologia, methodo scientifica pertractata, qua omnis cognitionis humanae principia continentur* (Francofurti et Lipsiae, 1736).

Secondary Sources

Adler, M., *What Man Has Made of Man* (New York: Longmans, Green, 1937).

The Problem of Species, Problems for Thomists (New York: Sheed & Ward, 1940).

Albertson, M. S., S.J., "The *Esse* of Accidents According to St. Thomas," *The Modern Schoolman*, XXX (1953), pp. 265–278.

Anderson, J. F., *The Cause of Being* (St. Louis: Herder, 1952).

The Bond of Being (St. Louis: Herder, 1949).

An Introduction to the Metaphysics of St. Thomas Aquinas (Chicago: Regnery, 1953).

Arnou, R., S.J., *Metaphysica Generalis* (Romae: Typis Pontificiae Universitatis Gregorianae, 1941).

Ayer, A. J., *Language, Truth and Logic* (London: Gollancz, 1949).

Blanche, F., O.P., "La théorie de l'abstraction chez s. Thomas d'Aquin," *Mélanges Thomistes* (Paris: Vrin, 1934), pp. 237-251.

Bourke, V. J., "Wisdom and Finality," *Proceedings of the American Catholic Philosophical Association*, XXIII (1949), pp. 1-9.

Thomistic Bibliography (St. Louis: St. Louis University Press, 1945).

Boyle, R., S.J., "The Nature of Metaphor," *The Modern Schoolman*, XXXI (1954), pp. 257-280.

"The Nature of Metaphor: Further Considerations," *The Modern Schoolman*, XXXIV (1957), pp. 283-298.

Carnap, R., *The Logical Syntax of Language* (London: Routledge & Kegan Paul, 1949).

Cassirer, E., *An Essay on Man. An Introduction to a Philosophy of Human Culture* (New York: Doubleday, 1956).

The Philosophy of Symbolic Forms, tr. R. Manheim (New Haven: Yale University Press, 1953), Vol. I.

Chenu, M.-D., O.P., *Introduction à l'étude de saint Thomas d'Aquin* (Paris: Vrin, 1950).

Chevalier, J., *La notion de nécessaire chez Aristote et chez ses prédécesseurs* (Paris: Alcan, 1915).

Collins, J., "Towards a Philosophically Ordered Thomism," *The New Scholasticism*, XXXII (1958), pp. 301-326.

Cunningham, F. A., S.J., "A Theory on Abstraction in St. Thomas," *The Modern Schoolman*, XXXV (1958), pp. 249-270.

Eslick, L. J., "What Is the Starting Point of Metaphysics?" *The Modern Schoolman*, XXXIV (1957), pp. 247-263.

Fabro, C., *La nozione Metafisica di Participazione secundo S. Tomaso d'Aquino* (Torino: Societa Editrice Internazionale, 1950).

Farges, A., *Théorie fondamentale de l'acte et de la puissance*, 7th ed. (Paris, 1909).

Finance de, J., S.J., *Être et agir dans la philosophie de saint Thomas* (Paris, 1945).

Forest, A., *La structure métaphysique du concret selon Saint Thomas d'Aquin*, Études de Philosophie Médiévale, XIV (Paris: Vrin, 1931).

Gehring, R. B., S.J., "The Knowledge of Material Essence According to St. Thomas Aquinas," *The Modern Schoolman*, XXXIII (1956), pp. 153-181.

Geiger, L.-B., O.P., "De l'unité de l'être," *Revue des sciences phil. et théol.*, XXXIII (1949), pp. 3-14.

La participation dans la philosophie de s. Thomas d'Aquin, 2nd ed., Bibliothèque Thomiste, XXIII (Paris: Vrin, 1953).

"Existentialisme, essentialisme et ontologie existentielle," *Étienne*

Gilson Philosophe de la Chrétienté (Paris: Les editions du Cerf, 1949), pp. 227–274.

"Abstraction et séparation d'après s. Thomas," *Revue des sciences phil. et théol.*, XXXI (1947), pp. 3–40.

Gilson, E., *L'être et l'essence* (Paris: Vrin, 1948).

Being and Some Philosophers (Toronto: Pontifical Institute of Mediaeval Studies, 1949).

Le Thomisme, 5th ed., *Études de Philosophie Médiévale*, I (Paris: Vrin, 1945).

La philosophie au moyen âge, 3rd ed. (Paris: Payot, 1947).

Introduction a l'étude de saint Augustin, 2nd ed., *Études de Philosophie Médiévale*, XI (Paris: Vrin, 1929).

L'esprit de la philosophie médiévale (Paris: Vrin, 1932).

God and Philosophy (New Haven: Yale University Press, 1941).

Christianity and Philosophy, tr. R. MacDonald, C.S.B. (New York: Sheed & Ward, 1939).

Réalisme thomiste et critique de la connaissance (Paris: Vrin, 1939).

The Unity of Philosophical Experience (New York: Scribner's, 1937).

The Spirit of Mediaeval Philosophy, tr. Downes (New York: Sheed & Ward, 1936).

Reason and Revelation in the Middle Ages (New York: Scribner's, 1928).

The History of Christian Philosophy in the Middle Ages (New York: Random House, 1954).

The Christian Philosophy of St. Thomas Aquinas, tr. L. K. Shook, C.S.B. (New York: Random House, 1956).

Thomas Aquinas and Our Colleagues (Princeton: Aquinas Foundation, 1953).

"Cajétan et l'existence," in *Tijdschrift voor Philosophie*, XV (1953), pp. 267–287.

Painting and Reality, The Mellon Lectures (New York: The Bollingen Foundation, 1957).

Glutz, M. A., "Being and Metaphysics," *The Modern Schoolman*, XXXV (1958), pp. 271–285.

Goichon, A. M., *La distinction de l'essence et de l'existence d'après Ibn Sina* (Paris: Desclée de Brouwer, 1937).

Hamelin, O., *Essai sur les éléments principaux de la représentation*, 2nd ed. (Paris: Alcan, 1925).

Hamm, V. M., "Form in Literature," *Thought*, XVII (1942), pp. 255–269.

"Literature and Morality," *Thought*, XV (1940), pp. 268–280.

Heidegger, M., *Existence and Being*, tr. R. F. C. Hull and A. Crick; ed. W. Brock (Chicago: Regnery, 1949).

Henle, R., S.J., *Method in Metaphysics* (Milwaukee: Marquette University Press, 1951).

"Existentialism and the Judgment," *Proceedings of the American Catholic Philosophical Association*, XXVI (1946), pp. 40–53.

Hoenen, P., S.J., *La théorie du jugement d'après St. Thomas d'Aquin, Analecta Gregoriana*, XXXIX (Romae: Univ. Gregorianae, 1946).

Hollencamp, C., *Causa Causarum. On the Nature of Good and Final Cause* (Quebec: Laval University, 1949).

Isaac, J., O.P., "La notion de dialectique chez Saint Thomas," *Revue des sciences phil. et théol.*, XXXIV (1950), pp. 481–506.

James, W., *The Meaning of Truth* (New York: Longmans, Green, 1927).

Joad, C. E. M., *Return to Philosophy* (New York: Dutton, Inc., 1936).

Johann, R., S.J., "A Comment on Secondary Causality," *The Modern Schoolman*, XXV (1947), pp. 19–25.

Jolivet, R., *Essai sur les rapports entre la pensée chrétienne* (Paris: Vrin, 1931).

La notion de substance (Paris: Vrin, 1929).

Traité de Philosophie, Métaphysique, vol. III, 3rd ed. (Paris: Vittle, 1946).

Kierkegaard, S., *The Sickness unto Death*, tr. W. Lowrie (Princeton: Princeton University Press, 1946).

The Concept of Dread, tr. W. Lowrie (Princeton: Princeton University Press, 1944).

Klubertanz, G., S.J., "Being and God According to Contemporary Scholastics," *The Modern Schoolman*, XXXII (1954), pp. 1–17.

"The Teaching of Thomistic Metaphysics," *Gregorianum*, XXXV (1954), pp. 9–13, 192–201.

Introduction to the Philosophy of Being (New York: Appleton-Century-Crofts, 1955).

The Discursive Power. Sources and Doctrine of the Vis Cogitativa According to St. Thomas Aquinas (St. Louis: St. Louis University Press, 1952).

Kossell, C. G., S.J., "Principles of St. Thomas's Distinction between the *Esse* and *Ratio* of Relation," *The Modern Schoolman*, XXIV (1946), pp. 28–36.

"St. Thomas's Theory of the Causes of Relation," *The Modern Schoolman*, XXV (1948), pp. 151–172.

Lauer, J. Q., S.J., "Determination of Substance by Accidents in the

Philosophy of St. Thomas," *The Modern Schoolman*, XVIII (1941), pp. 31–35.

Lonergan, B., S.J., "The Concept of Verbum in the Writings of St. Thomas Aquinas," *Theological Studies*, VII (1946), pp. 349–392; VIII (1947), pp. 35–79, 404–444; X (1949), pp. 3–40, 359–393.

Insight. A Study of Human Understanding (New York: Philosophical Library, 1957).

Lubac de H., S.J., *Surnaturel*. Études Historiques (Paris: Aubier, 1946).

Lyttkens, H., *The Analogy between God and the World* (Uppsala: Almquist & Wiksells, 1952).

Mandonnet, P., O.P., and Destrez, J., O.P., *Bibliographie thomiste* (Paris: Vrin, 1921).

Maquart, F.-X., *Elementa Philosophiae, Metaphysica* (Paris: Blot, 1938), Vol. III.

Marc, A., S.J., "Being and Action," *The Modern Schoolman*, XXVIII (1951), pp. 175–190.

L'Ideé de l'être chez Saint Thomas et dans la scolastique postérieure (Paris: Beauchesne, 1933).

Dialectique de l'affirmation (Paris: Desclée de Brouwer, 1952).

Maréchal, J., S.J., *Le point de départ de la métaphysique*, 3rd ed. (Paris: Desclée de Brouwer, 1944), Vol. V.

Maritain, J., *Distinguer pour unir, ou les degrés du savoir* (Paris: Desclée de Brouwer, 1932).

Sept leçons sur l'être, et les premiers principes de la raison spéculative (Paris: Téqui, 1934).

Court traité de l'existence et de l'existant (Paris: Hartmann, 1947).

Creative Intuition in Art and Poetry (New York: Meridian, 1957).

Art and Scholasticism, tr. J. F. Scanlan (New York: Scribner's, 1946).

Réflexions sur l'intelligence et sur sa vie propre (Paris: Nouvelle Libraire Nationale, 1926).

De la philosophie chrétienne (Paris: Desclée de Brouwer, 1933).

Science et sagesse (Paris: Labergerie, 1935).

La philosophie de la nature (Paris: Téqui, 1935).

The Degrees of Knowledge, tr. B. Wall and M. Adamson (London: Century, 1937).

Science and Wisdom, tr. B. Wall (New York: Scribner's, 1940).

A Preface to Metaphysics, tr. E. I. Watkin (New York: Sheed & Ward, 1940).

Existence and the Existent, tr. L. Galantiere and G. Phelan (New York: Pantheon, 1949).

St. Thomas and the Problem of Evil (Milwaukee: Marquette University Press, 1942).

Neuf leçons sur les notions premières de la philosophie morale (Paris: Téqui, 1949).

An Introduction to Logic, tr. I. Choquette (New York: Sheed & Ward, 1937).

An Introduction to Philosophy, tr. E. I. Watkin (New York: Sheed & Ward, 1947).

"On Human Knowledge," *Thought*, XXIV (1949), pp. 225-243.

"Sur la doctrine de l'aséité divine," *Mediaeval Studies*, V (1943), pp. 39-50.

Du Régime temporel et de la liberté, première partie: *Une philosophie de la liberté* (Paris: Desclée de Brouwer, 1933).

Martin, W. O., *The Order and Integration of Knowledge* (Ann Arbor: University of Michigan Press, 1957).

Mascall, E. L., *Existence and Analogy* (New York: Longmans, Green, 1949).

Masiello, R. J., "The Analogy of Proportion According to the Metaphysics of St. Thomas," *The Modern Schoolman*, XXXV (1958), pp. 91-105.

Maurer, A., C.S.B., "St. Thomas and the Analogy of Genus," *The New Scholasticism*, XXIX (1955), pp. 127-144.

"Form and Essence in the Philosophy of St. Thomas," *Mediaeval Studies*, XIII (1951), pp. 165-176.

The Division and Methods of the Sciences, Question V and VI of St. Thomas' Commentary on the *De Trinitate* of Boethius (Toronto: The Pontifical Institute of Mediaeval Studies, 1953).

Meyerson, E., *Identité et realité* (Paris: Alcan, 1908).

Muller-Thym, B. J., "Of History as a Calculus Whose Term Is Science," *The Modern Schoolman*, XIX (1942), pp. 41-47; XIX (1942), pp. 73-76.

Newman, J. H., *A Grammar of Assent* (New York: Doubleday, 1955).

O'Neil, C. J., "Practical Knowledge and Liberty," *Proceedings of the American Catholic Philosophical Association*, XXIX (1955), pp. 1-13.

"St. Thomas and the Nature of Man," *Proceedings of the American Catholic Philosophical Association*, XXV (1951), pp. 41-66.

Owens, J., C.Ss.R., "A Note on the Approach to Thomistic Metaphysics," *The New Scholasticism*, XXVIII (1954), pp. 454-476.

The Doctrine of Being in the Aristotelian Metaphysics (Toronto: Pontifical Institute of Mediaeval Studies, 1951).

St. Thomas and the Future of Metaphysics (Milwaukee: Marquette University Press, 1957).

"The Causal Proposition—Principle or Conclusion?" *The Modern*

Schoolman, XXXII (1955), pp. 159-171; XXXII (1955), pp. 257-270; XXXII (1955), pp. 323-330.

"The Intelligibility of Being," *Gregorianum*, V (1955), pp. 169-193.

"The Number of Terms in the Suarezian Discussion on Essence and Being," *The Modern Schoolman*, XXXIV (1957), pp. 147-191.

Paulus, J., *Henri de Gand. Essai sur les tendances de sa métaphysique*, *Études de Philosophie Médiévale*, XXV (Paris: Vrin, 1938).

Peghaire, J., C.S.Sp., *Intellectus et Ratio selon S. Thomas d'Aquin* (Paris: Vrin, 1936).

Regards sur le connaître (Montreal: Fides, 1948).

Pegis, A. C., *St. Thomas and the Greeks* (Milwaukee: Marquette University Press, 1939).

"A Note on St. Thomas, *Summa Theologica*, I, 44, 1-2," *Mediaeval Studies*, VIII (1946), pp. 159-168.

"The Dilemma of Being and Unity," *Essays in Thomism* (New York: Sheed & Ward, 1942), pp. 151-183, 379-382.

"Necessity and Liberty: An Historical Note on St. Thomas Aquinas," *The New Scholasticism*, XV (1941), pp. 18-45.

"In Umbra Intelligentiae," *The New Scholasticism*, XIV (1940), pp. 146-180.

Penido, M. T.-L., *Le rôle de l'analogie en théologie dogmatique* (Paris: Vrin, 1931).

Peters, J. A. J., C.Ss.R., "Matter and Form," *The New Scholasticism*, XXXI (1957), pp. 447-483.

Phelan, G. P., "The Existentialism of St. Thomas," *Proceedings of the American Catholic Philosophical Association*, XXI (1946), pp. 25-40.

St. Thomas and Analogy (Milwaukee: Marquette University Press, 1941).

"Verum Sequitur Esse Rerum," *Mediaeval Studies*, I (1939), pp. 11-22.

Philippe, M. D., "Abstraction, addition, séparation dans la philosophie d'Aristotle," *Revue Thomiste*, XLVIII (1948), pp. 461-479.

Prado del, N., O.P., *De Veritate Fundamentali Philosophiae Christianae* (Fribourg: Ex Typis Consociationis Sancti Pauli, 1911).

Pruche, B., *Existentialisme et acta d'être* (Grenoble: Arthand, 1947).

Raeymaeker de, L., *Philosophie de l'être. Essai de synthèse métaphysique* (Louvain: Éditions de l'Institut Supérieur de Philosophie, 1946).

Régis, L. M., O.P., *Epistemology*, tr. I. C. Byrne (New York: Macmillan, 1959).

L'Odyssée de la métaphysique (Montreal: Institut d'Études Médiévales, 1949).

Renard, H., S.J., "What is St. Thomas' Approach to Metaphysics?" *The New Scholasticism*, XXX (1956), pp. 64-83.

The Philosophy of Being (Milwaukee: Bruce, 1943).

Reichenbach, H., *Elements of Symbolic Logic* (New York: Macmillan, 1947).

Robert, J.-D., O.P., "La métaphysique, science distincte de toute autre discipline philosophique, selon saint Thomas d'Aquin," *Divus Thomas Plac.*, L, 3-4 (1947), pp. 206-222.

Roland-Gosselin, M. D., O.P., *Le De Ente et Essentia de S. Thomas d'Aquin, Bibliothèque Thomiste*, VIII (Kain: Le Saulchoir, 1926).

De Distinctione inter essentiam et esse apud Avicennam et D. Thomam, Xenia Thomistica, III (1925), pp. 281-288.

Rousselot, P., S.J., *The Intellectualism of Saint Thomas* (New York: Sheed & Ward, 1935).

Russell, B., *Problems of Philosophy* (New York: Holt, 1912).

Saliba, D., *Étude sur le métaphysique d'Avicennae* (Paris: Presses Universitaires, 1927).

Salmon, E., "Philosophy and the Unity of Wisdom," *Proceedings of the American Catholic Philosophical Association*, XXVII (1953), pp. 1-12.

"What is Being?" *Review of Metaphysics*, VII (1954), pp. 613-631.

The Good in Existential Metaphysics (Milwaukee: Marquette University Press, 1952).

"Metaphysics and Unity," in *Progress in Philosophy*, ed. J. McWilliams, S.J. (Milwaukee: Bruce, 1955), pp. 47-60.

Sartre, J.-P., *La nausée* (Paris: Gallimard, 1938).

Being and Nothingness, tr. H. Barnes (New York: Philosophical Library, 1956).

Existentialism, tr. B. Frechtman (New York: Philosophical Library, 1947).

Schwartz, H., "Plato, Aristotle, St. Thomas and Univocity," *The New Scholasticism*, XXVII (1953), pp. 373-403.

"Analogy in St. Thomas and Cajetan," *The New Scholasticism*, XXVIII (1954), pp. 127-144.

Sertillanges, A. D., O.P., *Le Christianisme et les Philosophies* (Paris: Aubier, 1939).

Simon, Y., *Introduction à l'ontologie du connaître* (Paris: Desclée de Brouwer, 1934).

Critique de la connaissance morale (Paris: Labergerie, 1934).

Prévoir et savoir. Études sur l'idée de la necessité dans la pensée scientifique et en philosophie (Montreal: Editions de l'Arbre, 1944).

Traité du libre arbitre (Liège: Sciences et Lettres, 1951).

"On the Foreseeability of Free Acts," *The New Scholasticism*, XXII (1948), pp. 357–370.

Smith, G., S.J., "The Nature and Uses of Liberty," *The New Scholasticism*, XXVI (1952), pp. 305–326.

Natural Theology (New York: Macmillan, 1951).

The Truth That Frees (Milwaukee: Marquette University Press, 1956).

"Intelligence and Liberty," *The New Scholasticism*, XV (1941), pp. 1–17.

"Avicenna and the Possibles," *The New Scholasticism*, XVII (1943), pp. 340–357.

"Before You Start Talking About God," *The Modern Schoolman*, XXII (1945), pp. 31–32.

"Science and Philosophy," *The Biologist*, XXXV (1952–53), pp. 72–79.

"Philosophy and the Unity of Man's Ultimate End," *Proceedings of the American Catholic Philosophical Association*, XXVII (1953), pp. 60–83.

Smith, V. E., "Wisdom and Science," *Proceedings of the American Catholic Philosophical Association*, XXX (1956), pp. 3–15.

Thiry, L., *Speculativum-practicum secundum S. Thomas, quo modo se habeant in actu humano* (Romae: Herder, 1939).

Tonquédec de, J., S.J., *La critique de la connaissance* (Paris: Beauchesne, 1929).

Vaux de, R., O.P., *Notes et Textes sur l'Avicennisme Latin aux confins des XII et XIII* siècles, Bibliothèque Thomiste*, XX (Paris: Vrin, 1934).

Vignaux, P., "Nominalisme," *Dictionnaire de théologie catholique*, XI, 1931, coll. 717–784.

Vollert, C., S.J., *On the Various Kinds of Distinctions* (Milwaukee: Marquette University Press, 1947).

Walton, W., "Being, Essence, and Existence," *Review of Metaphysics*, III (1950), pp. 339–365.

Wild, J., "A Realistic Defense of Causal Efficiency," *Review of Metaphysics*, II (1949), pp. 1–14.

Introduction to Realistic Philosophy (New York: Harper, 1948).

"Tendency," *The Journal of Philosophy*, XLIX (1952), pp. 468–472.

Wolter, A., O.F.M., "Causality," *Proceedings of the American Catholic Philosophical Association*, XXXII (1958), pp. 1–28.

Zedler, B., "St. Thomas and Avicenna in the 'De Potentia Dei'," *Traditio*, VI (1948), pp. 105–159.

INDEX

Absolute,
  nature, 258-261, 271-272
  any statement involves an, 292-297,
    315-317, 318
Abstraction,
  conceptual, 227-236
  of a whole, 230, 235
  of a form, 234, 236
  of absolute nature, 259-260
Accident,
  is loosely connected with substance,
    39
  is a component of a changing being,
    68-69, 81-87
  is caused, 89, 174
  which is knowledge, 149-153, 170-177
  esse is not an, though accidental,
    172-174
Act,
  negates the "is not" of the potential,
    33-34
  which is accident, 18-34, 81-87
  which is substantial form, 54, 68-69,
    81-87
  which is *esse*, 63-67, 69-71, 81-87
  multiple being's, is caused, 88, 89
  accidental, which is *esse* is caused,
    174, 175
  which is *esse* in knowledge, 203-217
  existential, and its modes, 283-284
Action,
  and passion in change, 17
Active potency, *see* Cause
Adler, M., 46, 53, 388
Albertson, M. S., S.J., 277, 388
Analogue,
  the, is known existential act, 180,
    181

Analogue—*Continued*
  God is known in knowing the, 180,
    181
  the, and analogy, 181-184
  source of our knowledge of the, 183,
    190-191
  is known before the demonstration
    of God, 181, 184-185
  how the, is known after the demon-
    stration of God, 185-186
  analogy of the, is a noetic version of
    causality, 191
  is a mean between the univocal and
    the purely equivocal, 194
  mathematical, 183
  why being is an, 203-217
  the attributive, 193, 207-208, 211
  the properly proportionate, 208-212
  of inequality, 212-217
Analogy,
  the moments of our knowledge of,
    194-195
  of natural signs, 193
  a noetic version of causality, 206
  vocabulary of, 207-214
Anderson, J. F., 10, 183, 201, 388
Appetite,
  is actuation of the appetible, 128
Aristotle, 8-9, 35, 54-55, 80, 95, 125-126,
    147-148, 168-169, 200-201, 252, 274,
    310, 328, 342, 366, 385
  on being as being, 1
  distinguishes metaphysics from other
    sciences, 1
  on the history of the problem of the
    one and many, 3-4
  asks, why the many? 5
  says "being" means several things,
    5, 12

Koninck de, C., 53
Kossell, C., S.J., 276, 310, 391

Lauer, J. Q., S.J., 391
Leibniz, G., 171, 321, 369, 386
Liber de Causis, 386
Living,
  is distinct in kind from the non-liv-
    ing, 46-48
Locke, J., 31, 386
Lonergan, B., S.J., 159, 169, 271, 392
Love,
  self, and other regarding, 356-357
Lubac de, H., S.J., 392
Lyttkens, H., 201, 392

Malebranche, N., 321, 386
Mandonnet, P. and Destrez, J. O. P.,
  392
Many beings,
  cannot explain one, 11-12
  possibility of, 60-67
  not necessary, 61-62
  are caused, 56-67
  in knowledge, 149-165, 203-217
Maquart, F.-X., 392
Marc, A., S.J., 9, 392
Maréchal, J., S.J., 9, 150, 168, 292, 293,
  310, 392
Maritain, J., 9, 55, 79, 147, 148, 168,
  169, 201, 217, 228, 234, 251, 252,
  348, 361, 367, 392-393
  on being as being, 1, 42
  on tendency, 44
  on problem of species, 53
  on essence and *esse*, 64
  on freedom, 134, 137, 142, 143, 150,
    152, 159, 162, 164
  on analogy, 183
  on equivocal cause, 188, 220, 222
Martin, W. O., 218, 393
Mascall, E. L., 183, 201, 370, 373, 393
Masiello, R. J., 393
Mathematics,
  analogy in, 182
Matter, prime, 49-53
  knowledge of, 233-234
  description of, 378-379
Maurer, A., C. S. B., 64, 79, 182, 201,
  213, 229, 231, 252, 253, 393
Meaning, 312, 313, 314-315, 328

Means, 115-119, 120
  knowledge of, 158-160
  relation of, to end, 138-139
Mechanism,
  commits a paralogism about nature,
    42-43, 47-48
  Aristotle on, 42
  Descartes on modern, 42
  Gilson on, 42
  Maritain on, 42
  Meyerson on, 42
  Simon on, 42
Metaphor, *see* Figures of speech
Metaphysics,
  is science of being as being, 1-8
  knowledge of the object of, 222-229,
    254-273
  Christian version of, 263-273
  Greek version of, 265-266
  science of, 268-273
Meyerson, E., 42, 55, 93, 160, 393
Mistake,
  about the moral good, 141-145
Motion, *see* Change
Muller-Thym, B. J., 170, 179, 393
Multiplicity,
  of being, 1-8
  demands a cause, 4-7, 88-94
  why, needs a cause, 14, 81-87
  within one being, 14-30, 81-87
  among kinds of being, 14-15, 37-54,
    81-87
  among beings, 14-15, 81-87
  reduction of, to unity, 190-191

Nature,
  is a composite of subject and its
    necessary traits, 40-41, 377
  Mechanism's explanation of, 40-44
  inanimate, whose end-object is
    fixed, 132
  animate, 131
  animal, 131-132
  man's, 132-136
  is fixed upon operation by tendency,
    38-41, 44-46
  absolute, 258-261, 271-272
  is *extra genus notitiae*, 286-287
  of being, 345-349
Necessary,
  and contingent, 39-40, 165, 171
  Aristotle on the, 41

404